22 ON PELELIU

22 ON PELELIU

Four Pacific Campaigns with the Corps:
The Memoirs of an Old Breed Marine

GEORGE PETO

with

PETER MARGARITIS

CASEMATE
Philadelphia & Oxford

First published in the United States of America and Great Britain in 2017.
Reprinted as a paperback in 2021 by
CASEMATE PUBLISHERS
1950 Lawrence Road, Havertown, PA 19083, USA
and
The Old Music Hall, 106–108 Cowley Road, Oxford OX4 1JE, UK

Copyright 2017 © Peter Margaritis

Paperback Edition: ISBN 978-1-61200-979-7
Digital Edition: ISBN 978-1-61200-528-7 (epub)

A CIP record for this book is available from the Library of Congress and the British Library

Printed and bound in the United States of America
Typeset in India by Lapiz Digital Services, Chennai

For a complete list of Casemate titles, please contact:

CASEMATE PUBLISHERS (US)
Telephone (610) 853-9131
Fax (610) 853-9146
Email: casemate@casematepublishers.com
www.casematepublishers.com

CASEMATE PUBLISHERS (UK)
Telephone (01865) 241249
Fax (01865) 794449
Email: casemate-uk@casematepublishers.co.uk
www.casematepublishers.co.uk

Contents

A Note from the Co-author

In the late spring of 2015, I decided to enter a U.S. Naval Institute 3,000-word-essay contest. The subject was to be any noteworthy U.S. Marine Corps event that had significantly changed American history. This would be a challenge for me, because for over 30 years, although my research specialty has been World War II, I had mainly studied and written about the European Theater. So I was getting into somewhat unfamiliar ground.

I talked to a couple of American Legion cohorts that were Marine veterans, and their consensus was that I do the essay contest about the controversial invasion of Peleliu in September, 1944. A Navy buddy of mine suggested that I should consult with an old World War II Marine veteran who lived here in Central Ohio, a fellow named George Peto. He was one of what they called the "Old Breed" and had actually been in the Peleliu operation.

I first met with George on June 24, 2015 in a Bob Evans restaurant, not too far from his home on the north side of Columbus. George and I quickly struck up a friendship, and I invited him to co-write the essay with me. We thought that we would make a good team, since I was an experienced writer and researcher, and George had not only actually been there in the thick of it, but had a remarkable memory about his experiences. And as everyone who met him knows, he enjoyed retelling them.

Our essay unfortunately did not win the contest, so George and I decided to expand our work and turn what we had written into a book. As we continued our research though, and as he told me more about his past, I listened, fascinated, marveling at his consistent, detailed memory of remarkable things that had happened to him many decades ago. I finally realized that a much better book to write would be about his life. I wanted to—I *had* to write about him, to preserve his memories for everyone, especially his daughter Nancy, his son George Lee, and his friends. He good-naturedly agreed, and so we were off.

One thing I found amazing was that despite the fact that he was 92 years old when I began interviewing him, George's stories did not vary much from one telling to the next (except perhaps for some added detail), and sometimes certain phrases were almost word for word. Another reassuring item was that his accounts on certain events were nearly always backed up by subsequent research on my part.

This book is the result. It includes George's exploits as a young boy, growing up in a very interesting, long-past period in American history. It follows him in his early career in the Marines, his intensive Pacific campaigns, and his interesting life after the war. I definitely have never met a man who has had as exciting a life as his. And I learned so much from him and our research about war in the Pacific.

There are points in the narrative where I have slightly dramatized his memories to give them more depth and to help give his story continuity. They are, however, all backed up by extensive research. And the stories are all absolutely true, written as he told them, which accounts for incorrect grammar.

I would like to thank a couple people for helping us in our endeavor. To Steve Ebersole for his encouragement, and for putting me in touch with this amazing Marine. My heartfelt appreciation to son George Lee Peto, for encouraging his father to undertake this project, and to daughter Nancy Peto for her wonderful support. Thanks also to Ruth Sheppard at Casemate Publishers for believing that George's story needed to be told. Last, my deep gratitude to my loving wife Mindy, who put up with my weird, idiosyncratic behavior during this time.

Peter Margaritis

Introduction

My name is George Peto. I am a World War II veteran. I have been a Marine for over seven decades, what fellow Marines would refer to as one of "The Old Breed." That means I am one of those ancient guys that joined the Marine Corps as a regular (not a reserve) before the outbreak of World War II.[1] I guess that there are not many of us left today. I read one estimate that stated World War II veterans are dying at the rate of almost 500 a day. Wow.

According to statistics, of the 670,000 Marines that served in the war, there are probably only 22,000 still alive today. Of them, only about a thousand are Old Breed, like me—about a sixth of one percent. Nearly all the guys who served and fought with me are now deceased. So I guess that makes me a part of a very small group indeed.

Sometimes I look back at my time in the Corps and just shake my head in wonder. I served through 32 months of war in the Pacific, and I was never even wounded. Heavens knows, I came pretty damn close to it dozens of times, but somehow I survived, although I did get pounded a few times, and dog sick a few more. According to the numbers, by rights, I should have actually died many times: maybe at

---

1   The term, now one of "toughened endearment" in the Corps, first referred to those regular career Marines who had fought in World War I, and who served as the initial cadre for the 1st Marine Division when it initially was formed in February 1941. The term later was broadened to refer to any regular Marine who fought in the division and whose service began prior to the outbreak of World War II.

Cape Gloucester by a sniper; certainly at Peleliu a dozen times, from all the intensive incoming fire we took; or Okinawa in the many advances that we made across the island. Yet still, somehow I made it through the war.

You know, I find it strangely ironic that thousands of my fellow veterans were wounded in the war, came back and were decorated for valor. Many (although not nearly enough) were fawned over by the VA (back when the VA was doing its job right), discharged with pomp and circumstance, and as rightfully considered heroes, have been recognized and honored for decades. Me, I served throughout the entire war, fought in four major Pacific campaigns, saw, experienced, and endured horrible things no human being should ever have to go through, and in the end, I was unceremoniously sent back to Great Lakes Naval Training Center, processed out, given a quick handshake, and told thanks a lot. I was given some battle ribbons and years later, because of the malaria I contracted during the war, eligibility for VA benefits.

Nothing else.

Well, not for several years. Slowly over time though, I have been lucky enough to receive many honors. A couple decades ago I began to tell schoolchildren in Central Ohio about my experiences, giving them an awareness of what my generation did to ensure the rights and freedoms that we enjoy. I feel good about that.

In the many decades since the war, I have had been fortunate to continue living an interesting life. I had a long career managing my own store, and was happily married for 65 years. I've been told that I can still be obstinate at times.

Maybe that is what has allowed me to stay on. Even now at the ripe old age of 93, I am lucky enough to continue to have an active life. I live with both of my children in my own house, work a modest garden, grow some flowers, occasionally go hunting—I still hand-load my own ammunition—and once in a while, I operate my log splitter for firewood.

In the last couple decades, as I talked to kids in school and fellow Marines, I was encouraged by several to record some of the things I lived through. I had written a couple of articles, but nothing substantial. Then in 2015, I met Pete Margaritis, an experienced writer and researcher, and after a couple of interesting conversations, he finally convinced me that perhaps such an effort might be interesting for some people to read.

So, I guess this work is the result of that. You know, recalling many of these events, I again wonder on how I lived through them. And that includes things that happened to me before and after the war. After going through this book I can imagine that someone will read this and think, "Holy cow. All of that couldn't have happened to him."

But it did. Every damn bit of it. The details that follow have been recalled to the best of my ability. These are some of the things that really happened to me.

George Peto

Sergeant George Peto S/N 317040
United States Marine Corps

CHAPTER I

Early Life

Neither of my parents was born in the United States. They both emigrated from Hungary. My father was born March 7, 1894, and Mom was born two years later. Pop could more or less speak seven different languages, so for one of his professions, he eventually became an interpreter for Municipal Judge Hunsicker[1] in Akron whenever the accused could not speak English. Even though Pop spent many working days in a courthouse, he was mostly an outdoorsman, and my brothers and I picked up this trait. It was one that would shape a good part of my character.

I was the third of four children. The oldest was Elizabeth Rose, born six years before me on August 25, 1916. She was a somewhat thin brunette with a high forehead. I remember her as being sort of prissy, typical for a female in those days. Next in line was my older brother Alex, born July 25, 1920, in Trenton, New Jersey. A year after Alex was born, our family moved to Akron, Ohio. The next year, on September 18, 1922, I came into the world, born at home, with my mom assisted by a midwife. Soon after, our family settled on a backwoods farm in the Portage Lakes area south of Akron, and on June 2, 1928, when we lived in nearby Barberton, Ohio, younger brother Steve was born, mom assisted again by a midwife. That's all poor folks like us could afford in those days.

---

1   Oscar A. Hunsicker was on the Akron Juvenile Court Bench from 1930 until 1940.

My old man had a wild streak in him that in his youth often got him into trouble. Having a motorcycle sure as hell did not help. Nor did being an alcoholic. Yeah, as he grew older, he drank like a fish and smoked like a fiend. (Luckily, smoking was a bad habit that thankfully none of his sons ever took up, although unfortunately, Liz did.) In fact, Pop did so many things in his life the wrong way. Yet somehow, the old man lived to be 92 years old. Pop was a great contractor, quite the entrepreneurial self-employed builder. I mean, of just about anything. I remember when I was a kid that my brother and I would often go out with him and help him build a house, or a garage, or a fireplace or something. Sometimes, we dug basements for folks. Whatever we could do to make a buck, we would do.

Earlier in his life, my old man had trained to be a cobbler. In later years, on the east side of Akron, he started his own shoe repair store, selling and repairing shoes. Unfortunately, Dad gave up the trade, because he was not making much money at it. Also, in his mind, even an expert cobbler was a still lowly profession, not worthy of his own talents. So he decided to give up the store and become a freelance contractor. Mom couldn't talk him out of his decision. In fact, she pretty much could not talk him out of anything. You just could not reason with him, especially when he was drunk. Anyway, Pop pretty much did as he damn well pleased.

And he could be one mean old bastard. Once when I was in grade school, I played hooky a couple times. I was hanging around the swamps with a friend of mine, Bob Rining, who lived down the street. Finally, my teacher, frustrated with me (as she often was), gave my sister Elizabeth a note to take home to my parents. Liz brought the note home and gave it to Pop, and he got mad as hell.

Determined to catch me in the act, he didn't say a word to me when I came home that afternoon, and nothing happened to me that night. So the next day, unsuspecting, I skipped school again and went down to the canal with Bob to take my beat-up canoe out for a ride. After a while, my father came down along the shore, spotted us, and stood on the bank, watching us idly paddling away, happy as a couple of larks. He did not even yell out my name: he just stood there, silent.

Finally, I looked up and saw him there glaring, and my heart skipped a beat. With a mean look in his eye, he wiggled his index finger, motioning me to come ashore. Taking a deep breath, we paddled over to the bank and got out of the canoe. Man oh man, that's when all hell broke loose. He beat the crap out of me going up the bank and all the way back to our house, some three blocks away. That did the trick. No more skipping classes. I never missed a day of school after that. I was never easy to convince to do things, and normally, I often did things with little thought of the consequences if they were not hurtful or fatal to anyone. But this lesson took. Boy, did it take.

During these years, Alex and I often fished with dad at Wingfoot Lake. One thing that I vividly remember around five years old was seeing all these balloons floating around in the sky. They called them "airships," but to me, they were big balloons. Most of them were those shorter blimps, although early on, we once in a while saw one of the huge, long dirigibles, like the German zeppelins. Before World War II started though, they stopped making those and were just making blimps. But because we lived so close to the Goodyear factory, we could clearly see the Akron blimp building from the lake. In the summer, you could see them flying around, and I swear, Goodyear must have had a blimp named for every month of the year. I'd just sit there in the boat or along the shore and stare at them. Once in a while, we'd see one of those big long dirigibles, like the *Akron* or the *Macon*. They'd glide on by, or sometimes hover near the ground as the ground crews worked to land them.

Life on our farm was primitive. We lived in a heavily forested area, with lakes, rivers, and swamps all around us. We were not far from the Ohio Canal, and we always kept a boat there that we used to go fishing or just exploring. We grew over half of our own food, and life as such was basic. For one thing, we had no indoor bathroom, and so going to the head in the wintertime was sometimes rather uncomfortable.

Country life like that was sometimes a challenge. For one thing we had bedbug problems. Not that this was unusual, because back then everybody in our area had bedbugs. My father though, was rather effective in controlling them. He just used a torch. It seemed to be an effective technique, and anyway, as poor as we were, we really had no alternatives. Chemicals for that sort of thing were not easily available back then; the only thing that you could buy came in powder form. That stuff was expensive, and anyway, it was not very effective against them.

Pop's treatment was unique. Every month or so, he'd take our beds apart, and we would drag them outside. He would then separate the mattresses from the frames. The mattresses were filled with straw, so the remedy was easy. We would remove the old straw and burn it, while mom boiled the mattress covers. We owned a couple of blow torches, which were common back then. Each one was about 12 inches high, with a six-inch-round fuel tank. In it we would put gasoline or kerosene. Then he would pump up the blow torch, turn on the fuel valve, and light it. With a flame about a foot long, he'd take the torch and go to one corner of the bed frame, where it connected to the springs underneath. He would then go down the line of the bed springs and cook them little critters. And you could hear them sizzle and pop as he did. When he was done, he would then take the bed back inside, and we would be good for another month.

Because we lived as primitively as we did, we had to spend a good deal of time outdoors. Pop often took me and my two brothers out hunting for food. Rabbit was a common course for our meals. I had my own first kill when I was nine years old, and after that, I was never too content indoors. I inevitably became an avid outdoorsman, and so I never really acclimated to indoor activities. School, an indoor activity, was always difficult for me, because I preferred to go roaming through the woods looking for adventure, longing to just go exploring. Often, as a young teenager, I would get a friend to go with me and just take off to see what we could see. I took along any sort of basic road map and kept it in my back pocket. We walked wherever our curiosity took us, sometimes hitchhiking across the state by truck or by train. We sometimes stopped for the night on a hayloft or in a barn, before starting off for home the next day. It was a blast for me, and my curiosity always seemed to lead me to something new.

This outdoor nature of course had its drawbacks. As a teenager, it made my holding any job difficult. That was a big problem, because back then in the early thirties, jobs were difficult to land. However, I was an excellent hunter, and many was the time I would happily go out hunting with my dad for hours on end.

As I grew up, partly because of how we lived, I developed a positive attitude on life, and more often than not, I would not take things as seriously as sometimes the circumstances would dictate. I usually preferred the grin or the chuckle over the frown and the growl, and most of my teenage friends considered me to be more or less a happy-go-lucky fellow. So if someone got serious on me, I would laugh. Over the years, I found that this sort of lighthearted attitude was a double-edged sword. Sometimes it worked in my favor; certainly with the girls. Sometimes though, it backfired and worked against me; mostly with authority.

I remember one time when I was in the second grade. My teacher was this beautiful lady. I thought she was prettier than any gal I had ever seen, and I have to admit, I was smitten by her. We were studying a classic poem, *A Tree*, by Joyce Kilmer, and in the middle of it, somebody

George (left) and Alex Peto as children, taken in around 1931. (Author's collection)

made a smart remark. Our teacher looked up from her book and sternly asked, "Who said that?"

The room was dead silent. She glanced around with a scowl, and started walking down the aisle, looking at everybody. She came to where I was sitting and looked at me. I was smiling.

She calmly concluded, "You're the culprit."

"No, ma'am. I'm innocent."

But she didn't believe me. We went on reading the poem. A little later, one of the boys in the back took a small wad of paper and threw it across the room, lightly hitting her in the back. She whirled around, now angry. The guilty party was openly defying her. "Who threw that paper?" she snarled.

Again, none of us said anything. She started walking up and down the rows of desks again, glaring. When she came to me, I just looked up and grinned at her. It had just struck me as being funny, and now I was trying to hide the grin by looking innocent. It backfired. She smacked me hard on the head. I saw stars.

By 1928, we had sold our first home and had twice moved away from the development sections. Now, we had moved into an area below Akron that was called the Portage Lakes, which included some eight lakes in the area. Living there, we were right next to the Erie–Ohio Canal. There were several reservoirs in the area that helped supply the canal, so water was always nearby.

In one remote area, there was a small dirt lane that went far back and eventually ended in an open area next to a swamp. The older kids used it as a lover's lane. The main road that goes south in that area, State Route 93, is called Manchester Road.[2]

We lived on a simple, beat-up farm near Nesmuth Lake[3] (we called it "Mud Lake") on the north side of Carnegie Avenue, the only crossroads in the area. Back then, the area was open country, with swamps all over the place. There was no civic development, and there were no paved

---

2 So named because it went through the small town of Manchester, about ten miles south of the lakes, between Canton and Akron.

3 Referred to in earlier years as Nesmith Lake.

highways; just dirt roads with pylon street markers, and some pretty maple trees alongside our road. We got some livestock that we took care of: a horse, some pigs, and even a cow. Our house was next to a swamp, and there was a drainage ditch nearby. Dad and I built a small shelter over it for some ducks I had caught.

It was around that time when I became aware of the fact that the old man had become a bootlegger. I remember the time, because I was supposed to have started school that year, but I did not.

From the time I was born until the time I joined the Marines, we lived on several different farms in south Akron, all in a five-mile radius. We did not stay too long in any location, and we had to move a good deal, and that was for one good reason: the rent would come due. My old man unfortunately seldom paid his bills, and paying the rent was an on and off thing for him. He would run up a debt, and then either could not pay or would not pay; so as a result, we sooner or later were forced to move.

I grew up making a number of friends. Probably the closest were the Getz brothers. There were three of them, just like there were three of us Peto brothers. Our two trios hung out a lot, often sitting at each other's family dinner tables. We shared most everything, and promised that we would always stay in touch.

My close buddy was the middle brother, Melvin Forest Getz—we called him "Waddy." The older one was named after their father, Seymour, so we called him "Danny." The youngest was Warren; we called him "Boysee."

Waddy was a little over a year older than I was, and the two of us got along great. As we grew to be teenagers, he developed a strong, muscular physique, one that he often bragged about. He had a right to, because he really was a tough son of a gun, a pretty rugged guy. As he grew older and bolder, he once in a while would go into a bar and start a fight by picking on the biggest guy. Once in a while he would lose and come out bloody and worse for the wear, but he always came out laughing.

I guess that I was in my share of brawls too. There was this one guy that I went to school with named Paul Dunlap. One day, he started bugging me, ordering me around. I kind of let it go, but the second day when he pushed me around, I started getting mad, realizing what was going on. He was just out and out bullying me. The third day he started in on me, I'd had enough, so I let him have it. We started fighting, and after about five minutes of trading punches, to my surprise, he started laughing. Me, I was fighting dead serious, but I guess he wasn't. We finally stopped, and we made up. We ended up being friends after that. Not good ones, and I never got to where I trusted him, but we respected each other.

Yeah, even as kids, we did a lot of fighting back then, partly because it was rough where we lived, and partly because that was one of the few forms of entertainment that we had. And boxing was not only condoned, it was often encouraged. There used to be carnivals or sporting events where boxing matches were set up, and you could enter for next to nothing to compete for prizes, which sometimes were sponsored by our schools.

We used to box a lot back then. Mostly it was for fun and to pass the time, sometimes just to get better at doing it. Remember, boxing was really popular back then, and tickets for a good boxing match would go for good money, just like folks today would pay a lot to see a good basketball game. So we would box at all these different places. There was one place in town that had a bar on the first floor, and upstairs they had a gym. So we would go there and box.

We would box at other places too. A number of grade schools and high schools had a Weona Club,[4] and every Wednesday night, the school would have a dance, or a set of boxing matches. Often, we would go and just box. Hell, all you just needed was a pair of gloves and a ring. Or, we played basketball. All you needed was some sort of hoop and a ball that bounced. What equipment we didn't have, we improvised. Just like hockey, for instance. For hockey sticks, we'd go down to the canal and find these big bushes growing along the banks. We would each find a thick branch that curved up and went out over the water, and we would cut it off. We would then take these wooden branches, dry them

---

4   Weona Club was a chain of over a dozen recreational centers that held social, dancing, and sporting events.

out, and then shape them with our knives into hockey sticks. And for a puck, we'd get an old tin can, put a stone in it, crimp the ends, and then beat it around. That was it.

In the spring and summer we played baseball. Again, just the basics. All you needed was an open field, something that passed for a glove, a bat or a stick, and something that could pass for a baseball or softball. There was this one big field near my house, and there was a path that went right through it. Just about every time I went by there were a few kids playing on one side or the other. There were never any adults or supervisors; just us kids.

We did other things to pass the time. Being around the Portage Lakes and the Ohio Canal, we swam a lot. There was one remote spot that we called the "B.A.B.," short for "Bare-assed Beach." It was along the old Ohio Canal, a half mile down and back through the swamps. Most of the time, the swamps kept cars from going down there, so we were safe. On warm days when we had spare time, we would walk over there, yank off our bib overalls, drop them on the bank of the canal, and hit the water.

The cops knew what we were doing, but couldn't get down there to catch us and run us out. Except sometimes, when the weather had been hot and dry for a while and a car could get down there. So the cops would every now and then sneak down whenever they didn't have to worry about getting stuck and try to catch us. Usually though, we would see or hear them coming and hide. There were these heavy bushes growing along the bank, and so when the cops came looking for us, we'd hide under the bushes.

One time they got wise to us and looking around, found our clothes. They grabbed them and then told us to come out, or else they'd take them. After thinking about it a bit, and after they warned us that we would get in more trouble and that they were leaving, we finally sheepishly came up out of the water. They then gave us hell, but they didn't take us in. They understood that that was our recreation.

There was a lot of stuff that we did as kids, and because we were so poor, we had to do some innovative hillbilly engineering. Luckily, we had a lot of material to work with, even if it was all junk. Sometimes, we'd go to the junk yard for things we needed, or find a junk haul someone had dumped. We often salvaged nails out of the boards. You see, back in those days, there were no sophisticated waste management services, especially out in the boonies where I lived, and especially not during the Depression. Often, folks just took their sacks of garbage out to the dumps and just pitched it, along with a lot of other junk that they didn't want. So we would get a lot of what we needed to fashion our own stuff.

For instance, we used to get a bunch of old bottles and play mumbly peg. Waddy and I often played, but sometimes Waddy's younger brother Warren, about my age, would play with us too. Warren, like his older brother, had a short trigger too, and would start a fight at the drop of a hat. That's the kind of guy he was.

Being out in the country, we also fished and hunted a lot. A lot of it was for our own consumption, but often we hunted to earn some extra money. In the early thirties, when I was around ten years old, my brother Alex and I for a while ran a muskrat line and trapped muskrats along this big, cattail pond. Since we could not afford to buy a trap, we did the next best thing: we stole one.

One day when I was down along the canal, I saw an empty muskrat line. Taking out my knife, I cut the line, lifted the trap out of the water, and took it home. Just like for ocean fishing, traps had to somehow be identified, and this one had the owner's name etched into the metal. So, with a file, I sanded off his name. Then I carved my own initials onto the metal, and *voila!* Our own trap. Alex stole another one, and now we were ready for business.[5]

We mostly tried to trap the muskrats for the fur. If we caught any, we would skin them with a couple of wooden roof shingles that we carved out to look like arrowheads. Then we turned the muskrat inside out, sliced all the meat off real good, and then turned it back the way it was. They we rubbed it with salt to cure it.

---

5   The pond in later years was dredged out and Coventry High School was built there.

We would then take the furs, dry them, and when we had three or four, we would sell them. The meat we would take down to Snydertown[6] and sell them for 25 cents apiece—which was a good deal for us, because those poor people there just loved muskrat meat. Then we would take the furs to some guy that bought them for a living and get $1.65 each. Of course, that was for a prime fur, with no holes or nicks in it. Otherwise, the buyer paid us less.

One nice thing about this was that Pop actually supported our operations. In 1932, he built us this little shed with a small roof that had two sloped sides. At the top of the shed we built a loft where we took care of some tumbler pigeons.[7] I drilled a couple holes into the side near the roof, and the pigeons would come in and live inside at the top. Behind it, Alex and I had a chicken coop where we kept dozens of chickens. There was a small stream back there, and we built a chicken coop right along the stream. Over the next six years, I also caught and eventually tamed some 15 or 20 mallard ducks and kept them there. To keep them from flying away, I would trim their wings on one side with a pair of scissors, so when they tried to fly, they'd get airborne and flip around and fall to the ground.

Despite the fact that in 1934 the country was in the Great Depression, I surprisingly had a lot of fun just living life. We were just outside of Akron then, living in an underdeveloped part of Kenmore.

When I was 12, we fished a lot at the lakes. Big drainage pipes that were three feet round would empty into them. We caught a lot of shad, but they were very boney. They were not fit to eat, but they were fun to catch. They would swim right up to us, and we would grab them for fun. If we could catch enough to fill a washtub, they would give us a whole five bucks.

Other types of fish we caught were good to cook and eat, like bluegill. Of course, we couldn't afford bait, but we did not need to. Waddy

---

6   Snydertown, located in the southern part of Barberton, historically for decades was a very poor neighborhood, perhaps the poorest section of Barberton, especially during the Great Depression.

7   These are (usually) domesticated pigeons renowned for their ability to "tumble" as they fly. This is done by rolling over or flipping around backwards in flight.

and I found out that an effective bait, especially for bluegill, was water crickets. We would rake the shallows near underwater grass or stones, and these water crickets would pop up. They were only about a third of an inch long, but they could get around pretty good underwater, and so they made great bait. We would hook one and toss it out over the water on a simple line, and them bluegill would love to take a lunge at them. Even better, we could catch a whole bunch of them and take them over to the bait shop, where we could get a penny a piece for them. So if you had a hundred, that was a dollar; pretty good money for those days.

Many of our fishing spots were way out in secluded areas. There was a rumor that the gangster Pretty Boy Floyd had a hideout there. Every once in a while, we might see some stranger back there, walking by at a distance, so I probably saw him once or twice.

Now Waddy would do just about anything for a laugh, and he loved to see others in some sort of distress. Sometimes, we would go out to a lake and gig for snapping turtles. We could get up to five bucks for one. Normally, we'd take out our old johnboat. One guy would stand in front and pole. The other one would do the gigging using a nice two-prong branch with the ends sharpened. Waddy liked to be in front. So he'd pole, and I'd gig, which worked out well, because I was better at that. When he spotted a turtle's head moving along the water making a trail through that green crap on the surface, he would steer the boat after it, and I would spear the thing.

One day, we were out gigging by Nesmuth Lake. I was at the stern this time, doing the poling. Waddy was at the front with the wooden gig. He spotted a turtle head gliding along, and told me to steer the boat over to the spot. When we got close, instead of gigging the turtle, Waddy leaned over, reached down, grabbed it, and threw up it into the boat, next to me.

He grinned and said calmly, "Here, tie this sonuvabitch up."

My eyes must have got big around as the turtle flopped there, and I said, "Damn!" I mean, this was one big-assed turtle. My first thought was to jump out of the boat. I grabbed a rope and when he opened his mouth to snap at me, I shoved the rope into his mouth and wrapped it around his head. Boy, I had some choice words for Waddy while he laughed his head off.

In junior high school, one of the most popular pastimes was marbles. Every kid had a sack of marbles, one of them little pull-string bags. At recess, all the kids would run outside. The marble players would get together, and the rest of the kids would gather around to watch. Then we would start shooting marbles. We had all kinds of games and once in a while, a contest. I considered myself a great marble player, and in the sixth grade, I fancied myself the marble champ in the school. That was my highlight of sixth grade.

I tried to participate in school sports, and one season I tried out for football, but as it turned out, I could not stay on the team, because you needed three bucks to pay for a doctor's examination.

I went to Pop, "I need three dollars to get that exam."

My old man hit the roof. He refused to come up with the money.

We were destitute. You just couldn't get that kind of money out of poor folks back then, especially from tightwads like my dad. Hell, in those days, it only cost a nickel to get into the movie theater, and he didn't even want to give me that. You know, they had them weekly 15-minute serials back then, and I just loved them. But I never got a nickel for Saturdays, and no money, no admittance. So of course, I'd sneak in. When the guy wasn't looking, I'd slip around him and get in that way.

Most of the time though, I spent the hours alone, wandering around, exploring.

Once I had the opportunity to work in the circus when it came to Akron. I was about 12 or 13 at the time. Waddy and I walked over to where they were setting up the tents and hung out with other local workers that they had hired for odd jobs. Actually, nearly all of them were hobos that lived in the "hobo jungles" around the swamp next to the railroad tracks near Waddy's house. We would often walk by their campouts and sometimes stop and listen to them talk.

We were enthralled with everything about the circus, and so like the hobos, we tried to get odd jobs, sometimes just working for free to get in and see the acts. This one year, we were "hired" to haul water for the elephants. The circus supervisor figured that we should do our jobs just for the privilege of being there, so we were not paid. Hell, they didn't even give us free admission to see the shows.

Naturally, that was not going to stop us, so that night we tried to sneak in. We knew the layout of the area where the elephants were kept because we had worked there, so that was the spot where we would try to get in. The only ones that tried to stop us from getting in were, surprisingly, the damn elephants.

Now growing up in the outdoors, I had seen plenty of dung in my life. But I had never seen elephant droppings before, and these elephants were full of them. The dung balls were huge, and not very round, but oblong. They looked like heavy, brown loaves of bread, or flattened volleyballs, with the ends sort of squared off. Well, as we tried to sneak in, a couple of them saw us. They started grabbing these dung balls with their trunks and threw them at us. I didn't know they could even do that.

Have you ever been hit in the chest with elephant crap? It's bad enough that they smell and smear your shirt, but the damn things will knock you over. Some gratitude for getting those monstrosities fresh water.

Still, I loved working there for the circus, and after watching a couple of the shows, I seriously thought about going off with them. But in the end, I decided to stay where I was. I sometimes wonder what my life would have been like if I had joined that circus.

I have to admit that back in the thirties, my brother and I were two ornery little rascals. You could say the same for the Getz brothers. I wouldn't say we were out and out delinquents, and we never did anything to try to hurt anyone. We didn't go out to roll anyone or beat anybody up. We were just having fun. Still, we often got into trouble just for the spirit of the adventure.

Take Halloween, for instance. No one went trick or treating—I mean, it was the Depression. People didn't have anything to give out back then, and it was a sure thing that no one could afford to give out candy. So we'd take some cow crap, tiptoe up someone's steps, and smear it all over the doorknob. Then we would knock on the door and run like hell. Whoever was home would open the door, come out and see no one. Hopefully, they would grab the outside knob to go in again, and thus get the crap all over their hands. Then we would ha-ha-ha and go off to try it again.

Then there was the time we faked a corpse along the side of the road. We just wanted to shock some folks for the hell of it. Waddy, Alex and I put together this dummy made out of straw, some leaves, and a few tree branches. We dressed it with some stinky old clothes that we had found in the dump along with a couple of old shoes, and tied a thin piece of rope to one of the legs. We smudged the rope with soot so that it would not stand out in the dark.

One spot we picked was next to a wooded area along this gravel road. The location was perfect. It was along a relatively clear stretch next to these swamps, with a cemetery on each side of the road. We got Waddy to act as lookout, so he would climb a tree and sit up there. We then would put the dummy alongside the road to make it look like a dead body, and string the rope down the embankment and into the woods. When Waddy spotted a car coming, he'd let us know. If a car stopped and the driver got out to check out the dead body, we would yank on the rope and pull the dummy into the woods. The body would seem to disappear, and there would be no corpse out there for the driver to examine. Hopefully, that would scare the crap out of the guy.

That first night, Waddy shimmied up his tree, and Alex and I placed the dummy next to the road, face down, looking like a corpse. We strung the rope into the woods and got behind a tree. Then we waited.

Sure enough, it was not long before Waddy whispered down from above, "Hey, someone's coming!"

Alex and I crouched down and waited. A car came down the road. It slowed down, and then stopped. As soon as we heard the car door open, we pulled on the rope and our dummy slide down the bank and into the woods with us. We heard couple little muffled sounds come from the guy before he jumped back into his car and took off like a bat out of hell.

We laughed hysterically, and then after a while, set the dummy out again. We did this a few more times, and usually the guy wouldn't see us. No, they would look for the body, not see it, and then freak out, jump back in the car, and take off in a swirl of dust.

One time though, the driver caught on and took off after us. But we were masters at getting away from folks, and once we fled into the swamp, usually no one would want to follow us. And even if they did, they would never be able to catch us. They certainly were in no shape to. No, the swamps were always our refuge.

Years later when I recalled that memory, someone asked me "Hey, what about the guy in the tree? You know, the one that was the lookout? Wasn't he stuck up there?"

I just laughed and said, "Well, that was his problem. He was supposed to be quiet up there. No one was going to think to look up in the branches, and if they did, they sure as hell weren't going to spot him up there in the damn dark. So all he had to do was keep his mouth shut and he'd be fine. Besides, I don't think any of them would be in shape to climb up the tree anyway."

A week or so later, we decided to try something different. This time, we fixed on using a purse. Times being what they were, we figured someone would stop, hoping that there would be money or jewelry in it. A guy would get out, and we would yank on the rope, and the purse would disappear.

We found an old beat-up purse in the junk yard. Hell, it even had a hole in it, but that didn't matter to us. We tied it to the rope, found one of our spots along the road, and tried it out one night. Of course, the gag worked, although I have to admit, not every time. Sometimes, the car would keep going. When that happened, we kind of figured the driver did not see the purse in the dark, or saw it and did not know what it was, or just got scared because it looked like a setup and kept going.

We did this a couple times, laughing our heads off afterwards. Unknown to us though, one of these drivers had been on his way to work at the Palmer Match Company,[8] which was down the road on the west side, across the street from the Akron Porcelain Company.

---

8   The company, located in Akron, was an Ohio-based corporation, named after Charles Palmer, who also founded the Diamond Match Company.

This guy went into work really mad. He told his co-workers about the missing purse, and said something like, "There's something fishy going on down there."

He must have got the whole damn company to come after us, because eight or nine cars pulled up. They kept pulling up and parking, and then these burly guys would get out carrying flashlights and stuff. Crap, there must have been over twenty guys out there trying to find us. Naturally, we got a head start and all took off down the swamps. Not that we needed any, because they were wearing regular work clothes that they probably were not too keen to get all muddy, and we kids were in rags, basically at home in the swamps. The swamp was dark, mucky, and there were a lot of pools of water that they would get soaked in, and bunches of big bushes that we could hide behind or run around. They didn't catch a darn one of us. But we could hear them up there beating the brush and yelling. They finally gave up and left.

We did other pranks from time to time, but the dead body thing was our favorite. And from time to time, we would pick a different spot to pull it off. Our favorite place was this one spot next to a factory. We liked it because there was a draw right there, and you could disappear down that draw right into the swamp. Hell, there was no way in the world anyone could catch us. And no one ever did. Good thing I guess, because if any one of us would have ever been caught, he would have gotten his butt beaten.

As luck would have it though, we screwed up again, because the second or third car we did this to was our own, and my dad was driving with a couple of his buddies. They stopped, could not find the body, and went off towards our house. We were scared now because it was Pop, and because the guys were talking about going to our house and getting a couple of shotguns to come back and to shoot those "rotten sonsabitches that are pulling this crap." As if that was not bad enough, they had been drinking.

Well, the hell with that! Alex and I took off, splitting up in the swamps. Poor old Waddy in the tree was on his own. I ran through the marshes in the darkness like my life depended on it—which at that point, I reckoned it did. I made it through the backwoods and finally got back home. Dad and his pals were in the living room having a drink of some local stuff they had brewed. They were talking some real trash, getting ready to go out again and look for whoever had pulled that off and shoot them. They were serious, too.

I waited in the living room and started to worry because there was no sign of Alex. The old man and his buddies finished their drinks and got ready to go out. I could tell that they were getting smashed. I began to freak out. My own father was about to go out and hunt down and shoot my brother, his eldest son. I thought about telling Dad everything, but I figured the shape he was in, daggone, he probably would have shot ME instead.

I was starting to go nuts, wondering what I was going to do, when I heard the back door to the kitchen quietly open. It was Alex, finally home, dirty from head to toe, but safe. Man, I sure breathed a sigh of relief.

Naturally, even though Pop and his cronies were still out there, they didn't find anything. No people, no purse. Them damn goofs, half lit, were mad as hell and out there talking all kinds of trash, and that they were gonna shoot whoever the hell it was, but we didn't care. We had made it home safe.

It was just as well though, that the phenomena of the phantom body along the road stopped after that.

We did other things as well during that time, and thank heavens for the swamps so that we could make a quick escape. Sometimes on weekends we would aggravate one or two farmers that lived in the area. We would on occasion go ride their horses. We would take some old rope and make a harness out of it. Then we would toss it over the head of one of his horses in the field and go riding off and play games. Sometimes we would get sticks and just like knights in medieval times, we would go jousting, charging our horses at each other. One time though, we must have miscalculated our steering, and our two charging horses hit head on, and both of them went rolling. It was a wonder we were not killed.

We also used to raise corn and stuff, and we'd sell produce up in the allotment that was bordering our area there. Often though, we supplemented what we sold with produce we would get from other folks.

With time we became bolder in our ventures. There were some fields where blackberries grew, and when they were in season, we would pick them to sell. We got ten cents a quart for blackberries and sixty cents a quart for black raspberries if we could find them.

And corn. My goodness, the corn. There was this one farmer that used to grow this sweet corn. Times being what they were, we thought that we would take advantage of that when the stalks were ripe. Waddy would climb this big maple tree on the other side of the road next to the cornfield, and when it was dark, we would go at it, picking what we wanted. No one could see us. Waddy could see a half mile down the road. And back then, a car wouldn't come by for a good fifteen minutes or so. It actually got to the point where we started picking corn in broad daylight. We always seemed to get away with it. Then we'd go up to the allotment and sell it. It wasn't exactly honest, but come on, what else was a poor kid going to do in times like that? I ain't proud of doing that, but I have to admit, it was kind of funny in a way.

My escapades with stolen corn came up again a few years later when I got ready to go into the service. Although I was 18, I still had to get someone to sign my enlistment papers. My dad would not do it, so I tried to get my grade school principal to sign them. He agreed to, and when I took the papers over to his house, he spread them out on the table, looked at them, and grabbed a pen.

Before he did though, he looked up at me with a squinty eye and said, "Listen though. Don't think you were fooling me when you were selling me that corn."

Waddy and I had a couple times stolen some field corn, or what we called "hog corn," because it was only fit for hogs to eat. But because the kernels were white, we sometimes passed it off to a few people—which included evidently, our principal—as "country gentleman" corn, which was a developed white sweet corn and looked just like what we had stolen.

All I could say was, "Uh, uh …"

He looked square into my face, pointed a boney finger at me, and said, "I knew you were selling me field corn."

I knew my face was red, and all I could do was look down in shame. I mumbled, "I'm sorry." I sure as hell was not going to tell him that besides selling him field corn, I often used to take peaches off of his tree, too. He had a peach tree out in the front yard, and every time I went by there at night, I'd go into his yard and help myself.

Sometimes, just being ornery, we'd go into a farmer's field where his cows were and milk them. We didn't carry a pail or anything. One of us would just lie under the cow, and the other one would grab its teat and spurt the warm milk into his mouth. Then we would switch places. Once in a while we got spotted by the farmer, and he'd get mad as hell.

Sometimes he would even get a rifle and take potshots at us. Once I was in his field and heard him bellowing. I looked up and saw him aiming a rifle. I took off for the swamp as I heard a shot. He fired a couple more times, and once I heard the bullet hit a tree nearby. I didn't know if he was missing me on purpose to scare me or if he was really trying to take me down, but I damn sure was not going to wait around to find out.

The Getz family lived a mile or so down the road on a farm going into the city. Their farm was located in a swamp near one of the Portage lakes. They lived in a cabin that the brothers and their dad, Seymour had built using some old abandoned railroad ties for the four walls. Seymour was a horse trader, and he used the land around the swamp for his horses.

Northward, behind Waddy's house and next to the swamp were a couple sets of railroad tracks, and on the other side were some open spots where the hobos used to camp out, the "hobo jungles." For me and Waddy though, this was a place that we loved to visit. He and I enjoyed hanging out with these guys, listening to them for hours, always wanting to hear about their neat adventures (when we were not looking for excitement ourselves). We would sit with them by their makeshift fires, often well into the evening. Sometimes we brought food, like maybe some fish we'd caught that day. We were naturally fascinated with their lifestyles, and so we would stay and watch them cook their meals and be all ears as these vagabonds told these tall tales of things they had seen or done all over the country. We'd get filled with the excitement that two boys could only imagine, as wild, stirring images rushed through our minds.

Sometimes we would even stay all night and have our own little campout with them.

Of course, this gave my old man fits.

He tried to tell me time and time again about how dangerous these guys could be. Still, the idea that hanging out with these vagabonds might not be a safe idea never occurred to us. For one thing, back then, being a drifter did not necessarily mean that you were dumb or a social outcast. Times were rough for everyone. A couple of these guys once upon a time had actually owned some money or had held a high position. But because of the Depression and other things that had happened to them, they for some reason had ended up on the road, bumming from town to town. Surprisingly, there were usually a couple guys in the group that had some education and had been somebody in the past. We figured the dangerous hobos usually stuck to themselves. Besides, back then, we were kids, and did not think that anyone would hurt us.

There was one group that we did fear and stay away from. It was back around 1927. At that time, we lived in a row of four or five flats about two miles from where we finally ended up on Wingate Avenue. We stayed in that flat for six months until, of course, the rent really got overdue. There was a big field behind us, and on the other side was the Goodrich Rubber Company. They had this big storage area with tall piles of old tires. You could always tell when you got close to it, because it seemed like they were always burning some old tires, and you could see the wisps of smoke and smell the burning rubber.

Well, one summer, some gypsies came into that large open area behind our flats. They just moved in and set up some tents. This really upset my mom and dad, because the popular belief back then was that gypsies used to steal kids. So we were told over and over: stay the hell away from those gypsies, or else we'd never be seen again. And let me tell you, it worked, because we never went near them.

When I hit my teens, I started taking an interest in girls. Now Waddy's dad grew corn in a field about a mile away and he would shuck all the corn on this one acre. Waddy and I played there a lot. Later on, in 1936, when we were in the eighth grade, Waddy got himself a girlfriend named Donna, who was in the seventh grade. He sometimes took her over to this acre to mess around. Even at that age, Donna was already a somewhat loose young thing, and so we sometimes each spent a session with her. One would play lookout, while the other was, shall we say, "getting familiar." She eventually got the nickname of "Cornshock Donna."

Her parents owned a home nearby. So sometimes when they were out working, we'd go over to her house and lock the front door. Waddy and I would take turns playing lookout. The only thing was that Waddy was not as diligent about the job as I was, and because of that, we once got into big trouble.

One day my dad got an old Durant car.[9] Now he was a wiz at mechanical stuff, and after working on it for a week or so, he was able to fix the engine. In the meantime, he took off all the body parts and the metal work. Then using a rusty old abandoned piece of plow equipment that he had found and pulled out of the ground, he built himself this sizable plow, with a big lever. Then he mounted the plow assembly with wheels onto the back end of the motor frame and somehow hooked up the drive. When he managed to get this monstrosity running, he drove it out to a field and began using it to plow the land. It worked pretty good too, and with it, we used to grow different sorts of vegetables, mostly potatoes. Dad used the plow to first dig up the ground, and then later to harvest the potatoes with the plow pulling them up. Man, at one time we had potatoes all over the place, and kids came in from all over the neighborhood to help us. We'd watch him overturn the ground, and then we would dig into it with our hands. For a while there, we had potatoes coming out of our ears.

As we kids grew older, we became bolder in our adventures. When I was 14, we began to perfect our train-hopping skills. Back then, trains

---

9   Durant Motors out of Lansing, Michigan, built automobiles from 1920 to 1929. It was later turned into a General Motors Fisher Body center, and subsequently built Buicks and Cadillacs. The factory finally closed in 2005.

were the major source of transportation for bulk goods, and Akron had miles of main tracks and spurs used for industry, especially along the Belt Line, which was a railroad line that ran between Barberton and Akron along a 15-mile stretch lined with a string of shops and factories. Where we lived, a few of the big companies had their own individual side spurs, where trains would drop off and pick up boxcars and flatcars of supplies. When they did, they moved very slowly, making them easy to hop on. The Akron Porcelain Company would get boxcars full of these dusty 98-lb. bags of some white powder to make the porcelain.[10] Waddy and I would sometimes be able to land part-time jobs unloading those bags for cash.

Once in a while, we'd hop on a freight train to help ourselves to products being shipped. One of our targets, especially in the fall and winter, were coal cars. Usually there were a couple in a train, because that was the main fuel that factories used. We would wait at a curve where the train slowed down, and when a coal car came by, we jumped on. We would climb the side ladders to the top and start throwing lumps of coal over onto the ground. When we had tossed enough, we'd climb back down the side ladder, jump off, and then walk back, gathering up the coal lumps to carry them back to our homes for our fireplaces. Coal after all burned much better than wood, and it beat the hell out of sawing and hauling green wood.

Soon Waddy's younger brother Boysee started coming along with us. Unfortunately, he was not as wise in hopping on, and the second time he tried, he was almost killed. He and I that day had spotted our train, figuring that we would ride it for a mile or two. After all, it beat walking. So, after several cars had gone by, we made our move. Coming out of the bushes on the left side of the tracks, we began running alongside the moving train, picking up speed. Each boxcar or gondola had two iron ladders on each side, one at the front and one at the back. Now the object was to run alongside the train until we got our speed up and came to the ladder that we wanted to jump onto. You'd grab the side rails with your hands and then jump onto the bottom rung footrest. When

---

10 Powdered kaolin.

you did, you had to grip hard, because between the train's continuing momentum and your sudden stop, there was a tendency for your body to swing around towards the back.

Boysee went first, and I was to follow him and jump onto the next car. Running behind him, I watched as he jogged up next to the train. But he screwed up, making three critical mistakes. First, when he made his move, he was not running as fast as he should have been. As he ran alongside the train, it was moving faster, and the boxcar was slowly passing him. Second, when he finally grabbed for the ladder and jumped on, he managed to grab with only his right hand, and not his left, and as he did so, his feet were not yet firmly planted onto the footrest rung.

The third and most critical mistake was that even though he should have known better, he chose the rear ladder of the boxcar to grab, not the front one. I had learned early on that this was important, because if you hopped onto the front ladder and your body did twirl around because of the train's momentum, you'd just swing around and smack into the side of the boxcar. All you have to do is hold on to the side rail for dear life. If however, you made your move on the *rear* ladder and your body swung around, you would twirl around the end of the car into the gap between the cars, and there would be nothing there to stop your swing. So if you whirled around hard enough, you could lose your grip and fall onto the coupling, and probably down between the cars.

And that's exactly what happened. The train's momentum swung Boysee into the space between the boxcars, and because he didn't have a firm hold of the side rail, the swing tore his grasp and he fell backward between the cars. Sliding off the coupling, he slipped down between the moving cars and smacked onto the tracks, stumbling over a couple ties as the second car rolled by above him.

I watched horrified as I ran up and crouched down to try and help him. But there was nothing I could do as the cars rolled by. Boysee got up to his hands and knees, and somehow or another, he quickly scurried over to the other side. Timing the speed of the cars, he lunged between the wheels of the car going over him and as he cleared them, he rolled over the track and down the embankment. He missed getting run over by the car's right rear wheels by only a couple feet. I breathed a sigh of relief.

CHAPTER 2

Before the Corps

The Great Depression of the 1930s caused hundreds of thousands of families to lose their homes and become nomads. Every day became a challenge to live. Looking for refuge, folks would often stop for the night or camp out for weeks in the flimsiest of shelters, often thankful to stay in some ramshackle shanty or falling-down shed, desperate to find enough food to feed the children. Because the burden of their plight disheartened many such drifting families, teenagers, by nature energetic, wanting to work, and to varying degrees ambitious, often decided to go off on their own, either to assist their family in some way, or to at least alleviate the burden on their parents. Then of course, there was the call of adventure, and because it had become so commonplace, the quixotic image of a carefree life on the road—which, of course, quickly faded after several nights under the stars, or after a number of missed meals. Also, as many youths found out, the makeshift camps that tramps and drifters stopped in overnight often included ruthless, callous individuals that had no qualms about cheating someone, especially unsuspecting youths. Most hobo jungles were aptly named. Teenagers found that the best way to strike out on their own was to get involved in some venture that offered them shelter, allowed them to travel, and at the same time, gave them a sense of purpose, all while the country struggled economically to get back on its feet.

As I started my teenage years, I guess that my outdoor style of upbringing had sort of instilled in me a strong sense of restlessness. I finally dropped out of Kenmore High School in June of 1938 at 15 years of age. Times were tough, and another depression had started, sort of like an extension of the big one that had hit us in 1929. So I decided to join the Civilian Conservation Corps, the CCC.[1]

One good reason was because we were poor and I needed some sort of work to support myself and help support my family. Another was just the fact that I could get out on my own and get to go out West for adventures, and also get paid for helping improve the land.

I think my going off was sort of inevitable. I had this wanderlust; I would have eventually gone off on my own anyway, going somewhere, anywhere, because I grew up as a rover. Joining the CCC was the chance I wanted to get away from home; I felt it was time.

A big reason though was to get away from my father.

There had been some trouble brewing with him for a while. Part of the reason was that I was now a teenager and my hormones were in play. Also I was growing to be a stubborn little cuss, and, as such, my resentment towards the way he treated all of us was increasing. Often, he would work on a job, get paid, and then go to a bar and start drinking his money away. Alex and I would finally have to go looking for him, sometimes finding him in an alley passed out. We then somehow had to get him home. What made it much worse was that hardly anyone could reason with him when he had been drinking, and he was doing more and more of that. Alex took his guff well enough because he was more obedient. But I became more and more upset with his cranky moods, and especially the way he treated mom.

---

1   The Civilian Conservation Corps was a federal-government-sponsored program initiated in March 1933 by President Roosevelt. Considered a critical component of his New Deal, it helped offset the ravages of the Depression and to stimulate economic growth within the country. The CCC employed young males up to the age of 25 on various projects designed to improve the land. These included working on roads, forests, flood plains, dams, and various agricultural projects, especially if they had to do with soil erosion and land conservation. Workers were sent to all parts of the United States to work on such projects for construction, farms, working camps, rivers, and parks. Laborers were provided food and shelter, and given uniforms. The CCC existed until the Depression ended and World War II began.

That is not to say that he did not have his good points. When he was sober, he usually was okay, although even then he had occasional moods. Sometimes, he would go a month or even two without taking a drink and was usually easy to get along with. Then he would fall off the wagon and go into one or more of his mean drunks. Afterwards, he would be sorry for what he had done, or just deny ever having been that way, sometimes even laughing about it with "Aw, c'mon. I wasn't like that," or "I didn't do that." I found out in later years that there was actually a term for that: a "periodic alcoholic."[2]

Things between the two of us came to a head in the late spring of 1938. We were living at 2941 Wingate Avenue at the time. We had built the house on a slant, so the front end was low to the ground. One day, we were working on the house, my father and I both standing on a scaffold. He noticed something that really upset him and somehow figured that it was my fault. So he started in on me. Yelling at what I had done, he gave me hell. Upset, and on the spur of the moment, I badmouthed him back. He got furious and tried to take a swing at me. I ducked, jumped off the scaffold and took off. Not knowing where to go, I finally went over to Waddy's house to stay there until the old man calmed down.

I avoided him for three days, staying with my friend. Finally, at my mom's insistence, I reluctantly came home. It was evening as I walked into the house, my radar up, ready for anything. The old man saw me come in and just glared at me. Mom, perhaps trying to divert trouble, told us that supper was ready. Everyone sat down, with me, still hesitant, coming into the dining room last. Pop as usual sat at the head of the

---

2   Also called "binge drinker," the term refers to an alcoholic that a good deal of the time appears normal and consumes little or no alcohol, but then suddenly drinks massive amounts for a period of time, during which they show a totally altered character. They then sober up and either show remorse or a lack of memory on their altered state. The normal periods of ordinary behavior and actions often fool people (especially those who do not live with them) that they do not have a drinking problem. They also often exhibit traits of a "blackout drinker," one who drinks until they pass out, and then later have no memory of how they acted.

table, and slowly, hesitantly, I sat down in my spot, which unfortunately was the chair just to his left.

Pop sat there giving me a dirty look. I tried to look penitent and did not say anything. That did not help though. All this time, he had been festering over my disrespectful behavior and then taking off and not being around to be punished. In a sudden fit of rage, he swung at me with his left fist. He landed a solid shot on my chin, knocking me backward off my chair and onto the floor. My head woozy, I slowly got up and gritted my teeth. I left the table and went to my room, swearing to myself that I would never ever let him hit me again.

Perhaps if that had been the end of it, I might have worked through his temperament. Unfortunately though, I soon realized that he was not satisfied. So for the next few days, I tried to avoid him. A week after that incident at the table came another. That day, everyone was gone. I was totally alone in the house. I fixed me a late afternoon snack and had just sat down at the dinner table when the front door opened and my father came in. I could tell that he'd been drinking and was in a foul mood.

I tried to stay calm. He walked into the kitchen and came out holding a large carving knife in one hand. He picked up a china plate and sat down at his usual spot next to me. Sitting there drunk, looking angrily at me, he took the knife and tapped it on the plate. Then he did it again, letting the knife edge hit the plate. He whacked the plate again, stronger this time, doing a slow burn, staring at me. Another whack and I noticed small slivers of china were breaking off the plate's surface. Another smack, and more slivers. Pop kept sitting there, glaring at me, slowly hacking this plate to pieces. Then he started muttering that I was a no-good rotten this and that, and once in a while slipping in a veiled threat.

Finally, finished eating and not knowing what else to do, I stood up. Pop began to stagger to his feet. Before he could fully stand up, I grabbed for his hands. Somehow, I got the knife away from him and tossed it to the floor. But because somewhere deep within me I still respected him, I decided that I would not hit him if I could help it.

Growling, he lurched at me, but in his sloshed condition, he was slow and unsteady. I grabbed him from behind. Pop struggled, but I had too firm a grip on him. Grimly I held on as he kept trying to break free. Pop was not in shape though, and being overweight, much older, and, of course, drunk, he could not get out of my bear hug. I could tell that he already was getting tired. Finally, in frustration, he stiffened his body and lurched backward. We both went flying back and fell into the side of the davenport, knocking it over. I held on though, and as we rolled onto the floor, I kept my bear hug around him. He could not get loose. Finally, drunk as all get out, as we lay there, he started crying, looking for sympathy, feeling sorry for himself.

We finally made our peace, but I realized at that point that I had to move out. Going over my options the next few days, I concluded that the CCC seemed the best way to do that. After all, Alex had joined a year ago, and had done well, working on projects in Ohio. He had worked on that big park in Akron, and then gone down to old Shonbrook village, staying in a cabin.

My joining would remove my constant annoying presence, make some money for the family, and let me go on an adventure somewhere, all expenses paid, and being away from the Akron area would do both me and Pop a lot of good. Everyone could save face. And I also hoped that he might treat my mother better if I got off the scene.

The only problem was that I was still 15 years old and technically too young to join by two years and three months. So I sort of "modified" my birth certificate to reflect an older age. I thought adding two more years would be believable, and close enough to allow me to join, because in a few months, I would turn "18" and then I would be (to them) totally legitimate.

It worked, and they took me, along with a few other kids in the area. However, they scheduled us not to stay in Ohio, but to go west to work on projects. I looked forward to going, and it reflected in my attitude. So I became even more cheerful than I usually was. My father told me many years later that a friend of his was also going into the CCC and hoped that he would run into me somewhere out West. He asked Dad how he would be able to recognize me. My father looked at him, made a face, and said, "You look around and see the guy with the biggest smile on his face. That'll be him."

Go west, young man

A couple days later, having packed a few things, I left home and boarded a truck along with some other guys, and we headed over to the Akron armory. There we took some tests before they loaded us up and sent us down to Fort Knox, Kentucky. We spent almost two weeks down there, taking classes on what we were going to be doing. Then we were given a lot of shots in both arms. The medics told us that if we got dizzy, to sit down real quick. I started getting light-headed so I sat right down and put my head in between my legs and stayed there until it passed.

After almost two weeks in Fort Knox—they do not let anyone go into their vault to look at all that gold—they loaded us up on trains and we headed west. I had hopped on trains before, but sitting in one was a new experience for me, and I loved it. We sat and watched parts of the country I had never seen before. The weather was great, so the views were fantastic, and I was like a kid in a candy store, watching the world go by.

Yeah, traveling was for me.

We finally made it out to Colorado and I got my first look at the Rockies. I stared at all those big mountains, those mile-high peaks. The train went across some high trestles that were over some really steep gorges. It was kind of scary for me, because we could see down pretty good, and I wasn't used to that sort of thing.

As the train started up another incline, we went around a bend to the left and saw in the distance another tunnel. Now you have to imagine. We were riding in these old cars that I swear must have been converted from old cattle cars. They were made of cheap wood, with wooden seats and simple thin windows, and that was it. We had found out early in our trip that whenever the train went through a tunnel, breathing became a problem. If you snapped the windows down to open them, then the heavy exhaust fumes from the steam locomotive's smokestack billowed into the car. We had trouble breathing, and man, all that smoke and soot. If you kept the car windows up, you avoided a lot of the smoke, but not so much the fumes, especially if the car was not airtight.

We had been through a couple dozen tunnels so far in our trip. Now this one we were approaching was called the Moffat Tunnel. We were told it was the longest tunnel in the world—about six miles.[3] So we got ready.

We heard the guys in the car in front of us holler, "Tunnel!" So we made sure the windows were up, and then all grabbed for something to breathe through. Those of us with handkerchiefs pulled them out and tied them around their mouths to breathe. I didn't have one, so I just pulled my shirt over my mouth.

We entered that long dark tunnel. The train was going slower because we were going uphill. We sat there in our seats, struggling to breathe as this black smoke swirled around the tunnel walls, and the windows of our old car, then in through the vents and around us. After a while, I thought that the damn thing would never end.

When we finally made it through the other side, we had tears in our eyes, coughing and hacking from breathing in all that exhaust. Some of the guys were gagging, trying not to throw up. We all saw that we had these dark rings and black grunge all over us. Our faces were dark with soot, some of us so much that all you could make out was the whites of our eyes. But man, it was a relief to finally come out.

After passing through the Rockies, we got off in a town in the middle of nowhere, called Price Utah. It was the closest railroad junction to where we were heading, but still about 120 miles from our final destination, a small town called Vernal, near the border with Colorado.[4]

Walking around Price in our dirty clothes (compliments of the tunnels), I saw a world of tan. This was the country's Dust Bowl, created from all the droughts that had recently hit the area. This town was a good example of that. There was just sand and dust. I mean, the streets were paved with brick underneath, but all you could see was this sand. It was everywhere. There were no trees growing anyplace, and I saw no grass to speak of, especially along the highways; certainly not like today. No, it was just miserable.

---

3   Finished in 1928 after five years construction, the Moffat Tunnel, named after early railroad magnate David Moffat, is located about 50 miles west of Denver, cutting through the Continental Divide some 9,200 feet above sea level for 6.2 miles.

4   About 175 miles east of Salt Lake City. The distance between Price and Vernal is actually 112 miles.

Dusty and thirsty, a couple of us walked into a drug store and asked the guy at the counter for a drink of water. But the only thing cold that he gave us was his glare as he told us that the only way we could get a drink is if we bought a meal. Well of course, we did not have any money with us. Hell, we were out there to make some. So we had to sit there outside and wait until the trucks came to get us and take us over the mountain.

The trucks finally came, and they loaded us up in the hot sun and drove us to Vernal, a small town of less than two thousand. We were told that this was a friendly town, located on the Outlaw Trail.[5] We were driven to our camp, No. 1507, a large compound. Near the front was the mess hall, the officers' quarters, and a small administration building. Down the center were eight barracks in two rows of four. That was where we would live and sleep. At the back of the compound were the garages, the truck parking lot, tool sheds, and some equipment.[6]

Because the program was run by the Army, our camp commander was an Army officer. After he gave us a welcome speech, we went to the supply tent, and the supply supervisor looked you over and issued you working clothes. Then we had evening chow and retired to our quarters.

The next day, we immediately started working on various conservation projects. If we worked away from camp, we took some smaller tents with us, and slept in them. In the hot summer, everywhere we went, we did projects in what seemed like the desert. Things were dry, and the

---

5   It was called a "friendly town" because back in the 1880s, it offered aid and sustenance to most outlaws.

6   The Vernal, Utah CCC project was established in 1935 and administered by the V Army Corps out of Fort Douglas in Salt Lake City (about 170 miles west-north-west). The camp's main focus was soil erosion and water conservation. The Vernal work crews also cleared roads during the rough winter of 1936–37 when county equipment failed. Other tasks included ranch and road repairs, and in the winter, taking feed out to starving livestock and rescuing families suffering from winter hardships. George and his co-workers going into town and spending what little money they had stimulated the impoverished local community's economy. When the CCC around Vernal finally closed down in 1942, it was heralded as one of the most successful projects of President Roosevelt's New Deal.

dust bowl stories seemed to be true. I was amazed at how arid everything was, and our soil conservation projects took on new meaning.

For one of our first summer projects, we were tasked to build this small reservoir. The engineer in charge picked a spot where there was a ravine that ran into the Colorado River. We cleared it out and then dug a three-foot hole across the end. A small group of trucks would go off to get clay and bring it in. We then dumped that clay into the ditch, and with these big poles, we stood over that ditch, added water to the clay, and kept mixing it all to build this core about 18 inches wide. That finally stopped the water from seeping.

Then we slowly built the dam and reservoir. Working onsite there in the hot sun, I found out that you did not have to be in prison to bust rocks, because that is exactly what we did. I spent long hours for about a month with these other guys, going around near that streambed, carrying sledge hammers to bust boulders and rocks for what they called riprap[7] across the front of our dam.

Out in the heat, our supervisors told us early on to cover our faces, because the sun was pretty harsh on us. Of course, there were some of the kids that wanted to prove that they were, you know, macho, and knew what they were doing. They'd work out in the open with no shirts or caps. The next day or two, they'd wake up with their faces puffed up, their backs and lips all sunburnt. So for relief, the medics would give them Vaseline to put on their backs and lips. And working out in the open, the wind would then blow sand onto their greasy lip sores and create scabs on the mouths of those dummies.

We had a simple routine. Every day except Sunday, we got up real early, made our cots, washed up, and ate breakfast. Then we were either trucked out to the worksite, or walked over if we were out in the field. The CCC provided us all the tools we needed, and the foreman made sure we did the work.

When we were at the camp, we had warm chow for our meals. When we were at a detached site though, warm meals were only for supper. At noon, they would give us a little brown bag. It had

---

7   A term for any layer of small rocks, pebbles, or concrete rubble laid around shores, streams, or bridge abutments to minimize water erosion.

in it a sandwich and a piece of fruit. The sandwiches were either cheese or peanut butter and jelly, and the fruit was usually an apple or orange.

Sometimes we would go eat in our tents to get out of the sun and away from the wind. The tents had screen sides, but of course, that did not stop the wind, and with it came the dust. Sometimes it would blow a light coat of sand on our jelly jar, so we would have to scrape the sand off to get to the jelly. That was pretty much all we got, because we had no refrigeration out there. Of course, there was water to drink, but we usually had to haul that out as well, so we would have to watch our intake. Then after lunch and a short rest, we would go back out and work on that dam again.

Because this was a federally funded program, and because we were still in a depression, the pay understandably was small. We were given $30 a month as wages. We got five silver dollars a month. The other $25 went to our families back home.

Whenever we got paid, we were also allowed to buy a CCC coupon book for a dollar. Inside were coupons that you could use to buy stuff cheap at the camp's canteen, which was a small cubbyhole store inside the mess hall. You could go there during the day and buy stuff like candy, pop, and cigarettes.

Despite the hard work, which I actually enjoyed, being out west was quite the adventure, and I had several interesting encounters with the critters in the area. We were paid little, but back then, a little was worth a lot more. On some Saturdays, when we had the money, we would hitch a ride to downtown Vernal, buy a couple bottles of Muscatel, and try to get drunk. Sometimes on weekends, our excursions went further.

Even though I was a teenager, no one really was picky about age restrictions on drinking, so I was able to get the occasional nip in whatever town we could get to. I remember one time, just for kicks, I walked into a rundown saloon with a small lizard in my shirt pocket. As I sat at the bar, the lizard crept out of my pocket, worked its way down my shirt sleeve, and onto the bar. It raised some eyebrows, but no one thought much about it.

Because I was a likeable fellow, I was able to make friends with the other young guys. Still, the fighting I went through in my pre-teen years paid off, because every once in a while, I would have to defend myself.

I remember one other guy there who for a while wanted to get into it with me. His name was Harold Hosey, and he slept in the cot across from me. It's funny that I can remember his name after all these years. He was a big old guy of Eastern European decent. Anyway, I had found this snake that seemed friendly, and after I had picked him up and spent the afternoon with it, I had decided to keep it as a pet. It was not deadly or anything, just a simple blow snake.[8] They were called that because if they were threatened, they sometimes would rise up, rear back, hiss, and puff their throat and make a blowing noise, like they were getting ready to strike. Of course it was not poisonous, so it was harmless.

The fact that it ticked off the other guys in my barracks just made it more attractive an idea. Harold in particular was really scared of that snake and was paranoid about the thing, and the longer I kept it, the more upset he became. He did whatever he could to stay out of our barracks whenever the snake was in there with me. I enjoyed its company though. I got a kick out of one time where I was walking down between the barracks carrying the snake and this dog came running up to me, barking and carrying on. Well that snake reared back and puffed up and then hissed. That scared the hell out of that dog, and it took off running. I laughed and petted my snake.

Finally, Harold had had enough. He threatened me, telling me that if I didn't get rid of that snake, he was going to whip my ass, and this and that. Now Harold was about ten years older than me, so that was going to be a problem. Luckily for me though, another guy in the barracks stepped up to defend me, looked at Harold, pointed to his chest, and told him, "Okay, but when you're through with him, I'm next." Harold

---

8   Technically, a western hognose snake. Their pattern and color are similar to that of a rattlesnake, although they are almost always gentile and not vicious. They feed on frogs and lizards.

George and his pet snake. Vernal, Utah, 1938. (Author's collection)

finally backed off, but to make peace with everyone, I eventually let the snake go.

It must have taken us a good part of that summer to finish that reservoir project. No barracks out there. No, we lived in those tents along that ravine, and at a distance, we could see you could see the Blue Mountains, which were a part of the Wasatch Mountain Range. As hot as it was during the day, we could look over to those mountains and see snow on the tops of them.

We worked hard out there, so when my 16th birthday came up on Sunday, September 18th, I figured that I deserved a break. That day, I went into town with three of my friends to celebrate. One of them was a guy named Cotton Drury. He was a fair-skinned lad, and the weather out west was not the best for his complexion. It seemed like his lips were always cracked from the Utah desert's dry heat, and because his skin suffered a lot in the sun, he looked a lot older than he was. As a matter of fact, for a young guy, he looked older than hell, even though he was 22 years old. Of course, I had only turned 16, so he looked aged to me.

We walked into town and saw that a few flocks of sheep had come through. There had once been no water in the area; that's what we built that reservoir for. Now though, the flocks would be driven through town, and that many sheep hitting that little town made quite a mess. When they left, there would be enough dung around to start a fertilizer farm … I mean, they were worse than geese.

We strolled into the town restaurant. Sitting at some of the tables were these sheep herders. That was a common occupation out there, and they would frequently come into town after work, like we did. Between the four of us, we ordered a bottle of our old standby, Muscatel. We had a few drinks and started to loosen up. The guys wished me happy birthday, and I felt good as I sat there slowly getting drunk.

Well, at least until some sheep herder in his late thirties sitting at the table across the aisle from ours started giving us a couple of dirty looks. I took a couple more sips of Muscatel, and looking around, I saw him again staring right at us. He sneered at me and said scornfully, "Look … look at him."

We stopped talking. As he kept looking at me, he made this nasty grin and said scornfully, "Look at that kid. He oughta be home with his mommy."

Bastard, I thought. It's my birthday.

I glared at him and grumbled, "What'd you say?"

He grinned. "You should be home with your mommy."

I somehow got up, and though I was a little unsteady, I walked over to his table, ready to go. "Get on yer feet, you sonuvabitch," I said defiantly.

He stood up and I took a swing at him. Cotton, who was standing behind me, also swung his arm and hit the guy dead square in the face. I don't know where on earth my swing went, but I had clean missed the fellow.

As this stranger staggered back, Cotton grabbed me by the scruff of my neck and shoved me towards the door. "Get the hell OUTA here," he growled, "before you get in trouble."

Even though I was drunk, I had sense enough to do what he said. So I staggered towards the door, and propelled myself outside onto the sidewalk. And wouldn't you just know it, our commander, the guy in charge of our entire CCC camp, was standing there. He was an Army Reserve second lieutenant and holy smokes, I almost ran into him as he stood there in uniform outside the bar. Normally, we never saw the so-and-so around the camp, but here he was now, bigger than life.

He looked down at me with a frown and asked me what I was doing and I told him I was celebrating my birthday. Then I left and went down the road lickety-split, back to camp.

A little while later as it got dark, a couple guys began waking others up. A couple more opened up the property room and began to issue pick handles.

"What's going on?" I asked.

"The town's picking on our guys, and you guys are going up to rescue them."

I was in shock. The other three guys had never made it out the restaurant. Or if they had, there were guys chasing them. The guys finally made it back to camp and the scuffle ended, but I sure did get razzed about it for a couple weeks. How about that, I thought. I'd turned 16 and started my first riot.

After about nine months working with the CCC, I was given a couple weeks of leave. So in March of 1939, I decided that I wanted to take a trip to California and go to the San Francisco World's Fair that I had heard about. I had a little money saved up, so I took a Greyhound bus and headed west. By the time the bus passed into Nevada, it was evening. We went along in the dark, seeing nothing but the road ahead and the night sky.

Then we began to see swarms of locusts hopping on the road and along the roadsides, and as we traveled, their numbers intensified. We had evidently run into some sort of a giant infestation. The more we went on, the thicker the swarm, and soon the bus began sliding back and forth along the road because of all the squished insects in the bus's tire treads and under the wheels. I had never seen anything like this before, and I just sat in my seat in wonder, shaking my head, amazed at so many thousands of these insects that were flying and jiggling and hopping all around the bus.

Driving became difficult, first to navigate, and second just to see the road. Finally, the driver had to pull off. We stayed there, watching these hordes wildly jumping around. They crawled all over the outside of the bus, and the windows were so thick with them, we could barely see the sides of the road. The biggest part of the swarm finally began to move on, and as the swarms thinned, the driver started the bus, and we continued on.

When we finally pulled into Reno, the bus took a couple hours' delay. As was my nature, I took a walk around the town exploring. One thing I wanted to see was the casinos.[9] I had never seen a professional gambling strip, and as I walked past the nightclubs, I saw sights that left me amazed. In those days, the casinos had lots of neon lights outside and all sorts of lamps inside, and these huge glass windows that let passersby stop and gaze in. Poor kid that I was, I was one of the biggest gawkers.

Each establishment had a number of gambling tables where all these people were playing cards, or roulette or throwing dice. I was amazed at all the stacks of money lying around. In those days, the casinos did not use chips. They only used silver dollars.

The bus continued on to San Francisco. There I went over to the World's Fair and managed to get a temporary job working odd tasks. I was paid little, but during that time, I got fed and free attendance to most of the features there, including the famous attractions. One thing I

---

9   Open gambling in Nevada had only been passed eight years before, partly as a result of the Great Depression, and partly because of the Hoover Dam project.

really enjoyed was watching a performance of Sally Rand,[10] even though I was only 16 years old. Her performance was a hit, and I really got a kick out of watching her glide across the stage.

Something that first surprised me was the number of gay guys around. You have to realize that back in 1939, that was a rather shunned practice, and in my life, I had never really been exposed to that sort of thing. Around San Francisco though, I was given a real experience. I guess the image of this fresh young smiling tourist teenager walking around was the sort of thing that appealed to them, or perhaps they thought that being with a guy appealed to me. At any rate, they would often pester me.

There was this bar on Broad Street called Dorsham's. I went in there on the first day in town. I happened to be wearing a cheap bowtie that I had found. To my surprise, a couple of guys tried to hit on me, and I could not figure out why. When the third one made a pass, I asked him what in blazes was going on. He finally told me that the bowtie was some kind of secret signal to other guys that I was gay. I immediately stood up and left that bar. Going outside, I ripped off my bowtie. I ain't worn one since.

I worked at the World's Fair a couple weeks or so and while I was there, I met a couple guys working like me. We talked about the dangers that this city seemed to have, so we decided to stick together for protection. The three of us left there at the end of the second day of work and took a streetcar to downtown San Francisco. We ended

---

10 Perhaps the most famous burlesque dancer, Sally Rand was renowned during the first half of the 20th century for her risqué dances. One trademark routines was an artful fan dance, something she had made internationally famous at the 1933 Chicago World's Fair. She would begin her dance in a flimsy although adequate nightgown to the tune of some classical piece of music such as Clair de Lune, elegantly twirling about with two tremendously large white ostrich-feather fans. She would then pirouette behind a translucent screen and toss off the nightgown. A backlight made the dark silhouette of her nude body clearly viewable. She would then dance out from behind the screen for the remainder of the number, and although the audience almost never saw any "critical" parts because of those huge fans that she strategically moved about, their imaginations filling in the blanks. When George saw her at the World's Fair, Sally was 35 and in her prime. She died on August 31, 1979 at the age of 75.

up going to Chinatown, because we had been told that you could get a room there cheap. I had to admit though, that the area made me kind of nervous. For one thing, there were some gruff, scary-looking people there, and a lot of them gave us some really cold, mean looks. Another thing was that I was not used to being in an environment where no one spoke any English.

We rented a cheap flop over some restaurant and while we were there, we hung out as a group. To be honest, we were afraid of them damn Chinese. We had visions of these short, fanatical Oriental guys in them black silk suits screaming and running around chasing us with hatchets. Needless to say, we were really leery being there.

I finally started back to my CCC assignment in Utah. It took a couple days to get there, hitchhiking along the only available route at the time, U.S. Highway 40. I got back to Vernal and back to work on locations far from any civilization. We always worked out in the middle of nowhere, dozens of miles away from even the smallest town, and it was always cold as hell out there, even though April was upon us.

One time, we went south to do a project near the Ouray Indian Reservation.[11] I was really surprised at how they lived. For one thing, their village was made up of these really small, low hutches made out of this molded adobe clay. Hell, I could stand next to one, and as short as I was, I could see right over it. They were like bowls in the ground. Still, they ate and slept in them, and you could see smoke coming out of some of them. We were told that these were the Ute Indians (pronounced "You-tay" but I called them "Yutes"). We drove through the reservation, crossed the Green River near Colorado, and kept driving way out into the damn desert. It was dark when the truck stopped. All 35 of us were told to get out, and to start pitching tents and to set up a spike camp.[12]

---

11 George is referring to the large Uintah and Ouray Indian Reservation, part of which is located around Ouray, Utah, about 31 miles south of Vernal. The northern tribe of the Ute Indian Nation lives on this reservation, and is the largest of the three Ute reservations. The entire reservation has shrunken significantly in size over the decades, and now is a fraction of its former size.

12 A temporary or secondary camp set up in the remote back country, not near but accessible to a main camp or base. Living provisions and logistical supplies must all be taken along.

George's CCC spike camp in Utah, fall of 1938. (Author's collection)

We used fallen logs for fire, and for water we brought our own, because there was none out there—we had a 500-gallon tank strapped onto the back of one of our three trucks.

We ended up working in that area for some three months. We moved our location once in a while, and so we saw more of those Ute Indians. I remember one time during the day, we went out and crossed the Green River, which is a lot wider than people think. As we started driving along the river, about 200 yards to our left were all these Indian women doing their laundry at the river's edge. There must have been twenty or thirty of them standing there, bent over washing clothes. As we came closer, they looked up and saw our small convoy coming down the road. I don't suppose that they had seen many people like us, so the sight of our trucks must have scared the crap out of them, because they quickly grabbed their wet buckskins and began running up the bank. Our trucks slowed down and we watched as these Indian gals ran like the devil was chasing them, back up the slopes and off to their village in the distance. Obviously, they were really terrified of us. I guess they had a right to be.

At night, tired, we would come in from a long day of work, eat, fool around for a bit, and then get ready for bed. We slept about four guys to each tent. Before you hit the sack, because the wind blew that sand everywhere, you had to scoop the sand off your cot before you crawled in.

There were some bad guys in the camp, guys that had seen the harder side of life and often seemed to have a chip on their shoulders. But we mostly avoided them, and sooner or later, most of them became outsiders, and eventually outcasts who left the CCC. Things were different back then. We all looked after each other, especially way out in the middle of nowhere. We formed our own little social groups, and then we often hung out together. Back then things were simple and not complex like they are today. Folks just looked after one another. We just kind of ruled ourselves. Nowadays, if people see someone dying on the street, they are apt to just ignore them and walk away. It pretty much wasn't like that back then, and the older ones made sure the younger ones were okay. I guess that in many ways, it was also a good time as well, and in some ways, a good time to live, a good time to grow up, as compared to the 21st century. People say that oh, those were tough times back then. But you know, by God, I wouldn't trade them for this kind of life today. Life was pretty uncomplicated. We didn't have all these fancy play toys that they have now. We didn't have anything. The work was hard, too, although I was in shape for it.

A second lieutenant ran the camp. We rarely saw him around though, except for formal ceremonies. The foreman in charge was an okay guy, although he could be a bearcat sometimes. He was just a civilian though, and he didn't have any authority over us. So his two army assistants were the authority. The leader was a husky sergeant, and the assistant a corporal.

I remember one Sunday sitting in our tents, grumbling about our lives. We had run out of fresh water. The worksite had a shallow well, and we could draw water out of it with this little pump. It was okay to wash with, but other than that, yech! It tasted horrible. It had a strong alkali base, and you couldn't drink it without getting nauseous. The water shortage, the working conditions, being out in the middle of nowhere, and the fact that they were really pushing us—all of this made us decide that afternoon to do something about our conditions.

We decided to go on strike. On Monday morning, when they blew the whistle for work, no one was to go out of their tent. We all agreed and spread the word: no one would do any work until our conditions improved. Sure enough, the next day, at 10 a.m., the foreman and his two assistants stood outside. The "485" (the sergeant) blew the whistle, and nothing happened. Nobody showed up. We all sat in our tents and waited.

He blew the whistle again. Again, nothing. So he stuck the whistle in his shirt pocket and walked over to the first tent. The rest of us got up and cautiously peaked out. He strode into the first tent and disappeared. After a few moments, here came four bodies flying out of the tent—zoom, zoom, zoom, zoom. They sailed out onto the dusty ground. Then the 485 came out of the tent and started bellowing. Wow, the center lane filled up with all of us ready to work.

That pretty much ended the strike.

As the weeks went on, we worked a number of projects. Our evenings were usually dull. We often boxed, sometimes until it was nearly daylight. That was about all we had to do. There was no recreation area, no horseshoe pits—nothing way out where we were. Once in a while, we went exploring, although we had to be careful, because there were snakes out there. Now and then, just out of boredom, we'd go out and chase jack rabbits and try to get them with just a rock. At night, if we were bold enough, we would take flashlights and go off hunting rattlesnakes. I never did that, but sometimes I would go just to watch.

If we were feeling bold, a couple of us would go on a raiding party. One night, not satisfied with the lousy meal that they had served, I and another guy decided to break into the back of the storage truck they were using as the pantry. We picked the lock and opened the truck door. In the back, we found several gallon cans of peaches and pears. We carefully grabbed a couple cans of peaches, tiptoed away from the parked truck, and took our cans down to a nearby gully.

We opened the cans, and with big spoons we had brought along, we began wolfing down those stolen peaches. Man oh man, did they taste good. We sat there in the gully in the dark, gorging on those sweet, juicy chunks. We made some disgusting slopping noises as we bolted our prizes, but of course, not loud enough to draw any attention from anyone in the camp.

We were having a great time until suddenly I heard a rattle nearby. I stopped and held up a hand to get my buddy's attention. He stopped eating and we looked at each other, listening.

There. There it was again—a faint but deadly sounding rattle. We of course assumed it was a rattlesnake. Man, we threw those cans up off our laps took off running back to our tents, and that was the end of that. The next morning the camp foreman and his guys tried to find out who had broken into the food truck. Thankfully, they never caught us; we had gotten away with that. It was a freebie.

We finished our projects in the late fall of 1938, and I was surprised when they then took us up into the mountains. We got up to such a high elevation that we reached parts covered with snow. We could actually walk in chest-deep snow to make a path. Then the sun would come out and hit it, and it would get so warm many of us would take our shirts off and get sunburnt from the rays reflecting off the snow.

The new projects were varied and interesting. We worked on roads and built cattle corrals on ranches using pine tree trunks that we had to saw the ends off. We put in wooden irrigation systems, and put up or repaired all types of fences. One of the toughest projects we did was putting up a ten-mile drift fence that went up and down cliffs and along the side of a mountain. It was hard work, and sometimes we had to put the fence up through solid rock.

The trucks would drive us to where they wanted the fence poles. The roads were at best gravel paths, so riding around up and down those mountains was a real experience. The truck would go along for a while, then drop two guys off. Each pair would scout around for a short low cedar tree and chop it down with these double-bladed axes. We would cut the ends off, carry it back to the road, and then go out for another one. Later on, the truck would come around and load the trunks up to take them off to be sawed down into fence poles.

Working on those wide open slopes during the day was quite the experience. Whenever I took a break, I would walk on top of a nice high hill for a great panoramic view. On a clear day, I could look out for what I thought was a hundred miles. And what would I see? Just about nothing but desert. Sometimes, munching on my sandwich, I might see far off in the distance some wild horses running, playing, nibbling on some shrubs. I'd sigh and smile as I watched them. Life at that point seemed great.

The grass grows high up in the mountains, and it gets thick and green in the summertime. Since there is nothing but desert below, the ranchers sometimes drove their cattle up to graze on this government land. So we built ten miles of that fence through those mountains to guide the cattle. Sometimes that fence went straight down to the bottom of a gorge.

I finally got the job of stretching the barbed wire for the fencing. I had a come-a-long with a pulley. I would hook it onto the fence post and using the jaws on the other end, I would tighten the wire from one pole to the next so that the other guys could then nail it down. I also had a big empty 50-gallon drum at the site in which I kept a fire going, so that we could stay warm. The guys hauled the wood up and I kept the fire going, as well as pulling up the slack with the come-a-long. I would say that all in all, I had a pretty good job.

We stayed up in the mountains on and off the whole winter. It snowed heavily, and a few times there would come a heavy snowstorm that pretty much brought most of the work to a standstill.

Back east

I finished my stretch in Vernal and came back to Ohio. Employment with the government CCC was a two-year contract, and the way the program was set up, if you worked for them for one full year away from home, for the second year, they would relocate you to a project somewhere in your own state. In June of 1939, now entering into my second CCC project, I was assigned to a farm near Fresno, Ohio, about 10 miles northeast of Coshocton, and just 60 miles from where I had grown up at Portage Lakes.

The farm was a huge government project.[13] There were about 15 of us from the CCC working there, along with other construction workers and engineers. My main job was to take charge of these beautiful Percheron horses.[14] I had never been around horses like this, so I enjoyed taking care of them. Not only were they beautiful, but they were friendly and easy to work with.

With a couple assistants, we strapped plows to the back of these wonderful animals and did a sort of excavation by digging out this large hole in the ground for the basement of a chemical lab to be built there. I also at times hitched one up to a wagon and hauled wheat around, for consumption by both the horses and us. To collect and process the wheat though, we used this huge combine to harvest it. It took about a dozen of us to work it. Afterwards, my buddy and I stood in the rafter of this huge barn, with the combine just below us, and we would feed that thing for hours at a time.

Whenever I had some spare time, I wrote home. I found out one day in a letter from Mom that Waddy's girl Donna had died of some weird disease, and I felt bad for her family. That night, I remembered the good times Waddy and I had shared with her. It bothered me that someone so close had passed away.

I could not know that this would happen a lot over six more decades.

Working with the Percherons was enjoyable, but towards the end of my tour, another half dozen horses came to us, and these animals were not as high bred. They were just pathetic-looking. These, we were told, were army rejects, and we were to make the best use of them that we could on the farm.

Riding the army horses was okay I guess, but they were not as enjoyable as the Percherons. I remember that there was one army horse that

---

13 CCC Project SCS-30, Company #1509, begun in June, 1937. Workers like George stayed at Camp William Green (named after the president of the American Federation of Labor), five miles northwest of the town.

14 A Percheron is a draft horse of French origin, similar in size and weight to a Clydesdale. Their color is usually gray or black speckled, and although they average 16–17 hands and weigh nearly a ton, they are docile animals, ideal for farm work.

was in much better physical shape than the others, but had a wild streak in him and could never be broken. But I had a wild streak in me, too, so I took this as a personal challenge, and decided to put this steed to the test. One of us was going to break, and I decided that it was not going to be me.

With my co-workers watching in amusement—a couple bets I think had been made—I took the animal to a 20-acre pasture and mounted a saddle on him. I steadied the horse, looked over at my buddies, and with a bit of a jump, I mounted him.

The horse immediately reacted. It bucked a couple of times, then took off pell-mell across the field. I held on for dear life as the horse made a dead run all the way to the end of the pasture. It then immediately whirled around and came back at full speed. Again, I held on tightly, wondering how this was going to end. My eyes watered to the point where my vision became blurred as the wind whipped around my face.

As we raced across the pasture, I saw the open gate coming up fast. Unfortunately, the horse's eyes must have watered and blurred too, because he missed the gate and ran headlong into the barbed-wire fence. The strands caught him in the chest and ripped open a deep gash as he fell heavily. I was thrown and went sailing over him, hitting the ground and rolling roughly.

Slowly, I got back on my feet, dizzy as hell. As I recovered, my co-workers went over to the horse, thrashing about, and freed him from the fence. I recovered, but the horse was in pain from the wound, and eventually the veterinarian had to put it down.

After several months working on that farm, I decided to return to high school. It was autumn of 1939 when I went back. I started attending Kenmore High in Akron. I was 17 by then, and I wanted to complete my second year of high school. On the first day, I was lucky enough to meet this lovely young lady.

That morning, along with my buddy Richard Tomkins, I was sitting out front waiting for the bell to ring, when this cute little gal walked passed us. She was a bit on the slim side, but well proportioned, and to me, absolutely gorgeous. The short skirt she was wearing only high-lighted her nice build.

I just shook my head and mumbled, "Damn, I'd love to get to know her."

Richard filled me in. "Oh, she's Phyllis Carpenter, and she's related to such and such."

Still staring at her, I said, "Uh huh ..."

Richard replied, "Yeah."

I said, "She's pretty. You know, I'd sure like to take that girl out."

Richard grinned and said, "You know, I could arrange that!"

I looked at him. "Yeah?"

Richard stood up and said, "C'mon. I'll introduce ya."

We grabbed our stuff and, walking rapidly, we caught up to her. Richard introduced me, and although I was a little embarrassed, we starting talking.

In the weeks after, I did whatever I could to get to know her better. Surprisingly, she took a liking to me. We finally started going together. We would go steady together on and off for the next seven years.

While I was in the Marine Corps, she wrote letters to me, and as the family got to know her, she would occasionally visit them. She even took a short summer trip with my mom. Phyllis and I did a lot together. Yeah, she was my steady girl. If I went somewhere with a bunch of guys and she could fit in, she would go along. Things like swimming jaunts and going into town. She was sort of like my right hand.

All during that time, people just accepted the fact that she and I were paired. I guess that during that time, I dated a few other women, but Phyllis never knew about most of them, and those that she found about, she did not seem to mind much. I guess that she figured that she had me hooked, so there was no need to worry about me finding another love. Strangely though, we never talked about the future, about getting married, probably because she knew my views on that. I had absolutely no intention of getting hooked until I had sowed my wild outs and the war was over. However, I did resolve to make a thorough inventory of the female species, so I decided that I would date a lot.

I continued that second year of high school. Some subjects I did okay in. Others, not so much. History was my favorite. Chemistry I hated. Music though, was the worst. For me, it was a disaster, and each year,

I would get a big red F—not that my teachers hadn't tried. This year was no different, and in the first week, as we sang, our music teacher would walk behind us while we were singing and listen to us. Finally one day after class, she called me aside and told me that she wanted to work with me on my music abilities to improve my grade. We went over to the piano. First, she told me that she was going to play one note and then a second one. She said, "You tell me whether I'm going up or down the scale."

I tried, but I guess I didn't do so good. Then she told me to try to sing each note after she played that key on the piano. I tried to sing each one, but I just could not do that either. We did this for a while, with her banging out a note, and me screeching out what I thought was the equivalent. Finally she stopped, shook her head and said to me, "You know what? You're tone deaf."

I thought she was crazy, but I didn't say anything. I just stood there.

Feeling sorry for me, she said, "I'll tell you what I'm going to do. I'm going to make you a deal. If you promise not to sing in class or in any of the concerts, and you behave and do the written work, I'll pass you."

I did what she asked. When it was time for the class to sing, I would either stay silent or just mouth the words. She turned out to be true to her word and gave me a D. I was happy, because that was the first time in music that I had not failed. When she had offered me this deal, I had initially thought she was nuts about my musical talents. Look, I knew I was no Bing Crosby, but on the other hand, I didn't think I was really that bad. Over time though, I finally realized that apparently she had been right. I guess after all it did not turn out to be a big deal, and I have learned to live with it. I was just not musically inclined, and after that, I never did have much use for music.

As a boy, I had naturally always been fascinated with cars. The first one I remember Pop having was this old black Model-T Ford. The battery was not worth a damn (and batteries were expensive), so to start it, he had two choices. He could push it down a hill, pop the clutch, and hope that it started right up, or he could use a hand crank on the engine, which in turn had its own dangers. For one thing, sometimes the clutch would not completely disengage, so when the car began to start, you could find yourself getting run over. Second, if you tried to hand-crank the engine and the spark was not set to the 'retard' position, when the engine caught, if you did not pull the crank out, the engine would yank it around. If you were holding the lever firmly at that point, the force could sprain or even break your wrist. I remember my father on many cold mornings, out there in the snow, cursing and muttering as he cranked over that damn cold engine.

And of course, the entire experience was even more dangerous when the old man had been drinking. Once when I was about eight, half drunk and running out of booze, he decided that he was going to go out and get more. He always liked someone to go with him, and so he looked at me and told me that I was going too.

As big as he seemed to me and as small as I was, I knew better. I stood up, looked right back at him defiantly, and said, "I ain't goin' nowhere with you the way you are."

He glared at me and said, "WHAT!?!" Insolence from any of his kids was something he did not tolerate.

I looked back at him, scared but determined, and said, "I ain't goin' with you."

He thought about that (as best he could in his condition), nodded, turned to my older brother Alex, and told him that HE was going to go with him. Al was sort of easy going and did not have the nerve to turn Pop down, so he gave in, and after the old man managed to get the car started, they took off.

I guess Pop was drunker than he thought, because they did not get very far. He drove right through an intersection on Manchester Road and hit another car. The Model-T was totaled; I mean it was gone. And Al was thrown into the windshield. Now you have to remember, the glass on cars in them days was not safety-rated like today, and so the glass splintered into a thousand pieces. One of those slivers went into Al's neck and nearly killed him. If the piece had penetrated a half inch over, it would have severed his artery, and he would have bled to death right there.

The police were called to the scene, and the next thing we knew, a squad car pulled up to the house. The cops told mom, "Your husband was involved in an accident, and your son has been taken to the hospital."

Jesus, what a jolt that was for mom. Well, Alex recovered, and though the old man was charged and had to appear before a judge, he never had to go to jail. Part of the reason I am sure was his position as an interpreter for Judge Hunsicker. I think that did get him out of a lot of stuff.

My fascination for wheels continued. As kids, we sometimes rode the bumpers of cars or better yet, trucks. Yeah, back then, our motto was anything that moved was fair game for us. We would often stand near an intersection, and when a car approached and stopped, we might run to the back of the car, sit on the bumper, and ride like that for several blocks. Of course, that was not without the obvious dangers. Finally, when I was about 12, the car I was riding on turned and I went sprawling onto the black gravel road. My knees were skinned and I had a couple serious cuts on my left hand. That put the end to that type of stunt for me.

As the years went on, both my father and my older brother managed to get their own cars. At 13, I resolved I was going to get in one and take my first drive ever. So one day, when no one was around but me, I went over to Alex's car and managed to start it up. I got in, put it in low gear, and took off up Wingate Road. Ahead I could see the Waterloo intersection approaching. I was happy as all get out. I was driving!

When I approached the intersection, I tried to shift gears, but I was no good at it, and the car stalled and died. Determined to keep going, I started it again in low gear. When I tried to shift though, I stalled it again. I started the car again and made it to the end of the road. I managed to turn around and start back. No matter what I did, I could not get the damn thing out of low, and every time I got enough nerve to shift, it stalled out. So finally I drove it back to where it had been parked, never getting out of low gear. When I finally turned it off, I could tell that transmission was really hot. Of course, I never said anything to anybody, and luckily, nothing on it had broken down.

I finally bought my first car after I returned from the CCC. I was 17 years old living in Wooster in the fall of 1939. My prize was a 1929 Ford with a rumble seat, and I paid $30 for it, which seems dirt cheap today, but back then, was a lot for a kid like me. I did not keep it too long, and soon traded up for something much better to travel back and forth from Wooster. My second vehicle was this beautiful tan 1932 Model-A Ford convertible, complete with these big hubcaps. And I got it really cheap; I only had to pay $35 for it. Of course it needed some work, and I often found myself pushing it to get it started.

Like that one time Mom got herself a short little unexpected joyride.

I had been working on the car that morning, and now I needed to start it. Of course, the battery was no good on it, so it would have to be push-started. I could do the pushing, but I needed someone else to steer and to start the engine when it got going. The only one at home was Mom, and she had never driven a car in her life. That did not stop me though, and I finally persuaded her to reluctantly assist.

The car was sitting on a gravel road near the top of this hill. The road had a downward slope before it turned into our drive. There the slope became steeper, and finally bottomed out in a creek.

Mom got in the driver's side, mumbling, "I've never driven a car in my life."

I turned on the ignition key for her, closed her door and then told her, "Mom, I gotta push this damn thing, but I gotta have you in there."

So I set the magneto and explained the clutch pedal to her. I told her that when I gave her the word, she was to engage the clutch again with her left foot, and when I shouted "Okay, now!" to pop the clutch to put the engine in gear. I said when the engine started, to push the throttle adjustment lever on the right upward to idle the engine. She looked confused, but she said she thought she understood.

I got behind the car, and gave her the word to step on the clutch. She did, and I began to push the car downhill. It began to pick up speed, and when it was going about ten miles per hour, I shouted, "Okay, now!"

Mom popped the clutch and the engine started. I shouted for her to move the throttle. Mom though, instead of pushing up on the lever to idle, pushed it down—driving mode—and with the extra gas to the engine, the car took off down the slope, leaving me standing there in the middle of the road. I began running after the car, shouting and waving my hands, while Mom, desperately trying to steer, yelled back, "What do I do NOW?"

The car kept going, now moving at a good clip, but mercifully, my mother had enough foresight to turn the wheel into our gravel drive; a good thing, because if she had not, after a block or so, she would have gone right into the Ohio Canal.

The car continued down our drive to the bottom of the hill and with a *whoosh*, drove right into that creek. The Model-A went right across the creek bed, throwing up water on both sides. As it started rolling up our driveway, it thankfully stalled. As I ran up the driveway, Mom slowly got out, soaked and looked shaken. She had had the crap scared out of her, but she began laughing her head off. I mean, I don't think I ever saw her laughing so hard. I came up to her, started laughing too, and hugged her, glad that she was still in one piece.

Finally she looked at me and, shaking her head, she said, "Never again, George. Never again."

Now Waddy had this big old junker that looked like a convertible gangster car. My brother Al had somehow been able to buy an old four-door sedan, and I of course had my tan '32 Model-A with the big hubcaps. This one day, feeling daring, the three of us took off racing east down Carnegie Avenue, roaring towards that little bridge that went over and onto the hotel, our cars abreast of each other. Naturally, it was a race, and we were all wide open, with these three cars side by each, headed pell-mell down that dusty, gravel road towards this bridge that was only two cars wide. Because the bridge was arched, you could not see if another car was coming your way. If one was, there would be a crash.

I was in the middle, so I was pretty much committed, whether I wanted to be or not. Thank God, no one was coming the other way, and so Waddy on the right and I both made it over the bridge. Alex, though, was on the left and about ten feet back, and began to realize that he was not going to make it and was about to smash into the metal abutment on the side of the bridge. So at the last second, he veered off. Unable to stop in time, he and his car flew headlong into Nesmuth Lake with a big splash.

Luckily for him, he did not go in too far, and it was still shallow where the car stopped. His motor though, was well underwater. Always ready for a breakdown though, we all carried rope and stuff with us, because none of us could afford a tow. So Waddy and I drove back, hooked up the rope to each side of Alex's rear bumper, and slowly pulled the car out of the lake.

We figured that the hotel people must have seen the crash; hell, it happened in plain sight. But they never came out to yell at us, and as far as we knew, the police were never called. Not that we would have given a damn. What the hell. We were kids. Of course, on the other hand, we were smart enough to not stay around. So we towed Alex's dripping car back to our place, and a few days later, he actually had the damn thing running again. Of course, the cushions were soaked and took a long time to dry out.

I will say, though, we did our best to maintain our cars. It seemed like we were almost always working on them. The cost of running them was expensive, although fuel was cheap in those days. I remember there was this filling station on Route 76, coming into Barberton off Highway 224. Gas there was two gallons for a quarter. Then after I got our gas, I would walk over to the pit that the repairman stood in to change the oil on a car. In the pit was this barrel that he used to drain the oil. I would go down into the pit, grab the bucket down there, and dip it in the barrel. The owner did not mind, and it was free oil for me.

I still had another half year to go in the CCC. I was assigned to Camp Anthony Wayne, just outside of Wooster, Ohio in the fall of 1939.[15] I continued my education. I took several courses at night school, included typing. I kept dating Phyllis, and though she lived in Akron and I was in Wooster, we saw each other a lot. Either she would come over and visit me, or I would go home and see her. In fact, I was at her place as much as I was at mine, and she came to my house anytime she wanted. In the meantime, I sometimes dated other girls, but I don't think she ever dated another guy in all those seven years.

During the day, because I had a chauffeur license, I served as our crew's driver, taking us to and from the locations in an old truck. Every

---

15 Camp Anthony Wayne, designated Camp 584, began in mid-June 1939. It was one of nine camps in the country tasked with Project SCS-33 (Soil Conservation Camp #33). The camp was located about a mile and a half southeast of Wooster, Ohio, on the road to Fredericksburg. The site is now part of the Ohio Agricultural and Research Center.

day, I hauled some 35 guys out to that day's work site. We helped farmers learn how to strip crop over hilly country to keep water erosion down. We helped build a government conservation laboratory (which is still there today, doing soil conservation services). Once in a while, I was allowed to run a hydraulic jackhammer to help dig these huge craters.

I was also the crew's official blaster, since I had certified explosives training in Utah and certified to give first aid, as indicated by my Red Cross card (which I carried in addition to my dynamite blasting card and my chauffeur license). Driving the crew to a site every day. I'd bring the dynamite and the blasting caps, setting them in the front seat with me, and driving as carefully as I could (all of course, which was illegal, but I didn't know where else the hell to put them).

Our job was to clear fields with explosives as needed by blasting stumps and big rocks. For a large boulder I would secure the dynamite sticks to the top of the rock, run two wires into the bundle, and then cover them up with a thick mud pack. I then ran the wires back into the battery detonator and hooked them up to the terminals. Making sure everyone was clear, I would give the warning and then set off the charge. Because of the thick mud layer, a large part of the force of the explosion would be directed downward and would split the rock. After that, it was simply a matter of hauling the chunks away.

Tree stumps I treated differently, depending on their size. For the big ones, I usually planted the dynamite below the stump. I remember one time we had to clear the stump of this monster of a tree. The stump itself was tall, and had a massive girth. Up to the task, I planted 20 sticks under the stump, setting them in at a slight angle. My helpers put out the word, and a local deputy even had stopped traffic along a nearby road while I prepared. I ran the two wires to the detonator as always. I checked the sticks once more, making sure everything was set up correctly. I came back to the detonator and connected the two wires to each terminal. With the circuit live, I shouted the word to everyone around to stand clear. Finally, I pushed in the plunger, and the dynamite exploded. I watched in wonder at what I saw. With that many sticks, that entire massive stump went up ten feet into the air. My eyes wide,

I could not help but think that it looked like a huge dirty molar, roots and all. Quite unforgettable.

By the summer of 1940, World War II was well underway. I knew that someday I would be drawn into the military, whether I wanted to or not. War was on the horizon. Europe was in the middle of it, and everyone in America knew that sooner or later, one way or another, we would become involved in it. The military was already starting to expand, and factories were gearing up production. No, war was coming.

So with all this in my mind, I began to think about joining the service. I was certainly no keen patriot. Still, the service had its advantages. For one thing, the steady pay and food was appealing to a dirt-poor boy like me. More than that, I guess that my desire to travel instilled in me a hankering for some real adventure. I was like that—rambunctious and antsy.

I was in Wooster with my last CCC hitch coming up. It was September 1940. I convinced a buddy of mine that it would be great for him too. We got permission from our parents to join, so together one day, we hitchhiked up to Cleveland and walked into a recruiting office to sign up. I wanted to be a Marine.

We talked to the recruiter, some guy in an immaculate, sharp uniform, and we liked what we heard. So we talked it over and decided to join. We signed the preliminary papers, and everything was going fine until we went through the standard physical qualification examinations. We were both in great health, and I passed with flying colors. Unfortunately though, my buddy failed the eye examination because he was color blind. Thinking about it, I decided that I did not want to go into the service alone, so we reluctantly left. It was too late to go home, so we stayed overnight. We were too poor to rent a room or find a cheap boarding house, so we went over to the Cleveland jail and spent the night in one of their cells.[16] It was the first time for me doing that, but it would not be the last. The next day, we returned to Wooster.

---

16 During the Great Depression, it was not unusual for indigents to ask for overnight shelter in the local jail, especially if the weather was bad. The police were

Shortly after that, I relocated up to Akron and moved into Alex's apartment at 2273 17th Street in Akron. My first job was with the Troy Laundry Company. I busted my ass 12 hours a day for just 25 cents an hour. Then because I had a chauffeur license, I got a job driving a truck during the day. I helped out at a bar part-time at night. Normally you have to be at least 21 to do that, but since my chauffeur license indicated that I was, I qualified—even though I had just turned 18.

I spent the rest of the winter of 1940 there in Akron living in an apartment with Alex. I worked odd jobs and in general just hung out. I then became a self-employed truck driver for this Greek who owned a trucking firm called the Hanna Trucking Company. He had three old broken-down trucks, and I got a job driving one of them. As a freelancer, my job was to park the truck every day in this lot and wait. If a job came in, I would have work. If one did not, I did not, and so I was not paid.

One night, my truck broke down, and the Greek, knowing that I needed the money and that as a good driver he might lose me to a real job, asked me if I wanted a second job, to assist his daughter. They owned this small bar located on the southeast corner of Highway 93 and Kenmore Boulevard, and his daughter ran it at night. She needed someone that night, and could I help out—that is, if I could tend bar. Sure I could, I told him. What the hell. A job is a job.

He took me over to the bar, introduced me to his daughter, told me what I would be doing, and left. She and I hit it off right away, and together, we started working that bar at night. Although she was a short brunette, she was really built. I mean, like a real Greek goddess. Naturally, I began to flirt with her from time to time, but she decided right away that since she was older than me by a few years, that I was too young for her. I tried a couple of times to score with this sweetie, but no success.

I worked at the bar for about a month while my truck was being repaired. When it was fixed, I assumed that I would go back on the

sympathetic to the plight of the poor, and anyway, it made better sense to let them sleep locked up, rather than roam the streets and get into trouble.

road. The Greek though, wanted me to keep tending the bar. He liked me, evidently. It was a good thing that he did not know that I was after his daughter.

Finally I confessed and told the Greek that I was really only 17 years old, and not 21 like he had assumed. He was shocked, replying, "My God! I didn't know that!" So I had to go back to driving again, and that is how my days passed during those cold winter months. I went back to freelance truck hauling by day—when the piece of crap did not break down—and some going out at night on my meager pay. In the meantime, the Marine Corps kept sending me enlistment brochures, and I read about how awesome it would be to be a part of the greatest military service on earth.

Seattle bound

By March of 1941, World War II was into its second year, and the Axis reigned supreme. With the exception of Great Britain bravely standing alone, the rest of Western Europe had fallen. Greece and Yugoslavia were about to go down as well. Most of the Baltic and Eastern European countries were either aligned with the Third Reich or were about to be. In the Pacific, Japan was winning its war of aggression against China. Korea, the Marianas, the Carolinas, and the Marshall Islands were all now Japanese territories. French Indochina had been invaded in 1940, and Japan was now becoming bolder in its claims for a new Pacific empire. Tensions with the United States were mounting, and an American embargo would only promise to bring the economic confrontation to a head within a year.

In the spring of 1941, wanderlust got the better of me. Generally unhappy, I decided to quit my truck-driving job and head out west. I was disgusted with my life, the weather was cold, and I was driving that miserable, unreliable old dump truck as a part-time freelancer for that grouchy Greek. When I was not hauling around gravel and asphalt, I was sitting for hours in the Greek's office shack or in my truck waiting for another assignment so that I could get paid—not that I was getting that much. No, I needed a change in my life.

My plan was to make my way to Seattle, Washington, get a job on a luxury liner, and hook up with some rich broad. I asked Alex if he wanted to go too. I figured we could really have a blast out there, schmoozing with a couple of rich babes. Alex declined though. So, disgusted with the dump truck that I was driving, the nasty, smelly asphalt, and the lousy pay, on a cold, rainy morning, alone, I left Akron and headed west. Strangely though, two weeks later, Alex decided to take off and go west too.

Without even bothering to quit my job, I just left Akron. I hitchhiked across the top of the country, determined to get to Seattle. Early on I got a ride from a guy driving another gravel truck. He picked me up on U.S. Route 30. He was headed northward into Wisconsin, and then westward from there. So I nonchalantly tossed my suitcase in the back, on top of the gravel, and got in with this friendly truck driver. Unfortunately, when we eventually made it to Minnesota and I got out, my suitcase in the back was gone. It had evidently fallen off somewhere along the way. So now the only clothes that I had in the world were on my back.

I made my way through Wisconsin, where there are a lot of fishing lodges and resorts. Then my luck changed for the better. I was picked up by some college professor and his wife headed west to see Yellowstone National Park. With my chauffeur license to prove I was a good driver and my smiling ways to convince them I was a good kid, I talked them into letting me be their driver. That way, I told them, they could enjoy the trip much more. They agreed, and so we headed west. We had a great time along the way. Once in a while we listened to the radio, and a few times we sang songs. Mostly though, we just talked a lot.

I took them up through several northwestern states, and they in turn bought me meals. We toured through Yellowstone. While the professor and his wife marveled at all the wonders of the park, I concentrated on keeping us on those narrow mountain roads and not falling down the sides and into the steep ravines. We rode around Yellowstone for about a week, and they were going to pay me to return home with them, but I had to keep going. So I reluctantly left them.

I then made my way over the northern end of Montana across a lot of dry, open areas. I hitchhiked during the day, and when sunset approached, I did what I had to finding myself a place to bed down. I had found out early in life that, to my surprise, if you stopped in a small town in the evening (and you did not make a nuisance of yourself), the local sheriff would let you bed down in their jail for the night. The cells were simple, usually with two cots. The deputy would almost always leave the jail cell unlocked, so that you could let yourself out in the morning and leave whenever you wanted to.

I kept going. Sometimes at night I slept in a haystack, or a bundle of shocked wheat. I hitchhiked northward on into Washington, and eventually made my way up to Seattle. I spent some time bumming around the docks just to learn a depressing fact: while it was true that the shipyards were hiring part-time, unfortunately, the type of job I wanted was not available. Odd jobs on luxury liners were non-existent. Everyone knew that war was coming to the U.S., and speculation was high that we would become involved in conflict with Japan at any time. The Japanese had been at war in China since 1933, and with our country now evoking a partial embargo on them, tensions were high. Therefore, the steamship companies, until further notice, were not conducting any luxury cruises in the Western Pacific. So the only job that I could get was to paint the ships.

Bull, I thought to myself. I ain't gonna do that. How the hell can you meet a rich fancy broad doing that kind of a job? According to what I had read in the Hollywood magazines, the only way to connect with a rich broad was on a luxury cruise. And painting the hulls was sure not going to do that.

I finally left Seattle and hitchhiked south through California. I made it to the southern end of Modesto, and there I managed to buy some more clothes. Unfortunately, that took the last of my pathetic funds, so now I was flat broke. I got down to Hollywood and stayed for a while, still looking for one of those rich dames. Unknown to me, Alex had changed his mind and had come out to the Los Angeles area on a "bummin' trip." It was a big town even back then, and we never bumped into each other, but by funny coincidence, he and I each sent postcards home to our sister Elizabeth in Akron, who wondered why we were both in the same area and had not seen each other.

Towards the middle of summer, I decided that I had experienced enough adventure: I was ready to go home. I left Los Angeles and started hitchhiking eastward, across Arizona. Yuma was interesting. I remember seeing all these little shacks with slanted roofs, and in front of one was a Mexican snoozing with his sombrero over his face. That's all I remember. Nobody out in the sun, nobody walking around. Just here and there a guy alone, sitting in front of his shack in the sun.

I kept going, northeastward across New Mexico, Texas, and then Arkansas. Although I always looked for opportunities, because I moved around alone, I was always on my guard. This was especially true after crossing the Mississippi River, because I remember as a kid being told that conditions in the depressed South were pretty bad, a lot worse than what we were going through in Ohio.

I remembered wild stories of guys going down there and just disappearing, or getting their cars sabotaged at restaurants or filling stations so that they needed to be repaired (and parts purchased) by some local yokel. You pulled into a gas station and when the attendant checked your oil, he would pull or cut a hose or a wire, and then tell you that your car needed to be fixed. I did not have a car, and so being on foot, I figured I would be even more vulnerable to somebody trying to somehow take advantage of me, being a stranger passing through.

Traveling through Mississippi, I sometimes came across a group of sweating guys working next to the road. Each man had an ankle bracket connected by chain to another guy, and they all wore simple uniforms of white and black horizontal stripes. With hoes, rakes, shovels, and bags, these gangs were working odd jobs along the roadside, like picking up trash, cutting grass, raking, pulling weeds, and making minor repairs to the roads. You know, back in those days, they did all that by hand. Overseeing the prisoners were these guards riding on horses, really nasty-looking fellows carrying these mean-looking double-barrel shotguns; definitely guys I did not want to even think about messing with. I was told that these groups along the road were the infamous Southern chain gangs that I had heard about.

This was my first experience with the South.

After that, whenever I could, I tried steering clear of these chain gangs, although sometimes I had to walk through one or two. I could see the convicts sometimes look over at me as they worked, and if I looked up at a guard, I would see him glaring back at me with cold eyes. I just smiled and kept on walking.

After a couple encounters like that, I became convinced that traveling down here for a happy-go-lucky guy was definitely not for me, and my wanting to get back to Ohio developed into a really strong drive. So I continued making my way northward, sometimes sleeping at night in the back seat of a car in a parking lot or better yet, in the trunk in a used car lot, because the dealers never locked the trunks. Otherwise, I would find me a nice tree to bed down under, or a nice haystack, or three-foot stalk of wheat.

I finally arrived home. Alex was already back. We sat that night and wondered what the next months would bring. I had been generally calm and lackadaisical about life up until now. Now war was about to break out. What would I do with my life now?

I was about to find out.

CHAPTER 3

Marine

By the summer of 1941, I decided that I needed a change in my life. I was still intrigued with the idea of joining the Marines, especially the parts about traveling and being able to see the world. I wanted to enlist, but I did not want to go in alone. I wanted someone to come in with me.

The idea of the Marines stayed with me. Alex, who was a year and nine months older than me, had received some sort of a draft notice at the end of 1940. While he did not have to report for military service immediately, it was a formal letter stating that it would only be a matter of time. He was just being officially notified. We suspected that he would be called up just after he turned 21, on July 25th. Still, it seemed plain that the government was giving him some time to make the appropriate preparations to his life.[1]

---

1   In November 1940, two months after the Selective Service Act was passed and some 13 months before Pearl Harbor, the first American draftees were scheduled to be inducted into military service. It was soon realized by the War Department that not all of the 800,000 selected for service by mid-June 1941 could get sworn in. This was partly because the American government was not yet spun up to receive, handle, and process so many men, and partly because there was a definite upswing in volunteers for the military at that time. Added to this of course was the uncertainty of when or even if the United States would go to war, although it was seen by all that entry would not be long in coming. Thus some individuals, like Alex Peto, although declared fit for military service, would not immediately be notified to report for duty.

We both thought about his impending entrance into military service, now evidently no longer an option for him. His letter would probably come at the end of July or August, and mine probably would come some months after that. Alex's choices were simple: the Navy was out of the question, so he could join the Marines, or let the Army induct him. Whenever I occasionally received a pamphlet from the Marines, I would show it to Alex, and he would read it. We talked about the Marines again in early August, and about the possibility of joining together, and I could tell that he was starting to lean in my direction.

One day, Alex finally said to me, "C'mon George, let's go together. Let's join."

"Well hell," I told him, "that's what I've been trying to do!"

But Alex was not satisfied with just the two of us enlisting. He wanted us to go in with a bunch of our friends. So we decided to try and talk a couple of them into it.

"Let's go see our buddies," he told me, "and we can all go in together."

I agreed. I felt so much better now that I had a plan. I mean, I had for some time decided that the Marine Corps could be my next big adventure, but I did not want to go in alone. I had worked in the CCC alone for two years, and this time I wanted someone to go in with me. Now I had Alex.

The military service would be good for both of us, and with luck we could share it all together. Besides, the military would give us something we were not used to: three square meals a day and a nice shelter to sleep in.

Boy, was I proven wrong.

The more Alex and I talked about joining the Marines, the more enthusiastic we became. We were though, going to make an effort to get our buddies to go in with us; guys like Richard Tomkins and Waddy Getz, and John Siler, who at the time lived in the only other house near us, about a quarter mile away. Of the four of us, I was the youngest, although Richard was close to my age, but a year older. Waddy was as old as Alex, so his age was no problem. For years, the five of us had been close, sort of a gang within a gang. Alex and I knew that they thought the way we thought, that war was only a matter of time, and that we would all have to serve. So why not go at our choosing? Get in ahead of the rest? And of course, join the best service of the three?

Alex and I went out and talked to the other three about all going in together. We told them how advantageous it would be for them if they were already in the service when it broke out, and how we would do better as NCOs.

Sure enough, two of them, my childhood chum Waddy Getz, and Richard Tomkins, were eager to go in with us, and agreed to accompany us to the recruiter. However, John Siler did not like the idea. He was going to stay out of the service, at least as long as he could. After all, he had a halfway decent job and was making money for his family. John worked making insulators in the Akron Porcelain Factory, and felt that it was not quite time for him to enlist.[2]

Before the four of us left for induction in Cleveland, and with our Marine recruiter as an accomplice, we thought we would try John once more. The Marine recruiter drove us in a government van to the factory on Cory Avenue to take a final shot at convincing John to join us. The recruiter gave us some last-minute advice, and then waited outside as we walked into the main building. We found John on an assembly line putting together insulators. He was working steadily, wearing a big white apron to keep the dust off. We tried to convince him to come with us, and our arguments must have been effective, because he waivered for a few moments before backing out. We nodded our heads in sad understanding, and one by one, we solemnly shook his hand, wished him the best, and bid him farewell. Talk about a corny guilt trip.

We left him, occasionally looking back sadly and walked outside, starting to head back to the van. Suddenly, the factory door slammed open and John hurriedly came out.

"Wait, you guys!" he shouted.

We stopped. He walked up to us, untied his apron, grabbed it, threw it off, and slung it over a rail.

"The hell with it," he told us, "I'm in!"

---

2   Today it is known as the Akron Porcelain & Plastics Company, and is still located at 2739 Cory Avenue.

We laughed and slapped him on the back. Happily, we all piled into the van, one big gang, and the recruiter pulled out of the parking lot to take us to the induction station in Cleveland. It was a happy trip and we joked all the way up, laughing about what we would do as Marines.

On August 5, 1941, just seven weeks before my 19th birthday, and as it turned out, four months and two days before Pearl Harbor, all five of us were sworn in to active duty in the United States Marine Corps.

I was still seeing Phyllis off and on, but at times I was more going through the motions than actually courting her. We were though, close friends, and could tell each other just about anything. Still, I guess in the end, it was a relationship of convenience for both of us.

Well, it was for me, because I had too much of a roving eye. For instance, the week before I left for boot camp near the end of July, I met another pretty young lady. We went out a few times over a couple weeks, and I guess that she fell for me in the worst way: this little gal wanted me to marry her. She tried her best to talk me into it and sweet-talked me silly for two days straight. However, I was definitely not ready to settle down. I mean, she was a great little gal to spend the evening with, but I was certainly in no mood to get married, especially since I was going into the Marine Corps, so I let it go at that. However, before I left her for the last time, I gave her a picture of me.

Unfortunately, that backfired on me, because a few weeks after Alex and I had left for boot camp, this girl and Phyllis bumped into each other one night, just outside of Barberton. There was this huge old building that was a dance hall that served alcohol, and mercifully, they were not particular to whom they sold their beverages. This hall would often have dances, and big ones on Saturday nights. There were many like this in those days, and invariably, they were usually located way out in the country. I would often go to this one with my buddies and have a great time.

This one night then, they happened to accidently meet and began talking to each other. I guess they liked each other right off, and soon they were sharing their lives.

Finally, the subject of beaus came up. One of them must have said to the other, "Well, my boyfriend's in the Marine Corps," and the other one probably had replied, "Well, so is mine." At that point, they each pulled out a photograph of their boyfriend, and of course, they both turned out to be of the same guy—yours truly. Phyllis got a big kick out of it, but the other gal (I cannot to this day remember her name) definitely did not. When I returned from the war, she would not even speak to me. Many years later, I tried to find her just to talk to her, but I never found her. She had moved, and I never heard from her again.

Boot camp

A couple hours after the swearing-in ceremony, we were all sent to Parris Island by bus. We were about to go through a grueling set of weeks together in boot camp. As soon as we got off the bus though, the first thing that they did was to split all five of us up. Funny, but after boot camp, I would never see John Siler again. So much for joining with my friends. Right after that, they gave us haircuts. The barbers were ruthless, and when they were done, you had less than a half inch of hair on your head (I was later told that it could have been worse. In the brig, they cut all of your hair off.) The effect was devastating on a lot of these recruits. Many of them had these real fancy hairdos that they often combed and greased down with hairstyling stuff like Brylcreem. So all that hair getting cut off really did a number on their heads—in more ways than one. It was like destroying their personalities, which of course, is what the Corps did.

Then we went over to the supply building; gruffly tossing stuff to us as we went down a line, they issued us our gear, complete with a sea bag and a helmet. It was one of those prewar salad bowl-looking helmets. We called it the "Frank Buck" helmet, because it looked like one of those old ivory pith helmets that we used to see him wear in magazines when he went hunting on a safari in Africa.[3]

---

3   Before the war, the Marines were issued the M1916 helmet, copied off the British Army design. Other nicknames included the "doughboy helmet," "tin hat," or more pejoratively, the "dishpan hat." It was replaced in early 1942 by the more familiar looking M1 helmet.

With our gear issued, they assigned us barracks. Most of them were these cheap, wooden buildings, which is what I landed in. We each had a cot and a big footlocker for our gear. As soon as we had our gear stowed away, they told us where the pails, soap, towels, and scrub brushes were located. Then they ordered us to start thoroughly scrubbing our wooden walls down. It was a thankless, gloomy job, and those of us that had become upset by the haircut experience were now joined by most of the other kids. Many were really out-and-out scared, and a couple of them said, "Oh my God, what the hell did we get into?"

They stayed agitated like that as we were scrubbing, but unlike the others, I found the whole thing amusing. They had been so enthusiastic coming down here on the train, laughing and shooting the bull, and gaily singing the Marine Corps Hymn. Now they were mumbling to each other, scared to death about what was happening to them as reality set in, and they began to realize that these boot camp instructors were like monsters. The more I looked at them, nervously scrubbing, the more it seemed funny to me. So many of them had really serious looks on their faces. One guy actually had a couple tears in his eyes. Looking things over, I thought that maybe a little levity here might go a long way. So with a chuckle, I grinned at them, opened my big mouth, and started singing, "From the halls of Monte-zuuu—uu-ma, to the shores of Trip-pooo-liii …"

Again, another one of those times where my sense of humor did not work, because the other recruits glared at me and started shouting stuff like, "Shut the hell up, man!" and "You sonuvabitch!"

Obviously, I was a different breed of cat.

I continued laughing and singing for a bit, enraging the other guys, but I did not keep it up for too long. Mostly, I quit because I knew that if the D.I. caught me singing like that, he probably would have thrown my butt in the brig.

I had luckily got some critically important advice before joining the Marines. I was told to never volunteer, and to never disclose to our "G.I. D.I. from P.I."[4] the many types of training and certifications that I had

---

4   "General issue drill instructor from Parris Island," what the drill instructors liked to refer to themselves.

received in civilian life. The various types of training that I had earned in the CCC, my chauffer's license, my qualifications and certification with explosives—all were to be kept secret. The reasoning was simple. The main purpose of boot camp, I had been told, was to break the individual down in every way: physically, in spirit, in habit, and in mental attitude. It was from this lump of a man that they wanted to mold their no-questions-asked fighting warrior.

As it turned, out, that advice was sound. Those few who did disclose previous training in various types of machinery or operations were ridden especially hard, and given much more extra work to do, or details to go on. It was almost as if they resented the fact that you had some outside experience, because you had not been taught to do what you did their way. To them, the recruit was not supposed to have any ideas of his own. That would maximize our efforts to fight in the most efficient way possible as a team, because that is what they were going to teach us. They had to break you down so that they could teach you their way. There was no room in the Marine Corps for preset ideas.

There was one guy in our recruiting class that had been in college. While he was not totally out of shape, he was a somewhat heavyset fellow. When he proudly (even a bit cocky about it) admitted to the drill instructor, the D.I., that he had been in ROTC, it was like he was suddenly marked. The D.I. after that rode him mercilessly. In everything we did, if one of us screwed up, we all paid the price. With this guy though, the D.I.s always checked to see if he had screwed up, and if he had, they would go out of their way to showcase him and make him pay.

In the end, he did not make it through boot camp. One day on the obstacle course, he fell and injured his leg. The medics hauled him off in pain, and he ended up with a broken leg. So they pulled him.

It was only after boot camp that we learned the drill instructors wanted to tear down any preconceived notions and experiences that we had acquired in life, so that they could rebuild us their way. That was one of the reasons for the haircuts. So to know what they were up against, they would try to trap us into admitting our past experiences, so that they knew whom to concentrate on.

For instance, they would ask, "Hey, are there any truck drivers here?" And sure enough, a couple guys would answer with a smile, thinking that they would get slated for special training.

Wrong.

"Okay," the sergeant would growl. "There are some wheelbarrows over there. Grab one and follow me over to the latrine."

Luckily, I already knew their strategy, so I very quickly learned not to freely give them any personal information, especially work experiences, and not to volunteer for special details, or unknown duty requests.

The D.I.s were brutal in their schedules and excessively harsh in their training. And they had absolutely no pity for us in their instructions. Me, I survived because I quickly developed an attitude, probably coming to a large degree from my experiences on my own. Suffering the pain and misery of boot camp with my fellow recruits, I had early on gritted my teeth and swore under my breath that these sons of bitches would never ever break me. I would not yield, I would not give in, and I would never give up. No matter how harsh the exertions were, I knew that I would either make it to the end or die trying. So I never fell out of a formation no matter how exhausted I was. Nor did I ever miss a day because I was too bone-weary to get up. I would be there standing when it was over, no matter how strong-willed the D.I.s were. It was me against them.

But man, did they make it hard for us, especially the first few weeks. I was told months later that one reason for this was to introduce the idea of inducing pressure and stress, so that we would have less tendency to freak out when we went into combat. Still, even if we had known that back then, it would not have made things easier.

In our platoon was this Jewish fellow, a guy about five or six years older than most of us. Probably because of that and because of his faith (there were a lot of prejudiced guys in the Corps back then), they really rode him hard. Somehow he persevered and managed to make it through each day with the rest of us.

One morning we were marched over to the medics' tent to get shots. And we found out that we were going to get a bunch of them. This was no fun, because they did not have those high-pressure jet injectors in those days to give you multiple vaccines at one time.

George when he was at boot camp, fall 1941. (Author's collection)

No sir. They gave the shots to you the old fashioned way: one at a time. So with our T-shirts off, we would slowly walk through the main corridor of this large tent, with a row of corpsmen standing on each side. You walked down the aisle, pausing at each station while the corpsman on each side of you would jab a needle in your arm and give you the shot.

It was not surprising that after that session, when we left the medical tent, our upper arms were sore and our heads a little groggy. We walked out into the hot sun, and lining us up in formation, the D.I.s began to march us back to our tents. Unfortunately, the gunny in charge was one of the more sadistic bastards, and looking at us, he growled, "Oh, don't feel good, eh?? Well, I will not stop until each of you SOBs drops. If you babies are sick, go to sickbay. Otherwise, you march!"

And we did. We marched all over the place, and drilled for a hell of a long time out there in that intense South Carolina sun on that damn hot August day. Soon, some of the recruits began to drop, too weary to move, and that D.I. would bitch at every one of them, sometimes giving them a swift kick.

Finally the older Jewish recruit in our group who had been slowing down in the paces groaned and collapsed. He dropped to the ground, falling on his back. The sergeant walked over to the recruit, and towering over him, he yelled, and then viciously slapped the hell out of him. The Jewish guy did not move.

Looking down at him, that husky sergeant paused and growled, "Well, I guess he ain't fakin' it."

We went on marching and left that poor guy lying there. A couple of corpsmen finally hauled the unconscious recruit off, I assume to sickbay (although I never knew if he made it there).

More of the guys began to fall out of formation and tried to stagger off to sickbay. As tired as I was though, I resolved not to drop out. Huffing and puffing, I gritted my teeth. No sir, I thought, them bastards ain't gonna break *me*. At that point, as far as I was concerned, it was me against the world, and I was going to march until those sons of bitches killed me. I kept on, somehow finding the energy to keep going. My legs ached and my body was in pain, but I grimly kept going.

Finally, the gunnery sergeant, really steaming because we had not all dropped out (less than half of us out of the original twenty), determined that was enough, and marched us back to our tents.

A day or so later, we were told that the Jewish fellow had left the unit and had been transferred to the "Casual Battalion."[5] The rest of us, now all trained and qualified as a rifleman, began to split up into different specialty fields. I wanted to be on the mortars, hopefully as a fire observer. Unfortunately, there was no school for mortar observers, so that was the end of that.

After weeks of what seemed like a terrible ordeal dished out by cold, ruthless D.I.s, boot camp came to an end. There was no ceremony or celebration—back then, you didn't "graduate" from basic training. You just completed boot camp and got reassigned. It was like getting out of jail: no big deal. When you were through, they just shook your hand, told you that you were now a Marine, and then gave you a new assignment.

---

5   The "Casual Battalion" was where misfits or other recruits that could not pass boot camp were temporarily placed. Within the first 90 days, if a recruit was diagnosed as mental, too out of shape, ill, captured after going AWOL, or otherwise not able to finish basic training, he was transferred here and assisted in his problems. If the recruit could not or would not make it within those 90 days, he was considered unacceptable. He was then processed out of military service by reason of "enlistment rejection" from boot camp without a discharge (and of course, without veteran benefits) and reclassified by the Selective Service, probably as 4-F (not qualified for military service). Naturally, many who ended up this way were elated to get out of what they no doubt had not expected; but surprisingly, many recruits were devastated by the experience.

Alex was given his orders: 7th Marine Regiment, First Marine Division. He was to report down to New River.[6] He immediately had to pack and after a handshake, he left for training there, to then go with the division to the Pacific.

Waddy Getz was sent to Balboa, in Panama. I never found out where my old chum John Siler went. Richard Tomkins was ordered to the field music school, located right there at Parris Island. It was not much of a music school though: all they taught those Marines to play were bugles. Richard begged me to volunteer to go too, and it seemed like a great way to serve in the Marines. Unfortunately though, I had never had any use for music. I had a lousy singing voice, and I didn't know how to play any kind of musical instrument. My music experience in school had been terrible, to say the least. So bugles for me now were out of the question. The hell with field music school, I told Richard. He was disappointed, but I didn't care. I'd shovel crap first before I tried to play any instrument.

As the rest of those in my platoon got assignments, I remained. The only one who stayed was Tompkins, who assisted me on the rifle range. Life was a drag. You couldn't just walk around the base. We were not under any circumstances allowed to go to the PX and buy some "pogey bait" or "belly wash."[7]

Instead of going west though, along with several other recruits, I was transferred to some rearguard company, and in late September 1941, we were ordered to New England for guard duty. The next morning, carrying our gear and rifles, we boarded a train and started rolling northeastward. Our thousand-miles-away destination: Quonset Point, Rhode Island.

---

6   Construction of the New River base began at the beginning of May 1941 on an 11,000-acre-section of land alongside in Onslow County, North Carolina. In 1942, the base was renamed Camp Lejeune in honor of John A. Lejeune, a hero of the Spanish-American War, decorated at the battle of Soissons in World War I, and later the 13th commandant of the Marine Corps from 1920 to 1929.

7   Slang Navy and Marine jargon. "Pogey bait" referred to sweets such as candy bars, and "belly wash" was vernacular for soda pop.

Quonset Point

Our train went up the Atlantic Coast and then over towards New York City, where we were going to have a layover. We got off the train at the Central Railroad Terminal in New Jersey and crossed the Hudson River by ferry into New York. We then marched right up Fifth Avenue to Grand Central Station, where we were to stay for the night. Off the main area of the station, we piled our duffle bags, stacked our rifles, and then we posted a couple guards. The rest of us then had the opportunity to spend the evening looking over the city, although none of us strayed too far away.

We reboarded the train and went up to Quonset Point, Rhode Island, where we reported aboard. We found the accommodation nice. The buildings were all connected, including the mess hall, the brig, the supply room, everything. It was a wonderful new building, and you did not have to go out into the cold to go to chow. After Parris Island, it was like being on a vacation.

There was of course back then no public address system, so all of the daily tasks on each base were ruled by the bugle. Our bugler had this knack of being able to stand in a certain spot in the central building, and when he blew the call, the sound would bounce back and forth across the walls and echo down all the hallways throughout the complex. So you could clearly hear him for reveille, raising the colors, chow, assembly, taps …

Just after I arrived at Quonset Point, I was ordered on a 30-day tour of duty to Hope Island, right in the middle of Narragansett Bay.[8] There I was given the assignment of guarding bombs in storage for the new naval air station that was being expanded back at Quonset Point. Unlike the nice, all-connected brick barracks that we had enjoyed though, those on Hope Island were plain, small, plywood shacks that had room for only eight people.

8　About two miles off Quonset Point, between it and Prudence Island. It was established in 1939 as a munitions storage area, so that the explosives for safety purposes not be stored on the base.

Hope Island was only accessible by ferry. Since all during that time none of us on the island was allowed to go on liberty, and the weather was getting worse, our off-hours options were quite limited. Mostly we sat around the barracks, and with not much to do, we had plenty of time to shoot the bull and get acquainted. Still, it was a long, long 30 days, especially if you had a girlfriend in town, like some of the guys did.

Around this time, I made friends with a fellow Marine, a guy that I would serve with for some three years. His name was Henry Vastine Rucker. We had both entered the service about the same time, only in different parts of the country. I was a Yankee from Akron Ohio, and Henry was a rebel from some town called Gaffney in South Carolina. We were both 19, and were both fresh out of Parris Island. From just about the first day that we met, we took a liking to each other.

Like I had figured it would be, guarding bombs on a small island in the middle of nowhere was a mundane job, and for the adventure-loving kids like Henry and me and a few of the others, it was positively mind-numbing. Not all of us there though were kids. One time we came off of duty there and found this old guy taking a shower. Assigned to our unit, he had been swimming around in the ocean and was now washing off the seawater. As he walked out of the shower I got a good look at him. Man, did he look old. He introduced himself to us. He was a World War I veteran. The proper term we used was "retreads." They had evidently taken him back into service. Now they had called him back to do guard duty so that the young guys like us could get shipped out.

There were only two exciting things that happened during my time there on Hope Island. The first one was after we had been there for a week or so. One of the guards came into our barracks one day, having stood guard duty. He took off his heavy coat and sat down onto his lower bunk. The guy above him was cleaning his weapon. Unlike most of us, this guy had one of the new M1 rifles. Most of us had those old .03 Springfields.[9] Anyway, the guy above, in the process of cleaning his weapon, banged the edge of the stock against the wall. Evidently he

---

9   The Springfield single bolt-action rifle, model 1903 .30-03 caliber, which became
    the official standard rifle of the armed forces on that year. It was heavily used in

must have forgotten that he still had a round in the chamber, and when he smacked it the rifle accidently went off. The bullet zipped down and hit the guy below in the end of his butt. We all had a good laugh over that one, even the guy who had been shot.

The second exciting thing happened a week later. One night, one of our sentries called in to report that he was pretty sure that he had seen, of all things, a submarine. He supposedly had spotted it in this little bay on the far end of the island. That caused a stir, because if the Germans were to land a raiding party on the island, we would be in big trouble. There were only 30 of us on the island, and all we had to defend ourselves (and those damn bombs) was our rifles, most of them those trusty old Springfields. It was quickly decided that we would have to get the drop on them. So on that cold windy night, all of us Marines prepared to lay siege to a German U-boat.

Armed with our rifles and wearing our Frank Buck helmets, heavy coats and gloves, we moved in silently around the suspected cove. As we quietly approached, a couple guys said that they thought they could actually faintly hear chains clanging and other noises they could not identify.

Moving up in the pitch dark, it was impossible to see anything. So the officer in charge told us that we were going to wait for daylight to come. Then at the crack of dawn, we would rush the sub, board her, and take her by force, either capturing or killing its crew members. We crouched there in the night for a few hours, chilled as the wind blew. Once or twice again, a guy ahead of us swore that he could hear chains rattling way off in the distance. Henry and I were as excited as a couple of schoolboys, and we whispered comments about the whole thing to each other in the darkness. Hey, if we captured a Nazi sub, we would be big heroes and probably each get a medal. We grinned at the idea. That would really be something to tell our folks back home.

The early morning hours seemed to drag on and on, and finally the sky began to get lighter. The noises coming from the direction of the sub had long stopped, and we now waited, getting ready to pounce. Daylight

---

World War I and was finally replaced by the M1 Garand in 1937, although the Springfield did see extensive use in World II as well.

broke over the cove, but a heavy fog kept us from seeing anything as we lay shivering in the cold behind boulders, our rifles pointed toward the enemy. Slowly the fog began to lift as the sun rose. The officer gave the word, and we started moving in on the cove. Coming up to it, we were surprised to find it empty. Nothing. No sub, no Krauts ... nothing but an empty cove.

Needless to say, there were 30 damned embarrassed Marines who returned to their barracks on Hope Island that day.

After our 30 days guard duty assignment was finally over, Henry and I were returned to the Quonset Point Naval Base on the mainland and we were allowed to go on liberty in Providence. Naturally, Henry and I tried to catch up on lost opportunities, so we over-indulged, and the next day, my head felt like it was going to fall off.

Later in October, my brother Alex got leave and hitchhiked up the coast to see me up in New England. Although he was not authorized to, he stayed at our barracks for a few days and slept in a vacant bunk, Alex wore on his uniform the French gears braid.[10] When we went out on liberty, a couple people noticed the braid and asked him if he was Canadian, which, of course, he got a kick out of (I have it to this day, although I still cannot figure out how I ended up with it). After a few days, Alex left to return to the First Marine Division, training at New River in North Carolina. I did not know it when we parted, but I would not see him again until after the war.

More guard duty assignments came, and I stood guard through Thanksgiving. It was during that time at Quonset Point that I occasionally came in contact with a certain 29-year-old lieutenant JG,[11] a fellow

---

10 The Croix de Guerre *fourragère* (a braided cord) was a French military decoration awarded a unit to recognize its actions in a war that France was involved in. Since the 5th Marines and 6th Marines had distinguished themselves in several battles defending France in 1918 (including the famous battle of Belleau Wood), U.S. Marines in those two regiments who had fought in those battles were authorized to wear the red and white braid. Alex of course, had not fought in World War I and was with the 7th Marines, so was not authorized to wear the braid.

11 Richard Milhous Nixon, the 36th president of the United States, was at the time 29 years old. Having accepted a commission as a U.S. Naval officer, lieutenant junior grade (O2) in mid-June 1942, he began his initial naval officer indoctrination at

that would someday become president of the United States— of course, who could know back then?—Richard M. Nixon. He was always a serious-looking guy, and to me always seemed to have a sour look on his face.

From our barracks, the view was beautiful. I could walk 200 yards and look out over the Narragansett Bay. On all but snowy days, you could look out and see islands on the other side,[12] some of them two miles away. Many was the time I would gaze out into the slot in between and watch an occasional destroyer go by, because there were a lot based there.

Some of us were good on liberty, and some just plain were not. For instance, there was one big tall guy in our group named McNolan or McNorris, or something like that. We just called him "Filthy McNasty," mostly because he had a foul mouth and a rotten disposition on life. Since he was a big mean guy, he would often go looking for trouble, which, when I was hunting gals, was the last thing on my mind.

One day, a few of us were on liberty in Providence. We had been bar-hopping when we went into this one place for a few more drinks. It was called the Five Points Bar, because it was located at the intersection of these five streets in the southern part of town. The gal that owned the hotel above the bar was in her seventies, but her daughter Charlene was only 32, and I must say, she was not bad looking for her age. So even though she was an older woman, I had started dating her. Okay, I was 13 years younger than she was, but what the hell, when it came to women I didn't play favorites with regards to age. And anyway, as long as I dated her, her mom took care of our room when we stayed there.

The Five Points Bar was a big place, with a long L-shaped bar on the right side. Next to it were the tables, with dozens of sailors sitting and standing around, all of them drinking. Hell, there must have been over seventy of them. On our guard, getting a number of dirty looks, we sat down in the back and ordered some drinks. I was there to have

the Naval Training School at Quonset Point. Following its completion, he entered Naval Officer Candidate School (OCS) and graduated in October, accepting a commission as a U.S. Naval officer, lieutenant junior grade (O2). Because of his prominence as an attorney, he was able to bypass the entry rank of ensign (O1).

12   Looking at Aquidneck Island and Prudence Island.

a good time, and did not want any trouble. McNasty though, being the foul guy that he was, evidently did, because he began to badmouth the sailors, bragging that he could whip any bunch of them.

Ho boy, I thought. Here we go.

One of them finally told McNasty he had better shut his damn mouth up, which of course, just egged him on further. He looked at them with a mean grin and said, "Screw you. I can lick all of you swabbies."

They looked at each other and sure enough, a bunch of them got up and decided to take him up on his offer. We all went outside, the sailors crowded around us, and some of them lined up to fight. After a few moments, one or two started towards him. McNasty growled and lit into the first guy, and then the second and third. Sure as hell, he took out about five of them pretty good. He was holding his own okay, but daggone, there were dozens of the bastards waiting to get their shot. Besides, he was starting to get tired and they were coming at him fresh.

Naturally, the fight expanded, and soon all of us Marines were in it. We finally took refuge by going inside the bar again, and moved to the back. You know, it's always nice to have a wall behind you, just in case you have to defend yourself. And with all these sailors coming at us, that was a good thing. Besides, we could hightail it out the back door if we needed to.

As the swabbies started towards us, we realized that while we had no worry about getting hit from all sides, we were essentially trapped. A minute later though, the police burst through the front door with their billy clubs, and man, I was never so happy in my life to see them. They broke up the fight, rescued us, and luckily turned us loose and allowed us to go on our way. But McNasty, beat up and bloody by then, was taken to the hospital. I have to admit though, he was fighting like a demon right up to when the MPs broke things up.

You would have thought that I would have learned to stay out of trouble after that, but it just seemed like trouble followed me wherever I went. A few weeks later, we were on liberty again. On this night, four of us ended up at a place northwest of the Five Points called the Homestead Café. Again, we had a table sitting in the back of the bar. I guess we hadn't learned our lesson at the Five Points, because although no one could attack us from behind, if trouble were to start, we would be blocked from getting out.

We had been there for a couple hours drinking, and I guess you could say that we were having a good time and in a pretty relaxed mood. One of us though, was further gone than the rest of us. In fact, he was pretty boozed up and had reached a point where good judgment had left him. At that point, he got up, staggered over to one of the booths along the wall, and began talking right to this woman sitting there. We knew there would be trouble and looked at each other, because the lady was obviously married and sitting next to her husband. And there was our buddy, openly putting the make on her, with her husband getting ticked off.

Well, this did not last very long, and after a couple minutes, the husband had had enough and told our drunk buddy to take a hike. He responded by exploding into a rage. He yelled that he was going to whip the crap out of the husband and beat his ass and this and that. Hearing his outburst, a lot of folks in there became angry and took sides with the husband.

It was then that I realized how much this was some kind of a local neighborhood bar, and that these folks were all regulars who all knew each other pretty good. So there we were, sitting in the back, with all these guys in the place now mad at us and standing up to defend this local guy and his wife. The three of us sitting down definitely did not want any trouble. The problem of course was to figure out how the hell we were going to get out of there without getting our damn necks broken. I mean, there were guys standing near the front door with clubs and looked like they really meant business. And again there was no back door escape. We were cornered again.

Okay we decided, it was time for us to make our move. So acting on what we had learned in the last few months, we each took off our webbed belt, made a fist, and wrapped the belt around it, with just six inches and the belt buckle at the end of it. We stood up and staring around, we slowly began to walk through that mob, this wedge of three guys. They glared at us, but they grudgingly parted for us as we walked towards the front. We grabbed our drunk buddy, apologized to the guy and his wife, and walked away as we told folks that we did not want any trouble. We reached the door and got the hell out of there. We just walked off quietly. Afterwards, we had to restrain ourselves from killing that S.O.B. for getting us into that mess. He was nuts. Just as much as McNasty.

War

At the beginning of December 1941, I was given an assignment to stand guard next to a large vehicle storage complex around Davisville, five miles west of the base.[13] In it were several acres of machinery-type trucks and construction equipment. I had the 0400 to 0800 watch, which was a miserable time to be guarding a bunch of trucks. I'd stand watch for four hours, get eight hours off, and then be on again and so on for three more shifts. I stood guard next to a small wooden shanty that bordered some woods. At that time of day, very few workers came into the complex. I was bored, to say the least.

About an hour into my watch on December 8th, as I stood there in the freezing cold in my dingy little hut, shivering in my winter coat, feeling miserable, trying to see, one little light bulb as my only source of light, a jeep came barreling down the road and around the corner. I saw some lieutenant driving. The jeep skidded to a stop, and I stared at him.

He looked at me and said, "Japan attacked Pearl Harbor."

Without another word, he took off again, roaring down the road, leaving me in dark silence. I stood there in the dark, stunned, speechless, wondering, trying to figure out what the hell had just happened. Japan? We were attacked? Was this the start of the war that everyone had been predicting? I looked down at my Springfield rifle. I had just ten rounds of ammo and no extra clips. What in blazes was my 19-year-old butt going to be able to do if I was attacked?

As the wind softly rustled through the trees, I looked out at the cold, silent, dark woods in front of me. My imagination went to work, as I began to worry. I could almost see dark, skulking figures moving around

---

13 The Davisville Naval Construction Battalion complex was created in early December 1941. The facility was used to train the Navy's new Construction Battalion, which would go on to become the Seabees.

way back in the trees. What the hell could I do if a bunch of Japs came out of those woods? I wouldn't stand a chance. I stood there, alert, worried, and still cold.

That was my introduction to World War II.

A few hours later that morning, after I was relieved, instead of going to get some rest, I was taken over to the main gate of a nearby work facility to do more guard duty. Along with a couple other Marines, I was ordered to guard some twenty of those semi-round Quonset huts. Each one had a mini-factory or work assembly section inside, in which a dozen or so civilians worked every day.

Although we technically were not at war (word of the declaration of war would not come until that afternoon), because of the Japanese attack on Pearl Harbor, new precautionary actions were initiated. When the workers came in to go to work, we now had to frisk them. We were told to be really thorough, too; insides of hats, pockets, cuffs, wallets, and shoes. We had to even check the workers' thermos jugs and make sure that they actually contained liquid. Needless to say, these guys were infuriated at this new set of security measures. It really upset them that even though they were good, staunch, patriotic Americans, they were all of a sudden no longer trusted by their own damn government, and personally, I agreed with them. So I resented doing what I was ordered to do, and I hated to humiliate them by checking their personal stuff. I did not for a moment want to hassle those folks.

After the work shift began, we were then told to go into the facility and patrol around. Smoking, which was a habit quite common and even encouraged in order to "be cool" in those days, was now forbidden. No cigarettes, cigars, or pipes, and we had to strictly enforce the rule. Again, there was more resentment from the workers, and we guards took the reaction of their discontent and although they did not blame us, they took out their frustrated emotions on us. This became a daily routine, and the whole thing quickly became for me a real crummy job. I decided right there that I would never want to be a cop, and that I had to find a better use of my talents.

In January 1942, the facility was given a formal dedication ceremony, and I was in the Marine honor guard for that event. And to make me feel better, on the 23rd, I was promoted to private first class.

In the months that followed, I did various types of guard duty here and there. On the plus side, I did get to go on liberty a lot, and several of us would go together. There was me, Henry Rucker, Emanuel James "Jim" Olivera, and a fine Marine named Jefferson Davis "Jeff" Watson, Jr. from Jacksonville, Florida. Quite often though, we would hit it off with the girls and go our separate routes. There was one gal in Providence that I dated for a short while. Her mother owned this hotel above Five Points. She was nice. Then there was this barmaid I knew at a rathskeller[14] in Fall River, Massachusetts. I liked her a lot, too. Still, I guess I was not the marrying type in those days.

One day that February, I was given the assignment of guarding a load of ammunition on a train. I was told that I had to sit on top of this boxcar with my .03 Springfield. I was told everywhere that train went, I had to go too as guard.

The day we loaded up in the railroad yard in Davisville was a cold one. My assigned boxcar was located about three or four cars back from the engine, and as the train started southward, I sat up there on the edge of that boxcar with the wind whipping at my face, hunkered down, shivering, freezing my butt off, and generally feeling miserable.

Finally, we made a stop and the train engineer walked back and looked up at me. "Hey, it's cold as hell," he said. "There's no need for you to stay up there freezing, Marine. Why don't you come on down here and get in the cab and get warm?"

Well, he sure as hell didn't need to ask me twice, and I told him gratefully, "That sounds good to me." So I climbed down off the boxcar and walked over to the engine. Wow. What a beautiful piece of machinery I thought as I climbed into the cab.

There were two guys: the old engineer and the younger fireman, who was fueling the engine. He would open the steel door at the bottom of the furnace and shovel in some coal from the coal car behind us. Then he would clang the door shut, and then turn around for another load. In

---

14 A type of popular combination beer bar and restaurant with a Germanic theme or pattern located below the street level.

front of the engineer was this large black iron bar that ran diagonally in front of his spot. He took a hold of it and looked over at me. Curious, I stared at him.

"This is the throttle," he told me proudly. "You use it if you wanna drive."

"Uh huh," I said, my mouth open. Wow.

He grabbed a cord and yanked on it. The train whistle blew with a roaring *whoo-whoooo*! I laughed when I heard it. Then he grabbed the throttle and pulled down on it, and I heard steam rush in somewhere inside the engine. Very slowly, the train began to move. I marveled as we gradually began to pick up speed. I intently looked over the pipes, little wheels, and dials in front of us as the engineer explained what they did.

I volunteered to help shovel the coal, and the fireman grinned at me as he handed me the shovel and showed me how to do it. I grasped the shovel with my Marine gloves and eagerly stood there.

He looked at me and said, "Okay, just get a good scoop of coal from behind ya there, and then turn around, step on that lever right there, and just shoot the coal in. Then ya just take yer foot off the lever, and the door'll close. It's that simple."

I grinned and nodded. I turned around, heaved my shovel into the coal behind us and got a good load. I turned again, walked over to the engine, and like he showed me, I stepped on that lever on the steel floor to open the door. When it clanged open, I shoved my load into the orange hot fire inside. Then I yanked the shovel back and let go the lever. The door clanged shut. I grinned at him again and turned for another load. Another shovel full, opened the door, tossed the coal in, let off the lever, the door clanked shut. Daggone, this was fun! It definitely beat the hell out of sitting on top of that damn boxcar, freezing my butt off. So I shoveled coal for about five minutes until the fire was good and hot. Then the engineer asked me if I wanted to drive.

I was stunned. Wow. My eyes wide and my mouth open, all I could do was nod. Me, driving that whole damn train. I had jumped a lot of them as a kid. Now I had the chance to *run* one!

He reached out to the iron bar. "This is the throttle," the engineer told me proudly, his glove on the end of it. "You use it to drive the train."

"Yeah?" I said, mesmerized.

The engineer grabbed the large diagonal iron bar on the left side that ran diagonally in front of his spot. "Like I said, this is the throttle. You use it if you wanna drive. You just take that bar and pull her down."

Pull it down. Okay. Hesitantly, I grabbed the big iron lever and looking at him, the back of the engine, and then at the lever, I began to pull down on it.

The train seemed to jump forward as the wheels started to spin faster. "Whoa, take it easy!" he laughed. "Easy."

I let off the bar a bit, and the wheels grabbed onto the track and the train began to speed up.

Holy crap! This was great!

After about fifteen minutes of pure ecstasy, he took over control again. We ended up dropping our loads off in some small town, and then through a series of switches and side tracks, we turned around and made the return trip. Since there was no ammo on the train now, I figured that I did not have to sit up on top of that freezing boxcar. Besides, I damn sure liked riding with the engineer and fireman, and they welcomed my company.

At the end of the trip, the truck that came to pick me up had trouble finding me, because the train was in a different position than before, and I of course had to stay with the train. But I had a blast doing that.

Winter turned into spring, and when summer came, I briefly served guard duty in Newport. Then I returned to Quonset Point, where I stood guard over various vessels that came into port. For those assignments, I had to stand watch on this long flat dock adjacent to the land. It was boring, and I remember those winter days being icy and cold as hell. Chilly winds came in right off the ocean, and I would have to stand watch out there, sometimes in snow.

I did more months of boring guard duty at government facilities, next to trains, submarines, and various ships along the East Coast. One of those vessels in the early spring of 1942 was this huge aircraft carrier,

I think the USS *Hornet*.[15] I stood guard next to the gangplank walking back and forth in the dirt for one night. It was pretty cold and dark, and even wearing that heavy wool overcoat that hardly let me move, I was still chilled.

I found life there at Quonset Point interesting. The commander of our Marine guard detachment was a Major G. H. Morse Jr., a really serious type of guy. In our spare time, he made damn sure that we drilled over and over. We marched every day and did the order arms until our arms ached. We practiced all sorts of rifle exercises, and we got really good. We could do all kinds of fancy stuff, including drills like the Queen Anne's Salute. We went through different marching formations until we got good, and then went on and on until we were excellent at marching and turning in blocks.

When we were not outside drilling or on guard, we worked on our .03 Springfields. I learned to wipe linseed oil over the stock and then slowly rub it into the wood. Repeated treatments customized the wood and built up coats on the surface, and as they did, the wood would really shine. Yeah, we polished those butts to the point where they were dazzling, almost like glass.

And oh, our uniforms. Anywhere we went, we had to be all spit and polish, and so we spent endless amounts of hours cleaning our blouses, pressing our guard pants, working on our covers, shining all our brass,

15 George is mistaken, because no evidence was found of the USS *Hornet* (CV-8) ever going to Rhode Island. Quonset Point had become officially operational as a Naval Air Station back on July 12, 1941. The *Hornet* was commissioned later that fall in Norfolk but trained in that same area until March 1942. At that time, she left for the West Coast via the Panama Canal, on her way westward to undertake the famous Doolittle Raid on April 18, 1942. Similarly, five of the seven U.S. aircraft carriers in commission at that time never traveled up to Rhode Island. One though, the USS *Ranger* (CV-7), did indeed steam up to Quonset Point on April 17, 1942, loaded with the Army's 33rd Pursuit Squadron, which included 68 Army P-40 planes. She then put to back sea on the 22nd, and delivered the squadron to Accra on the Gold Coast of Africa on May 10th. She returned to Quonset Point on May 28th and then made a patrol to Argentia, Newfoundland. She came back to Newport on July 1st, loaded 72 Army P-40 pursuit planes and sailed again for Accra on the 19th. So George had stood guard for the *Ranger*.

spit-polishing our shoes, and of course, cleaning and shining our rifles over and over again.

The summer went by, and we continued our guard assignments. To make sure we kept looking good, every Saturday, Major Morse and his executive officer would line our two rows up on the parade ground next to the barracks, and he would meticulously inspect us.

I remember one particular Saturday morning. Henry and I had been doing some serious drinking the night before, and now I was hung over, and my head was splitting. Still, I dressed with the rest of the guys and walked out to the parade ground, my stomach churning and my head swimming. We assembled in formation as we always did, and when Major Morse called attention, we snapped to. We stood there as he began his inspection, starting with the first row. As he slowly walked down the line, I struggled to stand there, my stomach growling. Oh please, I thought, let's get this stupid thing over with before I puke.

Morse finished going down the first row, turned, and began inspecting ours. I clenched my teeth as my head began to swim and I started to get queasy. He slowly continued down our line, finally passed me, and turned to do the last row. Finally, after what seemed like an eternity, he finished his inspection. He walked back to the front and ordered us to parade rest.

He then began some speech. He was saying something, but I could not make out what it was, mostly because I was hurting, struggling at this point just to stand there. My stomach was getting worse, my head was killing me, and I could tell that I wasn't going to stay long the way I was without letting go of whatever was in my stomach. I was getting desperate, and his talk did not seem like it was going to end any time soon. The time crawled, and I realized that I had to do something. But I just couldn't raise my hand and tell the major I was sick. He'd yell at me and probably throw my butt in the brig.

Things inside me were coming to a head, though. I knew that I was about to let go, and I could tell that this one was going to be a big one. Yet I just couldn't hurl chunks of food and old booze on the clean backs of the guys in front of me. Nor could I turn around and do that to the guys behind me. I was stuck in this damn formation. Still, I had to do something as the nausea increased. I realized that it was about to happen, and there was just nothing I could do to stop that.

Well, if that was the case, I thought, since we were a guard unit and were supposed to do everything smartly, I decided that if I had to get sick, I was going to do it and go down with some snappy style. I was going to let fly, but by God, I was going to do it in a military manner. Taking a couple deep breaths, I impulsively snapped to attention and presented arms. I then did a right shoulder arms, took a sharp step forward, did a right face, and began briskly marching between the rows. I was barely aware that the major had stopped talking, and no one else said or even mumbled anything as I marched. I knew though, that all eyes were on me.

Oh Lord, it was getting ready to come up as my stomach rumbled like a volcano about to let go. I smartly marched over to the end of the formation and made it a couple quick steps beyond. That was about as far as I got. I stopped as the stuff came up and my mouth began to let loose. I had to admit, struggling as I was, the force and distance of what flew out impressed me as I stood there letting it all out. Finally, as I gagged my last bits, I came to attention and wiped my mouth off with my left glove as best as I could. Shouldering my rifle, I did an about-face and sharply marched back between the ranks. Getting back to my spot, I stopped, did a left face, took two steps forward, did another about-face, and snapped back to parade rest. I still felt like shit, but at least now I'd survive, the good Lord (and the major) willing.

Still, no one said a word. I had to admit, it had been a classy act. Finally, the major began talking again, finished his speech and then dismissed us. We fell out and the guys began to laugh their butts off. I just looked at them, turned around, walked back to the barracks, and collapsed on my rack. Luckily, the major did not come down on me. Another bullet dodged.

One day, an examiner from the AIG[16] came up from Washington to inspect us. They usually came around to each unit every six months or

---

16 Assistant Inspector General. A senior member of the Marine Corps' Inspector General Office, charged with the inspection of all Marine units within his jurisdiction to ensure that Marine Corps instructions, policies, and doctrines are followed,

so, mostly to make sure that we were following Marine Corps policy. They also over the years had become a private sounding block for us enlisted. When they spoke to us, we were free to voice any complaints or gripes to them, without fear of reprisals from our officers. This AIG, a major, inspected us in formation, and then later went through our barracks. No one had any complaints for him, and really, we did not think that it would make any difference anyway, and griping was not worth the risk of somehow it getting back to the CO.

He inspected our standing lockers. One guy, maybe in hopes of someday becoming a recognized hero, had found a photo of the Medal of Honor and had cut it out, being careful to cut the paper around the edges of the medal and the ribbon. He then took that paper cutout and taped it to the inside lid of his foot locker. When the AIG opened the door and saw that medal hanging there, he must have assumed that it was the real thing, because he immediately stepped back, snapped to attention, and smartly saluted the image. He turned to the guy next to the footlocker and made a comment about his having the Medal of Honor. That recruit looked at the AIG and fumbling his words, told him, "Uh sir, that's not real, sir; it's just a photo."

We were all ready to crack up. I'm surprised I didn't start laughing.

The AIG glared at him, and if looks could kill, that Marine would have been a dead man. Still, that AIG did not say a damn word. Finally, he turned around and stormed out of the barracks. We all just shook our heads. We figured that he must have thought that the more he made a big deal out of this, it would in the end be the worse for him. Better to leave well enough along and get out. We only laughed about it later on, when it was safe. Naturally, the photo of the medal hit the trash that night.

---

and that all unit components are functioning in accordance with U.S. military policies. The inspecting AIG representative must ensure that all individuals in every unit, from the commanding officer down to the enlisted personnel, "promote Marine Corps combat readiness, institutional integrity, effectiveness, discipline, and credibility through impartial and independent inspections, assessments, inquiries, investigations, teaching, and training."

For a time, I did duty at Davisville, RI, six miles to the east, guarding storage facilities for the new Seabee facility.[17] Mostly though, my assignments kept me in the Quonset Point area. While at times I did guard duty in the same location for a period of time, I often got different assignments.

It was at Quonset Point where I had my first round of trouble in the Marine Corps.

General Court Martial

I was transferred to the Naval War College in Newport in the late spring and did various guard assignments there. We stayed in wooden barracks located on a high bluff, about a hundred yards away from and above the channel, a few miles north of the city.

Staying out of trouble was getting to be a task for me, probably because I was so ornery. And there at Quonset Point, it seemed to be a common thing for us Marines. There were probably about three thousand sailors there and only some two hundred Marines. Still, at any one time, you would probably find about twenty Marines in the brig, and only a few sailors.

I had already been disciplined twice now. The first time was in March. I went out on liberty and stayed out too long. I got back an hour late, and because of that, I was charged AWOL. After a short hearing, I was busted down to private.

Then there was another incident a couple weeks later. We were at Davisville. A corporal was bringing three of us back to the barracks after we had stood our watch. It was evening, and as we passed the flagpole and approached the building, we saw the color guard preparing to lower the colors. Our corporal told us to hurry up and get in the

---

17 A term derived from the acronym "CB" for "Construction Battalion," referring the Navy's construction units that were created immediately after Pearl Harbor in 1941. They were created to perform many and various construction projects for the military in forward areas, such as clearing land, constructing airfields, and building makeshift harbor facilities. Their first training facility was at Davisville, RI, which became operational six months later.

building before they sounded the call "Attention to colors." See, when that happens in the evening, if you are outside, you come to attention. When the bugler plays "Retreat," you salute, and remain that way as the colors are lowered. You can go about your business again as soon as "Carry on" is played.

We hustled towards the building. Unknown to us, the officer of the day was watching us out the window from his office on the second story of the barracks. He got annoyed as he saw us hustling, trying to avoid standing for the short ceremony. Just as we neared the front door, the attention to colors was played. So close.

We turned around, saluted, and stood there until it was over. Then we turned around and went inside. We were met by that officer of the day coming down the stairs, really steamed. He walked up to us and started chewing our butts off. We hadn't done anything wrong, but he hadn't seen us stop outside, so he assumed we had not. The corporal told him that we really had stopped, but he didn't believe him. And he didn't give a crap what we said. Instead, we all got what they call a "deck court martial."[18] It was a bum rap, and we all had to do extra policing duties on the base for a couple weeks.

A month later though, I got into really serious trouble. I had been transferred to a guard unit in Newport. One night sometime after midnight, I became ill. I had had a few drinks that night, but I was not drunk. No, something else was happening to me. I had either caught some disease, drunk some bad liquor, or had eaten some tainted food. Anyway, I was pretty sick. Unfortunately, I was scheduled to go on guard duty in a couple hours. I struggled to get ready and walked outside.

Standing next to the truck loaded with sentries, all waiting to be dropped off at their designated posts, I pleaded with the sergeant of the guard to get someone else to take my shift. I had a temperature, felt queasy, and I was vomiting. Hell, I was dizzy just standing there talking to him. I told him plainly, "I can't stand my watch. I'm sicker than hell."

The sergeant sympathized with me, but said, "Well, damn it, I just don't have an extra guy tonight here."

---

18 A mostly informal hearing, usually by just one officer, it is held for minor offenses.

I told him flat out that I would not be able to stand the watch. I could barely stand up, and that would not be for long.

He thought about it, and asked me, "Well, can you stand your watch long enough to post the rest of the unit? If you can, I'll come back and bring a guy to replace you."

My eyes drooping, I looked at him, sighed, and said, "Okay, I'll try to hang in there." So I got into the truck, and together with the other sentries, they took me out to my guard post, a small 4×4-foot shack that was next to a bomb storage lot. I began my 0200–0400 watch.

Standing there in the dark, I felt just terrible. I winced every so often at the terrific pain in my abdomen. I knew I had a fever and could feel the energy in my body draining away. Out there in the silence, I did not—I just could not—stand for too long, and slowly I slumped down some. An hour went by, although it seemed like four, and no one showed. The sergeant never came back.

I got sick again, to the point where I had to throw up behind the guard hut. Finished, I wiped my mouth off and came back to the front, weak and dizzy. Finally, feeling sorry for myself, I sat down on one of those storage crates next to the sentry box. All I could do was think about the sweet relief of just being able to hit the sack and just get some shuteye. Ah, just to be able to sleep it off in my cot. I guess I must have dozed off.

The next thing I knew, someone was shouting at me. I opened my eyes and saw a lieutenant standing in front of me. He must have walked up and seen me sleeping on watch. He yelled for a security guard, and under armed escort, I was taken to the captain of the watch. While the captain sympathized with me somewhat and agreed that I should not have been put on guard, he still was resolute in his determination and charged me with sleeping on duty. He then ordered me to the brig.

I was taken to a hut and put into a wire cage. I sat there on a makeshift bed made out of two boards, still sick as a dog, worried about the charge that had been brought against me. They could not bust me down, because that had happened back in March when I had come back late from liberty. They could though, charge me with sleeping on duty, and in the Marine Corps, that was a court martial offense. Asking around,

I had found out that those Marines who had been found guilty of the charge were spending a year of hard labor at Portsmouth Naval Prison.[19]

I was to be charged with a formal GCM,[20] although in my mind, I should not have even been made to stand duty, much less get charged. I spent nearly two months in that cage awaiting my hearing, at which time the charge was to be formally read to me. In those few weeks before the hearing, despite the fact that I had no access to facilities or anything, I decided that I was going to put my best foot forward. These bastards were not going to get the better of me. I figured that the best way to do that was to act like the Marine guard that I had been in previous months. We had drilled often, marched often, and when we were off duty, cleaned and pressed our uniforms. The brig was gonna make a lot of that difficult, but I decided I was going to do what I had been trained to do.

In the next week or so, I saw guys go in and out of the brig. Many of them were going to be processed out. Surprisingly, a number of them would sit there in tears, all broken up, crying about their fate. As I sat there, watching them feeling sorry for themselves, all I could wonder was, what the hell was so damn bad about being in the brig? I mean, it was just temporary.

I spent some time studying these young fellows. Most of them were barely old enough to shave and had probably sung in some church choir before the war had started. And when we got into it, I'll bet they were

---

19 The charge is a violation of the Uniform Code of Military Justice, Article 113: Misbehavior of a Sentinel or Lookout. In the Marines, today is normally punishable by up to ten years of hard labor at Portsmouth Naval Prison. One of the gravest offenses even in peacetime, if it occurs during a time of war (which the U.S. was in at that time), maximum punishment could be death, and George could ostensibly have been executed by firing squad (although during the war, no service member was executed in the U.S. for this charge). In George's case, the charge might have been the lesser charge of Article 92: Dereliction of Duty.

20 General Court Martial. The highest of the three types of military charge for an offense, reserved for the most serious of infractions, with the severest of sentences allowed. The intermediate level charge would be a Special Court Martial, and the least serious being a Summary Court Martial (for minor infractions, not considered a criminal trial, an SCM is presided over by only one officer, and punishment is quite limited).

the first ones to run down and join up, all proud and bragging about how they were going to save the country. Then they get to boot camp, see how rough it is, begin wondering what the hell they did, and then start to panic. Well, looking at these guys now, all I could feel was sorry for them. I guess that no one had told them there were no church choirs in combat.

During that time I exercised regularly, did not give the guards any lip, and made sure I cleaned up as much and as often as I could. At night, I'd remove my trousers and folded them between the two boards that I slept on. Naturally, each morning, they would not look as bad as they easily could have, and in the end, they stayed in halfway good condition, and I came out looking pretty decent.

At the end of that time, when it was my day in court, so to speak, I strode out of that cage with relatively pressed pants and a confident look on my face. Even the captain of the guard was impressed with me as I walked up to him like I knew exactly what I was doing and saluted him smartly.

I was taken to the hearing room and saw the captain in charge of the detachment. He was an old retired World War I veteran, one of the old guard, a retread who had been allowed to reenlist when the war had broken out. In a small room, the charge against me was formally read off.[21] The officer in charge of the hearing was the same captain who commanded the Marine detachment.

I was quite relieved (although I did my best not to show it) to see at the hearing the sergeant of the guard on the night in question, and he testified on my behalf. He verified that I had told him I was too sick to stand my post that night but had tried to anyway. He further added that I had for months served as a very competent sentry without any incident, that I was certainly incapacitated that night from illness, and that I should not under any condition have stood that watch. The

21 George was probably charged with either UCMJ (Uniform Code of Military Justice) Article 113 (Misbehavior of a Sentinel or Lookout) or Article 92 (Dereliction of Duty). Each of these charges normally carries a General Court Martial. Under the circumstances, he perhaps should only have been charged with Article 134 (the General Article), under wrongfully sitting down on post.

captain was impressed by my performance and admitted that there had
been extenuating circumstances. In the end, I was found not guilty for
that reason, probably one of the few that ever was let off for that type
of charge. There was however, one condition: that I be transferred south
to New River and from there, shipped out to a combat unit overseas
immediately. My orders were to specify that.

Which was, of course, what I had wanted all along.

I readily accepted the findings, and the hearing ended. But I knew I
had been shafted. They should have dismissed the charges and cleared
my record as soon as that sergeant of the guard had admitted in his
testimony that he had forgotten about me. After it was over, the old
retread captain called me aside. He told me that he sympathized with
me over what had happened and added, "You know, I'm gonna try to
help you all I can."

He added that even though I was being transferred from Newport to
Camp Lejeune, he was going to try to arrange for my travel orders to
read that I get there via my home town of Akron, Ohio. "So that you
can get a chance to see your folks before you leave," he said.

I thanked him sincerely for all that he was doing for me, and I promised him that I would not let him down overseas. Unfortunately, as it
turned out, the captain told me the next day that he could not justify
my detouring to Akron. It was just too far out of the way for them to
justify it.

During this short time, getting ready to leave, I tried to at least catch
up on what my buddies were doing. Jeff Watson, Jr. as it turned out, had
joined the Marine Raiders. I found out in 1944 that he became part of
C Company, 4th Raider Battalion.[22] Another one of our buddies, Jim
Olivera, ended up in K Company, 3rd Battalion, 1st Marines (K/3/1).
Henry Rucker was still at Quonset Point. It sure was hard to keep track
of friends in those hectic days.

As my orders to ship out were being processed, I must have seemed
a pretty pathetic case, because two Marines in the administration office
took pity on me. They took me aside and one of them said, "Look fella,

---

22 Originally 1st Raider Battalion, and later designated 4th Battalion, 1st Marines.

you can't possibly have any money, because you've been locked up for quite a little while."

It was true. I only had a couple bucks in my pocket when I had been arrested, and because of the serious charge, I had not received any pay these last two months. The two guys were sympathetic, and evidently felt somehow that I was not a bad sort of fellow. They told me that if I needed any money, they would loan me some. Providing that I paid them back later, of course.

I felt humbled by what they had just offered. I mean, these two guys didn't know me from Adam. I had just come off being charged with a court martial offense, and I was being shipped out. And yet, they were offering to chip in and help me out, not knowing if they would ever see me again, or if I would ever repay them. The bonds in the Marine Corps though, were strong, and I was starting to find that out. I thanked them for the offer and told them that I most certainly would pay them back. With that, they loaned me a few bucks—just enough to squeak by until my next pay.

It was a freezing, snowy day in December, 1942, when I boarded a train in Boston to head southward. I was on my own. All I had was my gear, my ticket, and the few bucks those two fellows had lent me. I had no idea what the new place would be like.

Camp Lejeune

The trip down along the East Coast was monotonous, and the train briefly stopped in Richmond for a layover. I walked around the platform, looking at advertisements. Even for Virginia, the December weather was cold, and as I walked around shivering, looking at some boxes stacked on the platform, I felt isolated. Standing there, reading some of the box labels, I again started to wonder what lay before me. I remembered the GCM, and how close I had come to going to prison.

On the other hand, I thought about the generous advance that those two clerks had loaned me and why they had done it. They had really taken a risk loaning me dough, and based on what I had gone through, they had no idea if I was really the type to return the money. I knew though, that one way or another, I would pay them back for their consideration and for taking a chance on me. Determined to weather this setback and wanting to be ready for what was ahead of me, I took a deep breath and went into the station to get warm.

The train let me off in Jacksonville, North Carolina, and I got on a small military bus, its only rider. The driver took me some twenty miles down, and finally we arrived at the new base, Camp Lejeune. Of course, no one called it that back then. It was just known to us as "Tent City," because that was just about the only type of structure that was up there. I was directed to the base's new barracks area, the New River barracks.[23] When I arrived, I reported in to the top sergeant there. He looked me over and without saying a thing, he took me into his office.

I stood silently in front of his desk as he opened up my record. He looked at my papers and must have seen the GCM charge because he went "Hmmm ..." and then glared up at me.

"Well I got news for you!" he barked. "You ain't going to act up in my outfit now."

The top then proceeded to read me the riot act, in detail. He ran a tight friggin' ship here and by God, there sure as hell was gonna be no damn foolishness in his friggin' command. Was that CLEAR?!? I had damn well better remember that my sorry ass was always going to be under his watchful eye, and if said sorry ass so much as slipped up even just a tad, he would bring the force of the whole damn Marine Corps down on my stupid worthless head. A whole world of shit would come down on me, and I, sure as God made little green apples, would not know what the hell had hit me. This by heavens was *his* Corps, and my worthless piece of horse-crap butt was not going to disgrace it.

I stood there, just took a breath and said quietly, "Yes, sergeant."

Growling, he checked a clipboard and then assigned me to a bunk in the far corner of one of the cheap, plain plywood shacks that had replaced the tents in the area a year before. I found out that I was the

---

23 Actually, the entire base was named Camp Lejeune in a ceremony on December 20, 1942. The New River barracks section was named after the river the base was next to.

first one assigned to this shack, so I quietly stowed my gear in the far corner, lay down on my rack, and relaxed, waiting for chow call.

About an hour later, I was half asleep when the door flew open with a crash. I looked up and along with a chilly gust of wind, in walked a Marine that somehow looked vaguely familiar. He saw me, dropped his seabag, and broke out into a big grin.

By damn, I thought, that guy looked a hell of a lot like Henry Rucker. Still half-asleep, I thought at first I was dreaming, or that my memory was playing tricks on me. But as the guy came towards me, I saw to my surprise and joy that it really was my old friend Rucker. Laughing, we greeted each other and gave each other a big hug. I welcomed him to our new barracks and helped him stow his gear next to mine.

This was just one of the good things about the Marine Corps that I was finding out. It was small enough that you were always seeing old friends or meeting new ones that had news of faraway places. We were just like a big family. I also would learn the down side of that over time when I would occasionally get news that buddies that I had shared many an adventure with had been killed fighting on this island or in that operation. The family thing in those cases made news that much more unpleasant to bear.

For the next two months, we took intensive light machine-gun training. The schedule was nice: one day training, one day off. Being a natural shot, I did well there. Rucker took to the training as well as I did, and we were soon both appointed squad leaders of machine-gun squads. For several weeks, we ran up and down those North Carolina hills, dragging our big old weapons around until they became part of us. We took them apart, cleaned them, and then put them back together time and time again, until we knew them inside and out.

There were a number of other advanced specialty training courses that I wanted to take, and I was older than a lot of other Marines there, so that gave me priority over them. I found out though, to my chagrin that I needed a high school diploma to apply for them. So I lost out on a lot of opportunities to advance my skills.

In the middle of my training, I finally was allowed seven days' leave to go home for Christmas before I was shipped off to God knows where.

It was Friday, December 18, 1942 when I began the trip home. Taking a suitcase with me carrying my dress blues, I caught the train. About ten miles east of Pittsburgh, the train made a stop, and always curious, I got out. I walked into a nearby pub for a quick drink, and that's when my troubles started.

Taking my beer over to the window, I was shocked to see that the damn train was gone! It had left without me. And worse, my suitcase was aboard. I ran outside and spotted a railway supervisor next to a trolley. I told him that I was going home on leave before going overseas, and that I had been on that train. The supervisor told me to hop on the trolley, and we set off to catch the train at the next station. I mean, he opened that thing up as fast as it would go, and that damn trolley was really rolling, bumping all over those tracks, a stiff wind in our faces.

We just missed the train at the next station, just south of Pittsburgh. I jumped down off the trolley, thanked the guy, and took off running. I spotted the train and ran for it, but as I got near, it began to move. Frustrated, I had to wait for the next one. When it finally came, I went aboard and took it to Youngstown.

Getting off that train, I went in to the station and over to the line at the ticket counter to find out when the next passenger train for Akron was due. When my turn came, I asked the guy behind the counter what time was the next train to Akron was scheduled.

He looked up behind the window and said, "It's just leaving."

"WHAT?"

"It's just leaving right now. That's it over there," he said, pointing out the window.

I thanked him and ran out to the track as the train began to move. The car doors were closed, but I sure as hell was not going to miss *this* train. I looked around and saw no one looking my way. So I quickly walked up past the rear cars and hopped up between two Pullmans. I got a firm grip, and held on.

The train gathered speed as I just stood there between the cars. Wearing my gloves and green coat, I was not that cold at first. But as the train continued, the chill began to set in. Within twenty minutes, I was freezing my butt off, wondering what the hell I was doing.

Suddenly, the back door of the car in front of me opened up, and a guy who was probably the train detective looked down at me. Evidently, someone had seen me climb up between the cars as the train had passed them and had phoned in the report.

The guy crooked his finger at me and said, "Come on in here, son. It's too damn cold to be out there."

Gratefully, I crawled over the coupling as he fully opened the back door to let me into the passenger car. I stood there, shaking. I assumed he was the train detective, but he said that he would let me ride into Akron. We talked a while as I began to warm up. He told me that there were worse ways to ride the rails in this weather. Even where I had been between the cars, it was a lot better than "riding the rods," that is, riding on the crossbars underneath the car. He told me stories of some guys who rode the crossbars, even in the winter. I shivered. I could never do that. That was just dumb. He called them "cinder dicks," because they rode next to the cinders along the track.

We pulled into Akron, and I finally made it to our house at 2941 Wingate Avenue, the last house at the end of the street, back by the frozen swamps. No one else could build there, because it was a flood plain, and every year the Tuscarawas River would flood at some point. Still, we lived there, and I had a nice stay with my family.

During my leave, I made sure that I saw my girl Phyllis, and we were able to have several nice evenings together. Her mom took a photograph of the two of us, which my brother gave to me years after the war. I also did get drunk a couple times. In fact, one night, I soaked up everything alcoholic that I could, because I knew that once I was shipped out to the Pacific that would be the end of the good times for a long time.

The days flew by, and soon it was time to say goodbye and catch the train to go back to Camp Lejeune. That turned out to be the last official leave I would get in the Marines. I returned to Camp Lejeune and took up where I had left off in machine-gun training. Besides getting to polish firing techniques, I spent weeks learning the proper care and operation of various types of .30 cal. machine guns.

I had one more brief chance to go home again before I was to ship out overseas. In late February 1943, our top sergeant told us that we would soon be headed west to join the war. Not totally heartless, he told us that if any of us did not live too far away and could convince him that we had enough money to make it home and back again, he would grant us a 72-hour liberty.

By then most of us only had a few bucks, and not enough for a trip home. So of course, being Marines, we improvised. A bunch of us pooled all our money together and gave it to one guy. He went in to see the Top, showed him the money, and got his leave. Then he came out and gave the dough to the next guy, who went in and did the same thing. And on and on.

That's how each of us got to leave the base and go home. I wanted to see my mom again, but I also wanted to see Phyllis one more time. Those of us traveling north had it much harder, it being winter and all. I had to hitchhike, and man, it was icy cold. I managed to find enough rides to get me to Akron, but the last fellow I rode with dropped me off on the outskirts of town at 2 o'clock in the morning. It was so friggin' cold. There I was in my dress blues and spit polish shoes, walking down U.S. Route 224 past the airport, in the bitter night, shivering, wondering what the hell I was doing. I would be able to get home just long enough to say hi to my mom, and maybe see Phyllis for an hour or so before heading back. Shivering, I walked down Waterloo Road, and finally made it home there at the end of Wingate Avenue. I could not stay long, but in the end, I felt that the trip was worth the effort, especially since I might never see them again.

American Samoa

I made it back to New River in time and continued machine-gun training. One day, just about the time I had established new friends and had become accustomed to our surroundings, in typical Marine Corps fashion, our top sergeant came into our shack and growled, "Okay, half you guys are shipping out overseas. So get yer shit together, cuz you're leavin' here in the morning."

We packed up and early next morning, we headed towards a troop train that sat on tracks right there in the camp.[24] We marched into the area and boarded the train from both sides. Rucker and I found seats next to each other in a middle car. We had no weapons with us. They had all been left behind in New River; even our rifles. It was just us and our kit, stowed in storage cars.

The train chugged westward. It took us some five days to travel across the country, and we stayed in those cars for that entire time, mostly in our seats. When the train stopped at a station, we were not allowed to get off for any reason. We had to just sit there. The whole time. Mostly, we spent the time talking, reading, or just staring out the windows. We ate, read, wrote home, and at night, slept sitting. There were no facilities to shower or bathe, so after a couple days, we started getting ripe.

Each pair of cars had two black stewards assigned to take care of us, although they actually did little more than serve us meals. Mostly, they just hung out with us, listened to our stories, and tried to take care of our needs. The meals that they served us were definitely nothing to write home about. They mostly consisted of box lunches or brown bag specials.

The only time we ever left our seats was to visit with other guys in the car, or to hit the head. This was something of a new experience for me. At the end of each Pullman was a tiny bathroom, which was nothing more than a small vented closet with a toilet seat in the middle. When you were done doing whatever you had to do, you stepped on a pedal to flush. There must have been some sort of a holding tank attached to the car, and the water would run into the bowl and flush your business out onto the side of the tracks.[25] One of the guys early on asked where the

---

24 This short railroad spur, called the Camp Lejeune Railroad, became operational at the beginning of 1942 and connected to the Atlantic Coast Line Railroad in Jacksonville, NC.

25 This back then was what was known as a hopper toilet or a drop-chute toilet, available on the more modern trains. The bowl allowed the waste to fall directly into the holding tank, which would periodically be flushed automatically via an electric solenoid whenever the train reached a preset minimum speed. Because of the external health risks that this type of removal system posed, these types of

hell all the crap went. I knew, because when I had been a kid walking alongside railroad tracks, I had seen random piles of crap along the tracks. So I told him how it worked. I also told him that this was why we were not allowed to go to the head when the train was in a station. It would not be very pleasant for those folks waiting for a train with big piles of poop sitting on the tracks in front of them.

We traveled through a good deal of desert. Naturally it was hot, really hot, so the windows pretty much stayed open. Holy cow, a couple of times we even thought that we were in Mexico. Sometimes we saw sand drifts blowing over the tracks.

We finally arrived in San Diego near the end of February 1943. We stayed there for a couple weeks in tents put up on the sand between the parade grounds. We trained hard during the day, but we were given liberty most nights, so for the most part we enjoyed the stay. Then I came down with, of all things, the stupid measles. After being laid up for three days, I really got worried, because the medics wanted me to stay in bed for another few days. I was starting to get paranoid, because I knew that we would be moving out soon, and I did not want my unit suddenly shipping out without me. We had become somewhat close, and they were the only guys in the Corps that I knew. So I definitely wanted to get the hell out of this hut to join up with them.

Somehow, on my fourth day in the medical ward, I convinced the doctor that I was over my measles, pleading that I felt much better, and that he could let me out early. I went back to the unit and immediately went on liberty with my buddies. That night, I met a strikingly lovely lady in a bar. An older lady—I was 20 and she was closer to 30—she was brunette and had a nice figure. She was the quiet type and did not talk much, but to me, she was a goddess. I was my usual flamboyant self, happy to be with such a fine gal. We immediately took to each other and ended up spending the evening together. When the bar closed, we went back to a hotel and she paid for our room. I remember having a truly amazing night with her.

---

waste removal were largely replaced in the 1950s, although many trains in parts of Europe still use this type of disposal.

The next morning, March 11th, I left the hotel and hoofed it back to the tent area where my unit was staying. I got there about dawn. Going through the concrete portals and walking out onto the sandy beach, I was shocked to find a deserted, open area. The tents were gone, the guys were gone, the unit was gone—everything was gone. No, wait. What was that in the field next to the beach? I ran over and saw that it was my packed seabag with my rifle on top.

Seeing just my gear laying there, I knew I was in big trouble. I had already been through a court martial once, and being AWOL[26] was no joking matter. If I missed a ship movement, that would be another court martial for me. Damn!

Starting to panic, I desperately looked around for any sign of where the guys had gone. Wait, what was that in the distance? Far off, about a half mile away, I could just make out a line of guys heading down the draw, walking towards the piers. Was that my unit? Were those my buddies?

Fervently hoping they were, I grabbed my seabag and rifle and took off along the shore. Huffing and puffing, I finally caught up with the men near the pier, and was so thankful to find out it was my unit. At the end of the line, I boarded the USS *Wharton*[27] just in the nick of time. Made it!

We set sail across the Pacific on March 12, 1943. We had absolutely no idea where we were going. Only our skipper and the ship's captain knew that. One thing about our trip that I was happy about was the fact that once we were out on the open sea, unlike most of my buddies, I did not get seasick. I never did. That first day, I saw a number of them get seasick, hanging over the rails. I thought to myself that if I stayed around

---

26 Absent Without Leave. After being AWOL for 30 days, an individual was declared a deserter, one of the severest charges that could be brought upon an individual, punishable in wartime by firing squad.

27 The USS *Wharton* (P-7, later AP-7) left San Francisco on March 5th and arrived in San Diego on March 7th. An attack transport, commissioned December 7, 1940, with a crew of 566, plus a combat force of 181 officers and 2,130 men, and a top speed of almost 17 knots, the *Wharton* had a distinguished war career, earning three battle stars, and was finally decommissioned in late March 1947.

them, I would too. So I went down to my rack and just lay there, feeling the side-to-side motion of the ship. My stomach happily stayed under control, and as I lay there, I thought to myself, so far, so good. A few hours later, when we had hit the open ocean, the ship's rocking subsided, or else I just became used to it. Either way, I was fine.

Because we were at war and the fear of Japanese subs was pretty real, our transport followed a zigzag course as it made its way westward across the Pacific. We were however, sailing without an escort. When our officers asked why we did not have one, they were told that we did not need an escort, since the *Wharton* carried a 5-inch gun and a couple 3-inch guns.[28] We could easily fight off any sub that was dumb enough to try to take us on in a surface gun duel. Of course, if one decided to torpedo us ... well, that was why we were zigzagging.

A day or so out to sea, after we had left California far behind us, I went topside and made a surprising discovery. Strolling along the main deck, I saw two familiar figures standing at the rail talking quietly. I recognized those two clerk corporals who had loaned me that money right after my GCM hearing back in Newport Rhode Island. Small world, I thought to myself as I came up to them and said hello. We all shook hands, and I visited with them for a while. First things first, of course. I asked them right off if they had received my loan repayment. They told me they had, and I thanked them again for lending me the money. I told them that I had been down and out, and their trust in me had gone a long way to help me out of my slump. They dismissed what they had done, saying that they were just doing it for a fellow Marine. We talked some more before I wished them good luck and continued strolling along the deck.

I thought to myself that although I was glad to see them again so that I could thank them for the great thing that they had done for me, I thanked God that I had been smart enough to have paid them back, sending the money out of my first paycheck. Otherwise, this encounter would probably have gone quite differently, and I could have found

---

28 The *Wharton* was armed with an open 5-inch/38 main gun, four 3-inch/50 guns, two twin 40mm AA mounts, and eight .50 cal machine guns.

myself in the Pacific, swimming back to San Diego. I never saw either of those two guys again.

I continued walking around the ship and bumped into some other buddies in my unit. There was Rucker, John Skoglie from California, the Swede, and another guy named Elbert Kinser. Raised on a farm, Kinser was exactly one month younger than I was, born in Greensville, Tennessee (naturally, "Tennessee" was his nickname). He was a quiet sort of fellow with a soft smile. He was certainly not the boisterous type, and he spoke with a soft tone.

Slowly crossing the Pacific, the ship pulled into Hawaii, and we all became eager to hit the beaches and fraternize with the Hawaiian girls. The captain, though, was having none of it. He anchored the *Wharton* some three miles offshore. It was just far enough to keep even the most determined of us liberty-minded Marines from jumping ship and trying to make it ashore.

We stayed there a day or so and then we got underway. After several days at sea,[29] we arrived on March 24th at the port of Tutuila on the island of Pago Pago in American Samoa.[30] We walked off the ship with our gear and were told that we would spend the next month there doing various types of jungle warfare instruction.

We marched over to this huge training area and were assigned to the 7th Replacement Battalion.[31] The protocol for our training was established at the very beginning of our stay. At the first session, our company was told to gather round two fellows. The one in charge was a short Marine captain who stood before us and told us to pay attention.

---

29 For some reason, the Marines being transferred to the Pacific on this vessel did not have to submit to the Line Crossing Ceremony, which all officers and crewmen undergo when they are crossing the equator for their first time. Perhaps it was because the *Wharton* was a converted luxury liner. George mentioned that there were several senior Marines onboard, and this might have been a contributing factor. At any rate, he never underwent the ceremony with King Neptune.

30 Western Samoa was a New Zealand territory. Eastern Samoa belonged to the U.S.

31 Several dozen USMC replacement battalions were created as an administrative means to transfer replacements to combat units in the field. They included the 1st through 12th and the 14th through 69th, which were all raised in San Diego, and the 13th, created on Samoa.

Standing next to him was this huge gunnery sergeant. I mean, this guy was a massive, dark-complexioned, 250-pound, six-foot-four-inch gorilla who stood defiantly, glaring at us.

He stepped forward and growled, "Is there anyone here that can whip me?"

We looked around at each other, then back at him. No one spoke.

He then defiantly took off his T-shirt and challenged us again. "Well … anybody?"

Still, no one said a thing. I mean, this guy looked like what today kids would call an Incredible Hulk. Over 200 men stood there looking back at him, all of us silent. No volunteers.

"Okay, then," he said. "You damn well do as we tell you."

The Marine captain added, "Anyone doesn't, you'll answer to him."

And that's the way it was. Nearly every weekday we went through our training, and even by Marine Corps standards, it was tough. During these instruction sessions, the NCO instructors in charge took complete control of our training, and barked out directions to all of us, even to our officers.

To simulate getting on and off a ship, we had endless exercises crawling up and down cargo nets until we were exhausted. We had hand-to-hand combat sessions and bayonet drills with real bayonets. I mean, sometimes guys actually got cut. And right there with us each time was the gunnery sergeant and his minions, shouting and cursing. They were effective, too. We were told that when you made a bayonet thrust, you had to growl. Thrust and "Grrr!" Thrust and "Grrrr!" And if you didn't growl, Gunny would yell at you, or kick you hard in the butt with the side of his boot.

We tried hard to do precisely what they said, and none of us gave them any lip. If you did, Gunny would either smack you along the side of your head, or slap you with an open hand. I mean, he was brutal. Needless to say, I followed their orders to the letter, and did exactly what I was supposed to do, and so I stayed out of trouble. Anyone who says that physical discipline will not keep you in line is full of bullshit.

I will say one thing for them. They absolutely did not play favorites. Every damned one of us was treated equally, junior officers included (although I noticed that Gunny wisely did not smack them around). After all, they were just part of our training.

I found the whole experience quite interesting, definitely a lot more than standing around for hours guarding a hunk of haze-gray navy metal. And I will say that the jungle training that I received there was some of the best I was ever given.

There were exercises where, with our M1s held at port arms, we were told to walk along various jungle paths, and shoot at any "Japanese" we saw. While it was effective training, it was also kind of amusing, at least to me. I saw it as an exercise in an outdoor amusement park. I would be walking on some path, and at certain points, some fellow hidden in the brush would push a button or pull a string, and a spring-loaded, life-size cardboard figure of a Jap soldier would be released. As soon as I saw the target pop up, I was supposed to take a quick shot from the hip, hit the ground, and then fire at him again. I like to think that my experience as a hunter made me a natural for this, and as I expected, I received a good grade. I will say though, I thought it was pretty comical, especially with some of these goofy-looking Japs.

We were given various other types of training. We learned how to conduct a patrol. We were shown how to string barbed wire, and there were a few sessions on how to set charges. Being qualified on machine guns, I was given a number of opportunities to polish my own skills on various types of machine guns.

We had to undergo live-round sessions too, crawling along a course, often muddy, and sometimes under barbed wire less than three feet high, with live machine-gun fire going off. Several gunners at the sides would fire 30 cal. machine guns and the live rounds would zip over our heads as we slowly crawled forward. It was deadly, too. If you stood up, you would be killed. Sometimes, to even more effectively recreate the realism of combat, they would add to the effect of being under fire by setting off around us mortar charges that they had earlier buried in the ground. The shells going off were just concussion rounds without any shrapnel, so they were mostly cosmetic and would not hurt you, unless you were lying right on top of it when it when off. That did not happen of course, because the guys setting them off knew where they were. Still, the explosions were effective in getting our attention.

As if all that was not enough, there was usually a sergeant on each side of us with a .22 rifle, and every time a guy's head got a little too high, these two sergeants would shoot a round as close to that guy as they could—without hitting us, although one guy down in the dirt swore to God that a .22 bullet actually bounced off his belt.

Sundays we were allowed to rest. We used them to just catch up on some sleep, take care of our equipment, wash our clothes, and in general get ready for the next round of the hellish sessions.

The training was exhausting, but at night, we once in a while were given the opportunity to go on liberty. Granted, the town[32] was no San Francisco or Chicago, so you had to make do as best as you could. I found in my exploring around the area that about a half mile away through the thick jungle was this little Samoan village. It was just a bunch of huts in a clearing, and in the center was this big wooden platform, about 50 yards long and 20 yards wide, and almost two feet off the ground. That, I found out on my first liberty, was their local social center. At night, several of the natives would gather there and talk about their day, and share some beverages, although there was no alcohol, and certainly very little food; certainly none that they could share with us. Sometimes the natives would have a social gathering, and most of the folks would attend.

There were very few native girls that stayed around, mostly because the locals feared what we Marines would do with them. Those that did socialize with us, even though most of them were not at all good looking, had their pick. We could not choose who we wanted to talk to: the girls chose. If they didn't pick you, you just had to sit there and watch the activities. The few girls that came into the area would walk around, smiling, and chat casually with the other natives. If a gal took a fancy to you, she would come up to you, smile just a little bit, take you by the hand, and lead you off somewhere to get to know you better. Usually, this meant just walking around, visiting some of her relatives and talking to them—which did us no damn good, because we did not speak a bit of their lingo. So you basically were at their whim. If you happened to get

_____

32 Pago Pago, est. population then was about 2,500.

picked by an ugly one—well, what did that guy say about war sometimes being hell?

One thing about these native girls: they had this quirk. They did not like facial hair, and whiskers were definitely out, unless you wanted to be left alone. So it was no beards, goatees, or moustaches. If you had not shaved for several days, you were out of luck.

These nocturnal activities were monitored by 50 husky Samoan native guards,[33] who functioned as the island's security force. Each guard, or *leoleo*, typically wore for his uniform a *lavalava* skirt,[34] and a simple uniform on top. Most of them were big natives carrying .03 rifles, and I must say, they treated us fairly. So we felt secure with them providing security for both the natives and for us.

One thing interesting about the island was that there were no snakes on it, at least none that I ever saw. That was not typical for islands out in the Pacific. While the natives sometimes put large stones around the entrances to keep small varmints from entering, their huts were all built on the ground, because there were no snakes or other such crawlies. Later on, when I was sent to other islands like New Guinea, this was certainly not the case, and the natives had to build their huts on big stakes in the ground. But not Samoa.

One night, I was sitting in the open area and this nice native girl came up to me. I smiled up at her—back then, I had a smile the gals loved—and she sweetly smiled back. Then she gently took my hand, and we began walking off. We strolled around the huts for a while. She took me all around and talked to all of what I guess were her friends and relatives before we eventually ended up at her family's hut. They were lucky enough to have mosquito nets. I looked inside and saw this woman, probably her mother, sleeping on the ground. We quietly crawled underneath the mosquito net. Without making a sound, we lay down on the ground as well. We embraced for a while as we looked at each other before kissing some. Eventually, we got up and she took me outside.

---

33 Known as the Fita Fita Native Guard.

34 A *lavalava* is a common Polynesian garment worn below the waist. It typically is a long rectangular piece of cloth (cotton for the better quality, calico for lesser ones) made of wrapped around and worn as a skirt. It is tied at the top by tying into a knot the upper corners of the cloth.

Kissing me again, she took me over to this tall, drooping palm tree near the hut, leaned back on it, and staring into my eyes, she held her arms out for me. I figured out that she wanted to mess around, and somehow that she had this crazy idea that if we made love while she was standing up, she wouldn't get pregnant. I could not understand that, but hell, at this point, in the randy condition that I was in, who was I to argue with her?

Unfortunately, a short time later, as we were still kissing, her father, who turned out to be a huge guy, came walking by, so that stopped that. I stood up and quickly straightened out my clothes. To my relief, he didn't get excited about what he had seen us doing, and she stayed calm while they chatted. Then her father stared at us once more, turned, and went into the hut to sleep. We walked back to the hut too and went in. Holding hands, we lay down with all of them. At this point, I was amazed at the whole thing, and naturally, I was too leery of doing anything beyond just holding her. I stayed with her until just before daylight, mostly just snuggling and snoozing. Then I said goodbye to her, crawled out of the hut, and returned to my unit. Nice people.

When our training was concluded, we were told we were shipping out. Incredibly though, we found out that instead of going into combat or even into a preparation area as we had been expecting, we were instead going to the beautiful wonderland of Down Under—Australia. Melbourne, to be precise. Where the girls outnumbered the guys, at least according to some of our "knowledgeable" sources, by five to one.

Yeah, we knew then that we were in for a great time.

Australia

We boarded the American SS *Lurline* in Pago Pago Harbor on April 27th, and set sail the next morning for Melbourne. The voyage out was like nothing I had ever experienced before in my life. The *Lurline* was a luxury liner, the largest vessel of the Matson Line.[35]

---

35 Christened on July 12, 1932, the American SS *Lurline* was a lavish luxury liner. She could make 22 knots carrying 475 1st class passengers and another 240 in tourist class. Famous passengers included Australian Prime Minister John Curtin en route

For guys that had gotten used to sitting in muddy holes eating K-rations out of cans and munching on crackers out of wrappers, we felt like we were in another world. We sat at solid, round, decorative dining tables, with heavy white tablecloths. We ate—actually, the term to use here is dined—off beautiful heavy china with elegant silverware. We were served by waiters carrying pewter or sterling silver pitchers and dispensers of water or coffee, just like the rich folks. It was an experience I had only read about in dime novels.

On the way to Australia, the *Lurline* took us to the French port of Noumea in New Caledonia for about a week so that we could undertake a working party before continuing on. We were quartered aboard the ship and would disembark during the day for working parties. We would march to these warehouses and unload supplies, probably brought by our ship and by others.

One thing I remember in particular was that the water there in the harbor was crystal clear, and you could see down into the depths for quite a ways. In the early morning and evening, the crew on the *Lurline* would gather their food scraps, mash them all up, and then shoot the mess below the water and into the bay with compressed air.[36] I would stand on the main deck and watch with fascination as swarms of these fish, big and little, would immediately rush in for a feast. And of course, because the water was so clear, it was easy to see the fish dining and sometimes fighting for scraps so far down.

At the end of one day, after our working party was completed, we were offered a one-time liberty, and those of us that were not too tired from working decided to leave the ship for a few hours. After all, there

to America for a meeting with President Roosevelt, and in December 1934, this vessel took Amelia Earhart to Hawaii, along with the Lockheed Vega (strapped securely to the deck) that she had flown in across the Atlantic, and would soon fly out of Honolulu on her epic last, tragic flight. Pressed into wartime duties, the *Lurline* spent most of the war ferrying troops and war supplies across the Pacific. After the war, the vessel was sold to a Greek shipping company and renamed the *Ellinis*, she returned to being a passenger liner. She was finally broken up for scrap in Taiwan in 1987.

36 Ships in those days used ejector pumps to dispose of degradable food scraps in a sort of early recycling.

was nothing to do back on the ship. So I went walking around with a couple buddies.

One of the features of Noumea was a French platoon that was based there.[37] These French often paraded through the town, and they always did so in smart formation. I really got a kick out of those extravagant uniforms that they wore. They had all kinds of fancy crap on their jackets, and a lot of colored plumes in their helmets and all kinds of other stuff on their uniforms.

Probably because of us Marines and sailors, security in town was pretty tight. The houses all had tall wooden fences around them, so that you usually could not see into the yard, even if you were in the alley out back. And walking down the street, except for us Marines I usually didn't see a damn soul, especially not any gals.

At the other end of the wide main street, about three or four blocks down, was this large administration building, the largest on the island, which apparently was where the local government worked. On another street over, about three blocks from the town square, was a large pastel-pink house that was located on a small hill. And that was exactly what it was called: "The Pink House." While this pink stucco mansion was not exactly off limits to us, we were discouraged from going there, which, of course, made it a natural attraction for us Marines. We quickly found out through scuttlebutt that "The Pink House" was the town's only brothel, and I guess its reputation was quickly spreading throughout the military.[38] This explained the lines that I always saw there (especially on payday).

---

37 New Caledonia was a French territory until it gained independence in 1999.

38 The brothel, aptly named *La Maison Rose* or "The Pink House," was leased from the French Army, and run by one Madame Benitier. It became renowned during the war (and for many years after) throughout the armed forces of both the United States and the British Commonwealth. While the house was allowed to remain open for business, ostensibly for "morale purposes," it was strictly patrolled by military police and monitored by the island's medical facilities. Interestingly, the officers had their own entrance. Its reputation became so widely known that even James Michener after the war mentioned the Pink House in his epic Pulitzer Prize winning book *Tales of the Pacific*.

At the door were these MPs and a couple medics to check your private parts out. If you were healthy and you paid the 25 bucks entry fee, you got in. Then, later to get out, you had to give yourself a chemical prophylactic treatment with an EPT[39] kit in the presence of a medic or MP. I never had the desire to patronize the place—I mean, what on earth would Phyllis back home have thought? Besides, it was at the other end of the town, and I did not want to walk that far.

In the decades after I left the service, I learned that the Pink House's fame had spread throughout the entire Marine Corps. I found it quite amusing that, so many years after the war, any Marine veteran that I talked to who also happened to have stopped in New Caledonia would lean forward with a big smile and wide eyes and ask, "Hey, didja ever get to go down to the Pink House?"

We finally shipped out to Melbourne, Australia and arrived on May 10, 1943. As soon as we arrived, Rucker and I were transferred to the First Marine Division, and into the 3rd Battalion, 1st Marines. We were assigned to M Company, or as we liked to designate it, M/3/1.[40] This was the battalion's heavy weapons company, commanded by an officer named Captain Frank Simpson. The unit consisted of a headquarters unit, three machine-gun platoons, and a heavy weapons 81mm mortar platoon. Rucker and I were assigned to the mortar platoon, which consisted of a command unit, an OP section,[41] a battery of four 81mm

---

39 Emergency Prophylactic Treatment Kit or Pro-Kit, No. 9118000, issued during the war to prevent or treat venereal diseases. The active component was a tube of ointment with calomel and sulfathiazole.

40 Through the years, a tradition has been instituted that Marine regiments, regardless of their type, are referred to by their numerical designator and simply the word "Marines." Thus, the 1st Marine Regiment, a rifleman regiment, is referred to as the 1st Marines. Likewise in the 1st Marine Division, the other two rifle regiments, the 5th Marine Regiment and the 7th Marine Regiment, are referred to as the 5th Marines and 7th Marines respectively. The division's artillery contingent, the 11th Marine Regiment, is similarly referred to as the 11th Marines. It is also common for Marines to so designate their units, by company/battalion/regiment. Thus for example, Company F, 2nd Battalion, 5th Marines would be noted as F/2/5.

41 Observation Post. That component of a mortar or artillery group responsible for directing the unit's fire onto the enemy and observing the results.

mortars, an ammo squad, a communications unit, a forward observers unit, and two corpsmen.

We marched over to what was the Melbourne Cricket Ground at the southern outskirts of the city (we marched everywhere). It was a big stadium, and we pitched our tents out there. We were to live there some five months.[42] During that time, we spent a couple of months up in the mountains north of Melbourne, training. Although Melbourne itself once in a while got a little snow, it was much more frequent in the mountains. So between the cold and the warm weather around Melbourne, I experienced a variety of weather.

We newcomers soon became a part of the divisional family. The Guadalcanal veterans grudgingly accepted us in their own way, with a bit of snobbery. From time to time, they needled us about being the new guys, calling us the "Samoan Rats," and there was some cynicism about it. Also, if there was a shortage of something being given out, the "Canal" vets, being senior to us, always got first dibs. Still, they did eventually welcome us into the division, and we soon began to effectively train together to fight as a unit. I had always wanted to be with the mortars, and so the training was fun. Working with these awesome weapons was fascinating.

Our mortar platoon had two officers: 1st Lt. James J. Haggerty was the platoon leader, and 2nd Lt. Joseph Murphy was his assistant. Haggerty was not too crazy about him, and initially tried to drop him, but Lt. Murphy stayed with the platoon. Personally, I thought that he did okay by us.

Unfortunately, during our training Murphy had an accident on the firing range. He wanted to drop a few mortar rounds himself one day, just so that he could get some experience (and probably to brag to the other officers, and show Haggerty he was not a screw-up after all). Unfortunately, a couple of his rounds dropped a little short, and one of them unfortunately wounded a couple Marines. The two were taken to sickbay, and one of them ended up being crippled. Murphy, mentally

42 All national and state cricket matches in Australia were suspended during the war.

messed up by what he had done, swore that he would never fire another mortar round himself.

I was initially assigned as an ammo carrier, to fetch the shells from wherever they were stored up to the mortar crews, and to keep them well stocked. I also learned to be part of a mortar crew as well, and I had my share of feeding shells down that 81mm tube.

At night, liberty in Melbourne was as fantastic as we imagined it would be, and my memories of our time there are by far the finest that I have of all my experiences in the Marine Corps. The friendly people treated us great. I saw I was going to have a fantastic time there. There were shops that we go buy stuff in, and these trams that we could ride, which were small, about half the size of our streetcars, with small wooden benches. The tram station was out in the country, a big old barn platform, very primitive.

We discovered, to our delight, that the Australians had a great affection for us Yanks. They had already lost thousands of men in North Africa earlier in the war. When the Japs came into it in 1941 and started barreling down the South Pacific, the Aussies saw that they were in big trouble. They only had a couple divisions to defend their country. Things got worse when the Japs started bombing their northern towns, like Darwin,[43] and occupied almost all of the islands north of Australia.

So when the U.S. came into the war and moved down and took over naval control from the Japs in the area, the Australian people were very grateful for us, having, you know, saved their bacon. In a sense, they kind of adopted American servicemen. The country embraced us, and often they would fondly in the newspapers refer to us Americans as "our boys." In many cases, Australian families would take in U.S. servicemen into their homes or their farms, or treat them to special dinners.

Along with these close feelings came a good deal of respect for who we were, and for what we stood for. It was strange that when we walked

---

43 Several other towns were hit as well, such as Broome in March 1942, Horn Island several times, and Townsville, which was bombed several times later in July. All in all, the Japanese conducted nearly a hundred air raids on Australia, from the first most destructive raid over Darwin on February 19, 1942, to Parap on November 12, 1943.

down the street, they would often salute us as we passed. This really amazed us, especially since it didn't make any difference if we were officers or enlisted. That went for when we rode in their trams as well, which was a major mode of transportation for us. If we traveled by tram in units, as we passed folks on the street, they would come to attention and render a salute. The same if we came into a station.

We of course loved the attention we got, and reciprocated their affection as best as we could. Our division even adopted their unofficial national anthem, "Waltzing Matilda," as our own, and even today, when we have a big reunion, we go in singing the hell out of that song.[44] You know, funny thing, I found out years later that the song isn't about any gal named Matilda. It's about a hobo going around looking for work. Weird ...

Their feelings of gratitude of course went for the women as well, and with so many of their guys fighting in Europe and other places, they were often lonely and depressed, trying to keep their homes together. So they were more than happy to make us happy. And in oh so many ways.[45]

Several places had dances at night. And since the gals outnumbered the guys, and they were so fascinated by us healthy Marines—well, pickins were usually pretty easy. We of course, tried in turn to be polite and respectful, and since we were paid and fed so much better than Australians, we tried to be generous as well to those hard-pressed ladies. That of course, made things even easier for us Yanks as we carried out our battle plans on them, sometimes in small units, sometimes individually.

We were far from home and were sooner or later going into combat. So it was no surprise that several of the guys became "Australianized." They picked up their accents, their expressions, their habits, everything. Buddies were "cobbers" or "mates." The gals were "Sheilas." One guy,

---

44 After Guadalcanal, the 1st Marine Division was transferred to Melbourne in the spring of 1943. The song was soon taken up by the division's band, and they began to play it frequently. Eventually, as gratitude to the care and affection that the Australians had shown them, the division officially decided to make the song its battle anthem. Since that time, whenever the division ships out on a campaign, they play this song.

45 By 1943, there were a quarter of a million American servicemen stationed in Australia.

Donald Peck, had that brogue down pat, and sometimes we laughed our butts off just listening to him. A lot of our guys ended up marrying Australian gals, and they would often bring local newspapers from their wives back to camp to share with us single guys.

I remember early on, when we were given liberty, a bunch of us went downtown and then split up. Soon after that, walking down the street, I heard my name called. I turned and spotted almost half of the guys in my platoon at this bar. Laughing, they yelled at me to come over and drink with them. I had different ideas, though and was not going to have any of that. I wanted to meet some sweet gal and spend time with her. These idiots were going to drink themselves silly, then go back to the base and tell everyone about how great a time they had. Hell, they could do that on base.

Again they waved me over. I looked at them, smiled, and shook my head. I yelled back, "Are you guys nuts? Man, I got a broad I gotta go see." I had not yet found one, but I had plans to get one that evening.

They laughed and told me I could do that anytime.

I smiled at them and shook my head. "The hell with that. I have to listen to you bastards all damn day. I don't wanna drink with you now. I can do that any time. I got places to GO!" And with that, I was off. Sure enough, that evening, I found a sweet gal that I got to spend a few happy hours with.

Besides more training, there were other things we did while in Melbourne. So often though, I would enjoy the town with my buddies. Rucker and I went so many places together that the other guys in our unit started calling us the "Gold Dust Twins."[46] A little after we got to Melbourne though, Henry went through a new experience: he fell in love.

This gal was Russian and older than Henry by a few years. All the Americans called her "Mom." She ran her own restaurant near the cricket grounds, and it was a very popular place for servicemen, especially us

---

46 The term originally referred to a logo (racist by today's standards) depicting a pair of Black brothers ("Goldy" and "Dusty") on a popular cleansing product, Gold Dust Washing Powder. The term was broadened over the years to refer to two inseparable individuals who did most things together.

Marines. Our officers often had parties at her place, but the enlisted guys were more open in our admiration for what she did for us. Mom reciprocated the feeling, and we knew and appreciated the fact that there was not a thing that she would not do for any of us. However, as crazy as she was about Marines, she had a very special feeling for Henry. He in turn went bonkers, going head over heels for her. A bunch of us would all start out together, and Henry would drop off at Mom's. Then the Swede and I would go on into town and do our thing. On the way back, we'd stop and get Henry and continue back to the cricket ground.

At the beginning of July 1943, the commanding officer of the First Marine Division, Lt. General William Vandegrift, relinquished command of the division to take command of a new corps that was to be made up exclusively of Marines: the III Marine Amphibious Corps. Shortly thereafter, on July 10, 1943, his Assistant Division Commander, Maj. General William Henry Rupertus, took over command of the First Marine Division. His promotion would be a decision that would dramatically affect the division's performance; sometimes positively, and sometimes negatively.

As great as Melbourne was for liberty, during the week, we continued to train. There was this group of large hills called the Dandenong Range.[47] It was a rough place to train in, and although it was close to Melbourne, it was like going from Heaven to Hell. Our sergeants were ruthless, and my platoon lugged those damn mortars up and down those rough hills many times. We did get to fire them once in a while, but not enough in my opinion.

During this time, I came down with a case of blood poisoning, which happens when bacteria get into your blood. In my case, it came from a foot condition. In late June, we went on a hard one-week training mission up in those damn mountains again, just north of Dandenong, and we had been hard at it, running here and there, setting up positions, taking hills. Even though it was almost July, the weather was relatively

---

47 The Dandenongs are a low rolling mountain range about 25 miles east of Melbourne. Although they only rise up to 2,000 feet, they are renowned for their steep gullies, thick rainforest, and heavy undergrowth.

cold, because I guess, being below the equator, Australia's winters come during our summer, and vice versa. And up there in those mountains hiking around, it got cold. It even snowed a couple times. At night, we had to camp out in tents. After chow, until it was lights out, we would gather around the tent's only source of heat: a small pot-belly stove. We would throw charcoal briquettes into it and try to stay warm.

With all the moving around, my feet began to develop blisters. When I went to the corpsman, he would rub some lotion on them and give me some medication pads. He finally suggested near the end of one week that I go to sick call and be sent back to camp. But pig-headed as I was, I refused to fall out, even though that last day we were facing a very long 25-mile march back to the cricket ground. See, the official word had come down that if anyone made it through the week and did the march back to camp without falling out, they would get a three-day pass, and man oh man, I really wanted that pass. So I decided to stick it out, even though I had these big blisters. That Thursday night, I went over to sickbay for some more medication. The medic gave me more lotion and gauze pads to ease the sores on my feet, although by now, they were not helping much.

That Friday morning, I joined my column to make the march back, and by the time we were halfway, my feet were killing me. My blisters had popped and my feet had started to bleed. I fought off the pain, which had moved up my left leg, and somehow made it back to camp. By then, my boots were soggy from me walking in blood. I managed to gently get them off, and my feet were just bloodier than hell.

So I went straight to sickbay, and when Doc saw my feet, he ordered me to take my trousers off. Evidently, some germs had entered my bloodstream from the blisters on my left foot, and after a while, the infection had spread up my leg and into my genitals. No wonder the pain had become tremendous, Doc said that I had to go to a civilian hospital, so I was taken to one in Melbourne for treatment. To my surprise, the hospital turned out to be a just a group of some plywood shacks and tents.[48]

---

48 Early in 1942, with the United States now in the war, construction began on a new medical facility to replace the hundred-year-old downtown Royal Melbourne

I was taken to a ward, and the first thing the orderly did was to make me strip down. When I took my clothes off, I saw this big blue vein running up my leg to my crotch. Not only that, but there was a blue ball up there as well, which I figured was one of my swollen testicles. I figured that was definitely not a good sign. The orderly gave me a towel, and told me to wait on one of the wooden benches.

I had been sitting there for a couple minutes with a couple other guys, when the orderly came back and told me to go and take a shower.

I said, "Okay," and went over to the facility where they were located. I walked in and saw two rows of these wooden shower stalls. I set my towel down and walked into one. I had just started lathering up when I heard a knock on the door. Thinking nothing of it, I continued showering. Soon after there was a second louder knock.

"Yeah?" I said.

"Tea time," was his response.

I couldn't believe it. "What?"

"Tea time!" And with that, the guy left.

Strange thing about them Aussies. No matter what, some traditional patterns in their life were written in stone. It seemed that no matter what, they always took time out for tea. So I had to turn off the shower, put on my robe, and walk back out to sit on a bench and have some tea before I could go back and finish my shower. I was sitting there with just a towel on with about twelve other guys, and sure enough, this guy came around with a big hot pitcher and cups, and poured each of us a cup. So we sat there chatting, drinking our tea. Weird.

After my shower I was told to go into this small examination room, and wait for the nurse. A little self-conscious of my degree of undress, I took the towel and moved it down and around, so that she could see

---

Hospital. The new location was about a half mile up the road in the suburb of Parkville. At that site, while construction was going on, the Fourth General Hospital of the U.S. Army, which had disembarked in Melbourne in February, set up a temporary hospital at the construction site. As work on the hospital continued over the next two years, patients were slowly moved into the new facility. When George was admitted in July 1943, the new hospital was only half finished.

the blue vein going up my leg and the blue ball in my crotch, but not my other "essential parts."

A minute later, the nurse came in, a big burly gal. She brusquely grabbed the towel that was covering what little of me it could and flipped it off. She then examined me as I sat there, plum naked, really flustered. Then the doctor came in and the two of them talked about it a bit. Finally he told me that my blisters had become infected, and that the infection had gone into my bloodstream and caused blood poisoning. The clinical term was sepsis.

I stayed there in that ward while they treated me with pills. I had no problem urinating, which of course was a good thing. After four days, the inflammation in my testicle went down, the blue line faded in my vein, and I was finally allowed to rejoin my platoon. In the meantime, while I was in hospital, the other guys all got their three-day passes, but when I returned, I did not get mine. That stayed a sore spot with me, and I never forgot it.

The weeks went by, and despite the doses of heavy training in the nearby Dandenongs, we made out quite well and were in general satisfied with life. One day in August though, things changed. We had gone back to the hills and had done a number of days' training, hiking, and toting them friggin' mortars all over the place. Those things are heavy, and when we stopped at night, we were usually exhausted.

We finally marched back to the cricket ground on a Friday. My blisters were minimal, and I was relatively tired, but I was happy. We all began planning for our liberty. No one knew how many weekends we had left before we shipped off to war, so each one now was special to us. On this one, I was again going out with Rucker and the Swede. Henry missed "Mom," the Swede had a gal he was planning to see, and I had a few ideas of my own. So it was like a thunderbolt hitting us when Gunny announced at the last minute that none of us were getting liberty. Surprised, we asked why.

"Because I damn well said so, that's why," Gunny growled us. Funny, but gunnery sergeants never seemed to say a thing. They always growled or yelled. Our surprise gave way to anger, and we insisted that we know the stupid reason we could not leave the base.

Staring us down, he told us that we had been selected to do guard duty. Command policy dictated that ten percent of the base personnel had to stand guard, and our unit had been chosen to do it. Seniority was a big thing in the Corps, and evidently those guys that had been at Guadalcanal, considered senior to us, made sure that liberty passes went to them first. It did not matter that I was older than most of them. Age was not the consideration; time in combat was. They were the veterans; we were the Samoan Rats. The bottom line was that we were not getting any weekend liberty because all of them were going instead. What infuriated me was that the sergeants had waited until the last moment to tell us, as we were getting ready to walk out the gate.

Now we were really hopping mad. What the hell! We deserved to go out on the town too! We had really worked hard for it over the last couple weeks, training, running, climbing, practicing. And anyway, we knew we were soon going to be yanked off to war and very well might get killed. We felt that we were being taken advantage of, and it really pissed us off.

The more we thought about it, the more infuriated we became. It was not long after Gunny's announcement that the three of us had a conference, our own little private council of war. We grumbled about the situation and how unfair it all was. Finally, resentful and rebellious, all three of us—Rucker, the Swede and I—decided to go over the hill for a few days or so. What the hell, we might soon die anyway. We figured that we might as well make it worth our while.

We did some hasty planning and later slipped away into the night. We left the cricket ground and went over to Mom's restaurant. She had a couple rooms upstairs and was happy to let us stay there, giving us food and sometimes even cooking for us. Naturally, Henry spent his time with her. The Swede and I went into town, where we wined and dined the sweethearts of Melbourne.

Although we were AWOL, no one in authority knew where we were. So we continued with our farewell festivities, and soon a few days stretched into a week. We had a great time, but by the end of the second week, after having spent all our money, the three of us started getting guilt-ridden about what we had done. We had enjoyed ourselves while the rest in our outfit had continued training and standing guard duty. We became chastened for our transgressions, hung over, broke, and sick with worry over what punishment we would get for being AWOL. I was especially worried, because this would be my second big screw-up in the Corps.

We talked it over a few times, and finally, after agonizing analysis, we decided that we were going to go back to camp, voluntarily give ourselves up, and take what we had coming to us like men. Whatever punishment we were to get, we knew it would be softened, at least a bit, by the fact that we returned on our own, and were not brought in kicking and screaming by the shore patrol. Besides, once in combat, it all might be swept under the rug. Well, at least we hoped that it would.

The next morning, the three of us made our way back to the Melbourne Cricket Ground and turned ourselves in at the main gate. We told the sentries that we had been AWOL and requested that we be taken to the brig. We figured that we were going to be sent there soon enough, so we thought this might be seen as a good gesture, and also to just get the process started. Maybe we would spare some sergeant the effort of screaming at us.

Sure enough, they took us to the brig. About an hour later, our platoon leader, Lt. James Haggerty, came to see us. The lieutenant was about a year older than me. He was a mustang,[49] having gone through boot camp about the same time as I had. But then he had gone into OCS[50] and had received a commission. Lt. Haggerty had bright red hair, hence, the nickname "Red," although only the officers ever called him

---

49 "Mustang" is a slang military term for an individual who entered military service as an enlisted man and had served for a time as one before entering into some officer training process (such as OCS) or had somehow converted (such as a battlefield promotion) to a commissioned officer. Mustangs were generally older and more experienced than other officers of their rank, and they were generally popular with the enlisted men, who felt that they could better relate to them because hey had once been one of them.

50 Officer Candidate School. For Marines, this was an officer training school in Quantico, Virginia that screened and trained Marine candidates who showed superior leadership potential to earn a commission in the U.S. Marine Corps. The rigorous course was anywhere from 11 to 13 weeks long.

that; we never did, partly because it was inappropriate, but mostly just out of respect.

The lieutenant was a burly guy and did not take crap from anyone. Still, he did not seem to be a mean man. He was soft spoken, but authoritative. And he had this quirk. Most of the time, he loved to wear this plain, dark-blue baseball cap, and he was wearing it now as he came in. Part of the reason he wore it I think because he was in sports. He had played football and baseball in college in New York, and the blue must have been one of his team's colors. I also think he wore it just to stand out and to make a statement; sort of like telling all of us that he was not scared of us, and that he was the guy in charge.

We talked to him, told him we had seen the error of our ways and had surrendered ourselves. He assured us that he would have us out in no time. We smiled when he told us that they couldn't lock his men up. After all, we had a war to win. With that, he left, on his way to get us released, and our spirits rose.

After he left, we talked over our situation, relieved by what he had said. It looked like things would not be so bad after all.

That good feeling did not last for long, though. The lieutenant came back a while later, and wow, was he a changed man. Glaring at us, he started to really chew us out.

"But lieutenant," the Swede said, "you told us …"

"I don't give a shit what I told you!" he shouted. "You assholes really screwed up this time, and as far as I'm concerned, you clowns have found yourselves a new home." With that he spun around and stomped out. We just looked at each other.

They kept us in the brig for 30 days on bread and water. Still, it really was not too bad. Somehow I had smuggled in a pound of butter, and the few of us there were going to make the best of it. That is, if we could keep the butter hidden. Always the quick thinker, I came up with a solution. In the middle of the floor was a drain. So I wrapped the butter in protective cloth. Using a piece of twine, I tied one end to the middle of the butter and the other to the drain cover. In the corner of the brig was an old water heater. One of us had an old mess tin, so we fashioned an edge out of the lid. When we received our daily ration of bread, we would take the butter out, cut some thin slices off it, spread them on the bread in the tin, and then put the tin under the water heater. I have to say, that was some of the best toast I had ever eaten. Well, it seemed so at the time.

We did this for a few days, and then the next day, we had to fall out for inspection. Which to me was dumb, because we were in the brig. How clean could we be? We stood there in line, and in strode our company commander, Captain Frank Simpson, escorted by a few Marine guards. Now this Simpson was a big burly so-and-so, and he always had a really mean look on his face. He came in and slowly walked down the line, glaring at each of us as he passed by.

One or two of the others must have given something away, either with a glance or a look, because as he stared at me, looked down at the drain, then back up at me again. He turned to one of the guards and told him, "Pull that thing up down there and let's see what's down there." When the guard looked at him, he repeated, "There seems to be something down there."

Two of the guards managed to get the drain cover off, and up with the cover came the package of butter dangling there on the string.

The guard handed it to the captain, who was standing right in front of me. When I saw him take the cover with the butter dangling from it and hold it up with a puzzled look on his face, I don't know why, but the whole thing suddenly just struck me funny. I grinned and then I started to laugh. Simpson started glaring at me, and as his eyes began to bulge and the blood rushed to his face, I could not help but laugh even harder. Now he was getting enraged, and the more he did, the more hysterical it seemed. Even while I was laughing though, I was wondering if he was going to whack me or kill me or something. And yet, to save my life, I just couldn't stop. By now I was in tears, struggling just to breathe, I was laughing so hard. Finally, he just gritted his teeth and stormed out of the cell …

The rest of the time passed quickly, and one day, it was time for the charges to be read. They walked me in for the SCM proceedings with a guard on each side, along with my other two brig mates who had also gone AWOL. I stood there at attention as the captain overseeing our court martial came in. I took one look at him and realized it was the same burly Captain Simpson, the guy that I had had the sewer drain incident with in the brig. He came in, sat down, and began swearing in the other officers for the proceedings.

I remembered the incident with the butter, and before I realized it, I was smiling again, a big broad grin. A few moments later he looked up at the three of us and he saw me standing there grinning. Sure enough, just like back in the brig, he began to get angry again. I stood there trying hard not to smirk, but the more I tried, the funnier the memory became, and thus, the funnier the situation now. I could just see him turning livid. This guy was really pissed off.

The charges were read, and the punishments were allotted. Rucker and the Swede each received extra policing duties. They would have to scrub floors and take double shifts in the galley and the mess hall. But I got the full brunt of his wrath. I was sentenced to 30 days—this time in solitary confinement—on only bread and water, with a meal every third day. In addition my pay was reduced by half for six months—all because I smiled at that SOB. I knew I was guilty and deserved punishment for going AWOL but after all, I had surrendered voluntarily. However, because I had remembered the drain incident and the whole thing now seemed like a sort of comic opera, I had just smiled at the guy, and so he had thrown the book at me. I later found out, there was such a thing back then called silent insolence. You could look at an officer mean, and he could charge you with that. I think I got charged under that, too. It cost me dearly.[51] I did not think it was fair, but I kept my mouth shut and did my 30 days without a squawk.

Well, maybe one. Soon after going into the brig, I did complain to the Officer of the Day, Lt. Haggerty, about Captain Simpson, and how he had cruelly confiscated our butter. Haggerty's reaction? He just shook his head and smiled.

Enjoyable as our time in Australia was, we knew it had to end sooner or later, and that the reality of war would come to us. As luck would

---

51 Also called "silent contempt." Covered by Article 89 of the UCMJ, disrespect towards a superior commissioned officer, which includes contemptuous language or, here, behavior.

have it, by the time my 30 days in the brig were up, the division was given orders to ship out to Goodenough Island in New Guinea.[52]

I was determined to have me one last fling in Melbourne before we left. My boss though, Captain Simpson, must have read my mind, because when my time was served, instead of being released, I was put in a holding cell. I was back to three square meals a day, but I had not been released. Of course, if they had, I would have headed straight for town to have one last memorable liberty. In my mind, I had served my sentence, and continuing to hold me was unfair.

So back to the cell I went, depressed, but still determined. No sir, I was not through yet. There is an old saying in the Marine Corps: "Don't beat your gums to me; tell it to the chaplain." So, I followed that theme and requested to see our man of the cloth.

The next morning, the regiment's Catholic chaplain arrived.[53] Under his arm he had several books on Catholicism, and proceeded to talk to me about the faith and how I should use it to correct the error of my ways. Obviously, he had totally missed the whole point of me wanting to see him. I had never been religious anyway, so I could see he was not clear on what I wanted. I tried in vain to correct any misconception he may have had about my asking to see him. I told him that I had served my time, and that I wanted him to intervene on my behalf. He finally got the gist of my complaint, and a sour look came over his face. He frowned, slowly shook his head, and waved his hand at me in disgust. I do not recall his exact words, but they were not very sympathetic. We talked some more, and then he left. I was played out at this point.

52 Goodenough Island is part of the D'Entrecasteaux Islands, located off the eastern tip of New Guinea in the Solomon Sea, and about 590 miles west of Guadalcanal. After being recaptured by the Australians, Goodenough Island, as of June 1943, became a supply center, and later a staging point for the conquest of New Guinea and New Britain.
53 Early in World War II, one Protestant and one Catholic chaplain were assigned to each Marine regiment, a few more chaplains for the division's support units, and one divisional Jewish chaplain. The chaplain George refers to was probably Father Matthew Keough, since he was the regiment's Catholic chaplain on Guadalcanal.

I mean, when even the chaplain turns you down, you've pretty much hit rock bottom.

Okay, so I had one more recourse. As far as I was concerned, what Captain Simpson was doing was not even legal, keeping in my cell past the appointed time. So as a result, I requested to see the Colonel himself.[54] This privilege, afforded any Marine at any time, was duly granted to me. That though, did not go well. The C.O. was not happy with me at all, and took Simpson's side completely. In fact, he used some rather choice words about me, and yelled at me in no uncertain terms that I was incorrigible.

"D'you know what that *IS?*" he roared with a furious glare.

I did not, so I told him, "No, sir."

He angrily stared at me and growled, "It means you ain't gonna change, dumb shit. Hell, if there wasn't a war going on, I'd have you shot."

I sighed, said humbly, "Yessir," and resigned myself to my fate.

After a few moments, he grumbled "Get outa my sight."

The guards took me back to my cell. Luckily, I did not have to wait too long.

Goodenough Island

The next day, October 10, 1943, two Marine guards, one on each side of me, escorted me in shackles to the pier and we boarded the USAT *Steinmetz*,[55] along, as it turns out, with my entire regiment. We were

---

54 The 1st Marines commanding officer at that time was Colonel William J. ("Wild Bill") Whaling. Formerly the executive officer of the 5th Marines, he took over command of the 1st Marines on February 10, 1943 and held it until February 28, 1944, at which time he was succeeded by Col. Lewis "Chesty" Puller.

55 *Charles P. Steinmetz* was a Liberty cargo ship classified as a U.S. Army Transport (USAT) vessel, one of a total of 2,700 Liberty ships built between September 1941 and September 1945. Commissioned in the Kaiser Shipyards in Richmond, California on March 4, 1943, it could only do at most about 11 knots. Armament consisted of a stern-mounted 4-inch gun and a few light antiaircraft weapons (interestingly, the armament was manned by U.S. Navy personnel, who had their own independent command aboard the ship). The *Steinmenz*, scrapped in May 1962, was

going to sail the next day for a place called Goodenough Island. Funny thing, though. Capt. Simpson did not go with us. I figured that to be a good sign.

Now out of the brig, the first thing I did after chow was to look up my good buddy Henry Rucker. I found him at his rack, and we caught up. I told him what had happened to me. He had pulled some light duty, and he told me the astonishing news that as part of his extra duty, he had incredibly been assigned guard duty for all of the officers' liquor and smoking items. It was all stored in a couple big lockers, and he was the custodian. Which meant that old Henry had the keys. Naturally, being a good Marine, he had decided to "liberate" some of the items. He had managed to confiscate a couple jugs of rum, as well as helping himself to several cartons of cigarettes. After he had stuffed his pack full, he had also secretly crammed my own pack with a couple of cigarette cartons as well. The problem with that was that old Henry did not tell me about the cartons that he had slipped me, and I would unfortunately not find out until it was too late.

It was a beautiful night, and after a nice chow, we sat on the fantail of the transport under the stars, staring at the ship's foamy wake. Rucker generously shared a bottle of rum with me, and we proceeded to get stinking drunk. We sat there on the stern all night, singing and recalling memories, and by dawn, we were asleep, definitely feeling no pain.

That morning, as hangover set in, the theft of the booze and cigarettes was discovered, and soon after that, we were all ordered to our quarters as the whole ship was searched. When they went through my pack, they found the missing cigs. I was dumbfounded, but quickly realized what had happened. Naturally, all my pleas of innocence were not believed, and I was confined to my rack. This time I was lucky enough to go before the battalion major. Thank God I was not going up before the regimental colonel again.

---

one of eight dozen transports and cargo vessels manned by Army personnel of the ATS (Army Transport Service), a division of the U.S. Army Quartermaster Corps. After the war, the ATS was absorbed into the Navy's Military Sea Transportation Service (MSTS), which in 1970 became the Military Sealift Command (MSC).

Early that evening, when they held "office hours,"[56] I made my case again and once more told them that I was innocent. I tried to explain to the XO that I had no idea about the cigarettes; hell, I didn't even smoke! But that just made him furious. Clearly he did not believe me. So as a consequence, good old Rucker got off light again: he was given a few hours of EPD scraping paint.[57] Me though, I got a deck court martial and was given five days' confinement to the brig on bread and water. In my mind though, I had the last laugh, because they later found out that there was no brig to put me in. Liberty ships did not have brigs. Still, some wise-ass figured out that a good equivalent was a coal bin on the upper deck, so I spent the next five days in that damn coal bin. In the meantime, on October 11th, exactly five months and one day since we had come to Melbourne's fair shores, the *Steinmetz* left Melbourne Harbor and sailed off to war.

I did my time in the coal bin on bread and water, and the sentence actually turned out to be eight days. Luckily for me, my buddies Henry and Skoglie would slip some food to me whenever I went to the can and they would stand guard for me while I ate. You know, there is an old saying in the Corps: if you want a good combat soldier, get one out of the brig.[58] If there was any truth to that, then I must have been quite the soldier. Maybe our platoon leader, Lt. James Haggerty, had heard the saying and taken it to heart. One day after I was out of the coal bin, he called me aside. We sat down, and he told me that he thought I was not a bad fellow and was not beyond salvaging. He said now that we were away from liberty ports and booze and women, I might turn out to be a good Marine. Maybe, he added, I could straighten up my act and try to be a good Marine.

I was surprised. How could the guy be so insensitive? I thought to myself I was probably the best-trained Marine in the whole damn outfit. I had been in the Corps for two years now and had trained a good part

---

56 Marine equivalent of the Navy's Captain's Mast.
57 Extra Punitive Duties. This is a form of non-judicial punishment assigned to an individual to perform cleaning duties after working hours, or in lieu of liberty.
58 Many Marines claim that a good Marine is one who has once been in the brig. Others embellish by adding "and has had the clap, and has gotten crabs".

of the time. I had accrued no less than five different specialties. First and foremost, I was a rifleman, and a crack shot at that. However, I had also qualified as a mortarman, a forward observer, a chemical warfare school NCO, and a machine gunner. I was proficient with all small arms, and had completed jungle warfare school in Samoa.

Still, as I thought about it more, I conceded that perhaps he was right. And despite all my training, I had never actually been in combat, something we were now on our way to. Maybe the lieutenant was right. I guess that it was time to get serious. Haggerty then told me that he knew I could be a great Marine. I guess that he must have seen some promise in me. He also said that if I straightened up my act, he would not hold my past against me. I have to admit that made a sizable impression on me.

He also said that he had thought about my role in the mortar platoon, and had concluded that with my outdoor background, I would make a good forward observer, despite the fact that I was a little small for the job.[59] He told me that he needed a good runner; someone who could act as his scout and be a lead forward observer. As I thought about it, he added that he needed someone that he could depend on, and that I could be a great OP man. He said that he would see to it—that is, IF I got my act together and got squared away.

I must admit that my first impression was that maybe he was just trying to get me killed. On second thought though, it seemed a great opportunity to redeem myself for my past indiscretions. I told him I agreed and then asked him one favor: that he assigned Rucker as an OP as well.

Haggerty thought about it and agreed. We had a deal.

Then he looked at me and said gently, "I'm not gonna hold anything against ya. That is, as long as you turn over a new leaf."

I told him I would. And for the rest of my time in the Corps, because he gave me another chance, I swore never to fall out of a formation or miss a day of duty if I could help it.

And I never did.

---

59 George was only 5'6" and weighed 125 lb.

We rounded the southeastern tip of Australia, sailing northward, putting into Sydney and Port Moresby. Finally on October 23th, after a voyage of some 2,500 miles, we pulled into a Goodenough Island in New Guinea.

The division was using the island as a staging and planning area for our next operation, whatever that was going to be. Unfortunately, for our own purposes, Goodenough definitely did not live up to its name. It was infested with thousands of these dark sand crabs that crawled around at night all over the beaches and over to our tents. They would crawl around on top of the tents, and inside them, and sometimes they would crawl into our boots. We had to shake our boots out in the morning to make sure none of the little bastards were in there. The crabs were hard to spot coming towards the tents, because they were usually hidden in the high grass that grew all over the island, grass that was well over eight feet tall and thick.[60]

Unfortunately, rats and mice of all kinds also lived in that tall grass. The worse part though, was that these vermin also lugged around these small ticks that carried a deadly typhus germ called scrub typhus.[61] We were told that it was 50 percent fatal. We might have been able to avoid the rats, except that we were always training, which involved a lot of crawling through that damn high grass.

Many of us began to catch this disease, and one morning, my buddy Rucker did as well. He came down with a fever, and was immediately admitted to the base hospital, which was actually just a bunch of mess tents. He lay in the tent for several days, feverish, with severe abdominal pain. A couple times early on when I went to see him, he did not even know who I was. The deadly typhus had done its work. We were preparing to leave for Finschhaven farther up the coast of New Guinea

---

60 Called kunai grass (*imperata cylindrica*), it was once only indigenous to the Western Pacific. The long, thin leaves grow to a point; the longer grass is often used by natives for thatched roofs.

61 A deadly form of typhus predominant in the Western Pacific, caused by tiny mites, and contracted in areas of heavy vegetation. Symptoms include fever, intense headache, muscle pain and gastrointestinal problems. Even today it is common in certain areas.

and to support the Australians as they captured it. Rucker though, would have to miss it. He would have his hands full just staying alive.

During that time there, I drew duty on an Australian vessel, the *Manoora*.[62] For a couple of weeks, we practiced night landings somewhere in New Guinea.[63] On that ship was the first time I ever had to sleep in a hammock. And I mean, that sonuvabitch was really deep. I had all kinds of trouble navigating into the damn thing.

After each exercise, we returned to Goodenough Island. As we continued to prepare for our operation, several of us worried about how Rucker was doing. Christmas was by now a few weeks away, and we were told we were going to leave the island soon. So I picked up a package from the Red Cross to take over to Rucker. It was partly a premature Christmas gift, and partly a goodbye gift to my friend. When I arrived at the hospital, which was in truth just a row of tents, I asked the corpsman on duty to see Henry Rucker. He took me to one of the tents and pointed to a lonely cot about midway down the ward. I saw my friend lying there. His eyes were closed and he was wearing nothing but a diaper. The poor guy had lost control of his bodily functions, and the overpowering odor of crap and pee was gut-wrenching. I stood there next to his cot and said hello. He smelled terrible, and as his eyes

---

62 HMAS *Manoora* (F-48) was an Australian passenger liner that was built in Scotland and commissioned in 1939. When war broke out, she was requisitioned by the Australian Navy and converted into an armed merchant cruiser. In 1942, she was reconverted into the first Australian Landing Ship Infantry (LSI). She served the rest of the war as a training vessel for landing exercises and saw combat in several operations. With her twin screws, she could make almost 16 knots. She had a crew of 345, but could land an additional battalion of 1,230 men in 17 LCVP (Landing Craft-Vehicle & Personnel) and two LCMs (Landing Craft, Mechanized). Main armament was a 6-inch gun, and she also carried two 3-inch AA guns, eight 20mm Oerlikon AA guns, and six 40mm Bofors AA guns. From March 1943 until mid-June, she undertook landing exercises with U.S. Marines.

63 All three regiments of the Marine 1st Infantry Division engaged in practice landings on the Taupota Bay beaches. Ringed in by jungle, they were located on the northern shore of Papua in New Guinea, to the leeward side of the D'Entrecasteux Islands. The exercises were to train units on landing procedures, to test out new equipment, and to observe and improve unloading techniques.

opened, he looked up at me, delirious. I was shocked to realize that he did not even recognize me.

I gritted my teeth in anger. Holding back, I tried to tell him that things would be okay, and that he was going to get well soon. But inside, I knew better. I stayed with him for a short while, and after a few minutes, I left the Red Cross box and walked away.

Seething, I went over to the corpsman. Had I been armed, I'd have shot that damn bastard, and I told him so. He told me that he understood, but assured me that there was nothing he could do for my friend. Poor Henry would have to lie in that pitiful state for another couple weeks, and like the others, only had a 50–50 chance of surviving. The corpsman told me that Henry was going to be transferred to a Red Cross hospital in New Guinea.

With a heavy heart, I finally left. I felt really depressed. Henry and I had gone through so much together. He had started to become part of me, and by now I knew him so well. We had shared so many good times down in Melbourne. I remembered him with that older gal he had fallen in love with, and the crazy things we had done.

I sighed, and returned to camp. I knew that I would never see Henry Rucker alive again.

CHAPTER 4

Into Combat

Like Henry, dozens of Marines were coming down with this typhus, and the command soon realized that unit efficiency was going down. My buddy the Swede always said he'd probably never see any combat, and he was right. He contracted the disease and was evacuated off of Goodenough Island. I only found out later that the Swede was sent back home. I would never see him again, in spite of my efforts to locate him after the war.

The division was losing too many men, and so we had to get off Goodenough Island soon. More and more of us were coming down with this deadly disease, or getting bit by rats. So we were going to be sent to a place called Finschhaven, located on the eastern side of New Guinea. This would be my first campaign.

Our entire division boarded these LSTs[1] and left Goodenough Island on December 13th. We landed three days later on New Guinea at a

---

1   Landing Ship Tank. These were shallow draft vessels designed first by the British and later put into mass production by the United States in 1942. Their purpose was to give the Allies the capability to move and land men, equipment, vehicles, and supplies across the ocean and land them onto irregular shores. The LST featured a large ramp built into the bow to allow the unloading of trucks and mechanized vehicles. A typical LST displaced nearly 4,000 tons loaded, and could make about 12 knots. Fully loaded, it only carried a maximum draft of about eight feet (three and a half at the bow). Most were lightly armed, typically with a 3-inch gun and several mounted machine guns, and carried a crew of about 100. During the course of the war, many were converted into other functions, such as repair

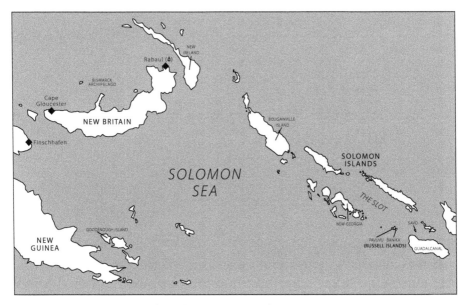

The Solomon Sea Area of Operations

place called Nascing, Alatu. Our role there was to be the reserve for the Australians, who were going to take Finschhaven at the eastern tip of Papua Island in New Guinea. The Australians had first landed on Papua on September 22nd, and had been fighting to take the area for almost three months now.[2] As their backup, we stood by, ready to give them any assistance they might need.

We sent out daily patrols in our area to make sure there were no Japs around. We were located about a mile and a half to two miles from where the fighting was taking place. The Aussies had gone in a few weeks before, and in our defensive perimeters, we often could hear

---

vessels, hospital ships, and a few even carried light reconnaissance craft that were loaded and unloaded by cranes. While LSTs were constructed also in the British Commonwealth, the U.S. by far exceeded all of them, eventually constructing about 1,000 LSTs. Most of those that survived the war were later either scrapped or put into mothballs.

2   On December 3rd, a detachment of Combat Team B left Goodenough for Cape Cretin near Finschhaven, followed on the 11th by the rest of the 1st Marines and all its attached units.

small-arms fire and artillery. We were later told by John Quinn, our company commander, that they had taken their objectives without too much trouble.

During this time, we hiked around quite a bit, doing all kinds of training exercises. One of them was going out at night and just sitting. For three weeks, when it was dark, we went out into different parts of the jungle two at a time to just sit there for a couple hours, listening to noises and take notes on what we heard. Bugs, birds, wind … we were training ourselves to hear and identify what we were listening to. Often we could hear off in the distance the Aussie attacks. But as it turned out, they did not need us.

In the daytime, we either did gun drill or patrol exercises to get proficient at each. On bad rainy days, we would clean our weapons, but no matter what the weather was, we slept in tents. Us forward observers were given map-reading courses and map exercises. We were taught skills on using a compass to quickly get our bearings and blend them with compass results to find map coordinates.

I began to realize that being a forward observer was probably the best job in the battalion. I was only temporarily attached to units to do my job, and as such, was often on the move to find myself a new observation post (OP), which was just a new position for me to call in our mortar fire onto a target and to observe the results. I had my own field radio that I took with me, and then was set up by three or four other guys in our mortar platoon. I often had my own radioman whose only job was to make sure that I had a field phone that worked. We trained constantly. There was no sitting on our ass. We did a lot of hikes to stay fit, and we walked all over those jungles.

In the Pacific, I found out that each island had some common but also different types of wildlife, different types of fish, animals, and plants. On Pavuvu, there were fields of these weird types of sensitive plants. You could lay them down by just touching them with your finger.[3] They had these long leaves, and when you touched them, they would fold and

3 The plant is called mimosa pudica (from the Latin word *pudica*, which means shy or bashful). It is sometimes referred to as the sleepy plant or shy plant. Technically a creeping annual or perennial herb, a part of the pea family, its leaves fold up and

the plant would sort of lay down. Because of that you could see where guys had recently gone through. A couple hours later, they would pop back up and look normal.

After some nine days holding our positions and conducting patrols, we loaded back up on the LSTs and sailed off to get ready for our next assignment. So as far as I was concerned, Finschhaven had not been much of a campaign. We had not stayed there long, and we had seen no action. However, we had been close enough to hear the Australians fighting some distance away. That gave us some taste of what we would soon expect.

Cape Gloucester

Critical for Allied success in their push across the Pacific island was the neutralization of the crucially important, centrally located port of Rabaul, located at the northeastern tip of the island of New Britain in New Guinea. The Japanese had captured this excellent deepwater port at the end of January 1942, and had immediately begun building it up as a military center for their operations in the South Pacific. By mid-1943, despite the many air raids that the Allies had thrown against it, the area had grown significantly, and was now guarded by some 90,000 Japanese entrenched there. The port was now being used as the main forward base for units of the Imperial Japanese Navy and Air Force. From this strategic citadel, the Japanese were able to control all of their naval and amphibious operations in the Solomon Islands, the Bismarck Archipelago, and New Guinea.

Clearly, this enemy fortress had to fall or at least be neutralized. However, conquest would not be easy. The port was heavily defended, and an attempt to take it would strain the Allied effort to the fullest. Not enough resources were available for that huge an endeavor, especially with a number of critical naval operations going on in other parts of the Pacific and in Europe at the time.

So with a direct assault nearly impossible, the Allies chose instead to neutralize Rabaul. In the fall of 1943, considerable air operations by the U.S. Navy had crippled Japanese airpower and naval power in the area. The Allies now decided to at least threaten the port with a surprise landing at the opposite end of the

droop defensively whenever they are touched or moved. Minutes later, they will slowly re-open. They also close up at night.

320-mile-long island of New Britain and slowly work their way eastward from there.

During this time, the division took the opportunity to conduct final training exercises in preparation for their upcoming crucial assignment: the invasion of New Britain. The Marines were going in on the western tip of the island to take Cape Gloucester with its vitally important airfield.

We were told that a place called Cape Gloucester was our next assignment. Ours was the preliminary operation to eventually take the entire island. Unlike at Finschhaven, the division would be in the thick of the combat, and this would be my first combat experience. Also, this would be the second combat landing for the First Marine Division: the first opposed landing had been at Guadalcanal in 1942, before I transferred in. The entire operation was to start on Christmas Day, of all times. We were told that, according to intelligence (which right away made us doubtful), the Japs would not expect us to land on a holiday. On top of that, we would be landing in their summer, when they get a ton of rain at that time, what they call the monsoon season. We would be landing at the start of it, another reason the Japs would also not expect a landing.

So anyway, one way or another, it was on. On Christmas Eve,[4] at Goodenough Island, we boarded the LSTs, and later that morning, we left for Cape Gloucester at the western end of New Britain.[5]

Right after we got underway, several of the guys started to get seasick. Since I had never come down with that, I was fine. Our gunny though, seeing all these guys get ill, got furious with them and cussed up a storm. It did not matter to them, because they already felt miserable. The next day, though, the gunny himself got seasick, and we all, even those guys still nauseated, laughed our butts off.

We traveled north-northeast all day and on the morning of Christmas Day, 1943, we approached the western part of New Britain. We sailed some seventy miles through a strait,[6] went around Cape Gloucester[7]

---

4   It was Christmas Day in the United States.
5   The convoy was recorded as leaving at 0600.
6   Dampier Strait.
7   The Japanese had no artillery in the area to challenge any vessels running the strait.

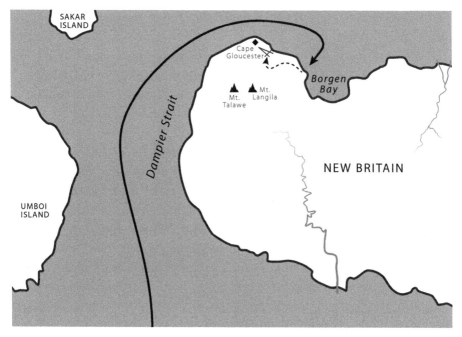

Cape Gloucester Landing, December 26, 1943.

and traveled past it without incident. We sailed clear around the top
part of the western tip of the island, turned south, and approached the
island. We were to land at Yellow Beach, near the top of Borgan Bay.

As we approached, we saw the pounding that the Navy was giving.
Finally the warships stopped firing, and several aircraft took over, bombing and strafing targets inland.

"Give 'em hell," I mumbled to myself.

A few elements of the 7th Marines were already going in just before
us to take the high ground. Our 3rd Battalion was getting ready to land
in the bay, several miles southeast of the airport. We were under the
command of Lt. Col. Joseph E. Hankins, who was an okay guy, I guess.
I had not had much contact with him, but he seemed fair. I was told
he was a little eccentric, and he enjoyed bringing his officers into their
mess tent and making them stand for chow. Then he would tell them to
sit there as he played guitar for them, but that was about all I knew. He
did believe in his men, and once growled with pride that as far as he was

concerned, every man in our outfit, even a lowly private, was capable of leading a rifle company into combat. I think that was something that could motivate me in the next couple years.

The monsoon season was underway, so naturally, it rained that day. The waves were rough as we approached the landing area, and luckily, despite the fact that we were close to shore, the anchorage was still deep. Because of that, the LSTs were able to get close to the beach. Some units landed in LCVPs.[8] Our LST though ran right up onto the beach, grinding on the sand as it shuddered to a halt and the front clamshell doors opened up and the ramp dropped down. Hell, we were not even going to get our feet wet as we got off.[9] Of course, that was offset by the heavy rain that kept falling.

Just before our LST ramp dropped, a sergeant in our group, nervous about the landing, had accidently chambered a round in his rifle and as we stood there, it accidently fired. The bullet ricocheted around the inside of the big compartment, startling all of us. We were up tight as it was, and the inadvertent discharge made it worse.

It was about a quarter after eight in the morning. The beach was called Yellow Beach, which, by the way, was not much of a beach. Several squads of infantry moved up, while my platoon started unloading equipment in the rain. At one point in the process, we actually lost a Sherman tank. Attached to the 7th Marines, it rolled down the ramp of the LSD[10] and started out. It tried to make its way through the muck, and soon it got stuck in a swamp and just sank down out of sight.

---

8   Landing Craft Vehicles & Personnel. Also referred to as "Higgins boats" after the designer, Andrew Higgins. This was a small landing craft used a great deal in amphibious operations during the war. Made of plywood and light metal, this 4-man craft with its shallow draft could bring ashore a 36-man platoon. With a 9-ton displacement, it was 36 feet long, 10 feet wide, had a maximum draft of 3 feet, and could make almost 12 knots. Over 20,000 were built during the war.

9   George was lucky again. Many Marines on other LSTs were not though, and they desperately tried to keep from drowning as they stepped off, loaded with their equipment into three to five feet of heavy surf.

10 Landing Ship, Dock. These were large 4,000-ton vessels used to unload landing craft by a large dock in the stern that could be raised or lowered. LSDs could of course also carry troops and vehicles in those landing craft, and were generally more

I did my part. I slung my M1 and grabbed a cloverleaf of mortar shells.[11] I carried the mortar pack down the landing craft ramp, onto the beach, and then inland to the ammo stack, which was about 50 yards away. Harry Owens carried a cloverleaf with me and stacked his next to mine. It all only took about five minutes, and we turned around and began heading back to the landing craft for another load.

We were walking towards the ramp when suddenly we heard approaching aircraft. We looked up and spotted two Jap planes diving down towards us to make a strafing run on the landing ships. We all immediately fell into the sand, as bullets zipped by around us. The Japs made two passes at us and then flew off. Harry and I stood up, brushed ourselves off, and went back to unloading.

There were several tanks and artillery on an LSD. They maneuvered the ship as close as they could to the beach and then fired artillery and tanks from it for gunfire support. Unfortunately, when it came time to fire close in, because of the height of the deck, they initially had trouble getting the guns to depress low enough for direct fire.

We kept hauling ammo, and eventually began taking the crates further inland. As we walked towards this thicket of bamboo and next to it was a big banyan tree. As soon as we cleared it, a machine gun opened up with a sharp *krrrr!* We could hear the bullets flying in, make clicking noises as they hit the bamboo.

Harry and I immediately dropped our crates and hit the dirt. My first thought was what were we to do? I don't mind saying that I was

---

seaworthy than LSTs, with a top speed of 17 knots. With a crew of 250, they could unload LCTs, LCMs, or DUKWs. For this campaign, the LSD George mentions was probably the USS *Carter Hall* (LSD-3, commanded by LCDR Cecil Blount), which later went on to serve during the Korean War and the Vietnam War.

11 Rounds of 60mm and 81mm mortar were packed in two-foot-long heavy card-board tubes, which were then grouped in a stack of three in a triangular fashion. Each group was then packaged as one container by placing over each of the three tube ends a cloverleaf, which was a sort of protective metal cap that had three cups to fit tightly over the tubes. The two end cloverleafs were in turn all connected by a rod that ran through the middle of and parallel to the tubes. The rod was secured to each end cloverleaf by a tightened hex nut or wing nut. In addition, there were sometimes metal straps secured around the tubes as well. The entire 3-round group weighed about 61 lb.

definitely scared. This was the first time that I was being exposed to intensive enemy fire. I knew that it would happen, but on this operation, I had not expected to get shot at so quickly. Like everyone around me, we just hunkered on down. We were both scared, but Harry, his eyes wide with terror, freaked out, yelling and shaking. The firing stopped, and we waited until some infantrymen came up and cleared the area. Then I went back to unloading gear.

Eventually, we formed up and began moving out. We had landed about 10 miles from our objective: the town of Cape Gloucester and its airfield. The plan was for us to advance through the beach, make our way up along the coast to the airport, and then attack that way. The good news was that we would hopefully surprise them and overwhelm them. The bad news is that this was not going to be an easy operation, because there were no roads. There was nothing but this really massive jungle and bad weather. Okay, there was this one small trail along the coast, but it was narrow, primitive, mostly overgrown, and sometimes hard to find. That was it. No natives in the area; just a bunch of Japs, mostly in the trees. The enemy fire was light, but we quickly found out that there were several enemy snipers ahead of us.

We found out after we landed that there had been some kind of landing snafu. At least it looked that way to us. Typical. We had landed to the left of the remaining 7th Marines coming ashore, instead of to their right as had been planned. So the units of the 7th would have to move across our front, and we'd have to slant off towards the right. As we crossed through each other, filtering into our assigned units, all I could think of was what a target for the bad guys. I imagined that the Jap snipers were laughing their butts off watching us crisscross like that, thinking, "Look at those dumb asses."

We cleared each other and began to move inland. Enemy sniper fire from the trees continued, and we took a few casualties. We ran across this one hut on sticks, and inside we found a Jap that had been wounded and was trying to get past us. He died in that hut.

As we slowly advanced northwest up that narrow coastal trail, we suddenly started to take machine-gun fire from our front. We heard later that K Company had unknowingly come up on a couple of camouflaged bunkers and a couple of machine guns had suddenly opened up on them. The company CO, Capt. Joe Terzi and XO, Capt. Phillip Wilheit, were killed right off.[12] They took a couple more casualties, but all of the Jap bunkers were finally taken after we brought up an amtrac and covered it as it ran over three of the four bunkers and pounded them flat.

We kept moving, and sure enough, those damn snipers occasionally took shots at us nearly everywhere we went. Despite the snipers though, we slowly slogged our way forward. It was a stormy day, and I was soaked from the rain. It was hard walking because of the mud. And believe me, there was mud everywhere.

That day we advanced up the beach and along that narrow coastal trail, and that evening, we set up a defense perimeter at the edge of a field of tall grass. In front of us, we slashed several fire trails with our machetes to have clear fields of fire. Unfortunately, the grass was infested with rats and even worse, these tiny mites that turned out to be carrying scrub typhus, just like on Goodenough Island. We knew that it was 50 percent fatal to, so we tried very hard to keep the little buggers off of us.

As it got dark, we made our defensive perimeter, clearing fields of fires in front of us with our machetes. Some guy later walked up to Jack O'Donnell, who was doing sentry duty. Jack was quietly sitting behind a .30 cal. machine gun that he had set up. Jack did not recognize the guy, but that was not unusual. We had taken a number of replacements in the last couple weeks before we had boarded for this operation. The guy now walked up to Jack, looked around, and asked him, "Hey, where's the front line at?"

Jack pointed in front of him and said, "It's right out there."

The guy turned around and started to walk that way, heading into the jungle. Surprised, Jack told him, "Hey, yer gonna get shot if you go out there!"

The guy did not say a thing and just kept walking. He disappeared into the night. It took Jack a while to realize that the fellow was probably a Jap.

---

12 Terzi and Wilheit were both awarded the Navy Cross posthumously, and later, the main Japanese resistance area, initially called "Hell's Point" was renamed "Terzi Point" in honor of K Company's commander.

In our unit were these identical twins: the Woodring brothers, from Paulding, Ohio.[13] Now I was not too crazy about these two, especially since I could not tell them apart, and because of that, they had conned me out of some money. One of them had come up to me a week or so before we had landed and asked to borrow five bucks. I had given it to him, but when I went to get it back after payday, I had a problem. I asked him, "Hey, when are you gonna pay me my five dollars?" and the twin told me, "Uh, oh, you must have given it to my brother."

When I later went to what I thought was the brother for the money, I got the same line. "Like I told you, that was my brother." A nice little scam, especially since I could never catch them together, and I'll bet I was not the only sucker that they had pulled it on.

That evening, we settled in for the night. We finished our defensive perimeter, munched on some rations, and fixed our sleeping spots. We knew it was going to rain, so we made sure that our hammocks were strung up off the ground. One of those Woodring twins had set his suspended between two tree trunks, about 10 or 15 feet from me. I did not have that option, so I had to set mine off the ground off a few tree branches stuck in the ground. It was uncomfortable and pretty unsteady, but at least it held up enough so that I could get some sleep. I carefully crawled in, flung the mosquito net over me, and despite a light drizzle, I finally dozed off.

Sure enough, this huge storm came on us.[14] It had been pouring down for a while there in the dark, with lightning flashing, when suddenly, a large branch above us that had been hit by a shell broke loose. With a sharp crack, it fell and landed with a leafy-sounding crash next to me, right across one of the twins. The branch hit him square and took him right down, pinning him to the ground. Luckily for him, being suspended between the trunks and off the ground kind of cushioned the branch's impact. Otherwise, if he had been near the ground (like me), the impact might have broken him in two. As it was, the impact crippled him up pretty bad, and the medics had to take him away.

We never saw him again (or my five bucks).

---

13 About 20 miles southwest of Defiance, OH, and 135 miles northwest of Columbus.
14 A monsoon was recorded hitting the area on December 27th.

The next day, the 26th, as we started advancing up the coast, snipers again started to take shots at us. We could not figure how they knew where we would be or what path we were taking. Hell, we didn't even know where *we* were gonna be, but somehow, they were always around us. The closer we came to the airport, the more intense the sniper fire was. Finally, our battalion commander, Lt. Col. Joseph Hankins, decided to just ignore the damn snipers and to keep moving towards the airfield. So that is what we did. Still, we did shoot at them if we had any opportunity, which I guess was just as well, because they sure as hell were taking potshots at us, and they seemed to be all around.

At one point, we began taking sniper fire from this big banyan tree that was at the other side of a 100-yard-wide grassy field. He was invisible in that damn tree and every time we tried to move or anything, he would crank off a shot. As we moved forward, we started to get worried. We figured that if he kept plunking away at us, sooner or later, he was gonna get a few guys.

Finally, irritated, I told a Harry and Corty, "Damn it, we've just got to do something."

The three of us decided that we were going to go get that sonuvabitch, although Harry was scared as hell. We started crawling through that tall grass to get close to the tree. Now this banyan was massive, with supporting branches all around the main trunk.[15] As we moved in, we scoured the branches. Once or twice he took a shot at us, so we knew he was still there. We would just have to flush him out.

I whispered to the other two to spread out (especially since I didn't want Harry with me; the guy was spooking out). We separated and began to crawl closer to the tree. We slowly positioned ourselves around it, one on each side, and one guy up the center. We sat in the grass and waited for him to take another shot so that we could locate him. We sat there for some time, waiting for him to fire. But he did not take a

---

15 Known as "aerial roots," these are banyan seeds, known as "stranglers" because they appear to be strangling the host trunk. The seeds germinate somewhere above ground and then grow downward.

shot. Evidently, he had seen us moving up on him, and did not want to give away his position.

Suddenly, a BAR opened up from the other side of the tree. Evidently, another Marine from one of the rifle companies had had the same idea. He fired two bursts, and sure enough, the Jap came sailing out of the tree and onto the ground. That ended our anxiety, and we returned to the trail.

The next day, the 27th, even though this terrific storm hit us, we gathered our gear again and started heading northwest. The rain came down almost horizontal. Normally we would have called it a cloudburst, but the damn thing did not let up, and often the rain came down in buckets. Still, we kept going up the coast through heavy mud, moving slowly up towards Cape Gloucester, with our battalion in the lead, occasionally taking sniper fire.

Finally that evening, off in the distance ahead of us, we spotted a Jap defensive line, located about a mile or two from the airport. It effectively stopped our progress. The enemy line on its extreme left turned into a butt of land that jutted out into the ocean. All along the line, the Japs had dug in an organized line of resistance. Until then, we had just come across some harassing sniper fire. This, though, was a determined stand that they were making to defend the airport. The whole line centered on this 75mm naval gun that they had set right in the middle.

As it got dark, we approached the enemy line, and as we moved closer, we started taking heavier small-arms fire, and some 75mm shells starting to come in.

Lt. Col. Hankins decided to take the position on the flank instead of attacking head on. He wanted to hit it immediately, but word coming down the chain of command was for us to delay until the next morning. We were thankful for that, and even though it rained that night, we managed to get some rest.

The next morning, we prepared for our attack.

Although Lt. Col. Joseph E. Hankins's idea to take the main line by attacking its flank was sound, it was estimated by the senior officers that the enemy position was too well fortified and had too interlocking a network to be taken easily. Therefore, the division commander, General Rupertus, ordered the attack be delayed until the next morning, so that additional support could be mustered. Rupertus immediately ordered his reserve, the 5th Marines, to come ashore and support the effort. He also called in additional artillery fire missions and air support for the upcoming assault.

The next morning, December 28th, it was raining as artillery from the 11th Marines began pounding the enemy line. They were supported sometime later by Army A-20 air sorties over the line. The Marines were getting ready to attack when another delay was ordered. This was to allow two platoons of M4 Shermans to move up to provide fire support. The process of getting in place of course was slow for the tanks because of the mud and the heavy jungle, so it took some time for them to get into position. Finally, at 1100 hours, Hankins's 3rd Battalion began their assault, with I Company and the Shermans in front.

We began moving up for our attack at 11 a.m.[16] on the 28th. The 1st Battalion was going to outflank the enemy and hit them in the rear. Our 3rd Battalion was given the thankless task of hitting them head on.

We prepared for the assault, and finally the word came down to move. Our mortar crew was set up, and the enemy positions pinpointed. I was assigned as a loader on one of our platoon's 81mm mortars.

We started lobbing shells as the riflemen advanced, and shortly after that, the enemy opened up on us. The assault slowed down as the riflemen moved up from cover to cover. Then the Shermans came up and the couple Jap 75mm guns took them on. The one in front of us though, was no match for our tanks, and where I was, I could barely see the Sherman, but it took that gun out pretty quickly. With that, the rest of our battalion stormed the enemy lines in a direct assault. After four hours of battle, we finally took out the Jap positions and captured the enemy line and what survivors were left fled into the jungle.

---

16 While George fought and worked in a military environment in which operations strictly followed the military 24-hour time notation, neither he nor his fellow Marines ever used that Armed Forces practice unless it was absolutely necessary. He once chuckled that the only two military time periods that he ever bothered to remember were 0700 (that was morning chow) and 1600 (which, of course, was liberty).

After this big assault on what we ended up calling Hell's Point, we secured our position. In the meantime, we kept firing mortars and artillery at the Japs that were retreating onto the airfield.

I spent all the battle and half of the night loading mortar shells. Hell, I must have dropped well over a hundred rounds down that tube. My arms the next morning were really sore. Unfortunately, because of our position and because the damn jungle was so thick, we could not see much of what was going on. We could see smoke rising in the distance where the shells were falling, but we could not tell if our mortars were effective or not.

The next day, we carefully walked around the enemy pillboxes and positions and examined them. I noticed that nearly all the Jap equipment that was not made out of metal was made out of leather. That included belts, pads, bags, and other stuff like that.

In front of us, along the main Jap defensive position, we got to look up close at that 75mm gun that had given us so much trouble. It was a naval gun, with a couple of seats on it for the operators.[17] In front were these cranks to traverse and elevate the barrel. The Japs had put the gun at this section of the line to stop the assault and to stop our tanks, but instead, it had been taken out by that one Sherman. After that, taking the rest of the positions had been relatively easy.

Now that we had taken their line, I walked up to the gun, and saw a couple dead Japs hanging from the spot. One of them was sitting in one of the gun's two seats, blood all over on his shirt, his arms down, his mouth open, his eyes glazed. Flies were already buzzing around his corpse.

We checked the area around the gun and found that this line of defense consisted of a couple dozen prepared Jap positions on each side of the naval gun. These positions were small, camouflaged four-foot-deep spider holes fortified around the front and sides with coconut logs.

---

17 The term "naval gun" was commonly used by Marines to describe unusual enemy ordnance encountered, such as this one with cranks and seats, not found with ordinary regular army field pieces. The gun taken here was possibly a Japanese Type 38 (1905) or Type 41 (1908) 75mm field gun, or perhaps a Type 88 (1928) dual-purpose 75mm mobile antiaircraft gun.

They sat about a foot above ground, and each had a lid that they crawled in and out of. The Japs sat in them and fired rifles out these slits in front. We had overrun them quickly, as a matter of necessity. After all, there was only one way to destroy it. You either killed them firing through the slit or by tossing a grenade. From the flank preferably, but you attacked them frontally if that was the only way. In this case, it had come down to that, since the 1st Battalion in their outflanking maneuver had gotten bogged down in swamps and bogs. So the only way we could get these bastards was head on. And it was a feeling I will never forget, because as scared as we were doing it, I was surprised to realize afterwards that it also was quite an adrenaline rush. Combat can do that to you.

We looked closely at each of these nests flanked out along both sides of the naval gun, mostly just to make sure that the Japs inside were dead. We found two bodies in each hole, and I was surprised at what I saw. In most of the positions, one or both of the Japs had evidently committed suicide. You could tell that they had by the way the bodies were positioned. Since the Japs were so short and none of them had pistols, the only way that they could kill themselves was to take off their boots, point their rifles into their mouths, and squeeze the trigger with their big toe. And that's how we found many, with their boots off, their heads splattered, and their rifles pointed the wrong way.

We talked about this that night. Evidently, the Jap soldier thought that if he died bravely in battle, he would go to heaven, or whatever the hell they believed was up there. So why had they not tried to die fighting us, instead of killing themselves? The only thing we could conclude was that they were scared shitless of us Marines. These guys must have believed what their propaganda had told them about us: that if they were captured by Marines, we would do unspeakable things to them. So when their buddy next to them was killed in combat, they actually out of fear of capture had chosen to commit suicide. This was even more surprising because doing that, they ran the risk, however slim, that word of their suicide might somehow get back to Japan, and their families would not only be dishonored, but in most cases, mistreated because of this shame.

I remember shaking my head once or twice. These buggers were sure as hell not helping their country that way. And I remember concluding that day that the story I had learned about the fearless, intrepid samurai warriors that the Japanese soldiers were was just a myth. Many were certainly not as brave as everyone thought.

I also realized then that we were going to definitely win this war, because you cannot win by committing suicide. What Patton had said was right in this case: you do not win a war by dying for your country; you do it by making the other bastard die for *his*.

After we took their main fortified line, their will to fight seemed to collapse, and there was little resistance after that. There were still skirmishes and occasional firefights, but nothing very serious as we moved up the coast towards our objective. After four days of combat, on December 30th, with our 3rd Battalion on the left and 1st Battalion on the right, we overran all the enemy positions at the airfield and took it. We raised the flag, and we all cheered.

We stayed in our position for a few days, building our defenses, regrouping. We found Jap bodies all over the place. A couple days after the battle, we tried swimming in this little river. Then it started raining, and soon Jap bodies started floating downstream. After a week or so, we were given the nasty job of burying their bloated corpses. They were everywhere: in the jungle, on the trails, in foxholes, in the streams; bodies surrounded by these big black flies, with maggots all over them, and they stank really bad. That sure as hell was no fun, and the smells made us gag.

Looking for bodies, one day I came across this little hill with about seven dead Japs on it, dead for weeks. They must have been Mongolians or something, because they were big fellows. Hell, this one guy looked like he was almost seven feet tall. I never saw such a big sonuvabitch in my life. From what I could see of how he lay, it looked like he had got shot just as he began charging down that hill. The others were all scattered further down.

Another corpse sat in a foxhole, still holding his rifle. It was a nice little .25 cal. piece, and I thought to myself that it would make a nice souvenir. Despite the terrible stench, I decided to take the rifle before I covered him up. I bent over and held my breath and pulled. I finally wrenched it loose, but when I did, the rifle came up with his hands still clenching the damn thing, and the stink that came with it was overpowering. Dizzy, I gagged, feeling like I was going to pass out. I stumbled and damn near fell in on top of him.

Reeling, I shook my head, grabbed that damn rifle and its "extras," and pitched it. Still retching, I tapped the corpse down with my shovel, quickly threw some dirt in the hole, and got the hell away from there to get some fresh air.

I finally recovered and went back to my grisly job. We found that we could not drag the bodies to bury in graves or holes, because they were too rotten and stank. All we could do was cover them up wherever they lay or possibly roll them into a trench. Oh man, did they stink.

We did this until we got all the Japs we found on that one side of the airport. I think to this day that that was one of the most tasteless jobs I ever had. Somewhere along the line, as we buried these bastards—who knows, I might have got it from one of them—I developed this fungus in my ears. I had seen fungus growing on my body a day or two before, but now it was in my ear. We had been playing cards, and all day I had noticed a slight ringing in my ears.

Finally, after I shook my head again, one of the guys said, "Peto, what the hell are you doing?"

I told them, "I got a ringing in my ears." Also, my ear was tickling. I mean, I really had this itch.

About an hour later, it started hurting and I decided I had to go see Doc. I went over to where he was in sickbay and he looked in my ears. "You've got fungus, " he said.

He took a thin piece of wire and wrapped a small wad of cotton around it, kind of like a Q-tip. Then he soaked the cotton in some sort of lavender liquid. He picked up this swab and then began to corkscrew it into my ear. He scraped off some goo that must have been in there as I flinched in pain. He finally took the swab out, wrapped the wire in some more cotton, soaked it, and then did it again. Doing this, he managed to scrape that fungus off, but wow, did it hurt, and occasionally I yelped in pain as a sting jolted my head. A pain like that, in your ear, through your brain, to me is the worst place to feel it. He carefully scraped all the fungus off, and then he made me come back the next day (which I damn sure did not look forward to). Then three days later, he scraped my ears again. As much as it hurt, I finally managed to get rid of it.

Besides the Japs and the wet crappy weather, one other interesting feature that was a constant in our day and one that worried us from time was, of all things, an active volcano.[18] This was a strange thing for me. When I had been out west before the war, I had seen a lot of mountains, and a few of them were old volcanoes that had been active hundreds or thousands of years ago. But this was the first active one I ever saw. And it wasn't that far away, either. It was located about five miles southwest of where we had landed, and there was always some gray smoke coming out of it.

Every morning when we got up, the first thing we did as we walked out of our tents was to go take a leak. We'd stroll over to the latrine and as we did our thing, we would be facing that way and look at that big old cigar, with smoke coming out of it like some kind of a natural chimney. If the smoke was no thicker than the day before and we didn't see flames shooting out of it, we figured that we had made it through another night and went about our business of fighting the Japs.

As we consolidated our positions around the airfield, we seemed to not have any significant air support, although aircraft occasionally flew around in our area. Still, some innovative fellows came up with an ad hoc solution. We had been given several observation planes to use. So the guys hit on the idea of using them as half-assed bombers. The pilot and observer filled their planes with grenades and dropped them as they flew over suspected Jap positions—the kind of stuff that those Marines did in the old banana wars down in Nicaragua in the twenties and thirties.

Of course, the Japanese returned the favor, and we would find ourselves on evenings getting bombed by Jap planes from nearby Rabaul.

18 The volcano, Mount Langila, is an offshoot of the larger and now extinct Mount Talawe volcano immediately to its west. Over hundreds of years, the active vents that once went up Talawe forged new channels northeastward and in doing so, created a new volcano: Mount Langila. As of today, this volcano consists of four craters, three of which are still active.

And then of course, there was always "Washing Machine Charlie."[19] He would come in around midnight and fly over us for an hour or two, before he finally dropped his one bomb and headed back home to Rabaul. The bastard never really hit anything; he just kept us from sleeping a lot.

The rain came down on us daily, sometimes in heavy downpours, making it hard to see things around you. Brooks turned into streams, and streams turned into rivers. Everything was always wet, and there was mud everywhere. Any semblance of a trail disappeared in soaked quagmires, while vines and underbrush made our forward progress very slow, so that we often had to struggle through the heavy jungle, sometimes hacking off branches in our way with machetes. You really can't see in the jungle too well, and it's hard to tell what the hell is going on.

We carried bayonets on one side of our pack and on the other side our machetes. We mostly used these at sunset to cut down areas of heavy grass to create fields of fire, so that the Japs could not easily sneak up on us. I know in the movies they show guys hacking their way through the jungle with their machetes, but that's just Hollywood. Usually we just walked around the heavy brush. Besides, if you just tried to hack your way through the jungle, you'd just wear yourself out. No, the machete was mostly just to cut the fields of fire at night.

We took breaks along the way, but it was almost impossible to get comfortable, sitting in the rain like that. Warm food was nearly impossible since fires were near impossible to start, although we did discover

---

19 The term was first used during the Guadalcanal Campaign to refer to the Japanese tactic of flying one aircraft over the American lines at night. The lone bomber, often a land-based Mitsubishi G4M (Allied designation "Betty"), would fly over the Americans partly to do reconnaissance, but mostly to just harass and irritate their enemy. To that effect, the bomber's engines were either naturally or intentionally set out of synchronization, producing a distinct, irritating drone, likened by some to the sound of an old washing machine, hence the derivative of the term. Although only one bomber ever flew the mission, several different aircraft and crews performed the function. The tedious buzzing engine noise, the barks of any resulting antiaircraft fire, and the suspense of waiting for the one bomb to drop did much to keep the Americans from getting a good night's rest, which, in and of itself, made the mission successful.

that the waxed paper around our K-rations burned nicely. Meals were miserable, and whatever we ate was soaked.

Sleeping was a real challenge, especially with those damn netted jungle hammocks (hopefully between two trees, and not sticks). One night, I was lucky enough to set mine up between two tree trunks in a clearing. It had rained some, so the ground was just one big marsh. I took my trousers off—I slept nude, because my underwear had rotted off of me days ago—set my hammock up, unzipped it, managed to crawl in with my blanket, zipped the mosquito net back up, and relaxed.

Naturally, about ten minutes later, I had to take a leak. Now sailing on the *Manoora* had confirmed to me that I was no good maneuvering a hammock. But the ground was just too damn messy to go walking around in the dark. So I unzipped the net, leaned over, and managed to get myself in position. And there I was in the middle of the night, doing a balancing act in my hammock on some damn island in the middle of nowhere, trying to take a piss. Suddenly, the whole thing struck me as funny as hell, and I started laughing my head off (it didn't take much to get me going). The more I thought about it, the funnier it got, and the more I cackled, waking guys up around me and everything. Naturally, I finally lost my balance, and guess where I ended up.

For two weeks after we had secured the airfield, the entire division stayed busy cleaning up the area. The word was that General MacArthur himself was going to come visit us. So we picked up trash, rotten coconuts, tree limbs and stuff, and cleared out jungle paths. But mostly we just buried Japs. Guys with kerosene and special equipment went around spraying puddles around the camps to kill the mosquitoes and other bugs.

Now I was no fan of this army bum to begin with. I had really been upset ever since I had heard that when he left the Philippines in the spring of 1942, he had decided to leave over a hundred nurses behind, and many of them were sick, and instead had taken all his furniture with him.[20] Now we were cleaning up for his visit. Finally, at long last, the day arrived, and we stood on a high bluff as we watched the destroyer

---

20 This rumor was never proven to be true, although one serviceman, Ralph M. Knox, who helped load MacArthur's B-17s for their flight from Mindanao, later

that he was supposedly on approach the island. The destroyer pulled in and docked.

Exactly a half hour later, the destroyer pulled out again. We were stunned. All that preparation and he had not even come ashore to see us. Man, were we pissed off.

I spent something like four months at Cape Gloucester, a good part of the time in some sort of combat, either moving up on Jap positions, or chasing the bastards all around that damn island. And I think that the worst part of it was that it rained almost every damn day. In one month in particular, it rained for 30 straight days. I remember one day after that, we were on patrol and the sun actually came out. I was shocked, happy, but shocked.

I grinned, turned to my buddies, and pointed to the sky. "Look, guys!" I shouted. "The sun's out!"

They paused and we all looked up. Just that fast though, the sun slipped away behind some dark clouds and disappeared for good.

"Thanks for jinxing us," Skoglie grumbled.

Soon after we took the airfield, we were told that the Japs were killing missionaries up the coast, and we were ordered to go up about 80 miles and take care of the situation. So our whole battalion loaded up onto a half dozen LCTs[21] and sailed along the northern coast of New Britain for about a hundred miles up. Our mission was first of all, to cut off the retreat of any Japs moving east from Cape Gloucester. Second, we were supposed to wipe out the Jap patrols trying to kill the missionaries.

We landed at this dock and were met by this Australian who lived there. He oversaw the coconut plantations for the industry owners on the island, and also doubled as a coast watcher. Working for him were these crews of natives that he had hired. He was to be our contact for the area and our liaison with the natives. Up the coast a short way was this little village, and the Japs had been harassing the people living there. So we were told to go up there, start patrols in that area and take out

---

attested to the fact that one of the four bombers was loaded with Mrs. MacArthur's furs and the general's pipe tobacco.

21 Landing Craft Tank.

any Japs we found. The Australian assigned a couple natives to act as guides for each of our units, and so we started patrolling with one or two of them with us. Because they knew the area so well, it gave us a huge advantage in checking the jungle out.

We set up in a camp that had been laid out for us, and the next day we started more patrols to find those Japs bothering the villagers, and to pick up any stragglers coming from the western part of the island.

Naturally, we took advantage of making friends with the natives. They lived in these small shacks that were no bigger than the size of a two-hole outhouse back home, and all of them were perched on these sticks. Several of their little villages had been abandoned. One we saw had a really fancy front entrance. The guy that had lived there must have been a hunter. He had killed several huge wild boars, and had mounted their tusks around the doorway.

One thing I noticed is that these natives barely wore any clothing at all. They had no footwear, and the only clothing the men wore was this wide woven belt, with a sort of two-to-three-inch-wide rectangular apron thing hanging down in front to, you know, cover their dingus. That's all that they wore. After a while, we decided that we were going to go them one better. So we took everything off. Shoes, socks, shirts, underwear. We were going around nude.

Well, we could see that a few of the natives didn't like the idea of us going around like that. Through that Aussie interpreter, we found out that they insisted if we wanted to go around like they did, we would have to put one of those aprons things on too. So we did, in order to keep them friendly, and to keep up our image as fair-minded Americans. Personally, I think they insisted that we wear them because they saw right away that we Marines had bigger wangs than them, and they didn't want their native women to try for a better time. Of course, those male natives would never admit that ...

While we were up there, I got to take advantage of the scenery. There were lots of tropical birds on the island, and you could often hear them cawing and squawking. And the water ... I had always been a good swimmer, and now it came in handy. I waded out into the surf on a number of occasions and went swimming around the reefs. At times

I could dive down some 20 feet or so and swim underwater around the beautiful coral that shimmered in the light, and that glowed in these fabulous colors. Of course, I didn't have any scuba equipment or anything. It was just a matter of holding my breath and down you go. Still, usually alone, I had a great time out there.

Of course, I saw a lot of fish, and so I got this practical idea to my adventure: food. I went fishing the efficient way: I took a couple of hand grenades and went out into the surf. I tossed a grenade out, it went *boom*, and up came the fish. That night, we had fish for supper, and man, it tasted good.

A couple of the natives added to our cuisine as well, and over time, they taught us how to fish. There was this one fellow who would go out into the shallows and dig around the bottom with his toes. Up would come a shell. He would look at it and determine if it was "ripe" or not. If it was, he would toss it out onto the sand. When he had a few of them, he would come out of the water, collect them and then take them over to a fire he had built and toss them in. After they had cooked for a while, he would pull them out, and we could suck the meat out of the shell. They were pretty good eating, too. I don't know what those shells were, but they tasted good. And anyway, I figured that if he ate them and didn't get sick, they were okay for me to eat.

Over time, our relations with the natives improved, and pretty soon, they were wanting to do stuff for us. They began to single us out and adopt us. It got to where one or two would hook onto to each of us and hang around, ready to do stuff for us. So, for instance, if I stood up and got ready to move out, my pair would pick up my pack and rifle for me and carry them along behind me.

It was funny. One morning soon after we had arrived, we had morning formation, and when we fell out of ranks, we turned about and there was a native behind each one of us. Our officers decided that this had to stop. But those natives wanted to join us.

Nighttime was interesting. When it was dark, huge flocks of these giant vampire bats flew above us, through the treetops. We never really saw them, just black blurs that sailed overhead through those big trees, flapping their wings and making squeaking cries. A couple guys were terrified of these things, believing they would swoop down, slash at our throats and turn us into vampires.

One night, we decided to shoot down a couple to see what they looked like up close. When a bunch of them flew over us, about twenty of us were lined up and ready, and so we opened up with our rifles at the same time. We must have shot off a hundred rounds of ammo, and in the end, only one damn bat came down. So much for our expertise at being crack shots.

We checked out this giant flying thing that we had shot. It really was huge, and I was impressed by its size. It measured over six feet across, with about a three-foot wing span on each side. While the body of a typical bat is the size of a mouse, this one was like a really big rat. I shuddered to think of flocks of these things swarming down on us.

We stayed for a month or so, cleaning out the Japs in the area, working with the natives and exchanging food with them: rations for seafood. I remember one day, one of those big native wooden canoes came up to the dock with the natives paddling. As it got close, we could see that there was a really nice native girl standing at the bow, with only a grass skirt. She was topless. You know, it was the custom. And man, she was well built. She had a nice set of jugs. For us sex-starved Marines, that was really a sight, and all we could do was stare. And she was right at the bow of this canoe, in plain sight and everything. Of course, it had to end.

All of a sudden, the native in charge—one of the Australian's assistants—saw her at the bow, and he let out with a yell. He started hollering at those guys in the canoe. Obviously, it was about the girl, because they immediately began to furiously paddle on one side, and that canoe spun around in just a few seconds, and man, all we saw was its back end as they took off. We never did find out what he screamed at them. Probably that we Marines were nuts and that we'd rape all of them.

Because it rained so much and this was a tropical environment, everything got moldy. Our uniforms could not take the weather, and soon our trousers and shirts began to rot, literally off our bodies. Our boots began to fall apart as our laces slowly shredded. Trench foot became common. On top of that fungus stuff in my ear, we had to put up with malaria mosquitoes, rats, and bugs carrying all sorts of neat stuff like that scrub typhus. Oh, and did I mention the ants? Red ones, black ones, big ones, little ones, millions of those nasty little things.

The 11th Marines Battalion commander said it right: "Hell, on this island, even the damn caterpillars bite." Yeah, we were all getting to be in bad shape.

Around February 5th, before we went up the coast, one of the last things I did was go exploring with John Skoglie. We went over to where the 7th Marines had advanced to our left, hoping among other things, to kill a wild boar, A sergeant a while back had killed these two boars, and the meat from them fed just about the entire battalion. We wanted to do the same thing, so there we were, out hunting. We walked through really heavy jungle, and soon we could hear the damn things moving about. We ran across their dung all over the place, but we could not get close enough to shoot one.

We eventually came across an area where the 7th Marines had fought an action. We slowly walked through the battle scene and saw all kinds of stuff. We found parts of various weapons, some ammo, hand grenades, and a few 60mm mortar shells. We also found a muddy boot with the foot still in it. It was a GI issue.

We decided to get rid of some of the ordnance lying around as per directives that had been given to us. This was mostly so that any stray Japs that came by would not be able to get their hands on it and use it. For a while we had a great time, throwing grenades down below and watching them explode. Sometimes we threw them at the same time, and other times one of us would throw a grenade just after the other. We had been doing this for a while when Skoglie pulled the pin off another pineapple and tossed it away. This baby, though, happened to hit a big tree just to his right, bounced back, and landed at our feet, the fuse burning.

I saw it land and immediately flipped backward over the log that was behind me and scrunched down. Skoglie saw it too and did the same thing. A few seconds later, the grenade went off with a loud *wham*! Dirt and grass rained down us. The danger over, we both popped our heads up, looked at each other, and started laughing. We looked at where the grenade had fallen, then at each other, and laughed even harder.

A while later, we were wondering how to destroy the 60mm mortar rounds. Skoglie reminded me of this story we had heard about an Army fellow in Italy named Commando Kelly. Someone had written this magazine story about him, and in it, this guy had dropped mortar shells out of a second-story window onto some German tanks below.[22] We figured that if this Kelly guy could do it, we could too. So we took some of those rounds and carried them over to this steep cliff.

Standing at the edge, we dropped two of them and looked away. Nothing but two shells clanging on the way down and thudding into the ground. So we tried dropping another. Then another. We couldn't get a damn one to go off. We sure dented the hell out of the casings, though. We later went back to the area and blew up the rest of the ordnance lying around.

Pavuvu

After the Cape Gloucester operation, instead of heading back to Australia, we were told that we were going to be shipped back to Pavuvu, at the northwest end of the Slot.[23] Our battalion boarded the USS *President*

---

22 Corporal Charles E. Kelly, 143rd Infantry Regiment, 36th Infantry Division, awarded the Medal of Honor (the first enlisted man for action on the European continent) for defending an ammunition storehouse against the German forces on September 13, 1943. Supposedly, as the enemy nearly overwhelmed the building, Cpl. Kelly picked up a couple 60mm mortar shells, pulled the safety pins, and using the shells as grenades, dropped them out a window. He ended up killing at least five of the enemy. According to accounts, he did this by first pulling out the pin for the propulsion charge, and then tapping the shell on the ledge of a window to get the second (safety) pin out. With the shell now activated, it was a matter of tossing the shell such that it landed on its nose.

23 Pavuvu and Banika (now Mbanika) are two volcanic islands in the center of the Solomon Islands, about 35 miles up "the Slot," northwest of Guadalcanal. Together they are referred to as the Russell Islands. These islands, once somewhat famous for their coconut plantations, were occupied by American forces starting in 1943 as staging areas for operations in New Guinea and New Britain. While Pavuvu seemed like a tropical paradise from above when division commander General Geiger saw it and decided it would be a great place for the division to recuperate, it proved to be nothing of the sort. There were no facilities at all, rats roamed

Hayes[24] and left New Britain on April 24th. We arrived at Pavuvu four days later.

We found a spot of clearing that was our assigned area and began to unpack. We were told some good news: we were no longer under the Army's command. We had been transferred out of General Walter Kruger's Sixth Army and were being released back to the authority of the Navy for the next operation. Naturally, everyone in the unit was glad. Screw the Army. We figured that the president liked us Marines, partly because we always got the job done, but also because one of his sons was an officer in the 2nd Marine Raider Battalion.[25]

The bad news though, was that Pavuvu was sort of like an undeveloped resort area in Hell. There was no accommodation, and conditions were to say the least, primitive, even by Pacific islanders' standards. Hot, humid, tropical weather, no buildings, no latrines, and no place to bathe. If you wanted to shave or wash, your helmet had to do. There were plenty of inhabitants on the island, but none that we cared to mingle with. There were rats and bugs of every make and model, including these big nasty, biting ants. On top of all that, there were these small black crabs that came out at night and got into everything. And there were no civilian bars, and, of course, no women. Definitely not Melbourne.

Grumbling, we set up our tents and tried to make the best of our new home. We went on working parties to clean up the area where we were staying and make it better livable. Quite a job, because it was a mess of jungle, infestations, and rotten coconuts.

---

everywhere, and the ground was littered with smelly, rotting coconuts which the Marines had to spend weeks gathering up and burning.

24 USS *President Hayes* (PA-217) was a President Jackson-class attack transport that was commissioned on December 15, 1944 in Newport News, Virginia. Later classified as an APA (Assault Personnel and Armament), she could make 18 knots with her one screw. In addition to a crew of 510, she could carry 1,400 troops into battle, as well as about 2,300 tons of cargo. She was armed with four open 3-inch .50 cal guns, and carried two 40mm twin mount Bofors antiaircraft guns and 14 20mm Oerlikon light guns. She went into mothballs in the fall of 1958, and in February 1973, she was sold for scrap.

25 36-year-old James Roosevelt.

Hell, even the simple act of taking a dump was an experience. We would dig a long slit trench for a couple companies. The trench was too wide to straddle, so you had to sort of perch your butt over the edge and do your thing. Naturally, etiquette was observed, so that you did not tick off some guy to the point where he would "accidentally" bump you over and down into the trench. When you were done, you covered your crap with a shovel full of some slaked lime. Later in the morning, after everyone had done his business, we would cover the crap up with dirt, as well as the damn crabs that fell into the trench.

It was while I was on some of these early working parties there at Pavuvu that I became acquainted with another Marine who had gathered some fame as a film star. His name was Bill Lundigan.[26] We first met him aboard ship on the way to Pavuvu. He had been in a dozen or so movies before the war, even as recently as last year, before he decided to enlist in the Marines. Now a combat cameraman, he also was in charge of our movies at night, while we sat on the coconut tree logs and watched. Last year, Bill had starred as a Marine in some movie about the early part of World War II in the Philippines,[27] and there were a couple scenes where he was mowing them down. So we would rag him by calling him "Jap Killer."

A couple weeks after we arrived, we started to receive a few reinforcements, and at night, I would either write a letter home, watch Bill's movie of the week (again), go off exploring, shoot the bull with the guys, or sit alone and think about stuff. I sometimes thought of Henry. Was he still alive back home? More likely, he was buried in some lonely grave on Goodenough Island. And what about the Swede and others? What had happened to them?

The campfire gave me no answers.

---

26 William Lundigan was an actor who starred in over a hundred movies in the thirties, forties and fifties. Some of his best works include *The Sea Hawk*, *The Fighting 69th* with James Cagney and Pat O'Brien, and *Santa Fe Trail*. In 1959, he turned to television and starred in a white space suit as astronaut Col. Edward McCauley in a science fiction show called *Men into Space*. Lundigan died of heart failure at the age of 61 on December 20, 1975.

27 *Salute to the Marines*, released 1943.

In early 1944, we were assigned a new regimental commanding officer: 46-year-old Colonel Lewis B. Puller. Halfway to becoming a legend by that time, he would go on to become the only fellow in Marine Corps history that would be given five Navy Crosses over his career. Today, he is considered by most in the Corps as the quintessential Marine. Having joined the Marines in July 1918 as a private, he had over the years gone up through the ranks as a maverick, until he carried the rank of full colonel and commanded the 1st Marines, my unit. To us, he was not just a great leader—Col. Puller was sort of a celebrity, since during his career he had worked closely and directly under what were today a number of very senior general officers, including four-star Admiral Chester Nimitz[28] and four-star General George C. Marshall.[29]

---

28 Col. Puller knew Admiral Nimitz from a decade ago. In early September 1934, then 1st Lt. Puller was assigned to command the 43-man Marine contingent onboard the flagship of the Asiatic Fleet, the 3-year-old heavy cruiser USS *Augusta* (CA-21) on China Station. Both the fleet commander, Admiral Frank Upton, and the cruiser's commanding officer, Captain Chester Nimitz, who taken over command in October 1933, insisted that the high-visibility flagship be the pinnacle of Navy command discipline. So a high degree of decorum was needed. Spit and polish were insisted upon every day. Nimitz had dismissed the lieutenant who had commanded his Marines because the man in his mind was unsatisfactory for the job, and the captain who took over from him was cached in soon as well. Puller's reputation for strict by-the-book discipline was known to many in that part of the world, and Captain Nimitz soon found that his third choice for his Marines was a winner. Puller measured up in every way to the commanding officer's expectations, as he quickly transformed his men into an élite ceremonial unit. The flagship's Marines began to win awards, which of course, quickly won Puller over to the approval of both Captain Nimitz and Admiral Upton.

29 1st Lt Puller had studied from September 1931 to May 1932 at the Army's highly regarded Ft. Benning Infantry School. George C. Marshall, then a lieutenant colonel, was the school's assistant commandant, and so Puller had many occasions to interact with the instructor. Eleven years later, Marshall, now a four-star general and the U.S. Army Chief of Staff, remembered Puller, now a hero of Guadalcanal, and sent for him to get his personal views and warfare concepts on how to conduct the war in the Pacific. Marshall was so impressed with Puller's ideas (not to mention his natural, direct, aggressive behavior) that he subsequently sent him on a tour of the States to share with other Marines his wartime experiences.

Col. Puller we soon found out was a gruff, brash leader, and he always spoke his mind, often peppering his words with some really salty language. He had taken over command of the 1st Marines at the end of February 1944, so I served directly under his command for some seven months, although I was around him for nearly ten.[30]

Somewhere he had picked up the nickname "Chesty" because he had this big barrel chest, and oh man, did he show it a lot, especially because he often went around without a shirt. We were, after all, in the tropics. Anyway, the name Chesty went with his type of aggressive personality. Even though he had this moniker, no one ever called the Old Man that. I mean, *ever*. This was not just because of self-preservation. We had too much respect for the man. His fellow colonels and the division commanding officer General Rupertus called him "Lewie." We just referred to him as the Old Man, the Skipper, or just plain sir.

Col. Puller's reputation preceded him. He was very popular with us enlisted, mostly because he had once been enlisted too, and he was always sharing what was going on with us. It didn't matter if we were in combat or in the chow hall, he was always there. You could be pinned down by enemy fire, and you'd turn around and see him behind you, often exposed to snipers, assessing the situation, talking to someone about getting fire into an area. There was a standing joke that it was a bad idea for the guys on the line to sometimes hesitate before advancing onto a position, because one guy might turn around, see Col. Puller standing next to them staring, and gasp, "Holy crap. There's the skipper. Let's move out and get the hell out of here."

He was a tough CO, but you could tell that his men always came first. And there were so many stories to back that up. One of the most popular ones was about the time he noticed this private saluting over and over to no one. Puller walked up to him and asked him what the hell he was doing. The private told him that he had forgotten to salute some lieutenant, who had ordered him to salute a hundred times as punishment. The colonel took the private over to the officer and told

---

30 Puller was with the 7th Marines at Cape Gloucester in December 1943, while George was in the sister unit, the 1st Marines. When Puller was promoted to temporary colonel, he was given command of George's regiment.

the lieutenant that a good officer always returned a salute, and so every salute the private gave was to be returned.

That's the kind of guy the skipper was.

Although our generals thought it would be a nice rest area, Pavuvu was a miserable place, what with the damn crabs, the rats, and the gazillion bugs all over the place. It smelled terrible from rotting coconuts. Oh, and the weather was tropical heat, which made for very uncomfortable nights. It was so different from those freezing cold nights back in Rhode Island.

The layout for the regiment was simple. The outdoor "facilities" were crude. Each company had two sections of tents, with the officers in one area, and we enlisted in the other. Similarly, the officers ate in their own mess tent, and we had our own. Main paths going all over were stomped out of the ground. Our officers, because they were officers, often got better "cushy" accessories than we enlisted, but Col. Puller had little stomach for that. He had a soft spot for the enlisted man and at heart, he was really one of us. To him, we were all one unit.

I remember one time when we first came to Pavuvu, a number of our officers managed to get mattresses for their cots. They weren't huge thick things, but they did make it more comfortable to sleep on. Well, after several of these officers managed to get one, Chesty put out a regimental order: all mattresses were to be turned in immediately. When the officers protested, the colonel growled at them, "If there ain't enough mattresses around for everyone to get one, then *no one's* gonna get one." I will be honest, it was amusing to see these lieutenants and captains grudgingly grab their mattresses and take them down to the base quartermaster and check them in. They were to remain there until enough mattresses could be given out to every man in the regiment. Which of course, never happened.

By this time, I had been placed in the 58-man heavy mortar platoon in 3rd Battalion's M Company (M/3/1). Now the Model M1 81mm mortar was the biggest and most formidable weapon that a Marine rifleman battalion carried; a buddy of mine, Russell Diefenbach, called them our "infantry cannon," and with the proper crew, this weapon could put out some serious firepower. Not including the shell that it fired, the mortar consisted of four parts.

First there was the base plate, which was a 45-pound, thick, heavy metal rectangular plate. It was what the weapon was mounted on. The barrel itself, in which the shell was dropped, weighed another 45 pounds and pivoted off the base plate at a set angle of anywhere from 40 to 80 degrees. The bipod which set the angle of fire and included the aiming device, weighed about 46½ pounds. Last, the weapon came with one or more aiming stakes. Now these were simple 1-inch-round wooden poles that were painted white, with black rings evenly spaced along each pole. Whenever a gun crew could not see any of the targets because their vision was obstructed, they would pound one or more of these stakes in the ground around the mortar and then use them as directional aiming devices to help them provide the unit accurate, although indirect, fire.

The platoon was commanded by a platoon leader, an assistant leader, and a gunnery sergeant. It was made up of two sections of two heavy mortars each, an ammunition team, an observation team, a communications team, and a couple of navy corpsmen, for a total complement of 58 men. While every one of us in the platoon was trained on operating these 81mm mortars, those who were not on the four gun crews received special training in their specific roles.

True to his word, Haggerty made Rucker and me two of the platoon's four forward observers (FOs), so we also received special training on spotting enemy targets, figuring out ranges and bearings, and then calling down the direct or indirect mortar fire on them, either by field telephone or sometimes by using those damned unreliable walkie-talkies.

I initially knew nothing about directing mortar fire, and while I learned that you can be trained as a forward observer, there was no school for it; hell, there wasn't even formal training. It was a matter of word of mouth and experience.

I quickly learned that it was difficult for anyone to accurately estimate sizable distances across any sort of broken landscape. It was especially hard to do in the jungle. Most guys could not do it well—could not estimate range. They didn't know whether they were looking at 50 yards or 200 yards. It had to pretty much be a God-given talent: you either had it or you did not. As it turned out, happily for me, I really had it. I'm sure that my years of experience as a hunter helped quite a bit, but the fact remained that I could figure out distances quite well. I do have to admit though, that it would take me three campaigns before I became an expert at it. Still, I can say with pride that I never dropped a short round.

Thus, I began to better learn my job as an FO. It was up to me to direct the fire of our mortar battery. As such, it was my job to go forward with a rifle company to find a good spot to direct the mortars, so I essentially had no purpose when we were on the move. Sometimes, our platoon leader would go with me, but usually he did not. When the riflemen stopped and set up a defensive position, I had to as quickly as possible find the best spot to observe where I wanted the fire placed. I soon learned that this was often difficult to do in jungle environments, where it was hard to see what was in front of you. Having a good eye for distance, the knack of figuring positions out by using my senses, and a keen sense of direction, helped tremendously. I discovered not to rely on what I could see, but also to listen to sounds and above all, to get myself in a good position where I could see a smoke round land.

Once I had found me a good spot, I would notify the platoon, and our communication guys would then run a set of wires to my position to attach to my field phone, and then leave me a spare set of batteries.

When the lines were set and connected, I was in business. If a fire mission was needed, I'd flip up the butterfly switch on the field phone and call into the network. My call sign became "Xray," and after a while, every officer in the battalion knew who that was. It was nice to have friends in high places.

I am proud to say that our mortar platoon was, in my mind, one of the best mortar platoons in the Corps. We could set up our weapons in minutes while the ammo was set out and the field phone set up, and I don't mind stating that I did quite well developing into a crack forward observer, usually getting our mortars onto the target within a couple rounds.

We trained for combat a good deal, and still, nearly every morning we were inspected. After chow, we would clean up as best we could and then fall out in formation with our rifles—we all had rifles, even the guys in the heavy weapons units, because every Marine was a qualified rifleman. We would be called to attention when our platoon commander came by, and then he would slowly begin going down the lines. As he passed each one of us, we would smartly bring up our rifle to port arms and open the breech for him to inspect the weapon for proper working order and cleanliness.

On Saturday, this became a semi-formal affair, and these inspections were special, because we were usually reviewed by the Old Man himself. He did this every Saturday for all the months that led up to our next operation. We would prepare ourselves that morning, and around 10 a.m., Col. Puller would come by. And since this was a true inspection, he would do us the honor of wearing a shirt.

While these Saturday inspections were semi-formal, they were to a certain extent somewhat informal as well, so we did not have to stand in formation or anything. Our rifles were not inspected because that was done every weekday morning by the platoon commanders, and if he checked those as well, he would have taken forever to go through the entire regiment to closely inspect each rifle. So we would leave our rifles in our tents. We instead would have our mortars disassembled, cleaned up, and laid out before us: the base plates, the tripods, the barrels, and the aiming stakes.

One time we had, as we did every weekend, prepared for him to inspect us, so we had all our equipment ready. That Saturday morning, as usual, we waited in our tents, because it was another hot day. When Col. Puller was spotted heading our way, someone snapped, "Here he comes."

Gunnery Sergeant Long bellowed "Fall out!" We ran out of our tents and over to the equipment. Each of us ran up to whatever piece of equipment we happened to go out to, came to attention, and stood there. Normally, as the forward observer, I was tasked with properly positioning the weapon's aiming stakes or using the field phone. But this morning, we just lined up willy-nilly, and I ended up next to our No. 1 mortar's thick steel base plate.

As Col. Puller walked by, he remained silent, looking at us, eyeing our equipment. Normally, he would stop every so often and say something friendly to one of the men. The colonel often did this during any kind of inspection, although I will admit that whenever he passed me, he would sometimes just smile at me. The skipper came along, inspecting the mortar components, and soon came by our section as we stood there at attention.

When he came to me, he stopped. He looked at me at my short thin frame and that big heavy rectangular base plate that was next to me. Then he glanced over to my buddy, Clarence Keele.[31] This guy was a Texan, and like all of them, Clarence was huge. He was a mean-looking, rugged, tough John Wayne kind of fellow, towering at six foot six inches and weighing about 270 pounds. Quite a contrast to me, a foot shorter and just 125 pounds. Clarence was standing next to me, holding a light wooden mortar aiming stake. Col. Puller again glanced at me and the base plate at my feet. Then back again over to Clarence standing with those puny aiming sticks, and then back to me again. He must have figured that my job was to carry the big heavy plate around. He smiled at me and said, "What are they doing son, picking on you or something?"

I just grinned back and totally intimidated by the man, I didn't say anything. He just smiled, shook his head, and went on. Obviously, the colonel had a sense of humor.

By June, the division was back up to strength, and we were trying our best to make Pavuvu survivable. We went back into training, and practiced to the point where we could almost fire the mortars in our sleep. Although I was an FO, sometimes I still went back to loading. For the first two campaigns we still took time out to train. We all took turns. Each guy had to know each job.

One of the weapons that the Japs seemed to be using effectively was what we called a "knee mortar."[32]

---

31 Cpl. Clarence G. Keele, from Runnels County, Texas. He attended Winters High School before joining the Marines in 1943. Keele would go on to serve in China with the division.

32 The Japanese "knee mortar," technically the Type 89 Grenade Discharger, was a versatile weapon that fired a Type 91 grenade or a Type 89 shell. The moniker developed from the fact that American intelligence initially translated the term from its manual as "leg mortar" (*jutekidanto*), because the weapon was carried strapped to one's leg. They also initially mistakenly concluded that the weapon could be fired

Using good old American know-how, our own guys were trying to rig some kind of a mortar weapon that could be shoulder-fired, like those weapon-development idiots were doing back in the States.[33] For that reason, one day, our battalion armorer took a spare 60mm mortar and rigged a stock for it, with a trigger to a firing-pin device. After making sure that it was all securely attached and hooked up, our company was asked to try out the new weapon. Whoever fired it would probably have to be braced for quite a kick. So Ernie Huxel, the gunner for the No. 3 81mm mortar, was the guy we chose to fire it, because he was one of the burliest guys in the platoon, with muscles all over the place. A few of us went with him out to an open area for the trial test-firing. After some instruction by the armorer and some joking around, Huxel grabbed the weapon and got down into a prone position. After checking everything out once more, he carefully aimed the weapon and then fired it.

It went off with a loud cough, and sure enough, the recoil of the damn thing was tremendous, especially because Ernie was in a prone position. Therefore, his entire body was behind the weapon, so his shoulder absorbed the full force of the kick. The whole mortar whirled up out of Ernie's hands, went sailing into the air, twirled around, and fell back onto the ground with a clanking thud. Ernie was thrown back and

---

braced against the leg, but when a soldier tried to fire a captured one that way, it broke his leg. The weapon went into production in 1932 and saw extensive service by the Japanese in the war. The 10-lb assembly was two feet long, with a 9½-inch rifled barrel and a base plate. Trigger fired, it was designed to be braced against a tree trunk or log and fired at a 45° angle. In emergency situations though, it could be horizontally braced and thus shot. The Type 89 shell was 50mm wide, weighed about 2 lb, and with an eight-second delay, had a range of about 500 yards. Shell types included high explosive (HE), flare, and smoke.

33 The Army had developed a shoulder-fired 60mm mortar, Model T-20. It fired a standard HE mortar shell with an effective range of about 600 yards. The weapon, which was a response to the effective Japanese 50mm Type 89 "knee mortar," would be tested on Peleliu. It did not perform successfully because carrying the weapon and ammo was a burden for the light riflemen, and it broke down frequently, and because the weapon's recoil was tremendous. The impact of firing it was so hard that even an experienced gunner had to be replaced by another after firing only a few rounds, or worse yet, sent to the medics for treatment.

Part of 3rd Battalion, 1st Marines on Pavuvu, August 1944. Henry Rucker is shown squatting in the bottom row center, directly below the palm tree. George is to the right of him. In a little over a month, over half of these men would be dead or wounded. (Author's collection)

rolled over on the ground, groaning, clearly in distress. We could tell that he was hurt. It's a wonder the damn thing did not break his shoulder.

So much for innovation.

In addition to our regular training, each of our standard Marine regiment went through a reorganization, which included disbanding each of the three battalion heavy weapons companies: D Company in 1st Battalion, H Company in 2nd Battalion, and my own M Company in 3rd Battalion.[34]

Up until now, the heavy weapons company had consisted of a headquarters section, three heavy machine-gun platoons, and our own 81mm heavy mortar platoon. The headquarters section was dissolved, and the three heavy machine-gun platoons were distributed onto the three rifle companies, as had been the light 60mm mortars. For 3rd Battalion, one

---

34 In mid-1944, this newest unit reorganization, entitled "F-Series," was promulgated to make the battalions more mobile and to give each rifle company better firepower, as well as allow better coordination of the heavy mortars. The redesign also included changes to the makeup of the rifle squads and the platoon headquarters. This theme would remain for the G-Series reorganization in May 1945. The concept of the battalion heavy weapons company though, would be restored a few years after the war.

platoon each went to Company K, Company I, and Company L. Our mortars became reassigned to the battalion's headquarters company. So of course, procedures for our fire missions were now different. This of course, allowed me to more closely integrate with the battalion officers, and ultimately gave me higher exposure in the battalion's operations. I would also more freely move around from one company to another for the best fire observations.

We slowly made Pavuvu somewhat livable, and our training went on and on. Sometimes, some of it seemed unnecessary. By now, I had accumulated a number of MOS codes in my Service Record Book.[35] My primary code of 645 (Forward Observer–Fire Control), 604 (machine-gun crewman), 607 (mortar crewman), and 870 (Chemical Warfare NCO), which I had acquired in training at Quonset Point. And of course, there was MOS 745—rifleman, a code that every enlisted Marine carried.

Socially, there was not much to do. Living in tents together, we got to know each other. So many of the guys I had known in the Cape Gloucester operation had been transferred. One nice thing though, was that one of my old buddies that I had joined up with had been transferred to the 3rd Battalion before me. My Portuguese friend Jim Olivera was with K Company, and we at least got to see each other once in a while. I just sometimes wished I could hook up with some other old friends.

We did have a couple interesting things happen. Once when we were sitting down to noon chow, some idiot decided to clean the grease off the concrete deck with gasoline. Naturally, the fumes filled the tent, the flames from the stoves ignited the gas, and there ya go. Instant panic as we ran out of the tent. The flames rose and the tent collapsed. The whole thing was burnt to a crisp and of course, we all cheered. All the

---

35 Military Occupational Specialty. An MOS is a numerical category to specify a training specialty. One's Primary Military Occupational Specialty (PMOS) was usually the regular job one carried out the most. An MOS of 737 denoted a rifle squad leader or a fire team leader. Joe LaCoy for instance, commanding the 60mm mortars, also had an MOS of 737. All enlisted Marines carried an MOS of 745: Rifleman.

officers ran over to find out what had happened. Col. Puller just shook his head and said, "Do you guys hate the belly robbers *that* much?"

One day, as I was shooting the bull with a couple of our mortar crewmen, I spotted a strange-looking lad come into camp. This guy was a pale fellow and really thin, but as he came closer, there seemed something vaguely familiar about him. He was pretty much bald, except for a few straggly hairs growing out of the top of his head. As this gaunt figure swaggered up the company street, that nagging feeling that I somehow knew him grew. My jaw dropped as I realized that the odd-looking creature I was staring at was none other than my old buddy, Henry Vastine Rucker.

"Henry!" I yelled as I ran up to him. Man, he had lost a good deal of weight from the scrub typhus fever, and his complexion was a pasty yellow; nothing like that Southern tan he used to carry. As fragile as he looked though, I gave him a big bear hug and he smiled as I stood squawking about how great it was to see him again. I had figured he was dead, and now there he was.

George's friend Henry Rucker in a grass skirt, taken on Pavuvu sometime in August 1944. (Author's collection)

We went over to my tent and he pitched his gear there. He told me in detail about how he had struggled with the typhus, how terrible it had been for him. I felt sorry for him when he told me how embarrassing it had been to have little or no control over his bowels.

We could not figure out why they had sent him back to the unit instead of returning to the States, because supposedly, scrub typhus was supposed to leave you with a bad heart—if you survived, of course. Evidently, his must have checked out good enough to keep him in theater, and they needed replacements badly. Still, I was just happy as hell that he was still alive.

I filled him in on what had been going on, and the landing that was coming up. Henry had joined us just in time for the Peleliu operation.

We immediately thought about how we could celebrate his return and what kind of brew we could get our hands on to toast the occasion. Unfortunately, all we could come up with were a couple big bottles of Aqua Velva. That night we found that while it made a damn good shaving lotion, it left something to be desired when it came to being sipped, even after we had filtered it through a couple dungaree shirts. So we mixed it with water and Kool-Aid so that we could at least get it down. We finished making our improvised brew, and soon after a couple weird-tasting drinks, the two of us were giggling like schoolboys and having a ball.

About an hour later, I realized that I could not lift my left arm, and groggy now, I concluded that I had sipped my fill. I staggered over to my rack and collapsed on it. Henry couldn't get to his. He was passed out on the dirt floor.

My hangover the next morning was—wow. And for the next three days, every time I belched, I swore that I could smell perfume. I vowed that I would never ever use (or drink) shaving lotion in any way, shape or form ever again.

CHAPTER 5

Peleliu

American strategists knew that liberating the Philippines sooner or later would be required to ultimately defeat Japan. To that end, taking the Palau Islands to the east seemed a key prerequisite. The Palaus comprised a group of islands and islets oriented roughly north to south for 100 miles. Strategically, they are located about 450 miles east-southeast of the Philippines and 650 miles north of New Guinea. Not only were they right in the path of the most likely main line of Allied advance, but one of the southern islands, Peleliu, had a large airfield that could be used to mount a major strategic bombing campaign. On the other hand, if these islands were bypassed, they could become a major threat to the flank of the Allied supply links as the Americans moved west.

General Douglas MacArthur had long figured that liberating the Philippine Islands as soon as possible was essential to the war effort, and thus taking Peleliu would be absolutely critical to the success of his momentous Philippines campaign. So at a summit war conference at Pearl Harbor near the end of July, before the senior naval advisors and President Roosevelt himself, he made his case. Despite misgivings from the Navy, MacArthur, in an impassioned plea, finally convinced Roosevelt that a major campaign to take the Philippines was paramount and absolutely essential to victory. Admiral Nimitz, in the presence of the president, reluctantly agreed to support the campaign.

Peleliu itself is the second to last southernmost island in the Palaus. Called "Periju" by the Japanese, this small coral-limestone island is only six miles long and two miles wide, shaped like a lobster claw—which is why in the invasion planning stages, it was often referred to as "the lobster claw island." In the summer of 1944, while other major operations were in progress, the Marines and the Navy began planning for what in their minds would be a smaller operation. The main assault would be made by the First Marine Division under Major General William Rupertus. He was convinced that the operation would only take three or four days, and that resistance would be initially moderate but not sustained. In this spirit of his unbridled optimism, he confidently told his officers that this would be a brief operation. He added, "We're going to have some casualties, but let me assure you this is going to be a short one, a quickie; rough, but fast. We'll be through in three days. Hell, it might take two."

History would record how wrong he would be.

As the days passed into the second half of August, we started getting briefings on our next operation. I don't think that any of us had ever heard of this island called Peleliu. Lt. James Haggerty, our platoon leader, and Lt. Joseph Murphy, his assistant, would gather us round and then take out this map. They showed us what the island looked like and where it was we were going to land, and where possible Jap positions might be.

We were going to go ashore in what we called amtracs.[1] They were basically armored transports that could float. We liked to call them "water buffaloes" because they were big and bulky, and looked like buffalo slowly going through the water. The only problem with them was that a lot of them were older models.

On Thursday morning, August 25th, our mortar platoon assembled at 8 a.m., and we took roll call at attention. Lt. Haggerty, standing in front of us, then said, "At ease. Gather round and sit down."

---

1   Amphibious tractors. Technically a Landing Vehicle, Tracked (LVT), it was essentially a seagoing armored personnel carrier, driven by a Navy coxswain in the forward part of the personnel well. It was propelled by a set of treads on each side of the chassis. Unlike other tracked vehicles though, it was watertight and had specially designed tall treads. Thus, it had the ability to also move through light seas, similar to an old Mississippi paddleboat. This unique dual feature of moving over land or water made it a versatile landing craft. If an amtrac came to an underwater barrier such as a coral reef, its treads allowed the vehicle to crawl over the coral until it was clear of the reef and able to continue on. Similarly, once the craft reached the beach, it could crawl up onto the shore before the men inside had to exit, giving them longer protection from enemy fire.

He told us that tomorrow we were going to board our assigned LST for our upcoming operation. He added, "You're free from now until 0800 tomorrow morning to say goodbye to your buddies in other units. Wish them success for their part in this."

He looked at us, smiled, and said, "Dismissed."

We did what he suggested. We took it easy that day and went around and told our buddies good luck. That night, after a movie, Col. Puller gave us one more pep talk, and I wrote one more letter home to mom.

The next morning, Friday, August 26th, we boarded LST *227* and got situated. We got underway and left Pavuvu after sunset. We sailed toward a staging area near Guadalcanal, getting instructions, looking to our weapons, and preparing for a mock landing. For three days after that, we underwent a dress rehearsal for the real deal.

We then boarded LST *227* on September 3rd, and set off northwest for combat. A veteran of several campaigns, old Two-Two-Seven had been given a new coat of paint and some updates.[2] Now loaded up with us Marines, jeeps, trucks, a water distillation unit, crates of ammo, fuel cans, crates of rations, and tons of other stuff we would need, she was now a lumbering mule plodding along, struggling through the waves. The joke that LST stood for "Large Slow Target" seemed appropriate.

As we sailed towards war, the briefings continued. We were again told that we were going to invade an island called Peleliu, in the Palau Islands. The first half of the operation, the most important, was to be done by our division. The plan called for the 7th Marines to land on the far right end of the beachhead, at what was designated Orange Beach 3. In the center, the 5th Marines were going to land on what was called Orange Beach 1 and Orange Beach 2. They were to move inland quickly and take the Jap airfield, which was a strategic target and the most important objective on the island.

Our own regiment, 1st Marines, was to land on the extreme left flank. The 2nd Battalion would land on the right at what was designated White Beach 2, and my own 3rd Battalion had the honor of anchoring

---

2   The modifications included a replacement gyroscope.

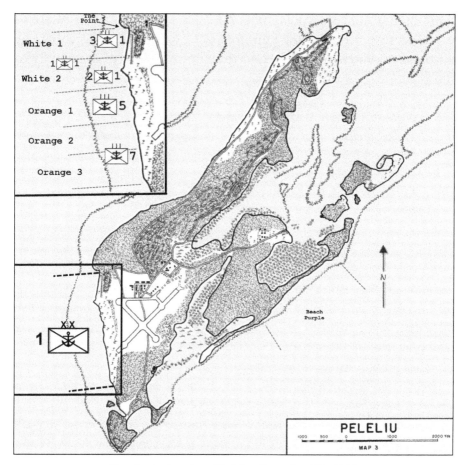

Plan for the invasion of Peleliu, September 15, 1944.

the entire beachhead's left flank at White Beach 1. The 1st Battalion would come in a bit later behind us. About an hour after we hit the beach, our artillery, the 11th Marines, would start coming ashore. With them would be our unit of Shermans, the 1st Tank Battalion.

In one briefing, our battalion commander, Lt. Col. Stephen V. Sabol, told us that the word was this would be a quick operation, and would probably be over in less than a week. That sounded good to us.

As we sailed towards war, the crew of the LST had battle station drills twice a day. Once in a while, a plane would fly by pulling a target, and ships in the convoy would have AA target practice.[3] The swabbies would let us practice on the guns too, until we began to show them up on the shooting. We were all glad though, that none of us were flying the plane.

On September 12th, at 0530, 22 minutes before dawn and three days before the scheduled landing, the U.S. Navy's Fire Support Force under the command of Rear Admiral Jesse Oldendorf began a three-day pre-invasion bombardment of Peleliu. The formation included five old pre-war battleships, four heavy cruisers four light cruisers, and 14 destroyers. Coordinating with the bombardment group to provide tactical air support was Rear Admiral Ralph Ofstie's task force of four escort carriers, soon to be joined by another six. In addition, three submarine wolfpacks formed a wide screen around the surface forces to report and engage any interference from the Japanese Navy. The invasion force had planned to shell the island for all three days before the landing, along with a cover-fire bombardment the morning of the invasion. The bombardment was steady and intense for the three days, and coupled to several airstrikes. Strangely, there was absolutely no return fire from the enemy, even though a number of artillery positions had been identified from earlier aerial recon photos.

Despite the full three-day bombardment plan, by 4 p.m. on the third day, all the identified enemy positions appeared to have been destroyed, both visually at sea and through overhead air reconnaissance missions. There was nothing else that had been spotted that was worth continuing the bombardment. To Admiral Oldendorf, firing at an empty jungle was just a waste of good ammunition. So because of this, and to save shells and wear and tear on his big guns for the huge upcoming invasion of the Philippines in the weeks to come, Oldendorf made a momentous decision. He decided to cancel the rest of the third day's shelling that had been both planned with and promised to the Marines. To that effect, he signaled his change of plans to Admiral Nimitz, adding that he had "run out of profitable targets." He sent a similar message to the unit commanders of the approaching First Marine Division on the evening of September 14th.

---

3 George's LST was armed with two twin 40mm gun mounts with Mark-51 directors (one at the bow and one at the stern), four single 40mm gun mounts, and 12 20mm guns.

When the senior Marine officers found out about the admiral's decision, they were furious (and would justifiably remain bitterly so for years afterward). They suspected that many of the enemy positions in the thick jungle all over the island had never even been identified, much less fired upon, and that many of those that had been were probably still at least partially functional. Even worse, the 14-hour lull in the shelling would give the Japanese a good deal of time to recover from the bombardment, prepare for the landing that was sure to come soon, and to rush reinforcements to the probable beachhead.

The Marines coming ashore would be sitting ducks for a well-prepared, patient, silently waiting enemy.

LST *227* sailed on, and as we slowly approached our target island group, the guys began to get tense. Many of them wrote last letters home. On Thursday, September 14th, around 10 a.m., Lt. Haggerty assembled us topside for a final briefing on tomorrow's landing. He went over our landing area on the map.

"The first wave will hit the beach at H-Hour of 0800. Companies I, K, and L will push inland 5,000 yards from the beach and dig in. We'll land at 0800 plus 30 minutes and set up our gun battery approximately a hundred to a hundred and fifty yards from the water's edge. The observation post will advance to the position of the rifle companies to direct mortar fire as needed."

He paused, and continued. "Our mortars will be the largest armament we have until artillery can be landed."

We thought about that as he went on. "Our observation post will also accommodate a JASCO[4] unit of naval officers who will direct fire from destroyers and the cruisers, until our own Marine artillery can be operational ashore."

He turned and pointed to a spot on the map inside the area marked White Beach 1. "At this line where the battery will be set up, aerial photos show palm trees, so you may need to clear a line of fire. You people in the ammo squads will clear the trees if it is necessary."

---

4   Joint Assault Ship Command Observers.

He looked at us and said, "Good luck, men. I'll go forward imme-diately upon hitting the beach with the observers. Lieutenant Murphy will remain behind as the battery officer."

He turned and looked at him. "Murphy, do you have anything to say to the men?"

Lt. Murphy, standing at his side, replied, "No sir." He was the quiet sort, and almost always let Haggerty do the talking.

"Okay, men. Again, good luck."

We spent the rest of the day quietly getting our weapons and gear ready. That evening, with about 12 hours to go before the landing, I began getting really nervous, so I went up topside and sat looking at the stars, wondering what the hell tomorrow would bring. I decided that if it was my time to die tomorrow, well then so be it.

I was thinking about things in my past when I saw a corporal walking along the deck. He seemed as nervous as me. I said hi to him, and we introduced ourselves. His name was Hugh E. Graham, Jr. He was a forward observer like me, only for K Company's 60mm mortar team.[5] We struck up a conversation, and I was pleasantly surprised to find out that he was from Cleveland, Ohio, not far from where I lived.

Hugh was as worried as I was, and both of us were too nervous to sleep. Besides, it was hot, smelly, and stuffy below decks. So we spent most of the night sitting up there on deck, in the fresh air and under the stars, talking about our lives, our backgrounds, some of the more adventurous things that we had done in our youth. I found it amusing that Graham, like me, had a knack for doing daring things early in his life. One of his biggest wishes, like me, had been to join the Marines. He was quite a bit younger than me. In fact, when he enlisted, he was just a kid, only 15 years old, but he had somehow convinced the Marine Corps that he was 17, so they had let him in. I laughed as he told me how crazy his mom had gotten when he told his parents that he had

---

5   Each battalion had one battery of 81mm mortars in its heavy weapons company, and three batteries of 60mm mortars, one in each rifle company. Unlike the four gun 81mm mortar battery though, the 60mm batteries only consisted of three mortars.

joined up to go to war.[6] We finally parted company in the early morning to get ready for the landing.

I never saw him after that.

The landing—Friday, September 15, 1944

The Navy's plan called for the 7th Marine Regiment to land on the far right end of the 2,200-yard beachhead at Beach Orange 3, with 1st Battalion (1/7) on the right and 3rd Battalion (3/7) on the left. Their 2nd Battalion (2/7) was designated as the division's reserve and would only be put in wherever and whenever needed.

In the center, the 5th Marines would land on Orange Beach 1 and Orange Beach 2, with 3rd Battalion (3/5) on the right, 2nd Battalion (2/5) in the middle, and 1st Battalion (1/5) on the left. They were to move inland and take the Japanese airfield, the most critical objective on the island.

The 1st Marines would land on the extreme left flank of the invasion area, at what was designated White Beach 1 and White Beach 2. The 2nd Battalion (2/1) was going to land to the right, and 3rd Battalion (3/1) had the honor of anchoring the entire beachhead on the left flank. The 1st Battalion (1/1) would follow them in succeeding waves. In an hour or so, the artillery in the 11th Marines would start coming ashore, along with the bulk of the division's tank detachment, which consisted of a few dozen Shermans.

We got up early on the morning of the 15th, and the Navy fed us a nice breakfast. They always did that just before they sent us off. For many of us, this would be our last meal, and the sailors knew that. So they went all out to make sure we had a great breakfast. This morning it was steak and eggs, and we really liked that, although I could tell a lot of our guys were nervous.

---

6   After Graham had fought at Guadalcanal and Cape Gloucester, his mother, frantic by now with worry, had written to him to inform him that she was going to write to the Navy Department and get him released because of his age. Graham had firmly written back to her, asking her not to do something she would be sorry for. Besides, he added, they had been told that after the Peleliu operation, many of the guys like him that had already fought on Guadalcanal would be sent home. So he wrote her to just relax, and that he would be home soon.

We finished chow and went back on deck to see what was going on. I looked over the side of the LST and watched the island get slammed by the bombardment. Actually, it was difficult to see anything but heavy black smoke and flames. It was hard to make out any spot of land, just the smoke where the shells were exploding.

A bit later, we heard over the main loudspeaker, "Now all Marines, stand by to disembark. Now all Marines, stand by to disembark."

We put on our gear, I grabbed my M1, and we started down the ladder towards the central area where the amtracs were. There were about 16 of them in the main hold.[7] Some had 75mm guns on them. A couple of them had flamethrowers mounted on the front.

Then we heard it again on that damn loudspeaker: "Now all Marines, lay to your debarkation stations. Now all Marines, lay to your debarkation stations."

We grabbed all our stuff and started moving down towards the amtracs. We each wore our combat boots, our typical green, herringbone twill dungaree trousers and helmets. Over our T-shirts we wore our standard green herringbone jackets. It had the Marine Corps stencil on the left side (no pocket), as well as our stenciled name. Many of us had our unit identifier (company–battalion–regiment) stenciled on the back. Since I had been in the heavy weapons company, mine still read M-3-1. Each of us had been issued two pint-sized canteens full of fresh water, and a medical pouch in our backpack. Most of us carried our M1s, and of course, our Ka-Bar,[8] which we wore on our right side, and because I was an FO, I had my compass next to it. Also, we each had all the ammo we could carry. Everything else we left behind.

We climbed down the ladders and slowly loaded our equipment into the amtracs. We piled in, and one by one, the engines were all started. Immediately, the air started to get cloudy with fumes. Finally, the bow doors began to open. Thank Christ it was almost time to leave. Me, I wanted to get the hell out of there. Have you ever been inside an LST with two dozen tractor motors going? If the noise doesn't drive you crazy,

---

7   A typical LST could carry up to 17 amtracs.

8   The 12-inch standard issue 1219C2 USMC combat knife. The term Ka-Bar refers to the knife's manufacturing firm, Ka-Bar Knives, Inc. (Olean, NY).

MORTAR PLATOON ROSTER
SEPT. 1944

PLATOON LEADER	- HAGGERTY		FIRST SECTION SGT.	- WOOD
SECOND LT.	- MURPHY		SECOND SECTION SGT.	- WARREN
GUNNY SGT.	- LONG		AMMO SGT.	- RZASA

FIRST SECTION

FIRST GUN			SECOND GUN	
GUN CAPT.	- O'DONNELL		GUN CAPT.	- McCLOSKEY
GUNNER	- SUTHERLAND		GUNNER	- WYATT
ASST. GUNNER	- RUSSELL		ASST. GUNNER	- SKOGLIE
LOADER	- DeSUTTER		LOADER	- LANDY
4th MAN	- McCREADY		4th MAN	- MILBURN
5th MAN	- LAMB		5th MAN	- CHISM

SECOND SECTION

THIRD GUN			FOURTH GUN	
GUN CAPT.	- MOLEN		GUN CAPT.	- MARONEY
GUNNER	- HUXEL		GUNNER	- OWENS
ASST. GUNNER	- MIKEL		ASST. GUNNER	- P.W. JONES
LOADER	- DIEFENBACH		LOADER	- MORIN
4th MAN	- HAYDEN		4th MAN	- LEISHMAN
5th MAN	- HURST		5th MAN	- R.G. KELLEY

AMMO. SQUADS

SQD. LEADERS	- GUZZARDO	- PARKER	- SHIPLEY
CARRIER	- ROBERTS	- EVERT	- PECK
CARRIER	- CALIGROVE	- KEELE	- WHITSETT
CARRIER	- MORAN	- SINGER	- BERCEAU
CARRIER	- JOSEPHOWITZ	- QUARTY	- LYNCH
CARRIER	- KISTNER	-	- CHEBOVICH

O.P. SECTION			COMM. SECTION	
SECT. SGT.	- REEVES		SECTION LDR.	- COOK
ASST.	- GIDDONS		ASST.	- R.R. JOHNSON
OBS.	- PETO		WIREMAN	- MILLER
OBS.	- RUCKER		WIREMAN	- SULLIVAN
OBS.	- DAWSON		WIREMAN	- MICELI
OBS.	- JACOBS		WIREMAN	- MONICO
			WIREMAN	- GULA
CORPMEN			WIREMAN	- CROSSBY
MEDIC	- ROMERO			
MEDIC	- CROWE	JEEP DRIVER	- STRINGHAM*	

The 3/1 Mortar Platoon roster as of September 1944, just before Peleliu. Note: Private First Class Stringham was later replaced by Capco. (Author's collection)

the exhaust fumes will. I'm surprised no one died waiting. My eyes began to water, and a bunch of us started coughing from the heavy blue fumes.

After some time with the amtracs revving their engines and us struggling to breathe, the ramp went down, and the amtracs began one by one to start crawling forward, down the ramp, and into the ocean. It was after 7 a.m. We could still hear the naval guns pounding the island, and from what I could see up front, there was a lot of smoke along the shore.

We were glad to finally get out of that big iron barn and down into the water, and the ocean breeze felt good as we started to clear our heads.

The temperature though was going up. It was already over 100°, and this was still morning. It was obviously going to be a hot day. On top of that, our amtrac was wobbling around in the water, and we realized that instead of choking on fumes, we would now have to try to keep from getting motion sickness.

Our amtrac slowly moved into position with the others to make their three-mile run to the beach. With our amtrac bobbing up and down on the waves, some of us began to get unsteady from that rocking and rolling. Between moving around in the water and just plain being nervous, a few of the guys got really ill and ended up upchucking that beautiful navy breakfast.

It was now around 7:45 a.m. Our amtrac joined others as we puttered around in a circle, with more coming over to join us. Then someone gave the signal, and we formed up in a line and began to move towards the island. As we headed toward the beaches, I could see a lot of smoke rising. The warships had been pounding the Jap positions for the last few hours. I liked seeing those battleships firing, like the USS *Iowa*, with her 16-inch shells *whooshing* overhead.[9] Supposedly, the Navy had hit them pretty hard over the last few days, but I knew better. This was not going to be a cakewalk.

I was in one of the lead amtracs, along with K Company commander Capt. George Hunt, and our mortar platoon leader Lt. James Haggerty, with his bright red hair showing under that damn blue baseball cap that he always wore.

I went over again in my head what I was to do when we landed. My job was forward observer for the 81s, so I would have to make contact with them as soon as I could to set up fire missions.

---

9   Sources differ on which warships were where and which shelled the island. Admiral Oldendorf's original main fire support force featured five old battleships (OBB), prewar dreadnought or standard battleships. Three of them were Pearl Harbor survivors: USS *Pennsylvania*, *Maryland*, and *Tennessee*. Also in the group were the USS *Idaho*, and *Mississippi*. In addition, there were four heavy cruisers present, four light cruisers, and a screen of 14 destroyers. A number of Marines (including George) swear that in addition to these warships, the USS *Iowa* (BB-61) was offshore at some time or another. George was sure that he recognized her, watching her fire 16-inch shells that roared through the air and exploded inland.

We kept going in, the amtracs all moving slowly. The Navy was still keeping up their bombardment and we were grateful for that. As we came nearer to the island, I could see in front of us a few hundred yards offshore white waves crashing onto the coral reef that surrounded the island. Our amtracs were supposedly designed to be able to waddle up to the reef, crawl over it, and keep going until they hit the beach, where they could creep up onto the sand and let us out onto dry land.

When we were about a half a mile from shore, we heard an artillery round whizz in from the island and pass low over our heads. We looked at each other and hunkered down into the amtrac, as the driver began to speed us up. We now approached the coral reef at a faster pace, about four knots. I began to notice splashes in the water around us. The Jap reception.

"That's Jap stuff," one guy said.

"You ain't kidding!" somebody else said.

Captain Hunt wrote about our approach after the war:

> Only the tractor commander, a Marine sergeant, was standing up, tall, lean, his broad shoulders bent over the machine gun mounted on the cab in front of him. He wore a leather helmet, and the square mouthpiece of his radio was fixed on his upper lip. I saw his mouth move as he was directing the driver. His voice was hoarse.
>
> "Go left ... Go left... That's right. No Bill, you're too far to the right; keep left ... Now steady, steady ... You're goin' fine ... Left more, left ... That's right, hold it there."
>
> Through the cab door, I could see the driver with his head jammed into the matted frame of the periscope. As he was stripped to the waist, I could see the muscles in his back strain when he shoved and pulled on the levers. The base of his neck bulged with his exertions, and the veins behind his ears stood out like whipcord. Sweat was streaming down his back, wetting the top of his trousers.

We came up to the coral reef. Although we seemed to be plodding along, we were going faster than I realized, because when the amtrac hit the reef, it felt like we were ramming a brick wall, and we all staggered forward, slamming into each other, trying to keep from falling. As the tracks began to grind into the coral, the amtrac slowly began to crawl over the reef, the engine straining as we inched forward. A shell landed nearby, and the driver shifted gears into low. Our nose began to creep up as the treads

took hold and we moved onto the reef, to the point where we began to
have trouble standing. The amtrac kept climbing up and we struggled to
keep from falling backward, until finally the stern was so low, sea water
began to splash up over our tail and into the well. Cold water start to swish
around our ankles and we started to stumble as we moved forward. Finally,
thank goodness, we made it over the top of the reef and fell forward with
a crash. We cleared the reef, and then began our final run to the beach,
about 300 yards away. We just looked at each other and shook our heads.

As we approached the shore, Jap artillery and mortar rounds intensified, and I could see geysers spew up as they hit around our landing
craft. Looking ahead, I could see that a couple amtracs had already been
hit on the reef and were now burning furiously, and there were men
around them desperately trying to make it to land. So far, we were the
lucky ones.

The temperature climbed and more shells occasionally landed close by
as we approached the shore, and sometimes a *pew-pew-pew* as machine-
gun bullets hit the water nearby. We finally made it to the beach, as the
amtrac crunched up onto the sand and stopped with a jolt. Our battalion
was the first to hit the shore, landing on the left flank at exactly 8:32
a.m., about two minutes after the scheduled H-Hour. We were followed
shortly by the rest of the regiment, then the 5th Marines in the center,
and the 7th Marines on their right.

*As George's 3rd Battalion approached the shore under heavy fire, the amtracs
carrying K Company and part of I Company for some reason began to drift
away to the left, separating from the main landing force. Thus, when they reached
shore, there was a considerable gap between them and the rest of the regiment.
They were much nearer the promontory of land to their left, where the Japanese
were waiting for them. It would take the rest of the regiment nearly 30 hours to
bridge the gap and link up with them again.*

We had finally made it to the beach. Unfortunately though, our amtrac
was one of the earlier models,[10] and did not have an exit ramp at the

---

10 The older model amtracs such as the LVT-1 or LVT-2, carried only about half as
    many men as the later models. After the amtrac hit the beach, the men had to exit

back. To get out, we had to climb out of the passenger well and go over each side. The eight-foot drop was not fun, especially if you had to land on something like sharp coral. A few moments after we landed, and with an occasional bullet clanking into the amtrac, we started to get out. I slid over the side and crunched down on a spongy, sandy coral surface. The jump was bad enough, but the guy that followed me landed partly on my back, driving me into the coral.

After I shook my head and got my eyes focused and back into their sockets, I stood up and ran forward as bullets zipped above us and occasional mortar rounds landed here and there. A bunch of us moved up the beach about 30 yards and dove into a tank trap that ran parallel to the shore. The tank trap quickly filled with other guys like me, and we all crunched down. More guys came ashore and those not immediately hit came up behind us, hitting the dirt and then starting to dig in along the sand. I recognized a couple guys from the No.3 and No. 4 mortar teams. I looked around and saw a number of bodies that were just lying on the beach or floating in the surf. A lot of them had K-3-1 stenciled on the back of their lifejackets.

I raised my head and looked around. Here and there in between the bodies were some dark lumps. I saw one near me, and crawling over to it, I saw that it was a half-buried mine. We had been told that the landing area might be peppered with mines and some artillery shells buried in the sand. Looks like intelligence had been right about that.[11]

I ducked down as I heard more shells land nearby. The noise seemed continuous. I again briefly popped my head up and looked around. The good news was that most of our amtracs seemed to be making it to shore. The bad news was that we were now taking a terrific amount of fire. There was some fire coming from a point of land sticking out

---

by climbing out of the cargo well, over the side of the craft, and jump down onto the sand or coral, a distance of some 10 feet. All of the newer models, such as the LVT-4s, mounted a machine gun next to the coxswain, and also featured a rear ramp to allow the men to disembark away from direct enemy fire.

11 Though a number of mines had been laid in the beach area, most fortunately either had not been armed or malfunctioned. This was primarily because many of the devices were quickly planted the night before by special Japanese swimmers, who in their haste (or ignorance) did not pull the arming pins.

far away on our right flank, but an amtrac that had been knocked out to our right was giving us some cover.

Luckily some logs were lying around in front of us to give some cover too, but it wasn't much, and we were taking some real heavy machine-gun and rifle fire from a coral ridge a hundred yards or so in front of us. On top of that, intensive indirect fire was coming at us from concealed positions inland, including light- and medium-caliber mortars and some artillery. But the heaviest and deadliest fire seemed to be coming from this point of land sticking out just to our left. It was effectively flanking us, and machine-gun, rifle, and some light mortar fire were pouring down on us. In addition, it looked like the Japs had at least one anti-boat gun there taking out the amtracs.[12] This 30-some-foot-high outcropping land mass was a position that we quickly dubbed "the Point."

I could see all around me Marines that were hit, pinned down, or struggling to get off the beaches and move inland. The Japs though, were really pouring it on thick, especially that enfilading fire that was coming from the Point. Casualties quickly began to mount. So much for the shelling the Navy had given them. Obviously, it had not had much effect.

By now everything was a mess and I was separated from almost everyone I had landed with. I spotted Lt. Haggerty and my morale went up a notch. We soon found our mortar communicators, Bob Johnson and Danny Sullivan.[13] Despite the heavy enemy fire, things were starting to

---

12 An anti-boat gun generally refers to a breech-loading artillery piece primarily used against boats, landing craft, and small vessels and mounted on a small vessel or, more commonly, a bunker. The term was mostly used in World War II in the Pacific theater to describe any one of a number of Japanese ordnance pieces mounted in island defensive positions to repel Allied landings. They were invariably single guns typically emplaced in concealed fortified defensive positions or bunkers. They ranged in caliber from 37mm to 200mm. Many were merely pieces removed from the turrets of lost or antiquated vessels. Many were Japanese 75mm field pieces set up in coastal positions to destroy incoming landing craft. Most had a dual- or even triple-purpose role: against landing craft and small supporting vessels, against attacking aircraft (AA), or as an anti-tank weapon against enemy armor.

13 Assistant Communications Section Leader R. R. Johnson and Wireman Danny Sullivan.

look up for our platoon. We seemed to have all made it to the beach with few injuries and were ready to get out and do our jobs. K Company was at the far left end of the regiment, covering our left flank, and thus the flank of the entire beachhead. The plan had been for us to advance forward up from the beach. Now though, we were going to pivot left and take out this one prominent 47mm anti-boat gun that was devastating the beach.[14] This gun was in a bunker protected by 10 feet of coral on top, with trees growing above, many of which were big and at least 20 years old. The only thing visible to us was a small three-foot-high by six-inch-wide slit for the gun to shoot through. One unfortunate tank made the mistake of getting in front of it. The anti-boat gun made short work of it, and it now sat there, a burning hulk (that knocked-out tank was still there on the beach when we left the island two weeks later).

I ran over to a sand trap and hit the ground, along with Bob Johnson and Danny Sullivan. As we continued to take fire, Lt. Haggerty turned to us and said, "I'll be right back." Then he slowly moved off towards the Point to contact Captain Hunt. He did not come right back though.

Others in our mortar platoon were having their share of trouble too as the Jap fire continued to rake our lines. According to James Hayden, the No. 4 man on the No 3 gun:

> When we landed on Peleliu, that's when the Japs threw that shell and hit that amtrac that brought us in, and Huxel[15] was on the top and was supposed to be handing us the mortar. Then Diefenbach got shot, then he handed it to me, then I got shot. Then Huxel—that bastard—threw that 50-pound base plate on top of us, and he jumped over the side.

Russell Diefenbach later completed the picture. He got hit as he rolled over the top of their amtrac and fell, landing next to the track. He lay there stunned as Ernie Huxel automatically handed off the base plate to him. Since Diefenbach was no longer there, the heavy plate fell and landed with a clank right next to him. Ernie finished unloading the amtrac and jumped down to the sand himself. He was immediately hit

---

14 This piece was a 47mm anti-tank gun, Type 1 (so designated because it was developed in the year 2601 of the Japanese calendar, which was 1941), created for use by the Japanese Army. It fired a 3-lb shell and had a range of about 3½ nautical miles.

15 He was the gunner for the No. 3 81mm mortar.

as well by shrapnel in the right leg and right shoulder. He crawled off onto the beach.

Russ Diefenbach though, was still next to the right-side track, and as the coxswain reversed his engine, Jim Hayden rushed over, grabbed Russ, and pulled him away from the amtrac. Otherwise, when the amtrac skewed to turn around, the track would have ground him up.

Hayden dragged Diefenbach over to Ernie's foxhole. He looked around for a medic and said, "Man. The Canal was never this bad!"

He waited a couple of moments, then he raised his head and yelled, "Corpsman! Corpsman!" Frustrated, he growled, "Where the hell are they? We have casualties."

He turned to the two wounded Marines and said, "Yogi, I'm gonna find the docs." He stood up and took off to get a medic. The two of them crouched down to escape the occasional incoming mortar and machine-gun fire. After a couple minutes, Huxel turned to Russ and said, "Diefenbach, you bandage me, and I'll bandage you."

Hayden came back with one of their corpsmen, Pharmacist Mate 1st Class Horace Crowe, who dressed the wounds with sulfanilamide and battle dressings. He gave both men a shot of morphine[16] and a little Lejon lemon brandy. He tagged them for evacuation and took off for another casualty.[17]

One thing that they drill into your head time and time again is that as soon as you land, you want to get off the beach as fast as possible. So I told Bob and Danny that I was going to find out what was going on. I picked up my "rusty-dusty"[18] and moved out. A Marine crawled up towards me

---

16 The pain killer was administered by pulling the cover off a small syrette, injecting the needle into the patient, and squeezing the tube containing the morphine.

17 It was Roman Berceau, a quiet, fair-complexioned 18-year-old ammo carrier with reddish-blond hair, who saved Diefenbach. He picked him up and somehow got him to the battalion aid station, which was at that point one big, busy mess. Both Lt. Cdr. Ketschner and Cdr. Christopherson were up to their ears in wounded, as well as occasional incoming fire. So after Diefenbach was given a shot of morphine and red-tagged for evacuation, Berceau grabbed him again and took him to the evacuation station, which at the time was under fire from a Japanese pillbox. Berceau shielded Diefenbach from fire until a flamethrower took out the pillbox.

18 Slang term for one's rear end.

in the weeds and the brush. He looked like he was shot up bad, bleeding here and there. As machine-gun bullets buzzed over us, he told me that he was a scout and had been ambushed when he had gone down a small incline, over a sand dune, and then down a small depression. Unknown to him and his unit, the Japanese were buried in the ground ahead of them in small spider holes. Over each hole was this sort of camouflaged lid with small holes to see and breathe out of. After he had moved past them, the Japanese had popped up behind them and had cut them to pieces. He asked me to pass the word on, to be careful, and to remember that the Japs were buried in the ground with lids. I told him I would.

I watched him go as he crawled back toward the Point. I looked around for a bit and crept back towards the beach. I did not see anyone familiar, but I still told the Marines around me about my encounter with the scout, and what he had said about the buried Japs.

I waited a bit, hunkered down with other Marines, taking mortar and artillery fire from inland, as well as rifle and machine-gun fire from our front and from the Point on our left. There were now Marines lying all around on the beach. Some were alive and lying low, some were obviously dead, and a lot of them I could not tell. Just to our right was that amtrac that had been hit and put out of commission. Off in the distance, several other amtracs were burning as well.

After a close mortar round hit, we began to wonder what the hell we were going to do, I looked up over the rim of my crater and was so glad to see Lt. Haggerty coming back to us, zigzagging as he ran. He saw me, came over to where we were, and crouched down. He looked around, took a deep breath, and said, "Okay, let's get going."

I asked him, "Where sir?"

He gestured to our left, and so we slowly started moving inland towards the base of the Point.

He went over to the mortar crews lying on the beach and told them, "You people, pick up those mortars and follow us when you get a chance."

He walked back towards the shore and then turned right, towards the Point. We few not actually assigned to mortars got up and began to follow him.

Our battery of 81mm mortars had only lost one of the three guns coming in, but even so, we would not be able to establish contact with them, being cut off as we were going to be. And anyway, they didn't have any ammo to fire yet. So for the first night, our mortar platoon would not be able to provide any fire support for K Company.

After some heavy casualties, the pillbox with the anti-boat gun were taken out around 9:30 a.m. Bob Anderson knocked out the gun with a rifle grenade.[19] The Point had finally been considered secure by Capt. Hunt's K Company at 10 a.m. Our small group got there just after and would stay with them until they were relieved.

The casualties were high. We found out that 2nd Lt. Murphy, our platoon assistant, had been wounded. A bunch of others had already been moved back to the beach. Our numbers were getting low.

After helping Capt. Hunt organize Company K to advance on the Point under heavy fire, Lt. Haggerty returned to us three in the mortar platoon and hunched down with us. He formed us up to move out. He asked us how we felt about staying with K Company to give them a much-needed hand since the mortars were not up yet, so we could not do our specialized jobs. We all agreed to help, and agreed to return with him to the amtrac and salvage whatever we found. We would bring what we could up to K Company's right flank and support them.

So sometime around noon, Danny Sullivan, Bob Johnson, Lt. Haggerty and I went back to that knocked-out amtrac that had been stranded on the beach next to us to scrounge up whatever extra weapons and ammo we could for the night ahead. Also with us was my new FO assistant, a young private. I can't remember his name, but I do remember that he was a green kid, scared to death, and complained a lot. I never found out after the war who he was, since he was only with us for a short time.

---

19 Leaning out of a tree, Corporal Robert P. Anderson, K Company, 3rd Battalion fired a rifle grenade at the gun's embrasure, but the grenade exploded against the concrete side. Leaning further out, he fired another one. This time, the grenade bounced off the gun's barrel and exploded in the bunker, setting off the ammunition there, and thus taking out the position. Corporal Anderson, K Company, 3rd Battalion, received the Silver Star on February 6, 1945, for this action.

The enemy mortars had lightened up some. They were now targeting guys that had moved inland on our right, so we took advantage of that. We waded into the surf and made our way out about 50 yards over to the disabled amtrac that had taken a direct hit from the anti-boat gun. It was also less than a hundred yards from the Point, so it was easy to see why it had been knocked out so early in the landing. It had been a sitting duck.

We waded in the warm, four-foot-chest-deep water, and crawled up the side of the amtrac and slid over the top into the center well. In front of the passenger well on the starboard side was a .50 cal. machine gun bolted to the deck. We were not going to take it for several reasons. It was firmly attached to the craft, and it would take too long to find any tools to disconnect it from the amtrac, it was much too heavy to lug around, there was no suitable way to anchor it to the ground to fire, and although we did not bother to look, there was probably not much ammo left to feed it.

Looking inside the amtrac though, paid off. The first thing we found was a Browning .30 cal. light machine gun[20] laying on the deck. I knew it would come in handy and I would be able to put it to good use, especially since I had trained and had qualified as a machine gunner back in the States. Danny was one of our mortar platoon's communicators, but he too happened to have qualified as a machine gunner. So between the two of us, we knew that we would be able to secure the company's flank with it. Along with the Browning, we found two cases of grenades and plenty of 30-06 ammunition. It could be used with the .30 cal, in any of the M1 Garand rifles, and with any BARs.

We offloaded the machine gun, two wooden cases each with a hundred grenades, and the metal boxes that each contained two belts of .30 cal ammo.[21] We began hauling the supplies inland to where K Company

---

20 The model the Marines mostly used was the M1919A4 Browning .30 cal air-cooled, belt-fed, recoil-operated machine gun. It fired the same .30-06 Springfield cartridge as the M1 Garand rifles, and could average 500 rounds per minute. It weighed 31 lb, and was 38 inches long.

21 For rifles and BARs, .30 cal ammunition came in crates of bandoliers, each with pockets that held ammo clips. For machine guns, two.30 cal 250-round

was located on the now-captured Point, about a hundred yards away. We found the company taking fire as they slowly consolidated their position. We made a couple of trips back to the burnt-out amtrac, taking off whatever we could. There was still some occasional mortar fire coming in, but it was not intense, and the shells were not landing in or near the water's edge.

We finished our last trip and distributed our haul. We kept some of the grenades and distributed the rest. Then Danny and I lugged the machine gun and its ammo over to the company's right flank, on the extreme right of the Point, where the land made an indentation, and very close to the knocked-out Jap 47mm anti-boat gun. We set up the .30 cal machine gun about 20 feet away, and made sure we had clear fields of fire. We then managed to hollow out a defensive position around the gun, building sides out of coral and tree trunks, and then setting up our boxes of ammo. When we finished, we sat in the position, trained the .30 cal out towards the enemy line, and waited.

There was no one to our right. We were it.

About ten minutes later, Lt. Haggerty came up and, checking out our position, he nodded in approval. He then offered to help us man the machine gun.

Danny and I looked at each other dubiously and shook our heads. "We'll be fine, sir,"

The lieutenant looked at that beautiful weapon and then back at us, petulantly. "Well, I can help too," he said. Obviously, he wanted a crack at firing the gun.

Still, this was no time for fancy demonstrations. I scowled at him and growled, "Look, do you know how to run a machine gun?"

He hesitated and replied apologetically, "Aw, come on George."

---

ammunition belts came in a disposable metal box painted semi-gloss olive drab (OD). The ammo box had a special bracket that allowed for it to be directly mounted and hooked onto the side of the machine gun. Many of the belts were woven or web, and as such could be repacked with loose bullets. Space in the box though was limited, and manual loading sometimes resulted in the two belts not fitting snugly in the box; one had to practice such loading techniques to get the belts to fit and the lid closed. The cartridges could also be manually pulled out of the belt and loaded into a rifle or BAR.

But I was in no mood to placate him. I said irritatingly, "Come on, shit! I want to know if I can count on you! Can you shoot this damned thing?"

He didn't reply, and I asked, "Did you ever train on it?" I had spent two months at Camp Lejeune firing them and taking them apart, so I felt qualified to consider myself somewhat an expert.

A little after dark had set in, the enemy began a series of infiltration attacks, and there were only about three dozen of us to stop them from retaking the Point. Our struggle to stay alive that first night had started.

Combat for the 1st Marines remained rigorous all day, and the casualties continued to steadily mount. On the beachhead's far right flank, the 7th Marines had made some progress as they struggled to advance across the southern area, but had done so against a determined enemy defense. It was only in the center that the division had made any significant progress. There, the 5th Marines had been able to move inland and had actually advanced onto the critical objective of the enemy airfield, when in the mid-afternoon, sometime just after 1630 hours, a Japanese counterattack had developed from the base of the hills.

The Marines had just started onto the airstrip when a force of over a dozen Japanese light tanks supported by infantry charged across the airfield at them, with many of the Japanese soldiers riding on top of the light tanks, screaming and hanging onto improvised bamboo handrails. The Japanese had some success penetrating the American lines, but at a severe cost to their infantry. Fortunately, the 1st Tank Battalion, the division's armor, had landed in the fourth wave[22] and could advance sufficiently to provide support. Between the superior American armor and the effective heavy weapons of the Marines (several heavy machine guns, bazookas, a couple 37mm anti-tank guns), as well as some tactical support from a single navy dive bomber, the assault was thwarted, and enemy force annihilated. However, the enemy charge did effectively stop the 5th Marines advance.

---

22 Most of Lt. Col. Arthur Stuart's 1st Tank Battalion's two dozen M-4 Sherman tanks had made some progress inland, although advancing off the beaches was difficult because of the terrain. Still, the Shermans were far superior to the Japanese Ha-Go Type 95 light tanks, which were little more than tracked, armored reconnaissance vehicles.

Overall, by the end of D-Day, casualties to the three Marine regiments had been heavy. There were some 210 dead, another 900 wounded, and a hundred or so missing. Moreover, the darkness brought the Americans little relief. All along the line came a series of quiet, deadly enemy infiltrations. In small groups the Japanese stealthily crept up on the Marine positions and in the silence of the night, tried to take out the Marines with bayonets and grenades. They seemed to come from nowhere, out of the dark. Grimly, the determined Marines held on in the pitch black.

By midnight, several units in the regiment had been decimated, and still they had not made any appreciable progress since the landing, with the exception of K Company, 3rd Battalion, which had landed with 235 men. Because of their proximity, they were given the thankless task by the company commander, Capt. Hunt, of outflanking the Point. After bitter fighting all day, they barely managed to do so, and with failing radios, facing heavy resistance, they became isolated. Capt. Hunt took a muster at about 4 p.m. K Company was down to just 75 men.

All that night, they would desperately fight off the Japanese trying to infiltrate their lines, often resorting to hand-to-hand combat. The riflemen had been exposed to nearly 16 hours of withering enemy fire, from the approach to the beaches to now sitting in pitch-black defensive positions awaiting more silent enemy attacks.

The division commander, Major General William Rupertus, still aboard his command ship, was unaware that the enemy had significantly changed his tactics from full-force, maniacal banzai attacks to slow, quiet resistance. Rupertus still believed, as he had maintained even before the landing, that the Japanese defenses would quickly collapse once their first line of defense had been broken, and vehemently insisted (and would stubbornly continue for weeks after) that his division needed no backup from the army infantry division currently sitting on the transports.

We stayed at our position, and as the afternoon turned into evening, the tide went out and the Japs began to approach us, some of them wading along the coral and moving in around us. Danny and I were both ex-machine gunners, so things went well until the Japs began to come up round our rear, and we became vulnerable on three sides. We kept our machine gun humping as the Japs became bolder in their probes along our line. I remembered my pompous conclusions back on Cape Gloucester that the stories of Japs being fearless warriors was just a myth and about how scared they must be of us Marines. Now, I thought to myself, maybe I misjudged the bastards.

Darkness fell, and the Japs continued to probe us. Although we were tired, Danny and I took turns on the .30 cal throughout the night, on watch. While one of us manned the weapon, the other one would try to get some rest, although with the occasional one- or two-man assaults and the occasional shelling, it was nearly impossible.

In the dark, the Jap attacks came periodically. Sometimes they tried charging a position, and we would fight them off with heavy fire. Sometimes, they would try to sneak up on our positions and either lob a couple grenades at us, or even worse, get up close and try to stab us.

Whenever the Navy threw up some starshell,[23] we would blast whatever Japs we could see moving towards us. We were on the right. In the center, Bob Anderson and Wilbur Beasley covered the line with a captured Japanese Nambu light machine gun. Like us, whenever they saw any Japs, they opened up on them.[24] Next to them though, Sgt. Perry Bandy and Gunny Joseph Schmittou were both wounded. To our rear, behind a pile of rocks, LaCoy's three 60mm mortars fired shells over our head—our only fire support. Capt. Hunt had specifically asked Joe[25] months ago to take over K Company's mortar crew, as well as be their FO, and now Joe proved that he was the man for the job. Their fire repulsed several Jap probes time and time again.

At some point, I realized that there was something strange about several of the grenades that were coming at us. A Marine would toss one, and a couple seconds later, another would come our way. I suddenly

---

23 Provided by the light cruiser USS *Honolulu* and three destroyers. All other close support vessels had moved off to evade Japanese submarines.

24 Anderson stated later, "I would open up with the machine gun at the running Japs. I don't know if I hit any or not, but I used up a lot of ammunition." At one point, the weapon jammed on him. Anderson began to field strip the weapon there in the dark, and incredibly, he cleared the weapon and reassembled it. Early in the morning it jammed on him again, but by then, the Japanese attacks had slacked off.

25 Joseph R. LaCoy, Lillian, Alabama.

realized that a lot of our own grenades were bouncing off trees and coming back at us. The timing was right, too. So I told the guys to stop throwing them, because they were coming back at us.

Over on the right, we stayed at our machine gun and the time slowly stretched into the early morning hours. If we could see them from the faint light of the starshell, we let them have it. In the darkness, whenever we heard any sort of rustling ahead of us, we would listen intently and maybe fire off a burst or two in the direction of the noise.

Danny's firing technique was different from mine, because he shot off more bursts, and they were longer. I told him a couple of times to cut down on his fire and to give the barrel time to cool down enough, especially since we were the only machine gun on the company's right flank. He listened to me some, but not enough I guess, and around 4 a.m., our .30 cal. finally burnt out on us. We had fired it too much and the barrel had become too hot. The mechanism finally jammed, permanently. We tried to fix it, but we could not. The weapon was now useless.

We looked at each other in the dark, and decided to get rid of the weapon. We picked it up and dragged it over to an embankment. We took a deep breath and then we pitched it into the tidal pool below, so that the enemy would not be able to find it and possibly repair it.

As a fire team, the two of us were now on our own. We grabbed our rifles and grenades and returned to our foxholes with what was left of Company K on the Point. During the rest of the night, we crouched there, firing occasionally at moving shadows in front of us.

Day 2

On the morning of September 16th, after the Japanese positions were pummeled by over 30 minutes of naval gunfire and tactical air attacks, the First Marine Division was ordered to advance along the entire beachhead at 0800. The 1st Marines on the left were ordered to advance northeastward up toward the base of the Umurbrogol Mountain, with 3rd Battalion on the left flank.

In those predawn hours of September 16th, we found out that the Japs had effectively silently overrun our left flank at the shoreline. They first bayoneted John Duke and killed him. They then began to infiltrate our line from there. They stabbed a flamethrower in 3rd Platoon, Fred Fox, pretty badly too, but somehow he managed to survive and crawl off into the surf.[26] However, the damage was done. The Japs had penetrated the left flank and there were now several behind us. Word went out that we were now totally surrounded.

Years later, when I recalled that night, I would tell folks that those GIs at Normandy might have had the longest day,[27] but for us Marines in K Company, that was the longest night.

The lieutenant organized our section into a roundabout defense, and after the Japs who had moved behind us were stopped, some of us began to root the bastards out, used thermite grenades to blast them away from the cliffs below. A few of them went screaming off into the surf. The rest of us remained on top of the Point, guarding it. Danny and I stayed on the right flank, near the draw, to make sure no one crawled over at us.

When dawn finally came, we thanked our stars we were still alive. There were just 18 of us Marines left at the Point. On the other hand, looking at all the bodies around the perimeter, some of them stacked four-deep, we figured hundreds of warriors had died for the Japanese Empire. We were informed later that, all told, we had killed nearly 500 Japs on the Point.[28]

Some of us began to patrol to finish taking out any Japs who had penetrated the line, and as we did, a new twist arose. A couple of the

26 Fred Kerwin Fox's exploit that night is detailed in Sloan's *Brotherhood of Heroes* p.162. Spotting a column of Japanese silently infiltrating along the shoreline in the dark, the Texan jumped down from his position into the surf and turned to warn the company. However, the Japs overcame him, and bayoneted him before he could get safely away. Still, he managed to fight off his attackers and sound the alarm before he passed out. In the dawn, he regained consciousness and managed to get a Marine on a nearby machine gun, PFC Andy Byrnes, to come out into the waves of the incoming tide and rescue him. Fox was later awarded the Purple Heart and the Navy Cross.

27 In reference to the Normandy invasion on June 6, 1944 and the title of Cornelius Ryan's classic book on it.

28 Capt. Hunt, along with Lt. Willis and Lt. Stramel, did a quick enemy body count, and including those enemy killed in the initial landing, there were over 450 dead.

guys came across this enemy corpse in front of our emplacement, seeing something that brought a rather disturbing revelation, something that indicated a change in Japanese night tactics. The dead Jap was close to one of our foxholes with a sack of grenades and an eight-foot bamboo stick with his bayonet attached to the end of it. That way, they could creep up on you and stab you from a distance with a lunge or toss a grenade. A new danger to worry about, new nighttime stealth tactics. They did not carry rifles; instead, they brought swords, or evidently, one of those bamboo poles and some grenades, sometimes a whole sackful, like this guy had.

Around 8 a.m., Capt. Hunt and Lt. Haggerty decided that it was time for us to try again to reestablish contact with the rest of 3rd Battalion. The two communicators in my mortar platoon, Bob Johnson and Danny Sullivan, decided to go back, find battalion headquarters and report. They'd grab some more phone wire, and string a phone line back to our position, so that I could establish contact with our 81mm mortars back on the beach and order support fire from them.

It was only some 300 yards back to the beach, but it would be through enemy territory. Bob and Danny grabbed their rifles and left. They disappeared into the jungle, working their way back to the beach as we went back to our positions, waiting for them to return with reinforcements. Unfortunately, they did not come back. As we held our positions, we began taking mortar fire. Although it was not intensive, it was steady. The sun climbed into the sky, and the temperature went up. We were hot, thirsty, and miserable. Relief would definitely not come too soon for us.

Finally, almost two hours later, Lt. Haggerty came over to our position and told us that Johnson and Sullivan had probably not made it back and had likely been killed. He looked at us and said, "I'm gonna go."

He looked over at where Capt. Hunt was at and yelled that he was going back to get us an amtrac and some reinforcements.

Capt. Hunt shouted back, "Yes, Hag, go ahead. Get through! Bring some more people up here … Anybody, I don't give a damn. Hurry, and take care of yourself!"

"I'll bring 'em up!" the lieutenant shouted. He turned to us and gave us one simple, last-minute instruction: hold the Point. Then he turned and began to make his way down the rocks, back towards the rear. Again we stayed at our positions and waited, while enemy mortar fire continued coming in.

But Haggerty did not return either, and by noon we were getting anxious. Company K (plus us three from the mortar platoon) was down to 16 guys, and in the daylight now, the Japs were periodically probing us for weakness. We began taking rifle fire, and an occasional grenade thrown at us. Luckily, a lot of them ended up being duds. Still, we knew we would not be able to survive another night like the previous one, not with our ammo low and the .30 cal out of action. We needed reinforcements, more ammo, and some heavy weapons. And some water!

Clearly, someone had to try again to get back to the rear. I was no good as a forward observer without my mortars, and since I could not just sit there waiting for the Japs to overrun us, I decided to go. Anyway, I did better on my own that most others, and I thought I had a good chance of making it back.

I took a deep breath, grabbed my M1 rifle, turned, and started back. The 5th Marines were nearby to our right, and I was going to go a roundabout way to them. It was only about 300 yards, but I was probably going to tack on another couple hundred yards to that. But I hoped, at least, it would be a safer route.

Slowly making my way to our right, I tried to circumvent any possible Jap spider holes. I covered a couple hundred yards, but in doing so, I managed to get disoriented, and got myself lost. With the combined sounds of mortar, rifle, machine gun, and occasional artillery explosions, the noise of combat was loud all around. At times it seemed almost deafening.

I snuck cautiously through the torn jungle, trying to look everywhere at the same time, tense, ready to hit the deck. I knew I was working my way southeastward to the 5th Marines, a couple hundred yards away. I sometimes caught glimpses of them off in the distance as they moved up, and I sometimes heard them talking far off.

Suddenly, a Jap machine gun nearby opened up with a barking sound. I heard bullets whizzing around me. I dived down behind a coconut log and took cover. I waited a bit, and inched over to the edge of the log. The Jap was using a light machine gun,[29] and as my helmet came into his view, he opened up again. I dived back behind the log, shaking. This happened several times. Every time I tried to crawl away or raise myself in a crouch to make a run for it, that damn Jap would lay on the trigger and open up on me again, his bullets chewing into the log right in front of me. Obviously, he knew exactly where I was, and this bastard was ready for me.

I lay behind that log, tired, nervously staring for some reason at these three sprigs of grass growing next to the log. I tried to think with all that noise around me. Mortar and artillery shells were going off periodically, and the sound of heavy gunfire was coming from in front of me and to my right. In the distance, I could hear the 5th Marines, talking, sometimes hollering.

Pinned down, stuck, parched, exasperated, scared, and so damned hot in that sweltering heat, I knew that I could not, I *did* not, want to stay where I was behind some stinking log. Sooner or later, one of those bullets would get me, either in the open or through that log. Besides, I really had to get out from under that blistering sun and somehow make it back to our CP.

Finally, after a couple more minutes of rest, working up the nerve to make a break for it, I took a few deep breaths, tensed, jumped up and began running towards the rear. After a moment or two, the Jap opened up behind me. I took off towards the beach, bullets whizzing by me. After a couple dozen rounds though, the firing stopped. Maybe he could no longer see me. Maybe he'd run out of ammo or was conserving it.

---

29 The Type 99 7.7mm machine gun was an air-cooled, light weapon originally developed for the Imperial Japanese Army in the late 1930s. An improved version of the lighter Type 96, it weighed 23 lb and used a top-mounted curved 30-round magazine and fired a Japanese 7.7mm cartridge (instead of the Type 96's 6.5mm cartridge) at a rate of about 700 rounds/minute. It proved to be an all-around favorite of the Japanese Army, and over 50,000 were manufactured during the war.

Maybe his machine gun had jammed. Either way, I was damn glad that he had stopped firing, and I kept running.

Scurrying through the brush towards the beach, I saw ahead this shallow crater with a Marine sitting in it. As a mortar round hit nearby, I instinctively dived head first into the foxhole, landing across his legs. Crouched down, I looked around and saw that my companion was a black engineer of some sort. I marveled at the fact that he was just sitting there in this three-foot crater, his legs stretched out, with his upper chest and head sticking out above the hole, a perfect target for any Jap rifleman.

Laying there across his legs, I said, "Hey man, you better get your head down, for crissake!"

He didn't say a word.

I yelled, "Get the hell down!"

He still did not say a thing. Sensing that something was wrong, I looked closely at him and saw a perfectly round bullet hole just above the bridge of his nose. He was deader than hell. This was the first black Marine I had ever seen in combat, and he was a goner. I was to learn later he was part of a shore party working with our regiment.[30] I shook my head, and thought to myself that I sure as hell was not going to stay in the same hole with him. I did *not* want to die with a dead guy. So when there was a pause in the shelling, I took off again and got the hell out of there. I finally managed to orient myself and saw the beach ahead.

I had finally worked my way back to the beach, but since I had gone a longer roundabout route, I figured that I was still some distance yet from the 3rd Battalion command post. I began looking for it, but could not spot it.

---

30 The concept of African Americans serving in the U.S. Marine Corps was a comparatively new idea. It was only in June 1942 that the first African-American recruits were accepted into Marine boot camp. Initially, they served in segregated units, often augmenting logistical components or becoming stewards. The dead Marine that George met was no doubt part of the 16th Field Depot, which listed the only two Marine African-American units in the campaign: the 11th Marine Depot Company and the 7th Marine Ammunition Company.

Finally, I saw McNulty[31] sitting on the sand. He was down behind a big wet log that had drifted ashore. He had built a small fire, and was now sitting next to it. All he had was his equipment and his pistol—no radio, no maps, no nothing. It was just him and his kit. And there was no one else from battalion staff with him.

I walked up to him, told him who I was, and that I was reporting to him.

He smiled and, to my surprise, said, "Can I fix you a cup of coffee?"

I was stunned. The temperature was over 110°, I was burning up, sweating, and here he was offering me a cup of hot coffee. I don't know why, but I accepted it—maybe to be polite to the major, and maybe because I was so thirsty any liquid would help.

He nodded and proceeded to mix a couple packets out of his K-rations and poured that into the water in the pot. The major was eager for news of our situation, so I gave him a full report. I went through about five minutes of telling him everything that had happened at the Point, how we had held off the Japs during the night, how they had infiltrated us, and how we had searched them out and killed them. I told him that K Company had managed to survive the night, but we had already been outflanked and cut off once, and we now badly needed water, and ammo, and more than anything, reinforcements. I told him about Johnson and Sullivan, and Lt. Haggerty all trying to get through before me and asked if they had made it.

The major told me that he had not seen Johnson or Sullivan, but that Haggerty had made it through and had started back for the Point with an amtrac, some supplies, and about two dozen replacements. We drank the hot coffee and talked another ten minutes or so. The major filled me in on the rest of the battalion and the progress we had made moving inland. The news he gave me was encouraging, and my spirits began to lift. Maybe we would survive this hellhole after all.

During that time, no one came around us, which surprised me, because I figured other folks would be working the CP. But it was just McNulty sitting behind this log, calmly sipping coffee. Although no

---

31 Maj. William McNulty, 3rd Battalion Executive Officer.

one came over, the firing continued, with an occasional shell landing here and there. I finally thanked the major for the coffee, and told him that I'd better get the hell back. He told me to tell the guys to hold the Point at all costs, and I replied, "Yessir."

I left McNulty's "battalion CP." Strange, but I still did not see that many people on the beach, certainly no one I knew. It was time for me to return to K Company, so I started back.

From the sounds of firing that I heard, I knew that we had renewed our attack that morning. Still, returning across the shore from the CP was not going to be easy, what with a few artillery and mortar rounds landing, or an occasional tracer whizzing overhead. I began to make my way northward, back along the beach. I had no sooner started moving when a Jap mortar team started working over the area. The bastards began to traverse the beach, and their barrage was effective as the shells rained down. I came up with a simple plan.

When a mortar shell landed nearby, I ducked. Knowing mortar techniques, I could tell that the Japs were blindly firing indirectly from an undisclosed position some distance away. I knew that firing for effect, they would work their shells across the beach with their pattern. So I decided that I'd follow the mortar rounds.

The shells came in steadily, and so as I started my way back to the Point, I timed the shells, and when I heard the next one coming, I jumped into a crater and wait for the round to hit. Then I would move until the next one approached. There was some occasional machine-gun fire as I began the 500 yards back.

Hearing another incoming mortar shell, I again jumped into a nearby crater. After the round landed, I poked my head up and I noticed to my right that the tank trap had in it a Marine with a war dog, a big one. There were not many dogs with the division, although we loved the animals, because they were useful for sensing the enemy.[32] This Marine

---

32 War dogs were integrated into Marine units in the summer of 1942 at Camp Lejeune, procured from the Army and from individual donors. The dogs could be no older than five years old, and had to weigh at least 50 lb. There were two such units assigned to the 1st Marine Division at Peleliu: the Marine 4th and 5th War Dog Platoons. Each consisted of about 50 men and 35 dogs of various breeds

handler was on his knees, holding the dog in his arms, soothingly talking to him. I could tell that the animal was not accustomed to combat, and was petrified from the sounds of the mortar explosions, because he would occasionally whine when one went off. The trainer was clearly concerned over his dog's fear, and was trying to console the animal, evidently without much success. Clearly, this dog would be useless for quite a while. That was the only war dog I ever saw in combat.

After a few more moments crouching in that hole, I moved on, still working my way off the beach, dashing between mortar rounds. As each shell landed, exploded, and crunched a shallow crater in the sand or the coral, I would rise to a crouch and shimmy over to it, trying to avoid the congestion of equipment, boxes, and bodies on the beach. Then I'd scurry over to the next crater, then the next ...

I had made some progress this way, but with so much noise going on at the same time, including whizzing of bullets overhead, it was difficult to judge when the next mortar round was coming in. And with the addition of occasional artillery rounds coming down here and there getting more frequent, I had to admit, I was just plain scared. Worming my way through the jungle around the Jap positions earlier had been one thing. But enemy shells were impersonal, and those damn things could not be outsmarted. I figured that the odds were that my luck sooner or later was probably going to run out, like so many of those guys around that had already lost out, some of them in a pretty gruesome way. Besides the many dead bodies, human body parts were strewn over the sand, and any one of them could be me at any moment ...

After another mortar round exploded nearby, I popped up again and ran over to another crater. This one was deeper than others, and I crouched down as a couple more shells came in.

(although Doberman Pinschers and German Shepherds seemed the best). The animals were used for message traffic, nighttime security, and on patrol to warn the owners of an ambush up ahead, snipers, or detecting enemy soldiers in caves. The animals suffered heavily in the campaign from a number of issues besides enemy fire, ranging from bruised feet on the coral to confusion and terror from artillery and mortar barrages.

I am sorry to say that up until now in my life, religion really had never played a large part of it. I could not remember the last time our family had been to church. Pop had not been fervent about the Lord, and I guess faith had never really been my cup of tea. Now though, with these impersonal mortar shells landing around me, I was scared shitless, and something inside of me though told me that if I was going to turn towards God, now was probably a very good time, even though I was quite a novice at talking to Him. Still, circumstances being what they were, I decided to try. It was a simple little prayer, but it did come from the heart.

I bowed down and tightly closed my eyes. I prayed to Him, "Oh Lord … please… if you can help me … now is the time to help." I took a deep breath and continued, "I am desperately in need. Oh Lord, please. Do something to assure me that you're there for me." I paused, and added, "Oh yeah. Amen."

I crouched down as another round came down off to my left. I guess that I didn't know what I expected to happen, but I was really waiting for something. A sign. Anything. The shelling continued though, and the Jap mortar crew thoroughly pounded the area around me as their machine guns up ahead chattered, stray bullets occasionally zinging over the beach. Here and there, I saw a guy or two running forward. One fellow got hit by a bullet and went down.

I sighed. Okay, I concluded. So much for religion. I was on my own.

At the next break in the explosions, I jumped up and trotted off to my left, going northward through this 300-yard patch of no man's land to another crater along the way. I jumped in and crouched down low. After a few moments, I looked up and assessed the situation. I was about 50 yards from the water's edge, and still had a ways to go to get back to the Point.

A thin curtain of smoky fog seemed to be everywhere, and there was a strong smell of TNT in the air. Gray clouds of smoke here and there blotted out some of the view around me. As I hunched down there, looking around, I managed to once in a while make out through the haze a Marine here and there struggling to move forward. I took in the area. There were some small piles of supplies, many of them fallen over.

Boxes stacked here and there, a few torn open. Along the beach, I could see several wrecked amtracs, smoke coming out of them, and around on the sand were a lot of dead Marines, and a few dead Japs. Here and there, further off, I could see dark chunks in the sand that I figured were either equipment or body parts, as well as a lot of fallen tree trunks and branches, shell craters, while all around, an occasional Jap shell falling here or there. It was a damn mess.

Then, off to my left in the murky distance, I saw two fellows walking towards me, parallel to the shore and away from the Point. One of them, a grizzled older guy, carried an M1 Garand. The other one was carrying a Thompson submachine gun. Like all of us on the beach, they had no rank on their shirts or helmets. They spotted me and approached me. The guy with the rifle slid into the other side of my crater, crunching the coral as he came down. The other fellow with the Thompson stopped about ten yards away from us and took a knee. He set the butt of his Thompson to rest on the ground and although he was exposed, he calmly started looking around.

I briefly gazed at the older fellow across from me in the crater and, to my surprise, I recognized our regimental commanding officer, Col. Lewis "Chesty" Puller. The other fellow had to be "Bo," his bodyguard. Sgt. Jan Bodey was one of the toughest guys in the regiment and an expert with any kind of weapon. He had been everywhere with the colonel since Guadalcanal, and over time, the two of them had become good friends, especially since Bo (like me, I guess) had a tendency to get in trouble occasionally. The colonel had stuck his neck out for Bo a number of times and gotten him out of the brig more than once.[33]

---

33 The bodyguard, Sgt. Jan "Bo" Bodey, was a Marine Corps reservist who had been mobilized when the war began. He stayed with Col. Puller throughout World War II. When the war ended, Bodey returned to San Francisco and stayed on active duty in the Corps, until one night he became tangled up in a street brawl in which he "allegedly tied two sailors together by their arms." Busted to private, he was allowed to remain in the Marine Corps Reserve, and when the Korean War broke out, Col. Puller remembered his friend and specifically asked for him to again become his bodyguard, only this time in Korea. The colonel's jeep driver was Orville Wright Jones ("O.W."), a man good with maps and who had a mechanical knack.

Now Bo, on one knee, briefly, unemotionally glanced at us, and then continued to scan the area. I guess he was the CO's lookout.

Col. Puller and I looked at each other. I was not sure if the skipper remembered who I was, but I could tell he was assessing me, most likely trying to figure out what I was up to, if maybe I was a straggler or worse, just shirking my duty.

What I figured he was thinking was a good guess, because right off, he asked me, "How're you doing, son?" Whenever he talked to any of his men, he would always address us as "son."

As another Jap mortar round landed, I told him what I was doing here, that I was one of the 81mm mortar forward observers, and that I was temporarily acting as a runner for K Company up on the Point. I told him how I had gotten lost on my way back to battalion, briefly ending up with the 5th Marines to our right, and how I had finally found Major McNulty on the beach. Now I was on my way back to K Company, still defending the Point.

He asked me what happened there, and I told him what we had done on yesterday, and about that long damned night, about how we had nearly been overrun several times. He asked what our casualties had been, and I gave it to him straight. I told him that we had killed one helluva lot of Japs, but that it had really cost us, and now we were down to less than a couple dozen men. We needed reinforcements and ammo badly. That was why I had tried to make it back. I told him that Lt. Haggerty had left before us, but he had never returned, so we figured he had been killed. Then I had tried to go back myself and find the battalion XO to let him know how bad things were.

"Any trouble finding him?" he asked.

"Damn right, colonel," I replied. I told him that I had gotten the crap shot out of me by a Jap machine gun as I was trying to get there, and that I'd had a hell of a time getting out of that mess. I then let him know that I had finally found Major McNulty behind a tree trunk on the beach, and that I had reported K Company's situation to him. Now I was now on my way back to the Point.

Col. Puller told me that he had just come from K Company, that he already knew where McNulty was, and that he was on his way there himself. He also told me that Lt. Haggerty had not been killed like I had thought, and that he had made it back to the beach and that he was okay.

I told him that I had found that out, having talked to Major McNulty. He had also confirmed that a support amtrac had been sent up to reinforce K Company, and that Haggerty had returned up there with it, along with some replacements and some more ammo. The company was sort of taken care of—at least for now. That was good news.

We talked some more, and he seemed satisfied with my answers. After almost ten minutes had passed, at the next break in the shelling, the colonel stood up. He looked down at me and said, "Take care, son."

I managed a grin and replied, "Yessir. You too."

He nodded, added "Good luck," and with that, turned and moved off towards the right, accompanied by Bo the bodyguard. The colonel was off to find McNulty, and then to head over to divisional CP.

I watched the two of them move off in the distance. Funny, but I never did figure out if the colonel had ever recognized or remembered me or not. Still, at this point, I didn't really care. It did touch me though, that he was concerned enough about me to find out if I was okay.

In the meantime, the mortar rounds had started again, and so, using them as a gauge, I began to crawl my way back towards the Point.

After some crawling and jogging, I finally made the last 300 yards back to K Company. I had planned to be gone for less than an hour, but it had taken me over two. The amtrac had indeed come up with more ammo and about 20 more men.

After that terrible second day, I never saw Col. Puller again.

In the afternoon, the LVT-4 amtrac Haggerty had managed to get arrived at the Point. The four black Marines from the 16th Field Depot manning it dropped the rear ramp door and began unloading crates of ammunition, grenades and a flamethrower. Also in the amtrac were over a dozen reinforcements, mostly men from K Company who had become lost the day before.

The amtrac also had a 55-gallon drum of what was supposed to be precious drinking water. What they pulled from in the drum though, was a brackish-tainted fluid that had a terrible, oily taste, and not even potable, much less palatable.

Most of those who drank any appreciable amount would get sick and retch.[34] *So the only way the Marines could get any water was to pick the canteens off the dead Japanese in front of them.*

In addition to their supplies, Captain Hunt commandeered the .30 cal machine gun from the amtrac, along with its ammunition boxes.

Later that afternoon, Company B, 1st Marines (B/1/1) moved forward and linked up with Hunt's K Company, to help them hold the Point. Additionally, Hunt established communications with the division's artillery and with the naval gunfire support coordinators. This would prove to be a lifesaver for the Marines that night.

I finally made it back to what was left of K Company at around 3 p.m. The amtrac had come and gone, carrying the extra supplies and reinforcements, and Lt. Haggerty was back by then as well. In my absence, the company had established wire contact with the remaining three 81mm mortar crews, who had actually been forced to move back to the beach area, because their minimum firing distance was 200 yards. Now though, they were dug in and ready for fire missions. The communications guys had strung a field wire from the Point back to them, so I was in business.

One of our communicators, Bob Johnson, eventually made it back the next day, and told us that the other lineman who had set out to find battalion HQ, Danny Sullivan, had been killed as they were working their way down to the beach. The two of them had been making their way towards the beach single file, and had come across the fire lane of a hidden enemy position. They had walked about dozen yards in front

---

34 Outside of each Marine's one-pint canteen, the only water supplies available for the operation came in 50-gallon drums that had to be transported ashore. Unfortunately, they had previously contained fuel and had not been properly steam-cleaned beforehand. Thus, the water in the inadequately cleaned drums was described as a dark color, and tasting very much like crude oil. Additionally, the drums were not completely filled, causing many of them to rust round the top, which further lent to the terrible taste (and color) of the water. As a result, many of the desperate Marines who drank the water became ill, and subject to cramps or convulsions.

of a Jap with a light 7.7mm machine gun on a tripod, and the Jap had opened up on them. They paused and decided to make a run for it across the thicket in front of them between the machine-gun bursts.

Johnson had gone first, running in front of the enemy position. Evidently the Jap was laying low with his weapon, waiting for one of them to cross his path. Johnson running by must have startled him, and he was gone before the Jap could pull the trigger. Unfortunately though, the enemy was now keenly alerted, and so he had been ready when Danny crossed. The Jap stitched him good, and Danny fell to the ground. Bob looked back and, seeing that Danny was dead, continued on.

Johnson made his way back to our mortars. Two of them had been knocked out, and the teams had no ammo ashore as yet. Since he could not find any himself, he stayed with them for a while, then went looking around the beach for some field phone wire. Sometime after that, he was assigned to another unit.

I too had probably crossed the same area, but like Johnson, I must have surprised the Jap as well. I was moving fast, and I was gone into the jungle before he could open fire. I had not been so lucky the second time though, and that Jap had pinned me down for a while before I had managed to get away.

Later that day, we took stock of the unit and what had happened to whom. While we had taken a lot of casualties at the landing, most of them had happened while we were taking the Point and during that night.

Two riflemen had died next to me last night as we had defended our positions: Arthur Graham, and a guy named Kenneth Kuld.[35] I barely knew them. Beasley was dead, having taken grenade shrapnel sometime that night. Sgt. Banford and Platoon Sgt. John Kovalt had been hit and sent to the rear. So had our platoon's Gunny Long, Sgt. Wood, who had

---

35 PFC Kenneth V. Kuld, from Tyler, Minnesota. Earlier in the night, he had alone stopped a Japanese assault on K Company's position and in doing so, had been seriously wounded by enemy shrapnel. Later in the night, defending the company perimeter next to George's position, he was killed. For these actions he was posthumously awarded the Silver Star.

been in charge of the 1st Section, and Sgt. Bandy.[36] Another guy who had been wounded and evacuated was a buddy of mine, Sgt. Joe Rzasa.[37] Joe had joined the Corps in 1939, and like me, had been in some sort of disciplinary trouble early on and been busted. He had worked his way back up the ranks again, and when I first joined the unit back in 1943, he was a sergeant leading the ammo squad.

Since he had no one who knew how to play cribbage (or wanted to) and I was sort of willing to learn, Joe had taught me how to play. I didn't really much care for the game, but he was a nice guy, and so I learned and we played many such games in Melbourne, becoming good friends as we did. Joe had a sense of humor, too. Along with the rest of our company, our platoon would get into Monday morning formation, and when it was his turn to give his ammunition report, he would march up to Lt. Haggerty in British style. He would snap off a fancy British salute just like they did, with his palm facing outward and his arm vibrating to a stop, and give his report. Sometimes he would use his imagination and bark something like, "SAH! I wish to report that three of our aircraft are missing!"

Many other guys from K Company had been hit that first day too, like Harlan Murray and Joe LaCoy, who had commanded K Company's battery of three 60mm mortars. An old buddy of mine who had been with me at Rhode Island, Jim Olivera, a BAR man, had been wounded too. I had known him back from Quonset Point, and the two of us had gone on liberty together a few times. I was told that he had been hit pretty bad and had been evacuated to the fleet hospital. I would never see him again.

On the other hand, Chuck Reeves,[38] the guy who led our platoon's forward observer section, joined us again. Chuck had been out on one of those close support rocket LCIs,[39] directing the firing of the rockets

---

36 1st Sergeant Lester R. Banford, Gunnery Sergeant Wellington B. Long, from Kinston, North Carolina, Sergeant Joseph E. Wood, and Sergeant Perry L. Bandy.
37 Sgt. Joseph J. Rzasa from Chicopee, Massachusetts.
38 Sgt. Charles L. Reeves.
39 Landing Craft, Infantry. Nicknamed "waterbug," this was a medium-sized amphibious assault ship normally used to land up to 200 infantry onto a beach. With

to support our landing. The 4.5-inch rocket launcher racks were secured to the decks, including where the side ramps were normally located. A Marine crew was assigned to electronically fire the rockets by pushing these buttons. Commanding them was Lt. W. A. Young, temporarily attached to our mortar company. He commanded the rocket unit because it was an important element in the gunfire support, and as such, only an officer could give the order to fire any of the rockets.[40]

Since the launchers were fixed and could not move, the only way the rockets could be aimed was to maneuver the ship to the correct direction. To do that, Chuck supervised, using, of all things, a broom handle as his aiming stake, and measured bearings off the compass he carried. He passed the word on the correct direction and azimuth to an assistant next to him carrying a sound-powered phone. The assistant relayed the information to the LCI's bridge, where they maneuvered the vessel to the correct bearing for the rockets. When they were lined up, Young gave the firing order, and a salvo of rockets would be set off against the Japs. Chuck later told me about that setup while shaking his head, because he had come up with the idea and had done all the engineering and the work. All Lt. Young did was give the order to shoot.

Over the first two days, they had fired off close to a thousand rockets. Then on the third day, the LCI struck a Jap mine, and as she sank, Chuck, Lt. Young, and the crew had to abandon ship and swim to shore. Now Chuck was back with us.

That night, the Japanese planned on making a substantial attempt to try and retake the Point. If they could once again secure this elevated position, they could set up mortars, automatic weapons, another 47mm anti-boat gun (still in its crate), and perhaps some light artillery to again outflank the White and Orange beaches and tear into their supply lines with withering, enfilading fire. The attack

---

a crew of 25, it had an empty displacement of 240 tons, was 160 feet long, 23 feet wide, and had a draft of 5.5 feet. Its two shafts could make a top speed of 16 knots in calm water. Some were outfitted for other roles, such as rocket support (designated LCI-R for rockets or LCI-G for Gunboat).

40 Young was an arrogant officer, disliked by the men. He was later wounded on Peleliu.

was scheduled for 2200 hours and was to be carried out by some 500 determined Japanese troops, supported by several mortar batteries. The enemy force was told to stop at nothing in rooting out the Americans and recapturing the Point.

That second night on the Point, there were only about three dozen of us there, including our OP assistant, Sgt. Joe Giddens. But now we had plenty of ammo, a couple more machine guns, the 60mm mortars, and I could call in our 81s if we needed them. Besides, there was Company B to our right. And I must say, even though we had been through hell so far and lost so many guys, our morale was still high.

As the sun set, we all were keyed up. It had become very quiet in front of us, and we kind of expected something to happen. Capt. Hunt told Lt. Haggerty to tell our battery to stand by, just in case. Haggerty got on our field phone and told the 81s to be ready to give support if needed. Of course, we only had three, since one had been destroyed the first day.

We reinforced our perimeter as darkness fell. Giddens and I had each taken one of the unit's two stretchers to lay on over the jagged coral ground. But the sergeant, probably wanting to score some points with Capt. Hunt, offered him his. The captain thanked him and lay it down at his command post nearby, just on the other side of what remained of a shot up mangrove tree.

A while later, Giddens, uncomfortably laying on the coral and I'm sure regretting his decision, walked over to me and said, "I want that stretcher."

Nervous, I had been concentrating on the darkness, imagining Japs crawling towards us. Startled, I looked up at him and defiantly said, "Well, you ain't getting this gawddamn stretcher."

He hesitated and grumbled, "Well, I outrank you."

I snarled back, "I don't give a shit. This is my stretcher. You gave yours away. If you're stupid enough to do that, okay. But you ain't getting mine."

Giddens growled but went back to his position. Fine. I was having enough problems staying alive. I heard Capt. Hunt quietly chuckle in the dark.

As evening set in and our positions were set, the Japs began to try to infiltrate our lines again. Then, several really intense firefights broke out, as Capt. Hunt yelled at us to let them have it.[41] We soon found ourselves desperately holding the bastards off. We used automatic fire and grenades, but the sonsabitches kept coming.

As the Japs closed in on us and we continued taking heavy fire, Capt. Hunt told Lt. Haggerty to again call in the mortars. Unfortunately at this point, the enemy was so close to us, any barrage would have to be called in nearly on top of us. Still, it had come to the point where it was a tossup as to whether we could hold our position, so the order was given. Hunt told Haggerty, "Red, put as many rounds in there as you can pump out."

The lieutenant got on the phone and gave the order. Then he turned it over to me. Estimating as best I could, "Xray" gave the mortar crews their firing orders.

About ten seconds later, our 81mm shells began to come in. The thunderous explosions flared up all round us, lighting up the night sky. Added to that was the firepower of Joe LaCoy's 60mm mortars (Joe continued commanding them, even though he had been wounded), located right behind us. We ducked our heads down as best as we could as the ground shook with the detonations. We could hear shrapnel angrily buzzing just above us. Tree branches were flung around us, and we were satisfied to hear some Japs screaming in the night.

A couple of us got some minor wounds from the mortars, but the effect on the Japs was devastating. Still, a couple dozen had penetrated our lines, and for a while it was hand-to-hand combat before they turned and retreated into the night.

Now it was our turn. We chased some of them into the ocean, and others onto the cliffs. Amazingly, we found about 50 yards from our position, still packaged in a crate, a second, brand-new 47mm anti-boat gun. After overrunning us, they had planned to set it in the original knocked-out bunker to again outflank the entire beachhead. They had

---

41 According to Hunt, he yelled, "There they are! They're com' on us! Give 'em hell! Kill every one of them!"

been so confident that they were going to take us that they had not even bothered to unpack the gun. That was dumb as hell.

Finally, we secured for the night.

Day 3

In just two days, the 1st Marines had taken over 1,000 casualties—about a third of their strength. Still, Col. Puller firmly gave the order for all three battalions to move forward up the northern coast of the island. The 3rd Battalion would progress up on the left. The 1st Battalion, reinforced by the division's reserve, 2nd Battalion, 7th Marines (2/7), would advance on their right. The 2nd Battalion would take the right and advance to the base of the Umurbrogol Mountain, or what the Marines had cursedly decided to call "Bloody Nose Ridge." The assault would be preceded by a half hour of naval gunfire support onto the mountain. At 0800, the attack would commence.

The next morning, the smoke from the night attacks had long cleared. We had killed a few hundred Japs that night. I personally gave up counting after four hundred. Capt. Hunt wrote after the war that he saw:

> 350 more Japanese dead sprawled before our lines. Their rear units, horribly mutilated by our artillery and mortars, had been lugging a 40mm gun, for it lay in their midst, scarred by shrapnel, an abandoned symbol of their efforts to recapture the Point ... In the countless gullies and basins in the coral Jap dead lay four deep, and on the level stretches they were scattered in one layer. They sprawled in ghastly attitudes with their faces frozen and lips curled in apish grins that showed their widely separated teeth and blackened gums. Their eyes were slimy with the green film of death through which I could see an expression of horror and incredibility. Many of them were huddled with their arms around each other as though they had futilely tried to protect themselves from our fire. They were horribly mutilated; riddled by bullets and torn by shrapnel until their entrails popped out; legs and arms and heads and torsos littered the rocks and in some places were lodged grotesquely in the treetops.

We had lost more guys yesterday too. Joe Giddens, our OP assistant sergeant, had been hit in one of the Jap counterattacks. He was evacuated.[42]

---

42 Giddens later received the Bronze Star for his actions that first day on Peleliu: "For heroic achievement as observer for the mortar platoon of a rifle battalion in the

K Company was now down to about 30 men, of which less than two dozen were well enough to make an attack.[43] They had lost one of their first sergeants, Joe Schmittou,[44] and because of their depleted condition, Lt. Col. Sabol ordered that they be pulled off the line and put in reserve. Relieving them was I Company.

Our mortar platoon's observation team transferred to I Company, and so I set up shop again, this time with them.

---

assault against enemy Japanese forces on Peleliu Island, Palau Islands, September 15, 1944. In order to observe and direct mortar fire, Sergeant Giddens, worked his way through an area infested with enemy snipers to an assault company isolated from the rest of the battalion. Upon reaching the unit and finding there were no communications with the battalion, Sergeant Giddens, with great resourcefulness, took command of a machine gun, and with other mortar observation post men, manned it during three fierce enemy counterattacks inflicting many casualties on the enemy. Seeing one of his men hit by shrapnel, Sergeant Giddens in full view of the enemy applied battle dressing and administered morphine, at the same time giving orders to his men manning the machine gun. His outstanding leadership, great courage and unswerving devotion to duty during a critical phase of the operation was of an inspiring order and was in keeping with the highest traditions of the United States Naval Service." Giddens, a veteran of Guadalcanal, Finschhaven, Cape Gloucester, and now Peleliu, would go on to rejoin the battalion in time for the Okinawa invasion, which would be his fifth Pacific campaign. From Okinawa, he would be sent back to the United States, where he would attend OCS and be commissioned a 2nd lieutenant.

43 By the time K Company was evacuated, it had been whittled down to just 78 men, including those in aid stations for various minor things such as superficial wounds, heat stroke, dehydration, or water contamination. It also included wounded that had been evacuated or in the process of being evacuated, and men who had become lost and had mixed in with other units. Nor was K Company the only unit with such heavy losses. After only three days of brutal combat, Company B, 1st Battalion, was down from its original complement of 242 men that landed to "19 men still on their feet."

44 1st Sgt. Joseph M. Schmittou, of Tennessee. Joining the Marines in 1937, he saw action at Guadalcanal, then at Cape Gloucester, where he earned a Silver Star after taking over as company commander and getting wounded in action (pinned on by Chesty Puller himself). He fought at Tuluvu, and now on Peleliu, before he would go on to serve in Okinawa and later, the Korean War (where he would earn two Bronze Stars). Schmittou retired from the Marine Corps after 28 years, as a master sergeant, returned home, became a deputy sheriff, and died in 1990.

Talking to the others, I found out that my buddy Henry had been wounded yesterday. He had been with L Company sitting in that tank trap that ran parallel to the beach. When they tried to get out and move forward, a Jap machine gun began firing at them. Henry got up and began running, and when he hit the crest of the hill overlooking the trap, bullets cut him down. But I was told that he was going to be okay. They had taken him to the rear, and he was getting shipped out to some naval hospital in the Russell Islands.[45] Poor Henry. It seemed like he couldn't catch a break for very long.

With K Company shattered, I was now attached as an FO to I Company. I would be with I Company for five days. As we began to take indirect mortar fire, our unit began to move north along the beach towards the steep hills to our right, which we had named (for good reason) "Bloody Nose Ridge." Every time we tried to move up though, the Japs would see us off the higher ridges in front and open up with their machine guns and mortars.

We were in a coconut grove when artillery shells began falling again. I dove down along with two other guys, into a sandy shell crater. One of them was hit pretty bad by shrapnel. I turned him over and lifted his shirt and saw a deep wound, with the blood just spurting out of him. I tore off a part of his shirt and tried to shove it into the wound to stop the bleeding. That was all I had.

Bob Johnson came by and had a syringe of morphine. I told him that I would try to give it to the wounded guy. I was nervous as hell because, first of all, I was looking at this guy's open wound. Second, we were in a combat situation, and third, I had never injected anyone before. Nervously, I took the cap off this small unit that looked like a midget toothpaste tube. My hands covered in blood, I pointed the syringe down and tried to inject it into the wounded guy, but the needle was bent just a little bit, and the more I pushed, the more it bent. I tried

---

45 Mobile Hospital #10, located on the island of Banika in the Solomon Islands, far across the strait from Guadalcanal. Banika, today formally known as Mbanika, is the second largest of the Russell Islands next to Pavuvu. Although technically classified as a mobile hospital, MOB 10 included over 30 surgical and medical wards, as well as a full laboratory, and could accommodate over 2,000 patients.

straightening it out again, and then injecting the guy again. But instead of giving it a good firm jab, I just pushed the syringe. Again the needle bent, even more. In the end, I just could not get the needle into him, and I felt terrible, what with him lying there in pain. Frustrated, tears came to my eyes.

The combat action around us intensified, and we were moving out. I finally had to leave the poor guy. He almost certainly died; I figure that he was probably dead before I was 20 feet from his hole. I never did know his name.

We had been working our way up along the shore when we finally stopped for the night and set up camp there in that coconut grove on the beach. They hit us just after dark, and attacked again through a good part of the night, but we were dug in and survived, taking only a few casualties.

We were though, overrun with these huge land crabs that lived on the shore and went crawling all over in the dark.[46] We had a hell of a time getting them out of our areas, smacking them with our helmets and rifle butts, and cursing them—which of course, made it easier for the Japs infiltrating our perimeter to locate us. Yeah, them damn crabs at night would crawl right on top of you and crawl all over your shoulders and scare the hell out of you. I mean, you didn't know if it was a Jap or not.

That night, I remember at one point in the middle of the night, one of our guys got it that way, that is the long bamboo stick and bayonet, in his foxhole. I suddenly heard this loud, terrible scream in the darkness as he was stuck with one of those gigs. It made the hair on the back of my neck stand up.

Sometimes even today, I hear that scream in my sleep.

The next morning, we took turns taking away the wounded and the dead. The stretcher bearers eventually came for the guy who had screamed in the night. He had been stabbed several times in his

---

46 These crabs lay their eggs in the ocean, and the babies finally crawl up onto the beaches and bury themselves during the day. They come out at night, especially after heavy rains, and feed on fallen leaves, ground plants, fruits, broken boxes of rations, and sometimes small pieces of dead meat.

foxhole. The medics went over to him in his foxhole, dead, bent over like a stiff pretzel. Rigor mortis had already set in. They pulled him out and laid him on the stretcher. When they lifted him up, he just rolled off the stretcher and hit the ground with a *thunk*. As disturbing as it sounds, when we saw that, we laughed our butts off. I know that it was morbid for us to do that, especially considering that this guy had been in our unit, but it was stress relief that we desperately needed at that time.

At the end of the day, Col. Puller mustered what reinforcements he could get and dispensed them into his decimated units. By next morning, 3rd Battalion would only be able to muster 476 men, less than half their original strength, and half of these men were headquarters personnel.

Day 4

On Monday morning, the 18th, our unit got up early. We regrouped and waited to be briefed on what we were going to do. Evidently, we were going to attack that damn mountain in front of us. At least today though, we were going to get some aerial help. A couple spotter planes had landed on the airstrip and were going to do some aerial recon for us. We would be in contact with them by radio.

I suddenly realized as we prepared to attack that it was my birthday. I was 22. Big deal. I thought how ironic it would be if I got shot today. The idea of getting killed on my own birthday on this lousy island depressed me.

We moved slowly up the shore along the northern side of the island, hitting the deck whenever we took occasional gunfire. As we moved along the beach, although tired, I was still alert. Col. Puller had decided not to go up the center of the mountain. That thing was 560 feet high, complete with gullies and ravines, although supposedly the top was flat.

Little by little, I clawed my way up those steep slopes, and I bet I struggled up every foot of that damn mountain, sometimes pulling myself up on vines and roots. Most of the time, we could not see where

The remnants of 3rd Battalion moving forward on September 18th. At far left carrying an 81mm mortar tube is Lionel "Frenchy" Morin (loader for No. 4 mortar); the next two carrying mortar tubes are Eugen Wyatt (gunner for No. 2 mortar) and John Skoglie (assistant gunner, No. 2 mortar). To his right is Orville Shipley (ammunition squad leader). (Author's collection)

the Japs were, as occasional rounds flew at us from two sides, bouncing off rocks, zinging past you.

We grabbed onto anything we could and kept moving up, tired, sweating, frustrated. We crawled up bit by bit, a foot at a time. When we finally got up there onto a level piece, we paused, looking out over the edge. We thought that we had reached the top, but sure enough, some 50 yards off, there was another ridge, higher than ours. And up there, them damn Japs had been quietly waiting for us.

After a few moments, the bastards opened up on us. Bullets began to fly all over the place, bouncing off tree trunks, logs, rocks, the ground around us.

We finally made it up close to the top, but we could not hold there, and finally we had to come down. Throughout the whole action, we got the crap beat out of us and took many casualties, as we struggled first getting up and then going down that damn mountain.

It was on that day that I found out why NCOs were given their choice of carrying a Thompson submachine gun or a 12-gauge shotgun instead of the usual M1. Me, I would eventually choose a Thompson, although some of the other guys would opt for the 12-gauge. I had thought it was just a matter of rank and privilege. On Peleliu though, I realized there was another effective reason, one that I would unconsciously use later on when we were on Okinawa.

The Thompson, I decided, makes for quite an intimidating image. As such, it makes a good enforcer for a sergeant's orders and if necessary, to "coerce" the men into following his commands—which to my way of thinking, makes those pistols that they give the officers a big mistake. As a hunter early on, I knew that a pistol was usually not a good weapon to kill with. And in combat, the larger weapon far outweighs the firepower of a pistol.

I concluded that a .45 isn't worth ten cents compared to a shotgun or a Thompson, or even an M1. As far as fighting the Japs, they might as well take those pistols and shove them up their asses. The only thing they are good for is that they're lighter and easier to carry. So what. Well, a .45 handgun might be okay to use against the Germans but it was no good against the Japs. That was because they just didn't stroll up to you: they usually came charging at you, screaming like crazy banshees. No, ours was an entirely different kind of war.

Anyway, today a sergeant from another company moving up with us pointed to a crater and told four of his men, "Alright, you sons of bitches, get in there and stay there."

The men protested. He finally waved the Thompson at them and growled at them to get in the damn crater and to hold it. They looked at the Thompson, shook their heads, and got into the crater. *That's* why our NCOs carried them.

I also think that this is why the Army came out with the M1 carbine, a shorter, lighter version of the M1 Garand.[47] The carbine was created

---

47 The main weapon of the Marine rifleman in World War II was the M1 Garand .30-06 (30-caliber round, Springfield 1906 modification). A semi-automatic rifle, it was 3 foot 7½ inches long, weighed 9½ lb, carried an 8-round clip, and fired a 3.3-inch-long cartridge at a muzzle velocity of 2,800 ft/second. Effective range was about 500 yards, although for an expert it was about 750 yards. About 4 million of them were made. In comparison, the M1 .30 carbine was a lighter version of the M1 rifle. It was shorter at only 3 foot long, weighed only 5¼ lb and fired a lighter 1.6-inch-long .30 carbine cartridge at a muzzle velocity of 1,990 ft/second.

to partially replace the .45 handgun. It is my guess that at seven yards, the average soldier cannot easily hit the enemy rushing at him, usually of being so nervous. The carbine had less potency than the handgun and the Garand, so it did not have the velocity, and the bullets, .38 specials, were jacketed. So they went right through the enemy, often without doing much damage.

By the end of the day, between all three battalions, the 1st Marines had lost another hundred men trying to take the outlying hills of Bloody Nose Ridge.[48] *Deputy General O. P. Smith described the terrain the 1st Marines were fighting up:*

> Ravines, which on the map and photographs appeared to be steep, actually had sheer cliffs, some of them 50 to 100 feet high. With nothing else on your mind but to cover the distance between two points, walking was difficult. There were dozens of caves and pillboxes worked into the noses of the ridges and up the ravines. It was very difficult to find blind spots as the caves and pillboxes were mutually supporting ... [and] housed riflemen, machine gunners, mortars, rockets, and field-pieces.

Days 5–7

In the early hours of Tuesday, we crouched in our foxholes and fought off a number of infiltrators trying to get at us, either with grenades or with their bayonets on those long sticks, like the one we had found that morning of the 16th.

The list of casualties was huge. So many that we had known were either dead, evacuated, or just plain missing. Hugh Graham, the kid I had talked to the night before the landing, had been killed by machine-gun fire on the 18th while assaulting a Jap mortar position with grenades.[49]

Carrying a 15-round magazine, it was effective at about 300 yards. Lighter but not as effective as the M1 Garand, it was designed for "specialized soldiers, such as artillerymen, airborne, or engineers." About 6½ million were made.

48 The western part of the Umurbrogol Mountain.

49 K Company commander Capt. Hunt, wrote after the war that Graham was found dead surrounded by four dead Japanese. Cpl Hugh E. Graham, Jr. posthumously received the Navy Cross for valor at Peleliu on September 18th. After his squad

On Wednesday morning, we prepared to move out again. We had no breakfast to speak of. Fires were not permitted. About all we ever ate on that damned island were K-rations. Me, all I ever ate if anything were the crackers. That was about it. My stomach was way too nervous for me to eat anything else. And water was at a premium, because of those crappy water drums they had brought ashore.

That day, we attacked again.

On Thursday, after we had given the Jap positions a preliminary shelling, we started crawling up that damn ridge in front of us. The going was sluggish, and like the last couple days, we again took fire as we very slowly pulled ourselves along this crevasse, up on tree limbs, vines, or exposed roots. At one point, I looked straight down and saw a 15-foot drop below me.

We started returning fire and then began to dig in and try to hold our positions. The enemy fire though, was coming from all around, and we were taking casualties. Like on the 18th, we stayed up there for about a half hour, until our position just became untenable. We couldn't leave the cliff without being exposed, but then again, we could not stay up there either. We were finally told to pull off the hill, so once more, we quickly and carefully went down the same way that we had come up. All the time we took fire, and a number of us were hit. What was frustrating was that we barely saw where their shots were coming from. It was hard enough to make out details in the jungle growth. And

---

leader took over command of the mortar platoon, Graham, according to his citation, "took charge of the squad and led his men through an intense barrage of hostile rifle, mortar and machine-gun fire in a bitter assault against strongly fortified enemy trenches. Fiercely hurling hand grenades, he succeeded in annihilating a Japanese mortar and its crew, then fearlessly leaped into a trench and engaged the enemy in hand-to-hand combat, inspiring his men to follow in a vigorous attack against the hostile position. Although mortally wounded during the violent close-in fighting which ensued, Corporal Graham steadfastly continued to direct his unit throughout the assault, insuring the complete destruction of the entire enemy objective before he succumbed to his wounds. His daring initiative and great personal courage in the face of grave peril were an inspiration to all his comrades, and his valiant conduct throughout was in keeping with the highest traditions of the United States Naval Service. He gallantly gave his life for his country."

the Japs were entrenched in these dugouts and well-prepared positions, blasting away at us.

And that's how it had been for us the last few days. Moving up was so exasperating. As soon as we managed to fight to the top of one slope, there was another one in front of us that was higher. And more of those damn Japs were dug in there, waiting for us.

We moved back down once more and set up for the night. We evacuated the wounded to the rear and exhausted, we lay back and rested. Most of us were too worn out to even eat our rations. One of the sergeants took a head count. Along with me, I Company was now down to about 27 guys.

Day 8

The next morning, we regrouped and just held our position. We took some sniper fire, and some artillery rounds, but mostly we just stayed where we were.

The 1st Marines had only been on Peleliu for a week, but most of us knew that our regiment was spent. We had been in combat almost constantly, and we had suffered massive casualties—55 percent. I found out later that these numbers were the worst that any Marine regiment had suffered in history. Some companies were down to just a few men; entire platoons had been wiped out.

We survivors were tired from having been pushed into action almost constantly, by day and by night, often isolated, sometimes low on ammunition, and under heavy fire. We had been subjected to terrible heat and humidity, contaminated water, and unreliable communications. We had fought a hidden enemy who only came out at night to silently slide into our shelters and slit our throats. And the worst of it was that we could not even get comfortable during the brief pauses in the action. Ever try to sleep on hard coral? And moving over it, we often cut our hands and clothes over those razor-sharp surfaces.

Finally, word came down that day that we were getting relieved.

I had been on Peleliu only seven days, and had seen more death and destruction in that time than in all my life. As a Forward Observer,

I had fought with two companies that had both been nearly wiped out. K Company had been shattered, and I Company was now down to just 22 guys. After we were told the sweet news that we were being relieved, I was told to leave I Company to go back to my mortar platoon.

I found out after the war that some navy bean counters had figured out that between us and the ships, we had averaged shooting off about sixteen hundred rounds of ammo to kill one enemy soldier.[50] That's a hell of a lot of ordnance to knock off one damn Jap.

On the afternoon of the 22nd, the Army began moving up to relieve us. The unit was the 321st Regimental Combat Team of the 81st Infantry Division.[51] As they moved in and took up our positions, we began to disengage from the enemy lines and start to withdraw. We made our way down to the beach, tired, and spent, and we looked that way. The army guys relieving us had relatively clean uniforms, and looked like they had been eating regularly. But we did not care. We were off the damn line at last.

We did not say much on the way down. There just was nothing to say. Besides, we were still in a combat zone, and you never knew if there were any stray Japs around. We quietly walked along the jungle trails like zombies, all of us lost in our thoughts. Too many of us had died on this rotten island.

As we were coming off Bloody Nose Ridge, I heard an engine. Round the bend came a Sherman tank moving up. It approached us and came alongside our unit. As I passed the tank, it stopped as the

---

50 According to one interesting source, the number of rounds expended was exactly 1,590, broken down as follows: 1,331 rounds of various .30 cal. cartridges (M1s, .30 cal. machine gun, BAR, etc.), 152 .45 cal. rounds, 69 .50 cal rounds, nine 60mm mortar rounds, five 81mm mortar rounds, one rifle grenade, ten hand grenades, six 75mm howitzer shells, five 105mm howitzer rounds, one 155mm howitzer round, and one 155mm gun round. And of course, these statistics do not include the many naval shells fired from warships, or the many bombs dropped in naval and Marine air support during the entire operation.

51 The 321st began relieving the 1st Marines on the 23rd, but it actually began the day before.

commander standing in the hatch took his bearings. I looked up at him and said hi.

He looked down at me, smiled, and said hi. Then out of nowhere, he asked me, "Hey, want a glass of tomato juice?"

I looked at him, surprised, replying eagerly, "Hell yes!"

He reached down into the tank and pulled out this container. I pulled out my cup and climbed up the side. Reaching down, he gave me a small cup of red tomato juice. I took a deep breath and then took a big swallow. Man, it tasted so good! I thanked him, and with a smile, be barked down to his crew, "Move out!"

As the tank rumbled off towards the front, my stomach began to churn. It had been in knots ever since I had come ashore, and I had been on meager rations for so long, the old gut was not used to this type of fancy nourishment. I belched once or twice, and then I started to retch. Finally, I threw up.

We moved on and eventually made it back to the beach just after dark. We were about in the area where we had first come ashore so long ago, about a hundred yards from the Point. We formed up as best we could. We were tired and worn down, both physically and mentally, and our esprit now just a faint ember as we just sat on the coral and rested for a while. I noticed that the amtrac that had been knocked out that first morning and that we had ransacked was still there. Funny though, but even with shellfire in the distance and that wreck sitting on the shoreline, the dark beach scene, with the waves lapping up onto the sand, seemed a serene backdrop. After all the carnage that we had been through, it seemed really bizarre, what I think they call surreal.

That day, I had developed another splitting headache, so I told the others that I was going to walk over to another nearby company to get a pill for the pain. John Skoglie, one of the gunners for our No. 2 mortar, looked up at me, got up and said, "I'll go with ya." He knew that it sure as hell was not safe to go anywhere on Peleliu at night.

The two of us walked down the beach to our right. We spotted a group of guys sitting about a hundred yards from that damn Point that had given us so much grief that first morning.

We walked up to them, and I asked, "Hey, you guys got a corpsman here? I need a codeine pill real bad. I got a helluva headache."

One fellow sitting down looked up at me with a tired, friendly smile. Out of the corner of my eye though, I saw another guy glance up at us and his eyes widen. He suddenly yelled, "JAP!" and pulling up his M1, he yanked back on the bolt, jamming a round into the chamber.

I was stunned, but as he began to swing his rifle towards me, his buddy quickly grabbed the weapon out of his hands.

"Stop!" he yelled. "He's a Marine," he told him firmly. The wild-eyed fellow checked his swing, looked at me and then at his buddy. His eyes went back to normal and he slowly sat down.

Skoglie and I stood there stunned as I realized what had nearly occurred. After all the crap I had been through in the last week, all that miserable heat, all the fighting I had been in, I had in the end nearly been killed by some stupid idiot that had mistaken me for a Jap. I was numb with shock.

I don't remember exactly what I said, probably mumbled something like, "Never mind," and turned round, and hustled back to my unit. The hell with the damn pill. My head still was throbbing, but I damn sure didn't need any pain pill *that* bad.

Looking back now, I can somewhat understand how the guy reacted. He had probably by then become a blabbering idiot, more than likely a mental case. I had walked up out of the dark with my jacket over my shoulders and huddled over. That must have probably set him off. But still, gawddamn ...

Skoglie and I went back to our platoon and sat down. My head was still aching, but I was pretty determined not to try to get any more medical help. The last time had been enough.

We stayed on the beach for an hour or so before we were given the word to move out. We began walking south along the shoreline. A lot of the wreckage that had been on the beach had been removed, as had nearly all the bodies from the first couple days. There were now large stacks of ammo crates and pallets of supplies.

We moved inland across the island, along the airfield, which the 5th Marines had taken, across the 7th Marines' line of advance, and onto a road past this small village,[52] towards Purple Beach at the southeastern part of the island. It seemed surreal moving through that area. And it was the only time I came across any barbed wire that the Japs had laid. We stopped long enough for our guys to lay down some more barbed wire next to theirs. I think that was the only time I ever came across a barbed-wire area. Hell, we never fiddled with that crap.

For the same reason, we rarely took our heavy machine guns along with us,[53] because we were always on the move. For us it was a matter of you get up in the morning, you eat, and then you attack. And at night, we'd set up our night perimeter and then the Japs would attack. Then the next morning we'd get up, eat again, and then try to take some more ground. And that's how it had gone for some eight days. It seemed like every day we had been on the move. So that's why we never took our heavy machine guns or stuff like barbed wire unless we got into a position and dug in and had no intention of moving for some time. But that didn't happen in this campaign, because we always concentrated on going forward, on moving on. After all, we were Marines.

Worn down, we reached Purple Beach just before dawn and were ordered to create a perimeter and dig in.

We made camp, set up some patrols, and mostly just slept, trying to recover from the nine days of hell we had just been through. The next day we rested, and they managed to make us a warm meal. Mostly it was just warm powdered eggs and potatoes. We sometimes got milk instead of water. But that was about it. No fruit, and definitely no chocolate. Purple Beach became a wonderful rest area. I guess that it had once been considered a possible landing area, but the guys in charge had in the end dismissed that idea. I think it was because there were only two roads leading out of there, and that was through these mucky mango swamps, and we would have been congested. Of course, the Japs would have had the same problems trying to get through those two trails to attack us.

---

52 Called Ngardololok, taken by the 5th Marines on September 21st.
53 George added that this included the water-cooled .30 cal machine guns.

On 27th September, an American flag-raising ceremony was conducted on Orange Beach 2, symbolizing that the island was secured. Although the battle of Peleliu would go on for another month, for the battered First Marine Division, the nightmare of Peleliu was over. The division, having lost 6,526 men,[54] would have to stay out of the war for at least five months before it again went into action.

Evacuated

We stayed on Purple Beach for about a week, trying to recover, licking our wounds, figuring out who we had lost, getting our heads together, assessing the condition we were in, and refitting.

It was near midnight on Sunday, October 1st, when we remnants of 3rd Battalion were ordered to get ready to leave the island. It was really dark, and as usual, with the heavy rains, there was no open sky for any starlight. We loaded up onto a 31-foot "duck"[55] and prepared to get underway to some ship offshore in the pitch blackness. There might have been more ducks moving out as well, but it was so dark and so quiet, we could not tell. At any rate, we did not see anything but the water around us. For all we knew, we were alone.

Once inside the duck's well, I squeezed away from the edge and made my way to the center of the boat. There I stood on the deck next to the two crewmen as they started the engine. We finished loading up, and with the coxswain at the controls, we slowly pulled back away from the beach. The duck swung round, and began chugging out in choppy

---

54 This includes casualties in the other battalions—tank, hospital, amphibious, etc. Numbers of course vary with sources. Another source puts casualties at 6,336, with 1,121 KIA, 5,142 wounded, and some 73 missing. The missing were all later ruled as dead, especially since because of the sustained heavy enemy fire, there was no chance to identify and remove many of the bodies before they drifted out into the surf and floated away, never to be seen again.

55 A misnomer pronouncement of the craft's official term, "DUKW." It was a 6½-ton amphibious transport that could carry a dozen men to and from shore. The odd term comes from the coding of the manufacturer (GMC): D because it was a 1942 design, U for utility, K for all-wheel drive, and W because the 6-wheel vehicle had dual rear axles.

waters towards the USS *Pinkney*.[56] As we navigated away from the beach in the dark, we noticed that the boat was taking on some water. We checked and found out that the bilge pump was not working. This quickly became a matter of concern, because it was a two- or three-mile ride out to the ship. Still, we had no choice but to go on, but we began to worry if we would make it before sinking.

Luckily, we reached the *Pinkney*, and pulled up next to the thick cargo net draped over her hull. We carefully prepared to climb onto the transport. Going up a cargo net is really hard to do at night, so we tried to be careful. We had no sooner come alongside the ship and started climbing up the cargo net when, to our shock, the water began to foam around the stern and it began to move. The damn thing was getting underway!

Those guys on the net jumped back down into the duck, and we began yelling up at the main deck. Our coxswain frantically began trying to maneuver us away from the moving vessel towering over us, so that we did not get pulled down into her wake. Unfortunately, as the *Pinkney* slowly began to move off, that is exactly what happened, and we drifted towards her stern. With the danger of our duck getting sucked into the

---

56 The USS *Pinkney (APH-2)* was a Tryon-class transport used throughout the Pacific war mostly as an evacuation and hospital vessel, although occasionally she was used to shuttle replacements out to forward areas. She began the Peleliu operation as an attack transport, although she later was used exclusively to evacuate wounded off the island. Originally the SS *Alcoa Corsair*, she was taken by the Navy and commissioned in May 1942 as the USS *Mercy*. She was re-commissioned five months later as the USS *Pinkney* and designated as an evacuation and medical transport. With a crew of 475, she could make up to 18 knots and carry almost 1,200 men in her compartments and wards. Like most transports, she was armed with one 5-inch/38 cal. gun on her stern, four 40mm antiaircraft twin mounts, and four 40mm anti-aircraft guns. Seriously damaged when she was hit by a kamikaze on April 28, 1945, she returned to the U.S. for repairs. In October, she returned to the Far East, carrying replacements to (now occupied) Japan, and began ferrying veterans back home. Earning six battle stars during the war, she was decommissioned in September, 1946, turned over to the Army, and converted into an AP (Auxiliary, Personnel) and renamed the USAT *Private Elden H. Johnson* (T-AP-184). She was finally sold for scrap in September 1970.

ship's propeller at any moment, seven Marines jumped over the other side and started swimming frantically away from us.

The duck swooshed across the ship's stern and over her screw, and as the boat swung round, we reached out and desperately pushed us away from the *Pinkney*'s hull. My M1 Garand was slung over my shoulder, and fearing that I might have to jump over the side like the other guys, I threw my pack off my back. When I did though, my M1 accidently slipped off my arm, hit the top edge of the duck with a clatter, bounced off the edge, and fell into the water. My ten-pound rifle that I had faithfully carried with me since the landing immediately sank down to the seabed. I cursed in the damn dark.

Slowly we began to swish out from under the *Pinkney* as it moved away. We kept yelling at the ship as she moved off into the dark, but no one above seemed to hear us. As the ship disappeared into the night, we began to circle round to pick up our guys swimming in the water.

With no other recourse, and with the duck still taking on water, we began chugging back to the beach at three or four knots, grumbling and cursing the Navy most of the way. I don't know how we did it, but we made it back without going under. We beached the duck, bailed out the water, and fixed that damn bilge pump. In the meantime, our radioman got in contact with the *Pinkney* and gave them an earful.

The ship soon turned about and came back. Still grumbling, we began chugging out into the pitch black again, and this time, everything went smoothly. The duck did not leak, we finally managed to spot the transport, maneuvered next to it, and wearily climbed up the nets without incident.

Naturally, the squids onboard were very apologetic and told us they were sorry. They just did not know that we were down there.

"Didn't you clowns hear us yelling?!?" I growled.

No, they had not over the ship's engines.

For the rest of the night, since the *Pinkney* did not have any available bunks, we sat around on the decks, jammed next to each other, with hardly room to move. At least for once it was not raining. None of that mattered though, because we were too tired to care. The sailors gave us coffee and some sandwiches, but most of us just tried to get some sleep. I dozed on and off, sitting on the afterdeck, my back against a warm bulkhead. Thank God it was all over.

We were later told that Col. Puller had been evacuated with us and was aboard the *Pinkney*. His old war wound from Guadalcanal had turned septic, and his leg had swollen up like a tree trunk. He could barely walk, he was by then feverish and in severe pain.[57] The colonel was immediately moved down to sickbay. They gave him a local anesthetic, and then the ship's doctor went to work on him. I was told that after a couple of hours on the table, the doctor finally pulled a two-inch-long slice of shrapnel out of his leg.[58]

Later that morning, Monday, October 2nd, we took on more Marines from the shore. The Navy gave us a great breakfast, and then we returned to the decks to sit and rest. At around 10 a.m., the *Pinkney* conducted a burial at sea. We Marines gathered round topside for the ceremony. There before us were laid out 15 of our comrades who had died onboard either that night or the day before. I found out that one of them was a guy from Akron, 27-year-old Walter Wade Hyler. We stood close by as our chaplain gave a short prayer. Then a bugler played taps as one by one, the board for each dead Marine's canvas-wrapped remains was tilted downward and his body slid away with a soft *shhhhht* into the ocean …

As I watched them slip down into the water one by one, I thought about their passing. It is strange what goes through your mind at times like that. At one point, I couldn't help but wonder what the canvas body

---

57 Peto remembers that when Col. Puller walked up to his crater near the beach on the afternoon of September 16th, the colonel seemed to be in good physical shape. He was not limping, nor did he show any signs of impairment. Thus, while the healed wound had already started to fester when the 1st Marines landed on the 15th, it did not become nearly unbearable until the 1st Marines were relieved.

58 According to one biographer, the colonel was given a local anesthetic, and after about an hour of surgical exploration, he found and removed a one-inch fragment that was next to the bone. The wound was left open a couple days to drain. The infection was cured and the swelling went down, and by the time the ship pulled into Pavuvu, the colonel, although still tired, was mostly his old, feisty self again, itching (literally) to get off the ship and back to his unit.

The burial at sea off Peleliu aboard the USS Pinkney, *October 3, 1944. (Author's collection)*

bags were weighted down with so that they would sink and not float. I found out later it was old shell casings.

We took on more Marines, and under the cover of dark in the early morning hours of October 4th, our ship got underway again and finally headed off towards Pavuvu. We were thankful that the hell of Peleliu was over, and that somehow we had survived. But there were a lot of our buddies we had left back there. I wondered what our next operation would be.

CHAPTER 6

Recovery

We left the waters off Peleliu and sailed southeast towards to the island of Pavuvu in the Russells, some 2,100 miles away. After a week at sea, our ship arrived there on October 10th. What was left of our battalion went ashore. We found an open area inland, recovered the gear we had left, and set up our tents. We then just sat and rested for several days. Col. Puller, much better after his leg wound was treated on the ship, naturally decided to ignore the doctor's orders to stay off his feet. We were later told that as soon as we pulled into Pavuvu and docked, he staggered out of his bunk, got dressed, hobbled off the ship with a cane despite instructions to stay in bed, and went back to commanding the regiment—well, what was left of it.

While Pavuvu had improved since we first arrived at the end of April, it was still no paradise. We had to renew our ongoing battle with the rats, the land crabs, and the bugs. Still, it was better than being in combat, and we began to recover.

As the 1st Marines began to recuperate, the men reached out to each other to determine who had survived and who had not. Small groups of three or four would visit tents in other units to see who was still alive and to talk about their experiences. The men often held small, informal wakes in the evenings and on Sundays in remembrance of those comrades who had died on Peleliu, and at the same time as a way of mentally dealing with what they had just gone through.

A few days after we had returned to Pavuvu, I decided to try to visit Rucker. He had been machine-gunned on Peleliu that second day and evacuated to the naval hospital on Banika Island, which was right across from ours. Hopefully, he had since been recovering from that wound. I wanted to see how he was doing.

It was only about 25 miles between Pavuvu and Banika, so the Navy had set up a shuttle ferry between the two islands, I took it across, and when I arrived, I saw that the hospital, even though it was only a series of tents, was well equipped and staffed. And I really mean *well* staffed, because, to my surprise, I saw several nurses. Some of them were natives—Banikan—but a few were U.S. Navy nurses.

I was stunned. I could hardly believe my eyes. It had been over a year since we had left Melbourne and its fair damsels, and we had not seen one white woman since then. So to see these American gals was like dying and going to heaven. With a smile, they directed me to Henry, and we both had big grins as we cheerfully shook hands. Henry told me that he was coming along nicely, and he introduced me to his nurse, an officer. She had obviously been taking good care of him, and the two of them had struck up a friendship. Lucky bastard.

The three of us had a nice chat. As it turns out, being a naval officer, she was allowed a ration of whiskey at the beginning of every month. Since she was not much of a drinker, she generously offered to share her ration with us. She told us to remind her at the end of the month, and if I could return, we could all party together. Henry and I looked at each other, grinned, and happily agreed. After a really great visit, I said goodbye and left the tent to return.

The ferry ran several times a day, so it was easy to hitch a ride back to Pavuvu. Today, I was going back on an LSD.[1] I got aboard and we got underway. Being the nosy type, I walked up to the bridge and began talking to the coxswain steering the ship.[2]

---

1   Possibly the USS *Gunston Hall* (LSD-5).
2   George undoubtedly means the ship's helmsman.

Curious, I wondered what it would be like to steer the ship. So I asked him, "Hey, do you mind if I try driving this thing?" He looked at me as I said, "Let me wheel that thing."

The sailor looked round, didn't see any officer, and said, "Okay."

I moved up to the wheel and he said, "Okay, you got two arrows here in front of you. Ya see them? You have to keep those two arrows lined up. You want them pointing to each other."

"Got it," I said with a grin. "Keep them together."

I took over the helm, and shook my head in wonder. As the ship began to drift off course, I would compensate, trying to keep the arrows together on the rudder indicator gauges. Finally, the coxswain, shaking his head, told me to look back. I did, and chuckled when I saw that our wake looked like some sort of a wiggly snake. Evidently, I had been overcompensating on the helm, and was zigzagging like hell.

I looked over at the coxswain who was laughing. "Well, what the hell do I do?" I asked him.

He shook his head and repeated as he laughed, "Keep the two arrows lined up!"

So I did my best, trying not to oversteer.

Suddenly from below, a deep voice (that I assumed was the Captain) bellowed, "What in the hell's going *on* up there?"

The coxswain quickly came up. "Damn! Lemme have that," and reached for the helm.

I stepped back and quickly sat down. You know, just in case the captain came up to the bridge. But he only did so near Pavuvu. Then he came up and ordered the ship to slow down to a crawl. I saw a guy walk over near the bow with a weight attached to a rope and began tossing it into the water and retrieving it. The coxswain told me they were taking depth soundings. Evidently, there were a lot of reefs around here, and there was a real concern about bottoming out. I thanked the coxswain for the adventure before I left the ship.

As we continued our refit, we did what we could to regain our health as well. Our battalion doctor was Lieutenant JG Joseph E. Christopherson.[3]

---

3   Lt. JG Christopherson, attached to the 1st Marines, won the Silver Star at Peleliu for his actions on September 16, 1944. He would win the Bronze Star for his

He was a quiet sort of guy, but we respected him, both as an officer and as a physician. Older than all of us at 35 and already an experienced doctor, his values were I guess different than those of us young enlisted Marines. He was not as coarse and he rarely cursed, and if he did, it sure as hell was not as much as us. So there he was, this navy doctor with us grimy grunts.[4] Every day he fought an ever-losing battle to try to get us to change our habits, especially our speech. Like this one time for instance soon after we had returned to the island, a few of us went in with different cuts and bruises. The favorite question the guys seemed to ask him was, "Hey Doc, how about putting some shit on this cut of mine?"

The first time he was asked, the Doc's eyebrows arched some and he didn't say anything in return. But when he had heard this a few times or so, he scowled and grumbled, "You know, all you characters who fill up my mornings with that crack are in for a big surprise. Someday, I'm gonna have a little tub of shit waiting for you, and when you ask for it, I'm gonna smear some on."

He paused and added, "Why don't you learn to say what you mean?" And then he smiled that dry smile of his.

The guy just looked at him and grinned. Naturally, his crack could not go unchallenged.

Sure enough, one of the guys grunted, "Well, who knows, doc. It might be better that the crap you're putting on us now."

As expected, that guy was told to go to the end of the line.

A week after I had visited Henry, I wrote a letter to his nurse friend to remind her of the whiskey ration agreement we had made. I knew that it would only take a few days to get there, right around the end of October. Since there was no classified information in the letter, I figured that the unit officer censoring our mail would have no problems with letting it go through.

---

actions on Okinawa. After the war, he returned to Mason City, Iowa, where he became a medical examiner for Cerro Gordo County until he died of cancer on December 28, 1964, at the age of 54.

4 Medical services in all Marine units have traditionally been (and still are) administered by U.S. Navy officers (doctors) and enlisted personnel (medics, orderlies), even in combat.

As it turned out, I was wrong. My censor I later found out was none other than our platoon leader, Lt. Haggerty, and after having read my letter and remembering my checkered past, he decided that perhaps it might not be a good idea for me to go over for that little shindig. That day came, and I had already secured my liberty pass. I dressed in my best uniform and was walking down to the dingy that would transport me over to the ferry, along with a half dozen other guys. This roundabout service was necessary because of all the submerged reefs along the shore, and a small boat could do it. As we neared the dingy, I spotted Lt. Haggerty standing on the shore next to the boat.

He put his palm up and told me, "You know, you can't go."

I looked at him, and all I could say was, "Huh?"

He said, "George, you're not going over there."

Surprised, I protested, "Whaddaya mean I can't go? I … I already got permission and everything."

"Well, you know, I got to thinking about it."

I waited in silence, stunned.

He told me he had read my letter and having thought about it, had figured out that I would possibly go over there and from a discipline standpoint, go astray. I tried to tell him that I had turned over a new leaf, but he wasn't buying any of it.

With a smile no less, he told me "You know, you're gonna go over there and yer gonna get a drink of that good whiskey, and see an American woman, and yer gonna lose it. One drink of that good whiskey and that woman will drive you off the wall, and yer gonna end up in trouble."

I tried to plead my case again, and that I needed to get over there to see Henry, but no good.

"You'll go nuts," he said, "and I don't want you to get in trouble again. You're not going." He added, "It's for your own good."

So, reluctantly, he had to cancel my second visit. But, he added, he knew that I would understand.

Bull. "Well, thanks for nothing," I growled and went back to my tent. Although looking back on it now, in his infinite wisdom, I guess that he was right at the time. Still, I was pretty PO'd at him for days. In any case, it did not make that much difference, because a week or so later, Henry came back, fit once again for duty.

Henry's return was a boost, but not just for morale. We had lost a good many men on Peleliu, and we really needed experienced Marines in the unit. Less than half of the 1st Marines who had sailed from Pavuvu had returned. With a few wounded returning to duty and a couple replacements, we still only numbered about 1,500, less than half our full strength. And in the following weeks, we lost even more as the entire division began to undergo a wide-scale reorganization. Some 4,800 of those that had served in the division since I came on were to be rotated back to the States.[5] In our regiment, most of those Marines who had fought at Guadalcanal in 1942 and had survived Peleliu were now shipped back home, having served two years overseas. That was a lot of guys: almost 50 percent of those that had survived.

Our division commander, General William Rupertus, was gone, having been relieved of command and transferred back to Washington. Well, good riddance to him. None of us had liked the grumpy bastard. His replacement came in on November 2nd, Major General Pedro A. del Valle. An artillery officer, he was no stranger to our division, since he had led the 11th Marines on Guadalcanal. After that, he had commanded the Marines' artillery in the Guam campaign. Similarly, the 1st Marines went through a command shake-up. Just after General del Valle arrived, our own commanding officer, Col. Puller, whose leg wound had acted up on him on Peleliu, was also transferred back to the States. He was popular with us, and man, were we sorry to see him go. He had always stuck up for the enlisted, and I remembered our encounter in the crater that second day on Peleliu. Puller was replaced by the regiment's executive officer, Lt. Col. Richard Ross, Jr.[6]

---

5   Some 246 officers and 5,500 enlisted that had served in the 1st Marine Division since Guadalcanal were sent home accordingly. Russell Diefenbach in his autobiography puts the number at 4,800, but that probably did not include wounded lying in hospitals.

6   On December 13th, Lt. Col. Ross, the temporary commander, was replaced by Col. Kenneth B. Chappell, who would lead the regiment onto Okinawa in April 1945.

Of the enlisted left in the regiment, I became one of the more senior NCOs. In the regiment, I was the senior forward observer.

The shakeup continued. The regiment received a whole bunch of replacements, about a few thousand,[7] and most of them were green kids that had never seen combat. As a matter of fact, many had been waiting for us there on Pavuvu when we returned. We used these new guys to refill our units. With these inexperienced recruits among us now, I stuck out even more as a senior Marine, even though I was only a few years older than them. Eventually the entire division would take on some 8,000 men.

Since I was one of the most experienced veterans in the battalion (remember, the Guadalcanal vets had been sent home), I became a sort of icon, especially since I was really getting good at my job. Groups of the new recruits would often like to engage me in conversation, just to hear tales about my life, both before the war and in combat. Sometimes, I would have fifteen or so guys around me, wanting to hear my stories, and of course things we had done on Peleliu was one of the most popular topics. Over time, the tales of my exploits spread, and at times many recruits who barely knew me would come up to me and start a conversation, just to later say that they knew George, that he was their pal.

Yet on the other hand, I usually found myself alone, moving around with a company as a rifleman until they got into position. Once I did find me a good observation spot, I could get my radioman, Bob Sprangle, to come up, and the wiremen would string a phone line for me to call in fire missions to the mortar teams. Until then though, there was no sense in dragging all that stuff around with me. So I was attached to whatever company was moving up, and until they were set and dug in, and I had found me a good spot, I was basically just a rifleman—well, certainly beefed up with my Thompson, but still a rifleman.

There on Pavuvu, I helped Haggerty reorganize the mortar teams, and we began to train with them to work together as a unit. I did sessions on map reading, disassembly of the .45 (ah, if only Haggerty would

---

7   The entire 1st Marine Division would take on another 8,000 replacements in
     preparation for the Okinawa campaign in a little over four months.

sit in on one), and stuff on the mortars. The communicators began to learn their jobs, and the phone guys practiced how to quickly string lines back to the mortar positions. We rehearsed over and over, and the better we became, the more support we could give to the troops. My radio operator, Bob Sprangle, tried to stay with me wherever I went, and I trained him how to keep our radio in good working order. Bob was some five years older than me but showed up next to me a good deal, and we got along pretty good. He had a cool temperament, and was slow to get riled. Whether it was in the middle of a bombardment or getting his ass chewed out, he maintained an even keel.

I was free to move around as I needed with any one of the companies, and once I had a radio, my call sign in the Division was "Xray," and I could communicate with anyone in the headquarters section of each of the three battalions, regiments, and even the division, as well as other attached units. I got to talk to so many people, and not just give them vital observational information, but also receive it too, which of course, made me popular with my buddies, because I was usually well informed on what was going on; that is, whenever I had contact through the field lines.

I was briefed on using secure communication techniques, especially since the Japs over time had improved their radio interception capabilities and could sometimes listen in on our conversations. So while any coordinates that they heard would mean little to them, attack plans, units, and personnel identifications and strengths would. Of course, they would have to understand English to make anything out of what we said. I sure as hell could not understand any of their Jap gibberish.

Just like I could not understand anything that those damn Indians in our division said to each other.

They were called "code talkers,"[8] and they seemed to be able to do their jobs communicating in Indian pretty good. They had joined our

8   Code talkers were Native Americans who famously served in World War II as radiomen. They were specially trained in communications to utilize their own native language to converse with each other and thus allow secure message traffic between combat units. Perhaps most famous of these were the over 400 Navajos who trained and fought with the Marines in the Pacific. Their finest performances

division around the Cape Gloucester operation, and over time, they improved their training with us. They were from the Navajo tribe, and there were always a couple of them attached to each battalion HQ unit, and a few more that worked at divisional headquarters. Naturally, whenever I heard them on the radio, I would have absolutely no idea what the hell they were saying to each other. For all I knew, they could have been talking about my mother. Still, I guess if trying to understand them drove me nuts, I could imagine what it would do to any Japs listening in.

There were two of these code talkers in our 3rd Battalion. The taller, thinner one was a guy called Dennis Cattlechaser.[9] Hell, I thought that was his nickname or his official Indian handle or something. I did not know until years later when I saw his name listed on a battalion roster for that time that Cattlechaser was actually his legal name.

These Indian radiomen had trained there on Pavuvu and now went on campaigns with us. Although I saw them around the battalion a lot, I noticed that they pretty much kept to themselves, and did not associate much with the white guys. They hung out together and did not talk much to us outsiders. Whenever they did, a lot of their conversation was just "yes" or "no," or more often than not, they just grunted as a reply or a reaction.

I will say one thing for them. Those stories that I had heard so many years ago about Indians and alcohol seemed to be true, because these guys drank whenever they could. Okay, me too, but what the hell. They would get loaded and then jibber what I figured was Indian gossip, or Indian chants. Hell, the bastards even had their own version

---

were considered to be at Iwo Jima and later at Okinawa. Not only was their obscure language impossible for the Japanese to decipher, but their rugged Western upbringing made them well suited for the harsh Pacific island climates. In addition, their culture of hunting in stealth and physical resemblance to Orientals frequently allowed them to penetrate enemy lines for short periods without being fired upon. Of course, this feature worked both ways, and thus it sometimes also made them difficult to be distinguished as being a friendly to other U.S. Marines.

9 23-year-old PFC Dennis Cattlechaser, who was from Tuba City, Arizona. He passed away on December 15, 1996.

of the Marine Corps Hymn (which drove the rest of us nuts when they sang it).

I remember one night a bunch of them Indians got loaded on some batch of jungle juice that they had either made or gotten a hold of. That night, I was hanging around with Bernie Huxel and Howard Quarty.

Now these two big guys lived about as far away from each other in the States as you could get. Bernie was from Oregon and Howard was from Long Island, and each of them was a really huge, burly fellow, about five ten. They were built like solid lumberjacks: in fact, that had been Huxel's profession before the war. Still, these two guys, although they were gruff and mean-looking, actually seemed nice fellows when you got to know them—well, Ernie was. Quarty was a boozer. He was okay when he was sober, although he had a chip on his shoulder that made him sometimes want to get into trouble when he had been drinking. He had already been married a couple times, and I think that it ate at him, making him a mean drunk. I believe that was also why he did not perform well in combat. He would fight anyone anywhere for any reason, and often started fights. But he sometimes seemed scared as hell in combat. Huxel looked out for him when he had been drinking, and the two of them had become really close buddies. I mean, they went everywhere together: wherever you saw the one, you saw the other.

So this night, I was sitting outside their tent with them, shooting the bull, when we spotted these two drunk Navajos walking unsteadily down the dirt lane between two company areas, talking their weird talk, singing Indian crap. Generally, they were being loud and obnoxious. Quarty, who sometimes liked to pick a fight, impulsively stood up, walked up to one of the Indians, picked him up, and just threw him across the lane. I saw the guy go sailing past me in the dark and land with a thud in the dirt.

Somehow, he slowly tottered to his feet and dusted himself off. Both of the Indians laughed and took of staggering down the lane. The three of us just looked at each other and shook our heads. Obviously, the Indians were as crazy as hoot owls.

On the other hand, because they were Indians, and because they seemed crazy, although the rest of us were fearless Marines, we learned that sometimes messing with them was not such a good idea. There was one time when a bunch of guys were playing a high-stakes game of craps in their tent. Dennis, who bunked there, had evidently that evening been into a fair amount of jungle juice that he and his fellow tribesmen had managed to make, and whether the experience for him had been a good one or not, he was now exhausted, and the noise from the guys playing was probably driving a spike right through his skull.

Finally, tired and probably hung over, Dennis decided that he had had enough. He got up, scuffed over to where the guys were playing, and dropped a boot right over the dice. He looked down at the guys and said tonelessly, "You go now. Dennis going to sleep."

Naturally, the guys reacted as you would expect, and started protesting.

"Cmon, Dennis! Knock off the shit! Gawddamit, this game's got a long way to go! Back off! Get out of the way, asshole!" Plus a few more choice words for effect.

The code talker though, was having none of it. He stood there with his foot on the dice. Narrowing his eyes, he repeated, "You go now. Dennis going to sleep."

The guys in the tent yelled at him again, and in even fouler language, told him to get his sorry ass off the dice and to leave them the hell alone before they beat the crap out of him.

Staring down at them, Dennis Cattlechaser simply turned and walked back to his bunk. Wordlessly, he pulled out his Thompson submachine gun from under his blanket, jammed a 20-round magazine into the bottom, and pulled back the action bolt. He walked back to the group with the muzzle pointed at them, and said again, stony-eyed, tonelessly, "You go now. Dennis going to sleep."[10]

---

10 The magazine was more than likely empty, because all live ammo is turned in to the battalion armory or the range officer when the day is over. Anyone caught with live ammo in their tent would be subject to disciplinary action. Of course, the men playing dice could not know if there were cartridges in Dennis's magazine or not.

The tent was clear in about three seconds. A few minutes later, the guys heard him snoring in his bunk.

I made sure during this time that I caught up on my letters. I was sending out quite a lot, because at the time, I was corresponding with five different women in five different towns. Lt. Haggerty, who was our censor and as such was allowed to screen our mail, got a big kick out of this. I guess that he figured I would get found out and one of them would shoot my butt when I got home.

He saw me writing to a few of them one day, and laughed. He asked, "George, how the hell are you going home to marry five different women?"

I looked up at him and laughed. "Damn, who the hell says I'm going home?" Of course, had I thought a bit about what I had said, I might not have laughed. Still, I think that by that time I had gotten used to my life in the Corps and even enjoyed most of it. And I found that I was even getting used to the combat. It was just another thing that I had to go through, waiting for my next liberty. I think that living outdoors so much had helped in that.

Being in combat as intensely as we had at Peleliu somehow had affected every one of us in one way or another, some more than others. A lot of the guys were on the edge. Several of them would panic at the littlest impulse; others just did their best to control the fear and do their jobs. Some guys just went berserk, either in combat, or afterwards. A few just quietly went haywire.

One of the guys in 1st Battalion went insane, but in a quiet, deadly sort of way. Their C Company was right next to my Headquarters Company, only about 100 yards away from us. One night, a Marine was attacked in his sleep and killed. His throat was slashed by what appeared to be a machete.

As the weeks went by, a nighttime killing happened a few more times. Every once in a while, a Marine sleeping under the mosquito net in his tent would be noiselessly slashed in the dark, hacked to pieces in the same way. Division ordered all the machetes collected, but that did not stop the nut. Two more Marines were killed, and another few were seriously slashed and eventually evacuated. None of those who survived the assault could identify the attacker.

Our command really became concerned, and each company began posting guards everywhere, walking around at night. Still, the butchery continued, although not as frequently. No one could figure out the killer's identity. Was it a Marine, one of our own? Or was it one or more Jap infiltrators? No one knew.

The guys began sleeping with one eye open, so to speak. This night-time executioner became known as the 12 o'clock Killer of Company C, and we were all uneasy about for a few weeks, wondering when—or where—the crazy bastard would attack next.

Finally, it came to a head one night when the killer decided to strike again. So once more, he grabbed his weapon—we guessed it was a machete that had not been turned in—and crept out into the night to find another victim. Unfortunately for him though, as he was skulking about, one of the guards armed with a Thompson sensed someone nearby.

The guard ordered, "Stop," and the marauder angrily charged at him brandishing his weapon, which appeared to be a large butcher's knife that the cooks used to cut meat. The guard just opened up on him and fired his whole magazine at the charging maniac. Half asleep, I heard the sound of the gunfire and thought, wow, that's a helluva lot of shooting going on. But it was too dark for us to make out anything, and no sergeant came running into our tent to get us up, so we did not get up to see what happened. Eventually, we all went back to sleep.

As it turned out, that guard stitched him good, and a couple MPs ran up to the body and fired their .45s into him as well. When they took off the killer's hood, they found out that the guy was one of C Company's mess cooks, and his weapon of choice was confirmed to be one of his butcher's knives. There were no more killings after that.[11]

Unknowingly, I had crossed paths with this crazy bastard a few days before his demise. He had always been somewhat of a fruitcake, and really did not have any friends. He had this habit of periodically walking

11 Russell Diefenbach added that the killer was also the division's boxing champion from the 5th Marines. A story based on the killer of Company C was written by Edward Slaughter and published in the February 1958 issue of *Male* magazine.

up and down the road between the company units and hollering nutty crap to the guys. On this day, I was walking with two of my buddies, the battalion Jolly Green Giants who went everywhere together—Bernie Huxel and Howard Quarty. The cook approached us, mentally in his own crazy world, snotty, oblivious, quirky, cursing and making nasty remarks. We stopped and watched him as he strolled by; he looked at us and made some smart-assed insult.

I was feeling sort of brave with my two giant buddies on each side of me, so I glared at him and replied, "Ah, you sonuvabitch, screw you. Yer crazier than hell."

The cook stopped, turned around and angrily stared at me, but seeing my two big friends, just glared, and kept on going.

Of course, I had no idea at the time that this was our mad killer. Had I known who he was, I sure as hell would have kept my mouth shut. And I suppose that it is just as well that they stopped him permanently a couple nights later, because in hindsight, I have a feeling I had made his list.

As the months went by, we began training again for the next operation. The senior NCOs like Henry and me did what we could to help the new kids along, trying to pass on what skills we had learned at Cape Gloucester and Peleliu. Looking back on those days now, I sometimes wonder what our motivation was. I certainly knew that the more trained these kids would be, the better all our chances of staying alive. On the other hand, having seen what we had at Peleliu, and with the upcoming operation promising to be just as bloody, many of us veterans, including those like me who had been lucky so far to have not been hurt, had resigned ourselves to the fact that we were probably going to die before it was all over. I was pretty sure that I would not see home again, although at that point, many of us had forgotten what home was like. Nor did I train day after day out of patriotism. Not really. As far as I was concerned, there was just no room for that flag-waving crap in a combat zone.

We received some more replacements. Some were green kids we had to train. Some like Bill Mikel, had been in for a while and were only now getting assigned to a combat unit. Funny thing, Bill initially was a quiet guy and did not say much. He told me why after the war. When he got orders to transfer to the First Marine Division, it scared the hell out of him. He had heard so many horror stories about us, and not knowing what to expect, it had really unnerved him.

I suppose we all had our reasons for diligently sticking to our training and improving our efficiency. I think at that point for me a good part of it was just a case of hating those Jap bastards. They had started this damn war, and they were the reason I was over here. All the misery we had experienced was their fault, and I was going to make sure some of them paid for that. So as far as I was concerned, it was easy to blame them and, from what I had seen, to hate them.

There was, of course, our Marine bonding as well, and that I feel was a key to all our motivation: the feelings we had for each other, for our comrades in combat, for our fellow Marines. It is something quite hard to explain to those who have never experienced the feeling of intense camaraderie and esprit in the Corps.

Six months after Peleliu, the word came down that we were about to saddle up and move out. The months of training were over, and each unit in the division was back to its peak efficiency. The replacements had learned well, and our morale was back up to where it should be.

We were ready.

CHAPTER 7

Okinawa

The final decision to invade Okinawa, part of the Ryukyu Islands, had been made back in early October 1944. Seizure of these islands would not only take the war right to the front doorsteps of the Japanese home islands, but it would also cut supply and communication lines to the rest of the Pacific. Okinawa, with its three main airfields, would also provide a base for a large bombing campaign against Japan, as well as serving as a springboard for the eventual invasion of the Japanese mainland, which was only 400 miles away.

Okinawa is one of the largest of the 200 Ryukyu Islands. Some 60 miles long, running roughly north–south, its average width is only 10 miles, and only 18 miles wide at the broadest part, the Motobu Peninsula.

The Okinawa invasion, like Iwo Jima, was planned as a huge, elaborate operation. The main landings would be preceded by the 77th Infantry Division securing the Kerama Islands, located about 10 miles west of the southern part of the island, at the end of March. On April 1st, this division would land on the lower west side of Okinawa itself and drive inland, the Sixth Marine Division to the north securing the beachhead's left flank, the First Marine Division to its right, the Seventh Marine Division below and to the south of it, and the 96th Infantry Division on the far right flank. The Sixth Marine Division on the left was to drive northward up the island, while the First Marine Division moved across the island and cut it in two. The Seventh Marine Division and the 96th Infantry Division were to pivot right and drive southward. The operational reserve included the 27th Infantry Division and if needed, the 81st Infantry Division could quickly be brought into the area for additional support.

In addition, on the other side of the island at the southeastern tip, the Second Marine Division was to make a feinted landing to draw enemy forces down the island to defend that beach. The Marines were then to withdraw and go round the island to support the main landing. The landings would be prefaced by a series of carrier strikes in February and March, and no less than eight days of severe pounding by a full surface fire support task force, which would also then remain to support the landings. Landing with the Marines would be a whole wide scope of specialized weapons and units, varying from flame- and fire-throwing equipment to new types of heavy weapons and fire support.

Many of the mistakes of Peleliu had been learned.

On Thursday, March 1, 1945, the First Marine Division began a week of amphibious training exercises for the Okinawa invasion. The units were taken to Banika Island and embarked for landing rehearsals, at Tassafaronga on Guadalcanal. For days, the Marines, supported by the Navy, practiced landing exercises and coordination logistical operations. Five days later, on Tuesday, March 6, 1945, a full-scale dress rehearsal of the landing took place. George Peto's unit, the 1st Marines, did not participate, but stood ready as the division reserve. At the end of the day, the rest of the division returned to the Russell Islands, and on Wednesday, March 7th, the 1st Marines had their own landing exercise, before returning to the Russell Islands. (The reason for the two dress rehearsals was twofold: first, the 1st Marines were not slated to go ashore in the initial waves, like the 5th and 7th Marines; second, there simply were not enough landing craft available to accommodate all three regiments simultaneously.)

On February 27, 1945, 3rd Battalion boarded the USS *New Kent*,[1] bound for Banika. It was an okay ship as ships go, not dirty or anything, but the heat below was almost unbearable, and most of us preferred to stay

---

1   The USS *New Kent* (PA-217) was a Haskell-class attack transport commissioned in mid-November 1944 in Richmond, California. She could make 18 knots, and in addition to a crew of 525, she could carry 1,600 troops into battle, as well as about 3,000 tons of cargo. She was armed with an open 5-inch/38 cal. gun on her stern, and carried four 40mm twin-mount antiaircraft guns and ten 20mm Oerlikon light guns. She went into mothballs in the fall of 1958, and in late October 1971, she was sold for scrap.

on deck. We soon put into Banika, and the next day, we practiced up and down cargo nets and into LCVPs.

Now climbing up or down a cargo net is a tricky thing if there are any appreciable waves, basically anything over a foot high. Going down is risky because starting off, you are pretty high up off the craft you are getting into. A slip at the top could kill you. And once you have gone over the side of the ship and are starting down the net, you have to be really careful, which is not easy when you are packing a heavy weapon, your gear, and ammo. And you have to not only be careful not to step on the hands of the guy below you, but also to make sure the guy above you does not step on yours. When you get to the right level, you have to wait for the boat to hit a wave crest before jumping down into it. Jump too soon, and you could fracture a bone. Jump too late as the boat is going down, and you could break something as well.

Going up a cargo net is not easy either. You have to time the swells and make sure that you grab onto the net when the landing craft reaches the crest of a wave. And when you grab, man, you better have a solid grip, because the landing craft will quickly drop down below you as the wave dips, leaving you hanging until you get your feet planted in the net. Conversely, if you grab the net at the middle of a swell, or worse, at the bottom of one, after you grab on, the boat will rise up and smash you in the butt. Then once you are on the cargo net, you are committed, one way or the other, because if you fall, you'll either break a leg dropping into the boat—assuming you land feet first; if you don't you're screwed—or worse, plummet into the water and be crushed between the ship and the landing craft. Yeah, going up a cargo net is a tricky thing …

The next day, March 1st, back aboard the *New Kent*, we left Banika and sailed over to Guadalcanal. There we took part in more training, more cargo net exercises, and weapons drills.

We did have one fun day. While hiking around, we found a watermelon patch. Some of the melons were ripe, and seemed to promise some good munching. The bad news though, was that there was an armed sentry guarding the lot. So the next day, as we were approaching it, I told Lt. Murphy to hold off and wait until the sentry walked down to the other end of the patch. Then I would slip down into the streambed next to it and sneak in. The group could go on, and when they came back past the patch that afternoon, I could jump back into the line. Skoglie wanted to go too, and Murphy smiled and said he would cover for us.

We approached the watermelon patch, and as the guard started off the other way, Skoglie and I slipped out of formation, crawled down into the stream bottom, and snuck into the field as the guys went on. After they left, Skoglie and I, careful of course to not be noticed by the sentry, dug into the watermelons. Man oh man, were they good. We spent the rest of the morning and part of the afternoon there, eating. We enjoyed them watermelons all damn day, laying out, resting. Hours later, we hid a bunch of them, thinking that we would come back later and get them. When our group came back in the late afternoon, we slipped out of the field, and down into the streambed. As the guys passed in single file, we rejoined the ranks.

As things turned out, we were relocated to another area and could not get back to retrieve the watermelons. However, Harry Owens (whose name alphabetically came before mine, so he was always in front of me), who had been the gunner on the No. 4 Mortar at Peleliu and had been promoted to be the platoon's ammo sergeant, did go back (although we never knew it at the time) and retrieved the stash. (At our 2006 reunion, and a few months before he died, Frenchy told me that he had gone back for our melons. Feeling guilty all these years, he offered to pay me back for them. I laughed and told him it was no big deal.)

On Wednesday, March 7th, the regiment conducted a full-scale mock landing. We got back into those damn Higgins boats and hit that Guadalcanal shore. It actually seemed strange to be landing and not getting fired on.

The next day, we sailed back to Pavuvu again and got there that evening. We immediately began loading equipment and supplies for the real deal. Jeeps, ammo carts, rations, water containers, shelters—all of it went over to the ships and down into their cargo holds. Priority was simple and efficient: the Navy used the LIFO process—last in, first off.

We made sure that the last stuff loaded aboard was the most important, and therefore would be the first things offloaded at the beachhead.

The next Monday, March 12th, we left Pavuvu again and sailed back to Banika. We put in there that night, and anchored up for a couple days, before sailing off to the Ulithi Atoll[2] on March 15th. We spent several days at sea, and I passed the time reading pocket mystery books that you could pick up for a quarter. The ship had some, and so did some other guys. One of my favorite series was Perry Mason. I would sit on the deck with my back against the equipment and just read about one case after another. I think that Perry's sense of duty for fairness and justice was something that struck a chord in me. I must have read over a dozen. Strange, but I had not read anything that thoroughly in years, not even the funnies.

On the night of Wednesday, March 21st after almost a week at sea, our convoy put in to Ulithi. It was pitch dark as we dropped anchor about a hundred yards offshore, and we all turned in.

The next morning we were in for a shock. After chow we went on deck, and as far as the eye could see were dozens of ships of all shapes and sizes. It was a massive fleet—battleships, cruisers, destroyers, transports, landing ships, hospital ships—and we just marveled at the awesome power of the Navy. One of the most amazing sights was the aircraft carrier USS *Franklin*,[3] anchored on our port side. Word was that she had been conducting carrier strikes some fifty miles off Japan just two days ago, and that she had taken a beating when a Jap bomber had popped up out of the sky and clobbered her. Under escort, she had limped back here to Ulithi.[4] Looking at her now, we could tell that she

---

2   Located in the Caroline Islands.

3   The *Franklin* (CV-13), commissioned January 31, 1944, was an Essex-class fleet carrier. Some 875 feet long, she could make 33 knots and hold up to 100 aircraft. She had been in a number of operations, including air support for the 1st Marine Division on Peleliu.

4   In the process of getting ready to launch over 30 more fueled aircraft warming up in the early dawn, the *Franklin* was attacked by a single torpedo bomber and hit by two 550-lb. bombs that penetrated her hangar areas, where another 22 aircraft were being readied for takeoff. The resulting explosions and fires resulted in over

was a mess. There were at least three good-sized holes in her hull, and you could actually see light through them. The island was burnt black and her flight deck—if you could still call it that—was off at an angle. We were told that they were still taking off dead and wounded. I sure as hell felt sorry for whoever had been on her when that attack had come.

The following day, they assembled us on the main deck and gave us an overview briefing on what was coming up for us. We were told that this upcoming landing was going to be a really important one. We were going to invade one of the Japanese home islands, one called Okinawa. This was going to be a huge operation.

For the next few days, we were allowed to go ashore to take it easy and to get some rest before the big show. Besides, there was not much trouble that we would be able to get into, because there was nowhere else for us to go. Ulithi was a really small, narrow strip of land. Every day we got a good look over the rails at the hundreds of ships at anchor, and like us, they all had to anchor offshore, since there were no docks.

As part of our pre-invasion rest, purely as a morale thing, the command decided to throw a big beer party on the 25th. Both the Navy and the Marines were included. There was plenty of good chow, and happily for the enlisted, a lot of beer. For us Marines, who had not had any alcohol for months, it only took a few beers to give us a buzz. For some four hours, for both sailors and Marines alike, we ate, guzzled beer, and played some ball. Naturally, after drinking like fish, we returned to the ship half blasted, and as you might expect, some fights broke out with the swabbies. We claimed later that the sailors began throwing us overboard as we came up over the cargo nets, and the Marines of course reciprocated. It was a real donnybrook for a while, until the officers and the senior NCOs from both sides finally managed to break up the fights and get order restored. Luckily, no one thrown over had fallen onto a landing craft, although several guys had sores from how they landed in the water. Still there were no major injuries.

Obviously, there would be no more picnics or beer parties. Well, I figured, what the hell. We were going into combat anyway. Besides,

---

one thousand casualties. Taking on a 13° list, she was towed out of the area and eventually, on her own steam, crawled back to Ulithi to undergo temporary repairs before proceeding back to Pearl Harbor, and eventually, Brooklyn.

truth be known, if there hadn't been sailors there, we would probably have found some army pukes to brawl with. And if there hadn't been any of them around, there would have probably been fights between the different regiments. Hey, I mean, a party is a party, right?

Along with the rest of the fleet, our ship, the *New Kent* weighed anchor and left Ulithi on the morning of March 27, 1945, headed for Okinawa. I passed the time reading pocket mystery books. One of my favorite series was Perry Mason. I would sit on the deck with my back against the equipment and just read about one case after another. I must have read a dozen of them.

Once in a while, I would just stand at the rails and watch our convoy move through the water, wondering what the future would bring. I saw a lot of flying fish. Every once in a while, a whole school of them, some 15 to 20 would go flying up out of the water all at once. They would rise up about ten feet and sail along for about a hundred yards or so, kind of drying up there, before dropping back into the ocean.

The Japanese were aware of the American fleet approaching the Ryukyus, but could do little to stop it outside of a few lackluster air attacks, which did some damage, but nothing serious. The weather though, began to be a factor as a typhoon approached the fleet. Some of the task units had to change their course, and there was a mounting concern among the senior officers that the storm would delay the invasion. This caused some confusion as well, because the task groups were now approaching the area on different courses than the ones originally planned. Thus, several of them were out of position as they arrived at the invasion area. These problems though were mostly minor. The storm did not directly move into the area, and on March 25th, the amphibious support force began shelling the island of Okinawa. Battleships, cruisers, destroyers, destroyer escorts, landing ships with rockets, all began pounding positions on the island.

Because of the storm, the convoys for the landing forces had modified their final approaches, and as a result of an extended effort, nearly all would be in position and ready for the invasion on the evening before the landing.

We began our final preparations as we got nearer to the island. There were more briefings. The good news we were told was that this would not be some half-baked operation like Peleliu had been. Instead of one

Marine division hitting the beach, the Japs were going to get hit with four Marine divisions and two army divisions. In addition, another army division would be in reserve to assist us if needed. The bad news was that there were a hell of a lot more Japs on this island than there had been on Peleliu, or even Iwo Jima. No, this was going to be one tough nut to crack.

We were told that this time though, we had the full support of the Navy behind us, and that even as we sat at the docks waiting to sail, they had already been pounding the beaches for over a week.

It was suggested to us that we cut our hair before we went in. That way, if you got a head wound, it would be easier to treat. So a lot of us got our heads trimmed, usually by each other. And let me tell you, none of these guys were what you would consider a good barber. But what the hell, this wasn't going to be a beauty contest. Our morale remained high, although, again looking back, I somehow sensed that things were a bit different than before. The carnage and savagery of Peleliu had done that, and the 1st Marines, I thought, would never be the same again.

You could tell a difference in this trip. Unlike our time at sea when we were on the way to Peleliu, the men now were subdued, quiet. There was very little laughter in the passageways, and our Marine cockiness that we had carried around boastfully in previous operations was now noticeably absent. And personally, I had a bad feeling about this operation, a feeling of some kind of impending doom that I could not shake. I knew that this would be a long bloody invasion, and those damn Japs would be even more fanatic. I mean, you did not have to be a brain surgeon to see that the closer we got to their homeland, the higher our casualties. They were still mopping up on Iwo Jima, and if half the stuff that was being printed and even a quarter of the scuttlebutt about that landing were true, we sure as hell were going to be in for quite a beating, no matter how big our forces were.

Gone were the days of those suicidal Japanese banzai attacks where those little bastards came screaming at us by the hundreds. Now the little shits were dug in, sheltered in reinforced underground caves joined by dozens of intricate tunnels, and just waiting for the Americans. Now they sat in interconnected fortified bunkers, well-supplied fortifications that they had been able to stock and strengthen over three years. And they crouched in the dark in them now, drinking sake, patiently waiting for us.

We had been given quite a number of replacements, and the new guys looked up to me, trusted in me, and thought that, since I had survived three campaigns without a scratch, maybe I had all the answers on how to survive in battle. How could I explain to these kids that I did not have much to tell them? Just use common sense, and hope that you would make it through alive? There were several times when a new guy wanted to have a one-on-one conversation with me, to either directly or somehow indirectly, pick my brain and find out those magical secrets of survival.

My simple advice to them was the same: obey your damn orders, constantly stay alert, don't make stupid mistakes like poking your head up at the wrong time or running around during a shelling, and to always remember what curiosity did to that cat. And I would usually finish up by telling them that in the end, much of it just depended on blind luck, on being at the right place at the right time.

I remember a few weeks after we landed, one of these new young fellows came up to me on one of the slopes and greeted me like I was his long lost brother. He proudly showed me his helmet that had bullet hole in the side. Evidently, the bullet had penetrated the metal and had spun round his head without penetrating his skull. He smiled at me as he showed me where the bullet had gone in, as proud of that damn helmet as he would be of a fine, award-winning Irish setter. Poor kid. That hole had probably used up half his luck in the operation. I never saw him again after that. He was probably killed and is buried under one of them simple, little white crosses on the island, keeping company other buddies of mine killed there.

As we began to get closer to our objective, the weather started to turn bad. Our transport began to pitch and roll in the heavy seas, and many of the guys became ill. I was fine though, and a few times I went up on deck to get some fresh air. I remember seeing some destroyers steaming on our port side, struggling even more than us to make headway. The one closest caught our interest, because evidently it had picked up a

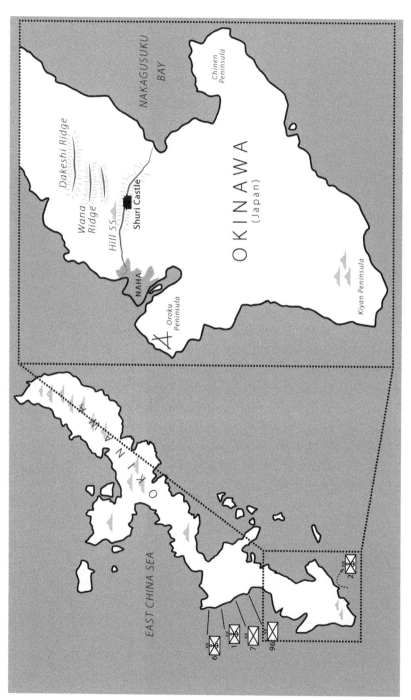

The invasion of Okinawa.

couple of escorts of its own. Leading the destroyer some fifty yards in front were these two dolphins. Periodically on a wave crest they would sail up out of the water, glide through the air for about twenty yards, and then slide back into the ocean again, with the ship following behind them. Fascinated, I must have watched them for a half hour or so before going below. That afternoon, I went up on deck again, and soon spotted them, still leading that tin can. I just shook my head in wonder and watched those dolphins having a great time.

I tried as much as I could to stay on deck during the rough weather and avoid going below. Conditions down there were pretty bad, especially in the mess hall, where you would see a lot of food spilled on the floor, making it difficult walking. It was a struggle just standing in line, waiting for your grub, and when you finally did, it was a challenge to get to a seat. You had to time your walk to a table so that you didn't go swerving off to one side or another, hoping that a really big roll didn't come.

The mess tables were wet from stuff spilled before. Every time the ship dipped into a deep trough, it would roll a bit, one way or the other, and trays and coffee cups would go sliding. If the guys sitting down didn't grab them, they'd end up on the deck. You sometimes had to lean one way or the other to compensate for a roll. You tried to get a quick spoonful of food in before a bad dip or a really big wave came and had to grab onto your tray. I usually ended up eating standing up, and somehow, I would manage to get most of my chow down.

Naturally, a lot of the guys got sick, and they tried like the dickens to make sure they did their thing in the head, or at least puke in the passageway, away from where we were eating. Still, the stench was pretty bad, and all in all, it was just one hell of a mess. We ended up eating as fast as we could and getting the hell out of there. Personally, I think they should have just served sandwiches or simple stuff, and held off making formal meals like that until the weather got better. Luckily, it was the swabbies who had to clean up the mess.

The weather finally let up, and at the end of March, we pulled into the invasion area and dropped anchor.

Tomorrow, it would be our turn.

The Landing—April 1st & 2nd

The invasion of Okinawa began in the pre-dawn hours of Easter Sunday, April 1, 1945 with the Allied fleet of some 1,300 vessels offshore, most of them to the island's west in the East China Sea. The weather was now perfect. It was a nice 75 degrees, with a brisk east-northeast breeze, visibility about ten miles.

For a week before the landing, Admiral Oldendorf's naval bombardment task force had pounded the island, firing some 13,000 heavy caliber shells (6- to 16-inch), and another 5,000 5-inch and 3-inch shells—which amounted to over 5,100 tons of ammunition.

Today, just after 0400, the commander of the supporting Task Force 51, Admiral Richmond K. Turner, signaled, "Land the Landing Force," and an hour and a half later, the huge naval support force of ten old battleships,[5] nine cruisers, 23 destroyers, and 177 gunboats once again began the pre-H-Hour bombardment of the beaches. Thousands more naval shells, rockets, and mortar rounds hit the island, a powerful naval bombardment that altogether actually exceeded that laid down before the Normandy landings. (Interestingly, three battleships, the USS Arkansas BB-33, USS Nevada BB-36, and USS Texas BB-35 were at both invasions.) At the same time, some 70 miles to the east, Carrier Task Force 58 was deployed to furnish air support and to intercept any attacks from the Japanese Home Islands.

The bombardment continued through sunup at 0620, and at 0745, additional tactical bombers from support carriers attached to the invasion force hit the island with bombs and a new weapon, napalm.

Finally, at 0830, while the Second Marine Division made a feint landing to the southeast of the island to draw off enemy units, the first waves of two Marine divisions and two army infantry divisions hit the beaches to the west of the island, followed by a wave of medium tanks. The men stormed ashore and discovered to their surprise that resistance was minimal. Those moving up the beaches found

---

5   Of the 17 OBBs in commission at the start of the war, only 13 remained active by the spring of 1945 (not including the USS *Wyoming*, which had been redesignated a Gunnery Training Vessel). While these vessels were inferior to those constructed during the war (although at the night battle of Surigao Straits on October 25, 1944, six of these vessels had decimated a large Japanese surface force), they still made excellent gun platforms that could well be used for amphibious gunfire support. As such, especially after being refitted, they played an essential role as primary naval gunfire support in all of the Allied amphibious operations.

the topography of the island was a welcome relief from the hot sweltering tropics and swamps of the islands in the Central Pacific. Here, the land was dry and green with regular trees (even pine trees) with a nice cool breeze coming in off the ocean. Maybe Okinawa would be different. Maybe it would not be the prolonged intensive battle that many were worried about. Maybe this would be an easy operation, and that attacking the Japanese on the day of the Lord's resurrection would be good for the Americans. It was though, also April Fool's Day.

On the morning of April 1st, long before dawn, I woke up to the sound of hundreds of these naval guns bombarding the island. Our 1st Marines were the immediate reserve for the initial landing, since we had taken the brunt of the initial punishment at Peleliu. So we were not slated to go ashore until late in the afternoon. Reveille was at 6 a.m. (although we were all awake by then), and mess call was a half hour later. As usual, the Navy gave us a good breakfast send-off of steak and eggs. After that, some of us went topside and watched the shelling with the sun coming up. We kept looking over the rail as we saw the first landing craft of the 5th and 7th Marines headed for the beach in front of us, with the 4th Marines and 22nd Marines to our far left. Over on the right were more landing craft as the Army began putting ashore two more divisions, the 7th and the 96th.

A while later, we heard over the loudspeaker: "Now hear this, now hear this. Good news from the beaches. Resistance is light, casualties are few … This is official from the beaches. Beachmasters have established landing party areas and stock points for supplies and material. Resistance consists of a few mortars and artillery shelling, and scattered small pockets of enemy troops."

We cheered. Maybe this would not be so bad after all. Coming ashore certainly was a helluva lot easier that it had been at Peleliu. We talked about it. Our guys had charged ashore, ready for the worst, and to their shock, the joke was on us. Enemy resistance was negligent. A couple shots here and there, and that was it. No Japs anywhere. It was like eagerly going to the dance and finding out that the band did not show up. After all that preparation, too. Surprisingly, despite the feelings of foreboding I had had earlier, I found myself feeling somewhat cheated. I had been looking forward to helping a few more of those Japs meet their maker. Well, the operation had just started. I told myself that there would be plenty of opportunity to get at them little bastards as we moved inland.

Man oh man, would that turn out to be an understatement.

Because I was an NCO now, I had been allowed to trade in my M1 Garand for some heavier firepower. The weapon I procured was an old-style Thompson submachine gun, model M1928A1. Unlike the later military version, this one had a neat-looking Cutts compensator over the barrel tip, with four fins on top.[6] Also, it had below the barrel a vertical wooden pistol grip in front. For combat, this was not as practical as the later models with a horizontal hand grip below the barrel, which acted as a hand guard against burns from a hot barrel. The Marines found that the wooden pistol grip was not as rugged as the handgrip and more susceptible to damage if a Marine hit the dirt and slammed the gun onto the ground. But man, what style!

When I first received the Thompson on Pavuvu, it came with the newer-style, standard-issue 20-round rectangular magazine.[7] Because I wanted more firepower, and probably because I had a bit of a flair for the theatrical, I decided I wanted one of those old-style 50-round circular drums, like those mobsters used to carry in the old Roaring Twenties. The drum was a bit heavier and a little noisier than the 20-round magazine that most other NCOs carried, but I felt that having those extra 30 rounds when I needed them would come in

---

6   The Cutts compensator, created by a couple Marine Corps officers who happened to be father and son, was designed as a recoil brake. The four vent fins at the top allowed part of the energy from the muzzle blast to be discharged upwards, somewhat counteracting the effect of the recoil, and allowing the weapon to be better controlled regarding muzzle climb when fired.

7   As a rule of thumb, if the cartridge case has no spring and does not feed the cartridge directly into the firing chamber, it is considered a clip. An example is the M1. The clip carries two columns of four cartridges, and the entire assembly is loaded into the rifle (when the last cartridge is fired, the clip is automatically expelled). If the cartridge container holds the bullets under pressure using a spring mechanism (which makes loading easier), and with it, feeds each bullet into the firing chamber, it is considered a magazine.

81 MORTAR PLATOON ROSTER 1945

	ORIGINAL ROSTER	REPLACEMENTS & ROSTER CHANGES			
	APRIL 1st to MAY 8th	5/8 to 5/11	5/12 to 6/3	6/3 to 6/21	6/22 to 8/14
1st LT. -	HAGGERTY	- HAGGERTY	- HAGGERTY	- HAGGERTY	- HAGGERTY
2nd LT. -	MURPHY	- MURPHY (W)	- BEALL	- BEALL (W) *	- BEALL
GUNNY -	GIDDONS	- GIDDONS ***	- BARRETT	- BARRETT	- BARRETT
PLT SGT -	WYATT	- WYATT (W)	- HOPGOOD	- HOPGOOD	- HOPGOOD
PLT SGT -	SKOGLIE	- SKOGLIE	- SKOGLIE	- SKOGLIE	- SKOGLIE
AMMO SGT-	OWENS	- OWENS	- OWENS	- OWENS	- OWENS
O.P. SECTION					
SGT. -	PETO	- PETO	- PETO	- PETO	- PETO
CPL. -	RUCKER (K)	- GOOD (K)	-	-	-
OBS. -	DAWSON	- DAWSON	- DAWSON	- DAWSON	- DAWSON
OBS. -	KUS	- KUS	- KUS	- KUS	- KUS
OBS. -	ACREE	- ACREE	- ACREE	- ACREE	- ACREE
OBS. -	McGUIRE	- McGUIRE (K)	- CELLI	- CELLI	- CELLI
1st GUN SQUAD					
GUN CPT -	LAMB	- LAMB (W)	- P.JONES	- P.JONES	- P.JONES
GUNNER -	MIKEL (W)	- DURANTE (W)	- R. KELLEY *	- R.KELLEY	- R.KELLEY
ASST. -	C.KELLEY (W)	- AVANTS	- HAYS (H)	- COMPTON	- COMPTON
LOADER -	DURANTE	- BERCEAU (W)	- COMPTON	- CONNORS	- CONNORS
4th MAN -	DWYER (K)	- H.JOHNSON (W)	- CONNORS	- H.JOHNSON *	- H.JOHNSON
5th MAN -	RAMIREZ (W)	- PIESKE (W)	- KEENER	- HTM JOHNSON	- RAMIREZ **
2nd GUN SQUAD					
GUN CPT -	LANDY	- LANDY (K)	- MIKEL *	- MIKEL	- MIKEL
GUNNER -	MILBURN	- MILBURN (W)	- AVANTS	- AVANTS	- AVANTS
ASST. -	HALEY (H)	- BROUSSARD (W)	- FRENCHIC	- FRENCHIC	- FRENCHIC
LOADER -	BROUSSARD	- E.HERMAN (K)	- DiRADO	- DiRADO	- DURANTE **
4th MAN -	E.HERMAN	- POLLOCK (W)	- HTM JOHNSON	- POLLOCK *	- DRECKMAN
5th MAN -	HTM JOHNSON	- HTM JOHNSON	- DRECKMAN	- DRECKMAN	- MILBURN **
3rd GUN SQUAD					
GUN CPT -	HUXEL	- HUXEL	- HUXEL	- HUXEL	- HUXEL
GUNNER -	DIEFENBACH	- DIEFENBACH (W)	- ESTES	- ESTES	- ESTES
ASST. -	ESTES	- ESTES	- ATHEY	- ATHEY	- ATHEY
LOADER -	CROOKS	- CROOKS (W)	- RADTKE	- RADTKE	- RADTKE
4th MAN -	HURST	- HURST (K)	- RIMMER	- RIMMER	- RIMMER
5th MAN -	McAVOY	- McAVOY (W)	- SCOTT	- SCOTT (H)	- CROOKS **
4th GUN SQUAD					
GUN CPT -	P.JONES	- P.JONES	- LEISHMAN (W)	- LYNCH	- LYNCH
GUNNER -	LEISHMAN	- LEISHMAN	- LYNCH	- C.JONES	- C.JONES
ASST. -	R.KELLEY (W)	- LYNCH	- C.JONES	- GEHRET	- GEHRET
LOADER -	LYNCH	- HAYS	- GEHRET	- GILMORE	- GILMORE
4th MAN -	HAYS	- COMPTON	- GILMORE	- GAYNESS	- GAYNESS
5th MAN -	COMPTON	- C.JONES	- GAYNESS	- J.NIXON	- J.NIXON

(W) - WOUNDED   (K) - KILLED   (H) - HOSPITALIZED
* - RETURNED TO ACTION - LT. BEALL, R.KELLEY, H. JOHNSON, MIKEL, POLLOCK
** - RETURNED TO DUTY LATER - RAMIREZ, DURANTE, MILBURN, CROOKS
*** - PROMOTED AND SENT STATESIDE - GIDDONS

Roster of 3rd Battalion's mortar platoon on Okinawa. (Author's collection).

handy. Still, I always carried a couple of the 20-round magazines with me as well, just in case.

I immediately went down to the divisional armament center and asked the procurement sergeant there if I could trade my standard magazine in for a drum. He was an agreeable sort, and they had been essentially told that for the upcoming operation to give us whatever we felt that we needed. So he agreed and went back, found a drum package, and slid it over the counter.

Thinking of Henry, I decided to push my luck. I asked him if I could get me a second for my buddy as well, for his Thompson. The sergeant looked at me, sighed, and said okay. I walked back to my tent with two drums. Even though I now sported that cool Thompson, I knew that it still always paid to have a backup, so I usually carried an M1 carbine as well. Not as potent as the Garand, but lighter, and it would do in a pinch.

We had noon chow aboard the *New Kent*, and after that we assembled on deck to move out. They wanted to get the regiment ashore before nightfall, so that we could dig in and prepare a defense. We began moving down the cargo nets onto the waiting boats below, and thank goodness, I did not fall. I was not though, lucky enough to get a landing craft, and I ended up having to jump down into a 35-foot whale boat, with a pointed bow, just like those we had trained in months ago. What the hell?

We started for the beach, and then, more bad luck: our boat skidded onto a submerged rock and ran right up the damn thing. After the prop spun freely for a few seconds, the coxswain stopped the motor. We just sat there, stuck, helpless, and open to any enemy artillery that wanted to take a shot at us. Luckily, the landing had gone well, and no Jap shells came over. Still, we must have sat on that damned reef for over a couple hours before another boat came by and pulled us free. Luckily, the boat had not sprung any leaks, so we went back to the ship.

Starting on the evening of April 1st and through the morning hours, Japanese aircraft launched a massive air attack against the American ships off Okinawa. The Japanese used both new and old aircraft in the raids, and some of the aircraft actually took off from fields on Okinawa. As the planes flew in towards the U.S. ships in the dark, they split up into single aircraft to present harder targets, and then made individual attacks. Damaged were two old Pearl Harbor survivors, USS West Virginia *and USS* Tennessee. *The British aircraft carrier HMS* Indefatigable *was hit by a kamikaze crashing into the base of her island superstructure, but fortunately, the bomb the plane was carrying did not go off, and damage was minimal. Also damaged were two transports, two LSTs, and two other vessels.*

We stayed on the *New Kent* that night. Sometime after dark, the ships in the harbor sounded general quarters. Evidently, there were a couple air raids coming in. I immediately went up to the main deck. I could see the sailors going to general quarters. A Jap air raid meant one thing: kamikazes. In response to that, the transports and the LSTs began to make smoke to mask their positions from the Japs. I didn't even know that LSTs could do that like a destroyer does, but evidently they could, because there it was coming out of them, just billowing out over the bay. Since we were anchored and not underway, it just puffed all around us in a dark, smelly cloud bank.[8] It was thick, too, and we choked a lot. Of course, it was worse below decks. Luckily, we did not witness any kamikazes that night, although I had seen a couple diving on our ships in the days before.

Early the next morning, April 2nd, we prepared again to go ashore. We had chow, and then went up to the main deck. We loaded up and began moving down the cargo nets onto the waiting boats below. Again, that 35-foot whale boat, with the pointed bow.

We started off for the beach, and this time, we went right in. We finally hit shore just before 1 p.m. The boat went up and beached. The whale boat had no ramp or anything, so we had to climb over the side. One of our sergeants stepped out of the boat and landed in a chest-deep hole. Carrying a lot of equipment and ammo, he went straight down into it. A few moments later, he came up sputtering, with seaweed over his shoulders. We laughed our butts off, and he cursed and yelled at us to get ashore.

I stepped out of the boat, waded through shallow water, and walked onto the sandy beach of Okinawa. At long last, I was ashore.

We assembled into our units. As with the guys the day before, we encountered no resistance. We organized there on the beach into the evening and then dug in. What surprised us was that, unlike the hotter

8   Ships either generated smoke by a) a simple device to infuse fuel-oil spray into the hot exhaust going up the vessel's smokestack, b) burning oil off special stern burners, or c) in some cases by special chemical smoke generators. The former made for a heavy dark grey smoke, while the latter created a much denser, white smoke. The smoke screens created by these amphibious ships were of the first type.

than hell temperatures of most the islands we had been on, that first night on Okinawa was actually cold. We hadn't prepared for that big a temperature change clothing-wise, and a lot of us ended up huddling in threes just to stay warm.

In the days following the invasion, thousands of destitute civilians on the island were homeless, in shock over the weeks of massive preliminary barrages and aerial attacks, the enormity of the American invasion, and the rapidity of their advance. Finding themselves caught in the middle of a savage battle, they immediately sought refuge in the safety of the American military's civilian control centers. Frantic and with their families and a few possessions in tow, they came to the Americans by the thousands for protection.

To accommodate these refugees and move them out of local stockades and put them out of harm's way, the U.S. military government officials swiftly began to build larger enclosed areas in villages or population centers under American control and that had not been totally destroyed. For example, just four days after the invasion began, there were over 1,500 civilians penned in in a barbed-wire stockade just south of Kadena, just to the east of the 7th Infantry Division's landing area. They were to be moved by truck ten miles southeast to Shimabuku, where they would be able to freely move around within the perimeter established by the Americans. Similarly, other refugee stockade areas were being evacuated to safer areas.

The next day, as we prepared to move inland, we spotted some civilian Okinawans walking around, dazed and lost. I remember there was this old grandma and her grandson, about five years old. The old lady looked like she was scared shitless, because when we spoke to her, she looked as though she thought sure as hell that we were going to kill her. You know, they had heard so many terrible things about us Americans. So this lady started crying her eyes out, talking incessantly in her language. We could not understand her, but you could tell that she was begging us not to kill her or the boy.

Eventually, Lt. Haggerty came up and tried to console her. She was still plenty frightened though, and stayed that way until we could get an interpreter. Through him, Haggerty told her that she and the boy would not be harmed. But you could see that she did not trust us. Finally, we took them to the rear, where they were put into a large enclosure. After a while, they had so many of them, this detainment camp would become a little city. I remember passing there some four weeks later as we moved down towards the combat area, and the enclosure was just full of folks.

It stayed cold that day, and we only had our green dungaree jackets to stay warm. We shivered as we moved on. We actually saw a few snow flurries the second evening, while we were dressed for summer. Our blood was thin from the tropical heat that we had been used to. That night, we had to dig into some hillsides to get out of the breeze. I was sure as hell glad that the damn Japs were not shooting at us.

We moved across the island in the next few days, but we only encountered scattered resistance and hundreds of refugees. Like at Cape Gloucester, the damn rain was frequent. Since we were now in combat, the hammocks we had been able to rig off the ground back then were now out of the question. We had to prepare defensive positions every night, complete with foxhole. With it raining so much, we often found ourselves sleeping in soggy holes, which of course, the bugs loved.

It was around this time that I contracted something called dengue fever.[9] I caught it while sleeping in foxholes half filled with water. I came down with a temperature and ached every time I moved. I was pretty much out of it for three or four days with cramps and a high fever. I had the scoots, and felt just terrible. All I could do was crouch in my watery foxhole every day, sweating with chills, puking my guts out. How the hell I survived it I'll never know. I guess that I was just too stubborn. I absolutely refused to go back to the medics, because I knew that if I did, they would have shipped me out. By then staying until the end had become a personal thing. Despite the horrors of this campaign, in some ways, I was having way too much excitement to leave just yet.

---

9   Dengue fever is an agonizing, incapacitating disease contracted by a mosquito bite that can be fatal. A virus related to West Nile and yellow fever, it is commonly contracted in the Pacific Islands, Southeast Asia, and Latin America. Symptoms include headaches, fever, vomiting, cramps, loose bladder, pain in muscles, and a rash. As yet, there is no effective vaccine to prevent getting infected from a bite.

So I suffered there for a few days, sick, throwing up, having the runs, before I started to feel better. Although the intermittent sounds of combat and explosions remained steady throughout the day, we had been out of action for a couple days. So I guess I had gotten sick at the right time—or the wrong time, depending on how you looked at it.

As I was starting to recover, I began to be able to get up for short periods of time. As least I had the strength to go somewhere else to crap, what with having diarrhea and all. So now this one afternoon, I gathered up enough energy to get up. It had not rained for a day or so, but the ground was still damp. I told the guys that I was going to wander off and do my business, so that they would not shoot me as a Jap when I wandered back.

I walked out about thirty yards or so to this ditch, squatted down, and started to do my thing. Off in the distance, I could hear artillery fire. Ours or theirs; I didn't know. All I know is that I really had to go.

I had just finished and was buttoning up when this massive explosion went off and slammed me against the side of the ditch. Straightening up, I started to hear what sounded like cow piles falling and hitting the ground. I slowly climbed out of the ditch, but looking around, I didn't see anything. So I made my way back to my foxhole, settled in, and got some shuteye.

The next morning, I was starting to feel better. I checked in with my platoon and was on my way back to my foxhole when, looking over at a plateau, I saw about fifty yards away this crater in an open field, one that might once have been a garden or something. This crater was huge—I mean, you could have driven a 10-ton truck into it. I decided that this must have been where that bomb or whatever had hit yesterday when I was in the ditch. Whatever had fired that shell, I sure as hell wanted nothing to do with it.

A couple hours later, I was on my way back to my foxhole from what was my first hot meal in a week, when suddenly, I heard in the distance a noise that was like nothing I had ever heard before. It was a *whooshing* sort of rocket sound that seemed to be getting louder and nearer. A shell of some kind, I guessed, but this thing sounded big and seemed to be propelling itself. Some kind of missile, maybe? And as it flew closer, it sounded like it was headed right towards *me*.

As weak as I was, I hit the ground and closed my eyes as this big bomb or whatever the hell it was came roaring down. It slammed into the ground about a quarter mile away with a tremendous detonation that rumbled the earth. Just like the one I had heard the day before. And in the distance, I could see stuff falling all around. I looked up and saw dirt and debris that had been thrown up by the explosion. I remembered what I had thought were cow piles falling around me yesterday, and I made the connection. Same weapon.

A couple minutes later, I heard another one coming in, but at a distance. Looking into the sky, I could actually see it coming down. It was some sort of Jap rocket that I figured by looking at it had to be heavier than a jeep. Judging by its speed, size, and trajectory, I figured that it couldn't have had a range of more than a mile or so. I could actually see it coming over, wobbling as it spiraled down and falling slowly, sort of like a miss-thrown football. You could almost outrun the damn thing it if you saw it coming in. Like the first one, it hit the ground with an explosive thud, and even at a distance, I felt the earth tremble.

I saw a couple more of these things come over at us, and boy, when they hit … It was obvious that these things had no accuracy, but damn, they were massive as hell.[10]

---

10   The weapon George refers to might have been a Japanese 320mm "Spigot" mortar, which fired a shell of 650 lb. It also possibly could have been a Type-4 400mm rocket mortar. The barrels were 10½ feet long, and the rocket-propelled 500-lb. shells could be fired to a range of just over two miles off a special metal rail. Judging strictly on his description though, he probably had been fired on by a 447mm (17.6-inch) rocket mortar. This weapon had to be fired off a 12-foot wooden rail assembly and only had a range of about a mile. The shell, as he described, was highly imprecise and very unsteady in flight. The warhead though was massive, a staggering 1,500 lb, and the shell's impact as expected made a huge crater. While this third choice seems to be the most likely weapon, most historical documents reported this mortar as only having been used in the Luzon and Iwo Jima campaigns.

On the night of April 14th, I had guard duty from midnight to 2 a.m. I assumed the watch in a foxhole on our perimeter with a new top-secret toy: something called a snooperscope.[11] It was some sort of special night-vision scope mounted on a special M1 carbine, and we could use it to see Japs trying to crawl up on us in the dark. Unfortunately, I found it clumsy to use, and hard to see into the forest. We had practiced with them aboard ship a couple times, and when we did, we could make out individuals clear enough in the night. In the thick jungle though, everything was just flipping around, and it was really difficult to make anything out. Nevertheless, I studied the jungle, looking for anything that I could make out.

Around 2 a.m., I was finally relieved, in every sense of the word. Worn out and still sick, I staggered from the foxhole and shook my head, my eyeballs rolling. I crawled back to my own wet foxhole and scrunched in for some sleep. That night we had a really hard rain, and it came down heavy for hours. I was so tired and delirious though, that I just slept right through it. When daylight came, I woke up to see a half dozen guys standing over me, staring down and laughing.

Soaked, I looked up at them and grumbled sarcastically, "What the hell is everybody laughing at?"

"We're laughing at you, dumbass."

I looked around and realized why they were laughing. I had been rel-atively comfortable sleeping in the warm downpour, lying there curled

---

11 The RCA-developed M1 Snooperscope came out in 1943. This was a modi-fied M1 Sniperscope with a primitive infrared scope and a handle in front of the clip. The 6-lb. assembly consisted of a 6-volt circular light with an infrared filter mounted on the front of an M1 Model T-3 carbine just below the front of the stock. The viewer was a modified scope mounted atop the carbine in traditional fashion, but with special brackets. Both the light and viewer were powered by a 16-lb. battery and power supply that the rifleman carried in a backpack. The scope was activated by an on-off switch on the stock and took a half minute to warm up. A modified version, the M2, came out in 1944, and about 150 were sent overseas to the Pacific. Many were used in the Okinawa campaign. On a clear night, it could effectively light up a night scene up to 120 yards away. The weapon was credited as being effective in decreasing the amount of Japanese infiltration into American lines.

up on my back as my foxhole had slowly filled with rainwater during the night. Now, only my neck and head were out of the water, my head resting on the dirt at the edge of the hole.

I grinned sheepishly and stood up, water running down my uniform. After a couple cracks about my sleeping habits, one of them said, "Oh, by the way, we just got word that Roosevelt died."

So, the president was dead. I was surprised, but not too emotional about it. I felt sorry for him that he had not lived long enough to see us victorious. However, I did not dwell on it at the time, as I had other things to deal with, like just trying to stay alive.

Those first two weeks in April, we had seen several more kamikazes come down and try to crash into our ships offshore. A few days later though, we saw one up close. Right around sunset, we spotted this Jap Tony[12] flying low. As he approached us, we took aim at him with our weapons. Surprisingly though, he didn't fire at us. Instead, he just wagged his wings, and as he flew thirty or forty feet over us, we saw him wave in the cockpit. He flew on for a bit and then crash-landed on a nearby river bank.

Surprised, we ran over to the crash site, and as we came up to it, we saw the pilot trying to burn his papers. We took him into custody and, surprisingly, he spoke English. It turned out he had gone to UCLA and earned a degree before the war. He told us that he was a kamikaze pilot who had decided not to die for the Emperor after all. His mission was to dive onto one of our ships, but he figured that living was a better deal. They did not give him enough fuel to make it back to Japan. So the next best thing, he figured, was to crash near us and be taken prisoner.

We stripped him and held him for a while, talking to him. He, of course, was very friendly, and told us about the shortages of salt and sugar back home, and how Tokyo was getting burned up from all the

---

12 Allied designator for the Kawasaki Ki-61 Hien ("flying swallow") Japanese fighter. It was nicknamed "Tony" (all Japanese fighters were given male names; bombers generally were given girls' names) because when it was first encountered by Allied pilots, it was thought that they were Italian in origin. About 3,100 Tony fighters were produced.

bombings. Finally, one of our interpreters arrived with a couple guards and took him away. So much for dealing with the Jap air force.

May 1st

Until April 21st, as the Sixth Marine Division pushed northward, General del Valle's First Marine Division, encountering little resistance, moved eastward until they reached Chimu Bay on the other side of the island. A few days later, after General Buckner's Tenth Army received a bloody nose approaching the fortified Shuri line in the south, the division was ordered to turn southwest and moved down to take over the western flank of the Tenth Army in its southern offensive. The Marines would be in place by May and fully engaged a couple days later.

The last week in April, we were ordered to start moving south. Until then, we had mostly been in reserve and had not seen much action; just a few skirmishes. At the end of April though, it would pretty much start hitting the fan. On the 30th, we relieved the 27th Division and began patrolling southward, where most of the remaining Japs were on the island. That day, as we moved into position, we took some light artillery and mortar fire. Nothing serious though.

That late afternoon, 3rd Battalion, after relieving 2nd Battalion of the 106th Infantry, attacked a town called Miyagusuku.[13] That very first evening we lost a couple guys. The GIs of the 27th had assured us that the village, which was just ahead of us, had been secured. We were a little leery, but as we had not found any Japs in our area, we for the most part took their word for it. Still, we sent a patrol in to make sure that the town was clear. As we suspected, they got caught in a firefight, and two of our guys were killed.

Some of our Shermans moved up and began blasting the village. Our heavy mortars had already set up by then, so as the FO, I rang up the mortar team and called in a fire mission. I told them to use white

---

13 Located about a mile inland from the Okinawan west coast and just inland of the Machinato airfield.

phosphorus,[14] and directing their fire, I made sure we systematically worked over the entire village. The phosphorus shells started fires in the structures, and the huts burnt up, as well as the Japs inside of them. Sure enough, the next day, when I Company went through the village, no shots were fired at any of us.

However, as soon as we cleared the southern end of the village, we caught hell from enemy machine guns and mortars. We took two dozen casualties, before our guys pulled back. I called in covering fire.

May 2nd

On Wednesday, May 2nd, we renewed our attack as we moved southwest across a draw, with our battalion to the left of 1st Battalion and east of the airfield.[15] Our guys met stiff resistance, and we took many casualties that day. I set myself up a couple of times in advantageous spots and directed our mortars on the Jap slopes.

That afternoon, I set out to find me another OP. I wanted to try to spot the location of a damn 150mm artillery piece that was harassing us. By finding where the hell that artillery was, I hopefully would be able to call in our mortars on it.

I moved forward with the assistant platoon leader, Lt. Murphy. It was just the two of as we went down about 80 yards on the other side of a cliff. We found this outcrop and on it was a six-foot circle of stacked coral about two feet high. The two of us worked our way over it and sat down. Below us was broken countryside. There was no

---

14 White phosphorus (WP) is a tactical chemical weapon primarily used to illuminate a target if exploded in the air, or to provide a smoke screen to hide movement or visibility if exploded on the ground. The chemical spontaneously ignites when exposed to the oxygen in the atmosphere, and as it quickly burns, it gives off intense heat and a dense white smoke. It also makes an effective incendiary, because it burns as long as it is in contact with the air, and often was used as such in the war. Contact with the burning fragments caused terrible, intensive burns on the human body. In wartime situations, it was often used for that purpose of taking out enemy positions as well. (Note: The Army used the slang term "Willy Peter" during Vietnam, but the term was not used in World War II.)

15 Machinato airfield.

one around us as our artillery sent shells over our heads behind the distance hills in front of us, while the Japs returned fire over to our side. I could see several draws ahead of me where the enemy might advance on us, and I thought right away that this was a good place for an OP. I settled in and called in by walkie-talkie, made a radio check, and made contact with my mortars. It was a good observation spot, but we were totally isolated, and Lt. Murphy was not crazy about the location.

He looked over at me, nervous as hell, and said, "You know, they could overrun us here. There ain't no one here but you and me."

I looked over at him, held up my Thompson and said, "What the hell you think I got this here for?"

"Yeah, but George, it's just you and me here," he repeated. He was trying every way in the world to convince me to leave that OP.

We sat there in silence. I was ready to call in a fire mission, but there were no targets in front of us. Murphy though, must have imagined that they were about to swarm us. After a few more moments, he shook his head and said, ""Let's get out of here. Let's go back."

Finally I told him, "Lieutenant, this is my job!"

"Yeah," he said, "well when that fire lifts, we're gonna get overrun."

Stubbornly, I told him, "Well, my job's up here."

He thought about that and replied, "I say we get outa here."

Frustrated, I told him bluntly, "Look, you wanna go back, go back."

As I thought he would, Murphy figured out some damn way to get out of there. He mumbled something about checking the lines and took off. Now I was alone.

I shook my head, lay down flat on the ground facing in, and got on the field phone. I made contact with communicator Bob Johnson and was telling him to hook me up with the guns so that I could get ready to call in a fire mission if I needed to. Suddenly above me, I heard this shell coming in, and I instinctively could tell it was going to be damned close. I'm telling you, it sounded like a big old friggin' train coming in, and this one was headed right for me. I knew it was gonna hit nearby, and so I started to scrunch down and braced myself.

Sure enough, that shell hit the embankment right behind me with a tremendous explosion that shook the ground. One piece of the blasted coral hit me on the backside as a part of the embankment collapsed and buried me.[16] A big shell, it must have been a 150mm, probably from that same son of a bitching gun that was shelling us. I had known that sooner or later, I was going to get hit from an incoming shell, but damn, this one was a real humdinger.

Groggy, my head spinning, I slowly began to dig myself out from the coral pieces. I looked down, I saw that while the receiver was still in my hand, the wire had been totally severed, and the rest of the field phone was nowhere to be seen.

With dust and smoke in the air, I dug myself out completely and carefully stood up. I shook the coral pieces off me, looking around. Covered with dust and now useless without the rest of the field phone, I staggered back up the ridge towards the rear, amazed that I could still walk at all. Uncertain on my feet, I slowly made my way back to the mortars, unaware that I still had that stupid receiver still in my hand.

Bob Johnson, who had been on the other end of the line, had heard through his receiver that shell coming in, and when it hit and contact with me was lost, he right away assumed that I had been killed. He told everyone around him, "I heard a shell coming and Peto got hit. He's dead."

So when I came walking back, stumbling in, hurting all over and looking like ghost, Bob saw me and understandably looked surprised. "Hell man, yer supposed to be dead," he told me.

I looked at him and said, "The *hell* you say!"

Another guy saw me and said, "Hey, we just heard you was dead!"

I looked at him, aching all over and said, "Man, I feel like it."

A few days later as we moved forward, I spotted that damn 150mm gun. It was at the base of this fortified cave bunker that had two thick iron doors and a set of rails going in. Evidently, the Japs would open the doors, somehow wheel the gun out, fire a half dozen rounds, and then wheel it back into the cave. It had been knocked out and its mounting

---

16 George believed that the back trouble he had for decades is attributed to this incident.

was broken. I saw it there off its tracks, lying to one side. This thing was huge, like a locomotive with a massive barrel coming out of it. I was damn glad we had finally blown it up.

May 3rd

In the early afternoon of Thursday, May 3rd, the action had let up, so some of the guys in the mortar platoon were resting in a clearing at the rear. There was some occasional enemy artillery, but nothing hitting close. Seven guys were relaxing under this big tree. With them was my buddy Henry Rucker. I was glad. Even though he was an FO like me, and these days acted as my replacement whenever needed, I knew that he had gone through a lot in the regiment over the last couple years. Because of that, and the fact that both Haggerty and I liked him, we preferred that he stay back with the mortars, rather than on the line. And anyway, I did my job much better when I was alone.

Now as I headed forward to find me a new OP, I saw all of these guys sitting there as I went by. What a target, I thought. I walked up to them sitting there, and shook my head. I yelled at them, "Damn. Spread out! You guys are all bunched up. One shell could get all of ya."

All seven of those guys looked up at me and laughed. They started giving me a bunch of crap, telling me, "Aw, we're fine," and "Go screw yerself."

Idiots. I shook my head, turned around and started to walk away, headed towards the front.

I had only gone about a couple dozen steps, starting up a ridge, when I heard this big round coming in. I stopped and hit the ground. I wriggled around to see it land real close, as I heard this deafening *Ka-WOOM* and the ground shook. I realized that the shell had fallen right onto that group of guys. It actually went off next to Henry Rucker, although I did not realize that immediately. The whole top of the big tree they had been sitting under had been blasted by the explosion and was gone now. The guys below all looked pretty bad.

I ran towards the nearest crypt. We had taken out the corpses and were using it as a combination bomb shelter. We had also set it up as a temporary command cave, and our officers were sitting in there. I ran in and told them, "You guys better get out here right away. We got some problems. I think a big one landed on some of our guys and they've been hit."

Just then, another Marine burst into the tomb and said simply, "Rucker's one of those that got the worst of it. He's dying."

My jaw dropped, and I immediately turned round and made a beeline to him. The platoon assistant, Lt. Murphy, happened to be sitting at the opening. Now Murphy was a big old bastard and had been a football player before the war. As I got to the entrance, he immediately stood up, put his open hand out, and gave me a big shove, knocking me backwards. I glared at him as he said, "Don't go out there. Don't go look at him." Evidently Murphy was afraid that I would go out and crack up seeing Henry. Which I would not have. I would have taken it in stride. I mean, I understood what was going on. Murphy thought he was doing me a favor, but he had read me wrong. Still, I did what he said and sat there, frustrated, concerned, my mind racing.

Henry had been a really close buddy since my early days in the Corps on Hope Island. We had had both entered the service about the same time and had enjoyed each other's company for many months, me being a Yankee from Ohio, and Henry a rebel from South Carolina. On and off for some two and a half years we had served together, laughed together, gotten drunk together. Poor old Rucker had been dealt a lot of bad luck during that time and had been in the hospital a lot over here in the Pacific. There had been that bad case of scrub typhus on Goodenough Island that had almost killed him. And then he had been machine-gunned on Peleliu the second day and had spent a couple months recovering from that.

Now he had been hit by this damn Jap shell out in the open and was dying as I sat there. They were going to quickly evacuate him to the rear. Just like when he had caught that scrub typhus on Goodenough Island; and later when I had seen him lying so pathetically on that cot in that hospital; and later when I had heard he had been hit on Peleliu; I now, once again, figured that I would never see my friend again.

The word of the hit eventually came to us. The shell had taken out all seven of those Marines. Three of them, William Nixon, Verle Lawrence, and Harry Bodong, had been killed instantly. Another, Charlie Kelley, the No. 1 Gun assistant gunner, had his foot blown off, and it was only hanging by a thin piece of skin. Bill Mikel took his Ka-Bar, cut the foot loose, gave it a pitch, and tried to slow the blood flow. Kelly though, wanted that foot back. He thought the doctors could sew it back on. "I ain't going nowhere without my foot," he growled. So they found it and put it in the stretcher with him.

John Dwyer died a short time later. Another guy, McAvoy, lost his leg as well. Rucker I knew had been badly wounded. I was later told that he had been hit internally, and that he had begged someone to cut him open because the internal pressure in his abdomen was tremendous and very painful. Giddens, now our platoon's gunny, had cut off Henry's web belt with his Ka-Bar, and that had relieved most of the pressure. Our two medics, Crowe and Romero, had then loaded Henry up onto a jeep ambulance that had come up and had gotten him out of there real quick.

I found out two days later that poor Henry died aboard the hospital ship the next day, May 4th. Supposedly, Lt. Haggerty had initially said with wonder, "I thought I was saving him, removing him from harm's way, and I sent him to his death." Still, he never made that comment to me, and I know for sure that Haggerty did not blame himself for Henry's death. Neither did I. We both knew that it was just the fortunes of war.

There was no time for us to mourn. The fighting went on. We moved up about 300 yards and dug in.

Isolation sets in

On the 6th, we were ordered to support 2nd Battalion's assault on what they called Hill 60. All morning long, along with 2nd Battalion's mortars, I called in fire missions on the enemy reverse slopes. When the tanks arrived at 2 p.m., they went in. Our coordinated attack was great, and the Japs were taken out in less than an hour. What we didn't know though, was that there were plenty more hiding in nearby caves and tunnels, and as they kept coming out, our guys started to take more casualties. I covered for them as they finally had to withdraw.

Sometime after Rucker had bought it, I dimly realized (but didn't give a damn about it) that my attitude towards everything was changing. While not a particularly lucky fellow, Henry—the guys used to call him "Boots"—had been popular, and he and I had been close. We had gone through so much together, both in battle and on liberty. We had enjoyed life together, and now he was dead.

I thought about how growing up, I had been such an optimist on life, taking life on, always ready to laugh at things. Henry's dying really affected me. The future looked dark, and my view on life at that point changed. I was not sure now who this new George Peto was, but I was fairly certain that I did not like his situation.

To make matters worse, I was really getting worn out, physically and mentally. When it wasn't raining or drizzling, we were getting shot at. The long periods of combat were starting to pile up, and like a lot of the older veterans, I found myself wondering when it was going to be my turn to die. It was no longer a matter of probably not or possibly, but one of plain when.

And the artillery ... the damn artillery.

I swear, from the time we went into combat at the end of April until the third week of June, it seemed like the artillery was going off every hour. If it wasn't theirs, it was ours. Boom, boom, boom. Heavier detonations, lighter ones. Artillery, mortars, bombs. At all hours, especially during the day. Incessantly, sometimes constantly. Most far away, but many nearby, and quite a few daggone close. After a few weeks, that really played on your nerves. How the hell we tolerated it I didn't know. And so many of our guys simply did not. They sometimes went yelling off into the woods, or just broke down and cried.

Too many of our friends like Henry were now gone. As a result, more and more, I began to stick to myself, and did not talk much to the guys. That was especially true for the replacements; even though a couple of them were nice guys, I avoided them. My fear of course was that if I did get close to them—especially the new recruits, who had a much greater penchant for getting killed—and if they got themselves killed, it would affect me even more.

At one time, I met these two new replacements. We talked some and just shot the bull, laughing. I soon found myself really enjoying their company. When I left them though, something in the back of my mind hit me like a bang. Would they get it soon? I mean, they were green as hell. Would they make it?

That's what went through my mind. Don't get friendly with them, I said to myself. Don't get to liking them. They may get killed. So after that I just avoided them. I made sure I never saw them again. It was a shame too, because they were a couple real nice guys, and I was one of those that made friends easy. But I did not want the pain of making new friends and then losing them the next day. Just like Hugh Graham, that night on LST 227 before we invaded Peleliu: we had just met and quickly made friends and spent the night talking, sharing our memories of Ohio. Then he was killed the next day.

So after that, I ignored them. I more or less stuck to myself. I did my job and talked mission to those I worked with, but that was about it. I became sullen, and started to socially isolate myself from the others. I mean, most of them were new guys anyway. And at night, alone, the more I thought about it, the more I mentally detached myself from the guys. I would look at them and see so many new faces. So many of my original buddies were gone after Peleliu, Cape Gloucester, and up until now in this damn operation on Okinawa. These had been guys that I had joked with, fought with, cursed with, gone on liberty and gotten drunk with, shared rations with in some remote jungle ...

I would sometimes sit in my foxhole at night and sigh, thinking about them, sometimes seeing their faces in my mind. So many of them now were either dead, badly wounded and repatriated, or transferred back to the States, like the Guadalcanal guys. Looking out now over a dim fire, I saw in the shadows new faces. Many of them were kids right out of boot camp; fellows that I did not know or barely knew. Most of them were guys I had not shared the excitement, the horrors of war with.

As the days went on, now not caring about much except doing my job, I became much more daring in combat. I actually started looking for trouble. I volunteered to be the first in line for any mission. If there was a chance for us to go out and shoot some SOBs, I was the first one up. And sometimes I took unnecessary risks to get my job done. My attitude was definitely skewed at that time.

My depression deepened even more when a week later, I found out
that another close buddy, Elbert Kinser, had been killed by a Japanese
grenade.[17] Elbert and I had been good friends. We had come across the
Pacific on the *Wharton* together. He had been a close friend of Henry
and me since Samoa in March of 1943, and together, we had gone
through some fun times in Melbourne. Later, we had fought together
on New Guinea. Now, just like Henry, he was dead.

Yes, I definitely changed after Rucker died. I decided that I did not
want any more friends. The kid who once loved life and smiled all the
time was now always unhappy with a constant frown on his face.

Around May 7th, we paused between actions and began stocking up on
supplies. I was standing on a ridge, and looking out towards the ocean.
I could see the fleet sitting there, and I could faintly hear off in the
distance the sounds of general quarters going off. That meant another
Jap air raid, which meant more kamikazes. I could see supplies being
ferried to the beaches as Jap planes flew high overhead and began diving.
I watched them as they aimed for the ships. So the small craft I guess
were safe. One or two planes would make it through the curtain of flak
and crash into their targets, each with a faint boom and a fiery cloud.

I was watching them when I heard a couple shells explode behind
me some distance away. Then a couple more came in. It finally dawned
on me that these sounded like they were navy shells, probably 5 inch.

---

17 Sgt. Elbert Luther Kinser, once with K Company, was killed on May 4th as a
platoon leader in I Company. Moving along a ridge with his men, they were suddenly attacked by Japanese on the reverse slope tossing grenades, and they quickly
became engaged in an exchange of grenades. He was cited for bravery for jumping
on an incoming grenade and absorbing the shock of the explosion to protect his
men. Buried in the 1st Marine Division cemetery on Okinawa, he was posthumously awarded the Congressional Medal of Honor. The medal was presented
in his home town of Greenville on July 4, 1946 to his parents by Col. Clifton B.
Cates, who commanded the 1st Marines in Guadalcanal (and who would go on
to become the Marine Corps Commandant in January 1948). Also attending was
the Tennessee governor, Jim N. McCord. Kinser's body was later reinterred to the
Solomon Lutheran Cemetery in Greeneville. The Marine logistical base Camp
Kinser on Okinawa is named after him.

Certainly not 8-inch gunfire from the cruisers, or 14-inch from the battlewagons. I knew what they sounded like. So that meant that the shelling was most likely coming from one of our own destroyers. Hell, we were getting shot at by our *own* guys. Friendly fire. Luckily, he had the range wrong (well, for now), or was shooting at the kamikazes and missing.

I cursed the damn Navy, shook my head, and looking around, figured that I'd better play it safe and go the hell over onto the other side. So I started over the top of the ridge to the landward side, and therefore get out of the way of their trajectory. I had just gone over the top when a couple of rounds exploded on the other side of our ridge, the ocean side. That meant that they were coming from Jap artillery. So which side of the ridge should I be on? Luckily, none of the shells came too close.

Since we had temporarily been taken off the line, we continued to try to recover, reorganize, and resupply our platoon. It was drizzling again (it seemed like it was always raining) that day when this new guy walked into our area. He was wearing a poncho and of course, had no insignia of rank, because none of us ever wore any. This stranger just walked up to where I was leaning against this tree and just started talking to me. So we chatted a bit.

He started to ask me all kinds of questions about this and that. I figured he was a nobody like me, so I freely told him how I would run the war. He mostly stayed quiet and intently listened to everything that I said. I figured that he was a new arrival. Maybe he was an MP or something, or even a noncom, someone that had just come ashore, and so he wanted the scoop on what was going on. I told him what I knew.

Then he asked me what the guys at the front were thinking. Hell, what better guy to ask than me? I was an FO that was pretty much in the know. I was not attached to any rifle company, and went around from one to another, getting information for our heavy mortars. Wherever I went, I had with me one of those big reliable 300 radios.[18] Unlike those pieces of crap we had been given on Peleliu, this was a big mobile field

---

18   The 38-lb. 40-channel Motorola SCR-300 (Signal Corps Radio, Model 300) was a versatile mobile field radio. Much more effective than the unreliable 6 lb. "spam can" (SCR-536; Stockman p.25), it had a range of some 3 miles, and could last

phone. When I got on it, with my call sign "Xray," I could get on the net and talk to any unit in the division. I nearly always had the scoop on what was going on, and as I had happily learned, that made my job one of the best in the battalion.

I figured that I knew exactly how to win the war, and I told him what I would do. Hell, we must have talked about ten minutes and I told him all sorts of stuff. If I ran this outfit, I would do this and that, and I sure as hell wouldn't do the other thing. If I was in charge, I would do this before an attack, and I would hit the Japs like this … He kept pumping me, and I freely kept giving him my opinion on any number of things.

Finally, another guy came up to us, and when I looked at him, I was surprised to see that it was Lt. Col. Richard Ross, the executive officer of the regiment. He looked squarely at me and said, "Son, do you know who you're talking to?"

I paused, looked at the stranger, and then back at the colonel. I shook my head and replied, "No sir, I don't."

"That's your new regimental commander, Colonel Mason."[19]

Surprised, I looked at both of them, and not knowing how to reply, I said impulsively, "The *hell* you say." Then I laughed, shook my head, turned and just walked away.

The two officers were speechless. They were probably wondering what the hell they should do. Should they arrest this guy for insubordination? I think though, that the Thompson I was carrying with that old-style 50-round drum probably persuaded them otherwise.

Many of the guys in the battalion who saw me around but didn't know me called me "that little guy with the big gun." I guess it was a sort of nickname. These two officers more than likely let me go because they figured I really did know who I had been talking to (which of course, I hadn't) and still sounded off in that blunt, nonchalant way because I was at the point where I didn't give a rat's ass. I mean hell, all Marines are somewhat crazy anyway.

---

anywhere between 8 and 10 hours on a battery. The Marines used it extensively in the Pacific from 1944.

19 Col. Arthur T. Mason had just taken over command of the 1st Marines from Col. Kenneth B. Chappell on Saturday, May 5th.

I walked off about a half dozen paces and, curious, I turned around. They were still gaping at me, not saying a thing, looking dumbfounded. Ross probably figured that I was losing it, a sonuvabitch who could tip over the edge and open up on him. I think by then a lotta guys felt that way about a lot of us older veterans.

May 8th & 9th

The next day, May 8th, the rain really came down, and no one did much except just sit and suffer in the mud. That morning though, a sergeant came up to me at my OP. I was sitting on a cliff a couple hundred feet up.

He came up to me and said, "Look, I gotta take a patrol out down there. If I get in trouble, I'll throw out a smoke grenade. Would you be able to cover me with a smoke screen so that we could get out if we need to?"

I nodded and said confidently, "I certainly will." By now, I had been there a couple of days, and I had the whole area plotted. I had target numbers and coordinates written down on my map, and could call out a fire mission to any spot down there.

He thanked me and left. Pretty soon, I could see him and his men move out. I kept my eyes on him from my cliff position and nearly always had them in my sights. They did not get into any action, and soon I saw them coming back. They waved at me as they went by. I felt like their protecting angel and waved back at them. It felt good knowing that the guys knew I was up here and able to help them out whenever they needed it.

At night, we did something we called harassing fire on the Japs, just to keep them from getting a good night's rest and to drive them nuts. About every hour, I'd wake up or someone would shake me awake. I would get on the field phone, and I would direct our battery to fire a half dozen rounds to wake the bastards up and hassle them. Then I would go back to sleep for an hour or so, get shaken again, and fire off another mission. I mean, what the hell. I was just sitting in a hole anyway.

By the 9th, a lot of our wounded were getting shipped out to hospital ships. Most we would never see again. There was one good fellow we did have back though for the Okinawa operation. Lt. Murphy, now our platoon leader, had recovered from his wound on Peleliu and was with us once more.

Unfortunately, not for long. On that day, he was hit again. We all heard this mortar round coming in, and so everyone dived for cover. Lt. Murphy and I ended up both leaping into the same hole. The shell hit close by and the shrapnel buzzed over us, missing me. Murphy though, caught some of it. Rolling over, he found out that he had been hit in the testicles and on one of his ankles. Bleeding, he struggled to get up, and in pain, he looked at me and said, "I'll see ya." Then he turned and began hobbling off towards the rear.

This left us now without a platoon leader, because Lt. Haggerty the day before had been transferred to be the divisional liaison officer to the battalion. When he found out Murphy had been hit, he immediately returned to us and took over the platoon.

As we moved around Shuri Heights towards the western part of Dakeshi Ridge, we often moved in open country, and so the Japs continued to shell us on and off. Some of it was effective, but most of it was not. We found out that they had another railroad gun located in a hidden, fortified bunker. Again, the Japs would open the iron doors, wheel the gun out, fire off a few rounds, then wheel the damn thing back in again and shut the doors.

May 10th

On May 10th, we were attacked by the Jap artillery again. Our battalion occupied this steep ridge, about 300 or 400 yards west of what they were calling Hill 55. Our ridge overlooked a narrow-gauge railroad track located below us.

Throughout the afternoon, after I had established my OP, I could see Jap patrols moving around. I called Battalion and told them I saw a Jap patrol working their way around in the brush. Later on, I saw more Japs moving around, and again I reported them to Battalion. I told them that it looked like the Japs were moving in on us, and that we were going to be hit that night. They took the message and said they would pass it along.

I was right. Sure enough, around midnight, the Japs started this massive attack against our line, and there was a big battle. They threw everything at us but the kitchen sink: I mean, artillery, mortars, and grenades. They played this weird banzai music from hidden loudspeakers, and as they charged, they played these wild bugles as they came at us, screaming and yelling in the dark, trying to scare the crap out of us.

We were halfway up this hill, about twenty yards from the crest, barely holding on. We fired at anything in front of us that moved, and took a lot of fire in return. Eventually, the attack petered, and we rested for a bit. But they hit us again at daybreak. We held our ground, and they finally pulled back.

During a pause in the action, I spotted a guy standing near our right flank. I asked him who the hell he was and what he was doing there. He told me that he was tech sergeant so-and-so and was in charge of the platoon in the next company on the hill just to our right.

Only as I looked over that way, they weren't there. I asked him where they were positioned, and he told me, "I had to pull my platoon off that hill."

I was surprised. I asked, "D'you mean to tell me that you guys pulled back?"

"Well hell, the shelling was terrible."

Damn! We were up there too, and we had taken that mortar fire as well. But we had not withdrawn. They had though, and by moving back, they had left our right flank hanging up there in the air, and the bastards had not even told us. Now we were sitting ducks.

"You guys should pull back, too," he said.

I glared at him. "No," I said. "We're defending this hill."

He only nodded.

I gritted my teeth. "Well hell then, if you're not gonna do anything, go back and get us some grenades. We don't have any. We ran out."

I was pissed, and it did not bother me that he outranked me. I had learned through experience a valuable secret. If you were in a tight situation, and you needed something critical done from someone, and they did not know who you were, then you should just act like you knew what the hell you were doing and that you had the rank for it. It worked here, too. He just said, "Okay" and with that, he took off. Sure enough, he soon came back with a couple cases of grenades. We distributed them among my men.

A couple hours later, I was still on that back slope about halfway up that hill, still at the apex between K and L companies. We were taking steady mortar fire, when a Jap with a light machine gun opened up on us from a hidden spot about fifty yards to our rear.[20] I looked round and saw all these guys standing around doing nothing, talking about what to do, while this Jap bastard was back behind us in this hole taking a bunch of shots at our line. I ducked as some of the damn bullets bounced around us.

Finally, I looked over at Lt. Haggerty. I said, "We've got to do something and we've got to do it now because that guy is going to get the range on us here and he's going to kill one of us."

Haggerty looked at me and said, "Well, whaddaya want to do?" He knew that charging the guy would be suicide.

I growled at him, "Somebody's gotta do something about this bastard, and we gotta do it NOW! We ain't got time to shit around and talk about it."

---

20 Most likely the enemy was firing a Nambu Type 96 light machine gun, designed to be fired from a sitting or prone position. An improved much more reliable model than the earlier Type 11, it was air cooled with a spiral cooling fin around the barrel and gas operated. It weighed about 20 lb, was 42 inches long, carried by a balanced wooden handle on top, and unlike similar machine guns manufactured by other countries, it had a mounting for a bayonet. The weapon used a top-mounted curved 30-round magazine and fired a Japanese 6.5mm Arisaka cartridge at a rate of about 500 rounds/min, with an effective range of about 850 yards. The Type 96 only had an automatic firing mode, though single shots could be taken by momentarily pulling the trigger. Going into early production in 1936, it saw extensive use during the war. Over 40,000 were manufactured, although the model was replaced a few years later by the larger Type 99 machine gun.

A couple more bullets whizzed by. I took a deep breath and said, "I'm going back there to get that sonuvabitch."

Haggerty hesitated, then said, "Well, I'm gonna go with you."

I said, "No you're not. I don't want you to go. You'll just get in my way."

He blinked and said, "What?"

Even though he was my lieutenant, I said, "You're not going with me. All you've got is that rusty, gawddamn .45 and you haven't had it out of that holster since we landed here. It's rusty and it probably won't fire." I paused and said, "No, I don't want you out there with me if you can't help me."

Well, he just put his head down and never said a damn word. Feeling some regret, I added, "Besides, you'd just get in my way out there."

I told the other guys what I was doing too, so that they would not shoot me while I was out there.

I thought about how I was going to do it. My plan was to creep down into those gullies in front of us then work my way over to get in front of him. There was no brush for cover, so I'd have to be careful. When he started firing again, I would know exactly where he was and would not miss him.

I took off and started crawling my way down the slope and through a draw, and damn if Haggerty didn't follow me. I just shook my head and kept going. I had no idea why he wasn't listening to me, but what the hell. He was an officer.

When we were in position, I waited. The Jap opened up again, and when he quit firing, I raised the Thompson and let him have it. I fired a full 20-round magazine at his position (I didn't want to use the 50-round drum, because it would take too long to reload it).

After I stopped firing, I lay there and waited. I knew that I'd gotten that sonuvabitch, but always being cautious, I wanted to make sure. It was a good thing that I did too, because after about ten seconds, he suddenly started firing again. Damn if I hadn't missed the bastard! A whole friggin' magazine, and I hadn't got him. I lay there, grumbling. He must have been behind a bunch of sandbags or something, because at that range, I couldn't have missed him.

Frustrated and knowing that I had just given away my position, I turned around to Haggerty. "C'mon," I said, "we gotta get the hell outa here."

The Jap opened up again, so we started to crawl back, me and Haggerty and that damn pistol that he never took out. He told me weeks later that he had gone along with me for one purpose: if I got hit, he was going to drag my ass out. He was not going to let the Japs get me.

We moved back down that big draw and when I figured the Jap was going to fire again, we hunkered down behind this mound that turned out to be a pile of canned fish: Japanese canned rations, and when that bastard opened up on us again, the bullets flew into those cans and man, there was Japanese fish flying everywhere. When he stopped, Haggerty and I, scared shitless, looked at each other with wet fish pieces all over us and began laughing like hell.

We moved back and finally got back to the bottom of the hill. As we stood there, that Jap started firing again, when this lone Marine came up to me and said simply, "Hey, I'll help you."

I was amazed. All these damn riflemen standing around, and only one sonuvabitch had stepped up to support me.

"I got a better plan," he said. "You cover me, and I'll crawl down along the edge of that ridge. When I get there, I'll slip a grenade in, and you come along behind me and cover me."

I looked around and agreed. I put another magazine in, and we started out. He crawled around into the gully, and I stayed back about ten yards behind him, covering him with the Thompson.

He crawled up there and when he thought the time was right, he tossed the grenade. It exploded, and then we came back down and around, and that was it. We never did get a chance to go in and find the Jap to be sure he was dead, because the battle continued. But we knew we had gotten him. There was no more fire from him. I thanked the Marine who had helped me, and he walked away. I never found out who he was, and never saw him again.

In the meantime, I knew sure as hell them Japs were going to advance onto that crest that was above us and then give us what for. So I went over to two new guys that were my runners, and that I was training to be OPs: James Kus and John Acree.

I jerked my thumb towards the top of the ridge and told them, "Cmon. We're gonna go up there and check things out." They just looked at me like I was nuts. I explained, "Hell, they're gonna come down onto that hill in a little bit, and then they'll be looking right down our throats." We had to go up to the crest and find out where the Japs were, and hold up there.

We moved up the last twenty yards and had just come over the top of the hill when something came flying at me, landing at my feet and rolling around on the ground sizzling. It was a Jap grenade, one of those with a handle. By the time I realized what it was and how close it was, it was too late to do anything. But the Big Guy up above must have been watching out for me, because the grenade just fizzed out. It was a dud.

Taking a deep breath, I moved off, raised my Thompson and opened up. As Acree and Kus started firing their M1s, I looked at the brush ahead of me and spotted some figures. I counted about five or six Japs. A few of them shot back, and then we saw them all take off down into the bushes. I again fired at them, but they were moving fast, and I couldn't get a real good fix on them.

Kus said, "I'm going down in there and get 'em," and started down the slope after them. "Get yer ass back up here." I growled. "You sonuvabitch, you stay here. If you go down there, we'll lose ya for sure."

He stopped and looked back at me. I could see he wanted to go down and get them, which to me would be stupid as hell. So I said, "We're defending this here hill. We ain't goin' down into that brush."

He and Acree took a position on each side of me, and I motioned for the rest of the unit to join us on the crest. We prepared positions and just stayed up there, holding the hill. Acree hooked up the field phone and fired it up. I contacted the first sergeant at 3rd Battalion headquarters and reported our position to him. I told him that there were a number of Japs in front of us. I was going to call in a fire mission for our mortars, but that I wanted to make sure that there were none of our own patrols in front of us.

After a few moments, he got back to me. There were none of our guys out there. So I called in the mission, and a few moments later the 81mm shells came down on the positions ahead.

We rested and held that point until later the day. Then the other company to our right and the rest of our own came back and joined us. As the hours went by, I walked around the crest and did my job as a forward observer. But I started to really get worried as I kept seeing on the slopes far ahead of us groups of Japs moving about, fortifying their positions here and there, and doing recon.

I contacted Battalion several times that day, and I told the first sergeant each time what I was seeing. "Look," I told him one time, "there's been Japs all day long movin' around out there, getting ready for something. I'm tellin' ya, they're gonna *hit* us."

Each time I reported something new, he told me that he would pass the info on to the Colonel. Sure enough, we were assaulted that night, and like the night before, we fought hard, defending our ground. I could only wonder how long we could last like this.

May 11th & 12th

The Shuri Line was the most critical enemy position on Okinawa. Located on the lower end of the island, it ran six miles from northeast to southwest across the island. On the Japanese left flank was the island's capital of Naha. In the center of the line, about 400 feet up along a series of hills and ravines, was the near-impregnable Shuri Castle, with the Japanese central command post deep below in bunkers. At the end of the right flank was what the Marines would christen Conical Hill. Orders on May 10th came down from General Buckner, commanding the U.S. Tenth Army. The Shuri Line was to be taken at all costs. Five divisions, including the Marine 6th Division on the right flank and the Marine 1st Division just to its left, would be in on the offensive. The main attack was to begin on the morning of May 11th.

In the early morning of the next day, the 11th, starting around 4 a.m., the Japs renewed their fire on us, and we took some more casualties. K Company and L Company were positioned along this ridge in a sort of wide-angle V, with K Company on the left, and L Company on the right. I was crouched down at the apex of this V, calling in fire missions to the 81s.

Jap mortar shells occasionally came over, and once in a while an artillery shell landed. We answered the Japs with our own mortars, and once again, I began to worry that the Japs would figure out their location and hit them.

When there was finally a break in the action and the smoke over the area had cleared a bit, I sat up and checked myself to make sure I was all right. Feeling around, I found a few small jagged holes in the front of my dungaree jacket. I checked the pocket inside, where I had a small leather-bound notebook, about 2 inches by 6 inches, that I kept firing coordinate notes in. Next to the pocket was an additional cloth slot to slide a pencil in. I pulled the notebook out and found that it had embedded in it several pieces of shrapnel. They must have come from one of the nearby mortar explosions. That little notebook had been right next to my heart, and if it had not been for that little notepad there, the shrapnel would have done a job on me.

I took a deep breath and put the lucky notebook back in the pocket. I did some more inventory. In my dispatch case, I had this small bottle of ink, smaller than the size of my thumb. I would take small pointed sticks and slot them, to use them with the ink as a sort of fountain pen to write with. I checked now and found a hole in the backpack and the bottle broken. Evidently, either a bullet or another piece of shrapnel had penetrated the cloth, shattered the bottle, and had gone right through the other side.

Once again, I had been lucky.

A while later, I started moving around, checking things out. I noticed that the Jap artillery fire was getting more accurate. Less than a week before, I had tried to alert Lt. Murphy that the bastards were trying to zero in on our mortars. "Them guns are going to get hit," I had warned him a couple of times. I could see the Jap artillery and mortar rounds going down, because they were big enough to actually see coming in. Closer in, I thought that I could see the knee mortar rounds coming in. So I had told Murphy once again that our mortars or the ammo dump were going to get hit, because the Japs' shells were landing closer and closer.

Unfortunately, when Murphy had been hit on the 9th and Haggerty had again taken over the platoon, they had never had a chance to talk about what was going on. Haggerty never got the warning I had given Murphy, so the mortars and the ammo cache had not yet been moved. And there they remained today.

Sure enough, a while later, what I had for days feared might happen did. That morning, as the Japs shelled us, we continued to return fire, including from our division's 75mm artillery. In addition, some navy Corsairs came in low and hit the Japs with some rockets, bombs, and even some napalm. Sometime after 10 a.m., the Japs stopped firing, and so we did too. We were told to take a break while we could, and we were glad to get it.

Before lunch though, around 11 a.m., the Japs started firing a few more rounds. About fifteen minutes later, that damn Jap railroad gun landed a shell right in our ammo dump, a direct hit. I saw it land and watched our entire stock go up in a fierce set of explosions. All our stuff began exploding, especially all the WP shells. Lord, you could see the smoke for miles. Those guys nearby not killed outright or knocked unconscious began to run off screaming in pain as the rest of our shells went off and bits of white phosphorus rained down on them. In just a few moments, we had lost about half of our platoon and some other guys, a total of about 30 Marines.

Six guys in the platoon were killed, including James McGuire, who had been Rucker's FO assistant, tall, quiet Clarence Hurst from the No. 3 gun, and Good, Landry, and Herman. Another 22 guys were wounded, including Russ Diefenbach, my assistant Bob Sprangle, Roman Berceau, and both our medics, Crowe and Romero. Gunnery Sgt. Giddens was evacuated with chemical burns from the white phosphorus.

The wounded included Gilder Kelley, two guys from the No. 1 Mortar: Gunner Bill Mikel and Charlie Ramirez, one of his assistants. Also wounded was Raymond Kelley from the No. 4 Gun, Three more, Howard Quarty, Kistner, and Haley, had to be hospitalized because of their nervous condition as a result of the explosion.

Mikel told me later that he was hit by a piece of shrapnel in the ankle, but as he was diving for cover, he sprained the ankle as well. He grumbled that the damn sprain hurt a lot more than the lousy shrapnel nick.

When the dead and wounded were finally taken away, I was the only noncom left in the unit. Since we had lost half the platoon, most of the guys on ammo runs were assigned to mortar crews. Lt. Col. Sabol ordered what was left of the unit to the rear to reorganize. And that's what we did.

Later that day, after we had evacuated all our wounded from the mortar platoon, a few of us went out on patrol to try to find a guy who was being tortured by the Japs. We had periodically heard him the night before, calling out for help. It was probably a trap, so no one had gone out to try to rescue him, and today we had been up to our ears in combat. Now with a break in the action, we decided to try and find the guy.

A patrol of us slowly moved forward. With us was our naval gunfire support officer, 1st Lieutenant Monk Myers. Off one of those destroyers, he had been with us since Peleliu, where he had earned a Silver Star, and we had gotten to like him. Tagging along with him was his assistant (we just called him Monk's bodyguard).

We finally spotted the guy lying down in this clearing. We figured that he was an American since he was wearing a Marine dungaree jacket. He was dead, and wow, he was a helluva bloody mess. His face was really swollen from the beatings that he had taken. The Japs had also bound him tightly with dry rope, and then had poured water on it, making the rope shrink, and of course, causing the guy a lot more pain before he had died.

Monk told us he was going to check the other side of the hill. He turned to his bodyguard, handed him his Thompson to stand watch, and started down the other way. A little bit later, we heard this small, sharp explosion. We went to check it out, and saw Monk lying dead. He had gone souvenir hunting, and had picked one up that was booby-trapped. Shrapnel had gone into his left breast and killed him.[21]

---

21 Years later, Monk's niece, Holly Beyer, wrote to George, asking how her uncle had died. According to George, "I really did not want to tell her the truth, because she had heard that Monk had died charging the Japs, or some other goofy story like

Sometime in the afternoon of the 12th, after we had repelled the Japs again and were regrouping, I was in my OP standing near the top of this hill, when six guys came walking around the bend up this big long grade.

The fellow in charge asked where George was, and one of the guys pointed over to me. The guy in charge walked over to me, and to my surprise, I recognized the regiment commander, Lt. Col. Sabol. He asked me how I was doing, and we started to chat. He wanted to know what the situation was, so I filled him in on what was going on. He had actually taken the trouble to come up to the front lines, because he specifically wanted to see who I was and what was going on.

Hill 55

Despite the fact that the 1st Marines had struggled against the Wana Ridge complex for two days and taken heavy casualties, on May 13th, they were ordered to attack and take a Japanese strongpoint labeled on their maps as Hill 55. It was located on the end of the southern ridge facing the Wana Draw. The Japanese had to hold Hill 55, because it was a key position in the critical Shuri defensive line. The 1st Marines were to coordinate their attack with the 7th Marines moving on Dakeshi Ridge to their north.

In the early morning, the area that these two regiments were to advance over was hammered by heavy guns of the Navy offshore, as well as by Marine artillery, mortars, and some 37mm guns. In the late morning, the 7th Marines began attacking Dakeshi Ridge, just to the north of Wana Ridge. At the same time, accompanied by some tank support 3rd Battalion started advancing as their assault on Hill 55 began. Capt. Bennett's 150-man L Company was in the lead.

---

that. I did not have the desire to tell her that he died in a dumb way, picking up a souvenir wired to a grenade. So I told her to write to get the report." Holly did. The report just indicated that Monk had died due to "massive trauma to the chest." Interestingly, Monk's brother was a Marine too and had been a stretcher bearer on Peleliu. When the war ended, he went home and in consoling Monk's girlfriend, took up a relationship with her. They ended up getting married a couple years later and gave birth to Holly.

On the morning of the 13th, I went looking for Lt. Haggerty. Our own mortar platoon, well what was left of it, had been relieved after they had been torn apart at the ammo dump on the 11th. So we had no heavy mortars to cover our companies moving up. The Army had some 4.2-inch mortars,[22] and we wanted to ask them if we could use them to cover our battalion. After all, we could do a much better job of spotting for them for our battalion than they could. And besides, I wanted a crack at spotting or, better yet, firing one.

I happened to walk by a tent when I heard coming out of it a bunch of hollering and cussing. I thought to myself, Jesus Christ, what's going on in there? So being naturally curious, I stopped, turned, and walked in the tent. I sort of realized it was officers' country, but I didn't care. I stumbled onto two senior officers. One was Col. Mason, our regimental commander, and the other was Lt. Col. Sabol, my 3rd Battalion commander. Mason was cursing Sabol out.

As I walked in, Mason yelled at him, "If you don't get your battalion's ass in gear, I'm gonna relieve you!" He stopped and they both turned and looked at me stunned, their jaws dropping (as mine probably did). Realizing I was way out of my element and had interrupted a personal senior officer dialog, I did an immediate about face and walked out. Luckily for me, no one hollered at me as I quickly walked away from the area.[23]

I went over to where L Company was, now commanded by Capt. Alton C. Bennett. I moved forward with them. That morning in the rain, the battalion tried to take Hill 55 with L Company in the lead, but even with Shermans supporting us, we took quite a pounding. Since we

---

22 The U.S. Army Model M2 4.2-inch mortar, a mainstay of Army units in the Pacific from 1943 onward. Technically a chemical mortar, it also fired HE shells. It had a maximum range of 4,400 yards and a top firing rate of about 5 rounds/minute. Like the 81mm mortar, it was moved in three components, with a total weight of 333 lb, which included the much heavier 175-lb base plate. Unlike the 81mm mortar, the barrel was rifled, and the shells were not fin-stabilized. Also, mortar platoons consisted of three guns, not four like the Marine heavy mortars.

23 Lt. Col. Sabol was subsequently relieved of command of 3rd Battalion on Monday, May 21st, and two days later, he was assigned to the 7th Marines as their Operations Officer.

had no mortars, all I could do was just shoot back at them. We eventually
fell back and used the tanks to carry back our dead and wounded. The
unit then tried to regroup. When L Company took muster, they only
had 36 men left.

I walked over to battalion headquarters where Lt. Haggerty was.
Together, we volunteered to go to the Army and see if they would let
us spot for their mortars. Battalion agreed, so we hitched a ride over
to rear areas of the 307th.[24] Luckily for us, they had agreed to help us
and had already been assigned to us. They loaned us a battery of three
4.2-inch mortar teams. We would observe for them, since our rifle
companies were still on the line.

I went back to L Company and advanced with them towards Wana
Draw. At one point, on the right flank in this wooded area and detached
from the unit, I started looking for a good OP. I stopped in front of a
large thicket. Crouched down, I carefully scanned the area in front of
me. I noticed something curious. Occasionally, far off, I saw this small
black thing bob up and then disappear. At first I thought it was a little
animal, like maybe a skunk or something. Whatever it was, it had to
be alive because it was moving. I knew from my hunting experience
that nearly all animals, both four or two legged, whenever they moved
through dense woods or jungle, even in dangerous areas, tended to move
along the easiest path of resistance, especially if it was a trail.

I stared hard ahead, and after a minute or two, I realized that moving
black spot was no damn animal. It was a black pouch of some sort
bobbing up and down, and gradually coming this way down through
the only opening in the thicket. Slowly but surely, this bobbing black
pouch or bag came towards me, and I realized now it was strung to the
back or the belt of a Jap, and that he was coming my way along the trail.
Across the thicket's one narrow open trail was a small opening. In it,
just ahead of me were these two logs. So I lay down behind the second
larger log, with the smaller one just in front about three yards. Little by
little, that black pouch moved towards me.

---

24 Army 307th Infantry Regiment, 77th Infantry Division.

While I did have my Thompson, I also was carrying an M1 carbine that I had picked up some time ago. Lying behind the big log, with my head slightly raised, I held the carbine up. With one cartridge in the chamber, I eased the safety off, and quietly waited. After what seemed like a long time, I heard the Jap slowly crawl over the first log just in front, and I could tell that he was creeping right towards me. I held the carbine at the ready, my finger just touching the trigger. I couldn't see anything behind that big log, but I knew that he was near. Then I heard him shuffle on the other side of the big log, and my body tensed. Man, this was combat up close and personal.

Finally, I heard the Jap start to crawl over the log that I was behind and I felt it shake slightly. His head appeared over the top, and his slanted eyes looked down into my eyeballs, as he took in the sight of both me and my carbine, with the muzzle pointed at his head less than a foot away. His eyes opened wide in surprise as I instinctively pulled the trigger. I didn't squeeze or anything. I just yanked on it, and the carbine fired. His head immediately dropped as he slumped down. I waited a few moments, not poking my head up, just in case he was not alone. Finally, cautiously, I gently raised up and looked around for any buddy of his, someone who might have heard the noise and was coming to see what had happened to him. I stayed put for a while and looked around several times. No one was there but me. And of course the Jap, but he was clearly dead as hell.

Then in the distance, I heard one of the guys say, "Okay, we're moving out."

Rather than stay and do something stupid like look around for souvenirs and maybe get shot while I did, I did not even touch that dead Jap. I wisely took off and joined the company.

A little while later, we were ordered to pull back. Lt. Haggerty suggested that we go down to battalion headquarters, find the colonel, and tell him we were going to start observing for the army mortar crew. So we went down to find 3rd Battalion headquarters.

We walked into this small gully near the tent and found four guys huddled together. They were all officers: Lt. Col. Sabol, our 3rd Battalion commander, and the three company commanders: L Company's Captain

Alton Bennett, I Company's Capt. Lawrence Hennessey[25] and K Company's Lt. William O. "Bull" Sellars.

Haggerty put his hand out and said, "You wait here. I'll go talk to them." I stopped about twenty yards away and crouched, waiting as I saw Haggerty go into the gully and join the group. He squatted down with them, and they all talked. Looking at them, I had to chuckle. The other officers were all wearing their Marine helmets, and Haggerty was wearing that damn blue baseball cap.

About five minutes later, they all stood up, and Haggerty came back up to where I was. He said, "Well, I got good news for ya. We're now officially in L Company."

What, again? What about observing for the Army mortars? Not quite understanding, I just looked at him and asked, "Where to?"

He scowled. "Well, we're not going to spot for the mortars," he said. "The Colonel put me in charge of L Company." He paused and added, "I asked him if you could come with me."

I just stared at him and my initial reaction was a sarcastic, "Thanks for nothing," I grumbled. Thinking about it though, I guess that I would really have been disappointed if he had told me to go back to battalion CP. If he had, I probably would have told him, "The hell with you. I'm staying with you."

As we walked back to join what was left of L Company, I asked him why he was taking over, and what about Capt. Bennett.

Without looking at me, he said simply, "Bennett's been relieved."

I stopped in surprise. "What?" I paused, "Why?"

We started walking again and he gave me the scoop. Word had come down that in the afternoon, Company L had been ordered to once again attack Hill 55. Capt. Bennett, the company commander,

---

25 Capt. Lawrence K. Hennessey of Schenectady, New York, who would be awarded the Silver Star for his actions on May 7th, was killed two weeks later with his radioman, Al Richards, as they were moving up the line. On May 21st, the two of them were making their way up a slope. They paused, and Hennessey told the radioman, "Wait here. I'm gonna take a look over the ridge. You stay here with the radio." Sadly, Hennessey never came back, and Richards later found his body. The officer had been killed by a sniper, shot in the head.

had protested. He was down to less than three dozen. They would be attacking a dug-in fortified position that was ready for them. They were *not* going to have any support from machine guns or from any mortars. Remember, our 81mm mortars had been devastated on the 11th, and our platoon had been relieved, and while the Army mortar crew had agreed to support us, it did not seem to be happening. Nor could they expect any of our covering artillery, naval fire, tanks, or even air support. On top of all that, they would be out in the open, really exposed to murderous crossfire as they attacked. And to make things even worse, all the Marines had to hit the entrenched Japs with were just their personal weapons—their rifles, grenades, and one BAR.

Capt. Bennett had told Lt. Col. Sabol that to attack up that hill that way was just plain suicide and had no chance of success. Lt. Sellars and Capt. Hennessey had agreed, siding with Bennett. Sabol though, had insisted that he make the attack. Politely but firmly, Capt. Bennett had refused to attack the hill again, not under those conditions.

Angry, Lt. Col. Sabol had relieved him of his command right there.[26] He then told Haggerty, "I'm putting you in command of L Company." Then he told him to do what Bennett had refused: to attack Hill 55.

Lt. Haggerty and I went back to what was left of L Company and prepared to attack. We assembled at the base of that narrow-gauge railroad track. Besides those 27 riflemen, there was me and Haggerty. Even though I was just a corporal, I was now second in command. Our weapons were few. Besides the M1s, we had some grenades, just one BAR, my Thompson, and Haggerty's rusty .45 pistol that he probably had not fired since Australia. We were not getting any tanks, artillery, mortars, or air support. Nothing.

Things just keep getting better and better, I thought sarcastically.

---

26 Capt. Bennett was eventually reassigned as the Executive Officer of the division's 1st Service Battalion on May 20th. He remained in the Marines and would later serve as the executive officer of Marine Aircraft Maintenance Squadron 33 (MAMS-33) in Korea.

Haggerty gathered us round and began his talk. "Men, here's the plan to take Hill 55. We're just gonna charge down that draw like the hammers of hell. They'll never know what hit 'em."

Squatting there, the men just looked at him silently.

"We're gonna take it before they know what hit them," he repeated. He paused, and as they looked at him skeptically, he then added firmly, "One way or another, we're going to take that damn hill."

He looked up at me and pointed. "And you bring up the rear and make sure that every man follows me." Standing with my Thompson on my hip, I nodded. Me and "Baby" would make sure that they did, but inside, I knew we were all dead men.

It was time. He took a deep breath, "Okay, follow me." He turned and started up the draw.

I have to give those guys credit. Every damn one of them, without hesitation, peeled off one after another and followed him. Not one of them hesitated, even though we all figured that this was a suicide mission. Who knows, maybe seeing me and the Thompson might have had something to do with it, but I doubt it. They were all good Marines. Still, I was glad that they were all moving out without a complaint. Haggerty and I knew one another, having been together for two years now, but all the others were new guys, probably replacements. Still, they seemed to accept us and our authority, and I was grateful, especially since this looked like a really bad idea. And besides, what could I have done if they refused to go? I wasn't about to shoot one of our own guys.

We took off in column and I brought up the rear. It only took us about five minutes to get there, a distance of about 200 yards, and when we got up the ten-foot-high ridge, we were lucky. We had completely surprised the Japs. Our luck did not last long. They saw us and opened up. I was standing next to this steep hill, and out of sight of most of them. On the other hand, I could not shoot at them either.

The incoming machine-gun and rifle crossfire intensified, and mortars started to zero in on us. Haggerty, over to the right, yelled at us to dig in. I could see him furiously trying to dig into the 10-foot-high coral mound. But the guys were digging in on the front side of the ridge, exposed to the enemy. There was dirt flying around all over the place, from the guys trying to dig in, and where the Jap bullets were hitting. Everyone soon went down, either to avoid getting hit, or because they were hit. We were sitting ducks, and the Japs tore into us. I was standing right up against the mountain side, so I was probably out of sight of the Japs above us. In the space of only five minutes, no one was standing.

We had probably lost two thirds of our group. Finally, Lt. Haggerty told us to pull back. So we all turned down the back side of this hill, carrying our wounded. Me, I was the last guy off to cover them, but just like before, the Japs could not see me and I could not see them, so I had nothing to shoot at. Finally, I started back, taking a different route down between the two hills.

Making my way down the hill, I saw two stretcher bearers come out from around this hill, carrying a wounded Marine. I didn't know any of them. A mortar round landed nearby, the two carriers dropped the stretcher and took off down the draw.

I stared at the guy who was lying helplessly on the stretcher. Looking around, I saw a straggler come running by. I gestured to him and barked, "Hey, come here."

He hesitated, and I repeated, "Come HERE!"

He walked over and I nodded to the stretcher, "You take the front."

"What?" he said, surprised.

I glared at him. "Come on. You take the front." I was in no mood to take any crap from him, and if he did not pick up the stretcher, I probably would have fired a couple rounds in the ground at his feet.

He hesitated, but then he bent down to the stretcher. He picked up the front two handles. I grabbed the back two and as we lifted the wounded man up, I growled, "Don't you drop this sonuvabitch."

Looking at the wounded guy, I saw that he was as white as a ghost. I wondered if he was already dead. We carried him back to the railroad cut. The medics stuck his rifle by the bayonet into the ground and started an IV for him. Then we slowly carried that guy back to the rear. We were the last ones out. Anyone else remaining was either dead or just gone. They would finally get the bodies out a day or two later, but they had to be escorted by a tank.

The whole thing had only taken 15 minutes, and now, not counting the wounded taken back to the rear, there were only 11 of us left. Lt. Haggerty and I had a conference right after that. He told me to take two men to locate the other two companies to set up for the night.

So three of us walked over to the other side of the railroad cut to this clearing. I turned to the two guys with me and told them that we were going to make a run for it and not stop until we made it to the other side. As we started running down, a machine gun suddenly opened up behind us.

Running between these two other guys, I yelled, "Keep going."

Suddenly, the guy on my right got hit in the hand. I actually could hear the bone snap as the bullet struck. He did not say anything and kept running. A few seconds later, the guy on my left slowed and said, "I think I've been hit."[27]

I grabbed him and said, "Don't stop till we make it to the gully."

We finally made it and jumped into the gully and ducked down as bullets zipped over us. I checked out the guy that had been on my left. He had been wounded alright, but it was one of those miracle shots that did not hit any organs. The bullet had struck him in the back on his left side and had exited through his chest. However, it had missed his left lung and had traveled through just above his heart. There was very little blood.

The guy to my right had a broken hand from the bullet that had hit him, and there was some blood running down his hand. I told them both to get back to the aid station, and they took off. That's the last I saw of them.

I checked myself just to be sure. No, even though I had been in the middle, the Japs had again missed me. I shook my head.

In the meantime, Lt. Haggerty ordered us to set up for the night on this small ridge. The nine of us dug in and set up seven gunpits. Terrific.

---

27 Based upon official Marine Corps casualty records, George later determined that the man who was to the right was Henry S. Wollard. The one on his left was Robert D. Wright.

Haggerty checked our position and then left us again to go looking for more men. He came back a while later with two stragglers he had come across. Then with a brusque "I'll see you later," he got up and left.

Now in charge, I did not even bother to check the IDs of the two new guys. I just set them up, off to one side. My Thompson next to my chest convinced them to dig in.

I got them situated, and then went back to check on the others, and to distribute some ammo for them. Then I lay down and took a break. When I came back to their end again an hour later, I discovered the two stragglers were gone. One of the guys told me that they had taken off as soon as I had disappeared.

It figured.

We located the other two companies and finished setting up on our small ridge two or three hundred yards out. We nine defended that hill all night. And it was a long one. Luckily, we did not get hit. The company on the left did, but not us.

The next morning, I gathered these nine guys, the pathetic remains of L Company, and handed over to the new commander, 1st Lt. Harry L. Zigler. Then Haggerty and I made our way back to my heavy mortar platoon. We were given 30 replacements and three new guns; our fourth was still unusable.

The Army battery never did provide us support. Damn Army ...

Wana Draw, mid-May

The Marines advancing southward knew that the village of Wana was a key point near the Shuri Line. Every direction from it featured a series of ridges. The major approach to the village was Wana Draw. This essentially was a wide, open, winding, twisting valley basin southwest of the village. Running roughly east–west, it was flanked by steep Wana Ridge on the northern side, and another ridge to the south, at the end of which was what was identified on the maps as Hill 55. Wana Draw would prove to be a killing ground for the Marines. Each of the steep ridges in the area was pockmarked with caves and holes brimming with Japanese riflemen, machine guns, mortars, and light artillery pieces, all of which had clear fields of fire and interlocking fire. The entrances and main paths

through the draw were peppered with mines and obstacles. The battle began on
May 15th with a day-long pounding of the ridges to each side by U.S. artillery,
mortars, and tanks. Then began a four-day assault on the draw and the ridges
to each side by the division's 7th Marines, supported by the 5th Marines.

According to the Tenth Army's Marine Chief of Staff, General O. P. Smith,
"Wana Draw proved to be the toughest assignment the 1st Division was to
encounter."

On May 15th, we started our attack at the foot of Wana Draw. It was
a really fortified line, and enemy resistance was stiff. We paused in an
Okinawan tomb, huddled, getting ready to resume our advance. As
we started moving up, I heard someone give firing coordinates. It was
coming from one of my counterparts, a forward observer for one of our
60mm mortar crews. He was about ten yards away from me, and I heard
him clearly give the firing orders.

A short time later, we started getting incoming mortar fire. Although
the men scrunched down, we began taking casualties, and I heard a
couple guys screaming and some shouts for a corpsman. I realized this
was friendly fire, and I quickly moved up and took up a forward position. When the mortar fire stopped, I moved back again.

My instincts were correct. The incoming mortar fire was because of
that forward observer who had called in the fire mission as he wanted to
cover the area in front of us, but he made a big mistake in his calculations
and had inadvertently given the order to bring the shells down on us. At
least a half dozen Marines were hit. He looked over at me and seeing the
look on my face, quickly put two and two together. He broke down and
cried like a baby. No one else ever realized what had happened, except
him and, me. The mistake really must have messed him up, because a
day or so later, they took him away, shell shocked (today they call it
PTSD[28]), and I never saw him again.

We started up a draw, and soon came to an area where there were
more tombs, very common for Okinawa. Around the front of each
was a two-foot-high stone wall. We were taking a considerable amount

---

28 Post-Traumatic Stress Disorder.

of fire from heavy machine guns, rifles, and knee mortars, so a bunch of us took up positions crouched behind these walls, and we began returning fire. I stopped shooting when I suddenly felt something slam into my right shoulder and knock me over. Figuring it was the guy next to me, I looked over at him, and he gave me this why-are-you-looking-at-me look.

I glanced down over my shoulder and saw that what had hit me in the back in a downward, glancing blow was a 2-lb. shell that had been fired from a Jap knee mortar. The shell was laying there on the ground, the fuse sizzling. Without thinking, and based on months of training, in the blink of an eye I automatically bent down, grabbed it, and threw it down the slope. Right after it left my hand, it detonated. It had only been in the air a half second or so, but there was enough distance to save my life. Otherwise, I would have been killed. Still, I had no time to think about my close call, and so we kept firing.

The next day, May 16th, we got the word that the war in Europe had ended, and we cheered a few times. That meant that the U.S. would now concentrate exclusively on beating the Japs, and so we would be able to go home sooner. That is, if we lived that long. In the meantime, we were getting the hell kicked out of us here. The artillery fire never stopped, and it seemed like every ten minutes or so something dangerous was happening near us. So there was not much to celebrate. Besides, we knew that sooner or later, we were going to have to invade Japan, and that was sure as hell not going to be any picnic.

That day, after having gone days without a warm meal, John Skoglie and I came across this chicken running around, and man, we must have spent a whole frustrating hour chasing the damn thing before we caught it and killed it. We started a fire, plucked the chicken, field dressed it, and stuck it over the fire. As the meat began to cook, word came down that we were advancing again, and I had to join up with I Company as forward observer. We were moving up Wana Ridge in preparation for an assault on the village of Wana. Our attack was to be coordinated with the 22nd Marines, who were hitting Sugar Loaf Hill[29] south of us.

---

29 Actually the apex of a triangle of three hills, it was designated on the maps as Hill 60.

I looked at the chicken, mostly still raw, and I cursed. Just my damn luck. I took off alone, and found I Company. Skoglie got to eat the chicken all by himself.

It rained solid for the next three or four days. It was miserable, a sea of mud, with open stretches of water all over the place.[30] We couldn't do much of anything, and neither could the Japs. Even trying to get into position in those showers was a real hassle. After a while, our ponchos were useless. Hell, it got to where there was more water under the damn things than there was on top of them. So we just tried to stay as dry as we could, and our guys spent the time lobbing shells over at the Japs.

I hung out with these guys from I Company; with many of them new replacements, I pretty much did not know any of them. We were taking a five-minute break, standing there in the rain, feeling miserable, when I saw in the distance a familiar face. Lt. Haggerty was coming up the trail, making his way through the mud. He caught up with us, and I took one look at him, soaked to the bone, and he took one look at me, standing there, dripping all over, and we both busted out laughing. Reaching into pocket, he pulled out a soggy K-ration of wrapped rolled oats pressed together in a round wheel and handed it to me. He knew I liked them.

He grinned and told me that he had been carrying that damn thing around for five days, waiting to run into me so that I could have it. Aw. I smiled and thanked him. That little incident of kindness meant a lot to me. We had over time become not just co-workers, but good friends. We looked out for each other. It was funny, but almost everyone else was half afraid of him, because he was this big burly bull of a guy. He got that from having played baseball and football so much back in college. All in all though, even though he looked husky and intimidating, he was actually a nice guy, and not cruel. We had become familiar with each other's habits. For instance, he almost tolerated my crazy occasional treks, and I in turn would sometimes rag his ass for not cleaning his .45 pistol.

---

30 The start of Okinawa's "plum rains" that typically drench the island in May and June.

By now, it had become a standing joke between us that whenever he occasionally lined us up for inspection to check the cleanliness of our weapons, he would get to me and look at my Thompson and then up at me. He would see that Go-ahead-pot-Try-to-call-the-kettle-black look on my face, make a funny face, then just the faintest hint of a smile broke on his face as he rolled his eyes and moved on to the next guy.

Around that time, Joe Miceli came into temporary possession of a jeep—okay, he stole it from the Army, but so what. He kept it going, and for gas, we used what I liked to call a "West Virginia credit card," which was a two-foot-long hose and a can. Always short of stuff, he loaned it to us, so that we could pay a visit to a couple nearby army units to "liberate" some supplies from them.

Lt. Haggerty did the driving. We took off towards the nearby army division, went up round a hill, and there in front of us was this big supply truck slowly going up the hill. Haggerty told me to jump up onto the hood of the jeep, and when he got right behind the truck, to hop into the back of the truck, then toss onto the hood any supplies that I thought we might be able to use.

So I crawled onto the jeep's hood, and when he got to where the jeep's bumper almost touched the truck's, I leaped into the truck. I looked round and found a number of boxes of food and other supplies. So I began tossing the stuff out of the truck and onto the jeep. The other guys grabbed the stuff and tossed it into the back of the jeep. When we were done, I jumped back onto the jeep, hopped over into the passenger seat, and Haggerty took off. We had a pretty nice haul. I chuckled over the fact that our own lieutenant had been in on our heist. Yeah, Haggerty and I got along. He was okay in my book.

It was raining again, and I had managed to find an old smelly blanket to try to stay warm under. I had cut a hole for my head like a poncho. Our mortars were back, and I had set me up an OP. I was sitting on a log looking out down the hillside when suddenly I heard a whizz and this deafening explosion. The concussion threw me backward as a piece of shrapnel, hot as hell, smacked into the blanket on my left shoulder, knocking me all the way over. Recovering, I reached around with my right hand and pulled a sizzling, half-dollar-sized piece of mushroomed metal out of a shredded hole in the blanket, burning my fingers as I did so. I took a deep breath and shook my head. If I hadn't been wearing that blanket …

I got up and straightened myself, shook off the wet dust, and sat down again. More Jap shells came over, but thankfully, none landed close.

I began thinking about the guys we had lost. Mostly those that had been killed. Many that were not wounded became casualties in other ways. Guys like Dale Dawson just couldn't take it. Dale had been one of the replacements back in mid-1944. He had been designated as a Forward Observer and assigned as my assistant. I had trained him for over a year, but whenever we went into combat, I never saw him. He was too scared, and always stayed back with the mortars. Which was fine with me, because I preferred to work alone anyway. Finally in early May, he had gone to Haggerty and told him that he just couldn't take it anymore. He was going crazy. So the lieutenant told him to just stay in the rear with the mortars and help out there. He did, but mentally he slowly unraveled. Finally he was shipped out, diagnosed with battle fatigue.

Another man in our unit who broke down was Carl Jacobs, a Jewish private from Cleveland. He just turned himself in to battalion headquarters one day, crying, telling them he was done for. They put him on KP and kept him in the rear.

Some guys just went crazy and had to be dragged away. Others went into shock and turned into zombies. Many just broke down. I once saw a kid in our battalion sitting next to the side of the road. I remember him as being a nice kid. Now, his rifle was on the ground, and he was quietly weeping. I stopped and asked him what was wrong. He just kept sitting there, his shoulders bobbing slightly as he cried. I started talking calmly to him, telling him that things would be okay. He just kept crying, tears rolling down his cheeks, an occasional whimper. He was clearly through. A corpsman finally came by, asked him if he was okay, and then gently walked him back. I never saw the kid again.

Over time, most of us, even the ones who stayed sane, started to develop little peculiarities. Sometimes this manifested itself through some really morbid incidents. Like one time, after a firefight, one of the guys took this enemy corpse and sat him up on a boulder. He pulled out a cigarette, lit it, and then stuck it in the dead Jap's mouth. Sitting next to the body, he put his arm over its shoulders. When we came round the corner, he smiled and started talking to the smoking Jap, as if they were good buddies and just passing the day.

We stopped and somebody said something like, "Are you *nuts* or something?!?"

He grinned and started howling, and we joined in, all of us laughing like hell at the sight of him and his pal, that dead Jap.

Then there was this nut job in K Company.

I don't remember his name after all these years. We just called him "the Greek," because he was. He had been with us back on Peleliu, and now here on Okinawa, he developed this weird habit of stabbing every dead Jap he came across with his bayonet, just to make sure the little bastard was not faking. He actually had a stick with the bayonet affixed to the end (like they used), and every time he passed a dead Jap body, he'd stick it with the bayonet. It might have looked amusing seeing him slowly walking along, stabbing each enemy corpse that he passed, if it hadn't been so weird.

He got worse as time went on. He never passed a dead Jap without stabbing the body. I could understand poking at one you were not sure about, but when the body had its intestines hanging out, there really was no reason to stab at it. After a while, the Greek's habit started to bother us. Finally one day, I saw him go by poking dead bodies, and I got fed up with this ghoulish ritual. I was tired and in a bad mood, and I was resting on one knee.

I scowled at him and yelled, "Gawdamn you, get the hell away! Quit!"

He whirled around and glared at me with a crazed look on his face, like a wild man. Angry, and bracing myself for a violent reaction, I tightened my grip on my Thompson. Go ahead, dirtball, I thought. He stared hard at me, and I knew he was on the edge of charging with that bayonet on a stick. But then he looked at my weapon and probably figured he would never make it. So, gritting his teeth, he turned, growled, and skulked off.

I looked at him walking away and thought to myself, "He's crazy." We did not cross paths after that, which is just as well. Anyway, the Greek did have a couple good points. He became one of our cave experts. Captain Hunt got him to crawl into a suspected cave like some sort of hound dog, with his rifle (and bayonet, of course) to root the Japs out.

On the evening of May 19th, the weary 7th Marines were relieved by the 1st Marines, who were to resume their fight the next day. 3/1, having relieved their counterpart 3/7, would assault the northern slope of Wana Ridge. To get into position, 3rd Battalion tied into 2nd Battalion's lines and assumed a defensive posture on the western edge of the ridge for the night.

On Saturday the 19th, we moved up to the line once more and relieved the 7th Marines. The next morning, we began attacking Wana Ridge. Just before noon,[31] two platoons of L Company, following Colonel Mason's orders,[32] started hauling these 55-gallon drums of napalm up the north side of the ridge, to I Company's positions. The idea was to maneuver the drums over to the edge of the crest, split them open, and then roll them down the steep slopes of the ridge, picking up speed as they rolled down. That napalm mixture would slop out as the drums spun, until finally they landed at the Japanese positions at the head of Wana Draw. The guys would then set fire to the mixture with some white phosphorus grenades and hopefully burn the Jap positions down there. It took us some five hours in thick mud to haul them damn barrels up the slope, but the results were great. Once the napalm was lit, a lot of the Japs were taken out.

That same day, our 3rd Battalion skipper, Lt. Col. Sabol, was relieved of command by Col. Mason. We never were told why, but some of us guessed that it might be because he was not considered aggressive

---

31 Reports indicated that the action began at 1140 hours.
32 The idea actually came from the battalion commander, Lt. Col. Sabol.

enough. Lt. Col. "Buddy" Ross took over command of the battalion on the 21st, and Sabol went over to the 7th Marines.[33]

On May 20th, our tanks got into some trouble. It hadn't rained that day. The sun was even out, and it was hot. A unit of Shermans was on the other side of Wana Draw, and they were taking a lot of fire from mortars and artillery. Three of the Shermans became disabled and needed help. The tank crews could not leave their vehicles, either via the top hatch or the bottom escape hatch, because if they tried they would have been easy targets for the Japs in their concealed positions.

They radioed for help, and I picked up the call. So from my OP, I targeted the area and called in the mortar crews for several white phosphorus smoke rounds to land on the enemy side of the area to cloud things up. Sure enough, a half minute later, the smoke rounds began to land, and after about seven or eight, the smoke made it almost impossible to see. The tankers got out and made it back to our lines. When they were clear, I called in the 81s to fire the 15-lb. rounds. That would at least pin down the enemy mortars.

The next day it started raining again, and man, it would come down on and off for the next week and a half. Everything was wet, and there was mud everywhere. Keeping things dry was almost hopeless. That day was a busy one, and our mortar platoon, along with the 60mm mortars in the rifle companies, were given quite a lot of fire missions. Our shells rained down over the opposite slope of Wana Ridge. We were later told that our fire had been effective.[34]

That evening, with the rain still coming down, the mortar platoon was pulled off the line. I was glad. Ever since I had been blown off that cliff on May 2nd, I had periodic headaches, and now they had started to get to me again. I had been having some groggy spells for a few days. I thought a codeine pill would hit the spot, so one morning, I told Lt.

---

33 Two days later, Lt. Col. Sabol replaced Major Holomon as 7th Marines Operations Officer. Lt. Col. James Monahan, who had commanded the division's Headquarters Battalion, took over Ross's job as Executive Officer of the 1st Marines.

34 The next morning, Company C, positioned between the 2nd and 3rd battalions, reported 140 enemy dead.

Haggerty where I was going and walked back to battalion headquarters and over to the aid station. Lt. Christopherson, our battalion doctor, took one look at me and I am not exactly sure what he saw, but I must have been a sight. He immediately said that I looked strung out. I just sat there, too tired to respond. He took another look at me and said, "I'm going to evacuate you."

"Huh?" I said, not understanding.

"I'm gonna send you back to a field hospital," he said simply.

I didn't know what it was that I had, so I asked him, "What the hell for?"

Doc told me that he thought I had malaria. If I had not been so exhausted, I might have just asked for the pill and returned to my unit. At the time though, his prognosis sounded like just what I needed, so I went along with his recommendation.

Doc tagged me for evacuation, and I sat and waited. Soon the ambulance came to take us back. Actually, it was just a scout car with a red cross on its sides, but what the hell. About seven or eight of us were loaded on, to take us back a mile or two to a field hospital that had been set up. As I rode along that afternoon, thankful that I was leaving the combat area, I took a closer look at the guys around me. I stared at the bloody bandages. Pangs of guilt gnawed at me as I realized that each one of these guys had one or more wounds, some of them serious. More and more this bothered the hell out of me, because they were a lot more deserving of getting evacuated than me.

It was starting to get dark when we pulled into the field hospital, which was really just a bunch of army tents. I made damn sure that all those wounded guys were taken off before I got off that scout car.

They took me into one of the tents and assigned me a cot. The doctor there finally got around to me and checked me out. He told me that I had malaria, and then ordered a medic to give me a codeine pill. I was tired, depressed, and had not slept in a real cot in over two months. I took the pill and went out like a light. Man, I just slept like a baby all night.

The next morning, I got up feeling so much better. I stretched, and then walked out the tent. I saw that even though it had been raining on and off for a week and a half, the sun was now shining. Even the weather was with me, I thought.[35]

Then I heard one of the medics say, "All right, all you guys who don't have a wound, fall out for shock treatment."

I realized what that meant. I was to undergo mental stability evaluation. I thought, uh-uh. Ain't no way that they were going to label me with that shit.

Then I found out that my unit had been called up that night. Guilt hit me again. Many of these guys I had served with for two years, and I now felt like I was just running out on them. It was true, the doctor had given me a free ride out, but at that point, I decided that I did not want to take it. I'm a stubborn guy, you know ... and besides, the platoon they needed me. They did not have an FO with any experience, and over the months, I had become very good at it, and unlike the thick jungles of Cape Gloucester and Peleliu, there was not nearly as much undergrowth here. The views on Okinawa were much clearer, making it so much better for me to do my job.

So determined to stay and still in possession of my Thompson, my compass, and my other stuff, I hitched a ride back to the front. Following the sound of the guns, I moved up to the line. It had rained so hard that nothing mechanical could move much. The jeeps, tanks, the trucks, wagons, were all stalled; there was thick mud everywhere.

I began walking forward. Everything was soaking. I finally caught up with the 3rd Battalion. I found my mortar platoon at the bottom of a hill next to the base of Shuri Castle, listening to the distant fire, getting ready to assault the Japs.

I said hi and they looked at me, surprised. I was stunned to find out that the bastards had not missed me. In fact, they hadn't even caught on that I was not there. So when I joined them again and they realized that I had not been around, their first reaction was that I had gone over the hill. I shook my head in wonder. Why the hell did I go back? I wasn't sure now, because I mean, I had not even been missed.

---

35 The weather cleared on May 28th.

Lt. Haggerty saw me and must have realized that he had not seen me in the last few hours. He asked me if I had gone somewhere, and rather than tell him that the doc had slated me for evacuation and that I had changed my mind, I just made up some other excuse to him. He just sighed and raised his eyebrows. I laughed. Oh well, I was back with them.

Shuri Castle

That morning, the sun came out, but that was short lived. We were each issued three emergency bars of chocolate. These things were big: six inches by two inches wide, and almost an inch thick. There was no time to savor them, though. The Japs were in retreat. So we took off, and sure enough, it started to rain again. There was an incredible amount of mud everywhere. Even the alligators could not move—the amphibious assault vehicles that is, not the animal, although if there had been any of those reptiles around, they wouldn't have been able to get around either.

We spent the next couple of days on the approach and then climbing up the ridge to Shuri Castle. Enemy fire that time kept diminishing, and around the 25th, we were only getting sporadic fire from the holding force. We were having problems actually assaulting the castle because it was so formidable, the key to their whole line. So we were expanding our hold along the ridge to isolate the position. It rained like hell as we spent a good part of the day slugging it up that damn ridge. The climb was really steep, with water pouring down on us as we struggled to move up. Finally in the late afternoon, soaked and really tired, we made it to the top of the ridge. The castle was far off to our left. Climbing up, we had taken occasional stray shots, and when we reached the top, a couple more Japs fired at us. Evidently, here they had left a couple snipers behind to slow us down. The castle was still firmly theirs. There was no mistake, though. They were on the run.

That night, we set up our defense perimeter atop the ridge in a spot near some steep cliffs. There were a lot of dead Japs up there, so we did some cleanup. We found an area where they had made a makeshift cemetery. They had buried a lot of their soldiers that had been killed, and they must have been in a hurry. Each grave were typically just a foot or two feet deep, the body dumped in, and then covered over with a small mound of dirt. Some of the graves had darkened body parts sticking out, and there were a lot of flies. Next to the area, we found a spot where they had set up some sort of a little field hospital. There were dirty, bloody rags and bandages all over the place, and a lot of syringes in the mud. The whole place smelled horribly. Evidently, they had taken their walking wounded with them. I can only imagine what they did to the ones that were too badly shot up to move.

The next day, May 26th, we moved forward again, following the retreating Japs. We moved down the ridge and going forward, we went down into this valley, with hills all around us. We came to a bridge that was out in an open area. We found it was covered by a couple of enemy snipers left behind to slow us down. We could not pinpoint where the shots were coming from, and in the end, we decided to run across the bridge one at a time. It took some time, because there were 55 of us. As each took his turn running across, we continued to look for the sniper. In the end, we were lucky. Only one of us actually got hit: Norman Leishman, the No. 4 mortar assistant who was from Santa Monica, California. He was six two and a good-looking guy, although he was pretty conceited and thought he was Mr. Hollywood himself. I remember that Norman liked to stand round a lot and smile, just trying to look "purdy." Anyway, he was shot in the ankle, and it was only a minor wound. They took him back to the medical tent, and he was back with us in just a few days.

We moved on, chasing the enemy southward as the days went by, and while we occasionally got into skirmishes, they were small.

The Army Air Corps tried to keep us supplied by regularly dropping stuff to us from the air. Those assholes were lousy shots though, because the wind would catch the chutes, and they would drift over the cliffs where we were and down into the valleys. Our fresh water came down to us in crates with these three-foot-long by eight-inch-round rubber tubes that we (for obvious reasons) called "condoms." As we expected, the crates often broke open on impact and or two condoms would pop up in the air and burst, spraying water everywhere. Bastards ...

One miserable, cold, wet morning around May 28th, we were sitting around under a couple tents. It was a drizzling cold rain, and we sat cleaning our weapons, and in general just trying to keep dry and warm up. We had been taken off the line because of the casualties we had incurred, so we were now reorganizing the platoon. We noticed in the distance Lt. Haggerty wearing a poncho, walking towards us. With him was this new officer. The two of them walked up to us and came under the tent. Lt. Haggerty introduced the newbie as 1st Lt. Curtis A. Beall (he pronounced it "Bell"), from Georgia. Technically, he was the new assistant platoon officer for our mortars, but was going to take over the platoon.

After brief introductions, Lt. Haggerty turned to me, and we began discussing the tactical situation, and how the lieutenant wanted me to do the fire missions. As we talked, I glanced over at the new officer. He sat quietly some distance away from us, looking at the two of us as we talked. He finally took off with Lt. Haggerty, and I did not see him after that.

Years later, at a reunion, I asked him about that morning, and why he had been so quiet and why I never saw him again after that; certainly never up at any of my OPs. He laughed and told me that he was new to the Pacific and did not know a damn thing about mortars. After having met me, he was sure that I definitely knew what the hell I was doing, and that I damn sure knew more about mortars that he probably ever would. So he simply decided that I was doing just fine, and that he was not going to interfere with what I was doing and screw things up.

I learned later that day that besides Beall, we received two new sergeants: Sgt. Hopgood and Gunnery Sgt. Richard Barrett. Barrett became the platoon's Gunny, and Hopgood was made the mortar platoon first sergeant.

The next day, May 29th, the whole division moved forward and attacked, trying to capture the main objective of the entire area: Shuri Castle, headquarters for the Jap Army on Okinawa. Taking it had up until now been almost impossible. Still, we were going up against it again. Well, I was back with my unit, and I was once again going to do my FO job for our heavy mortars.

This time though, we were going to do something different. We had experimented a couple times with a brand-new mass-fire tactic that we called "regimental mortars." We were going to try to coordinate all the 81mm mortars in the regiment by using just one forward observer, and today we were going to give it a try. I was going to direct the fire. When we were all set up, I got on the field phone with 3rd Battalion headquarters, ready to begin the firing missions. They somehow in turn were going to pass on my coordinates and instructions to set up simultaneous sequences with the other two heavy mortar platoons in the 1st and 2nd Marine battalions. So I was going to be the eyes for all 12 heavy mortars.

When I was ready, I gave the first firing order to our own platoon. The information was immediately relayed to the other two platoons via the 3rd Battalion headquarters, and all three commenced firing on the same target. I had planned on giving the castle area a good going-over before the infantry attacked. So I began by zeroing in on the coordinates of a large high-tension steel tower nearby. I was going to knock that damn thing down. A strange thing, though. With all them mortars firing, the tower stayed up. I could not knock it down. There were a lot of explosions next to it and a lot of sparks, but that damn tower stayed up.

I shifted my fire onto the empty moats around the castle, and pounded them. Then I concentrated fire on where I thought the main tunnels were beneath the castle, based on where I had been told they might be. There was also a nearby cemetery, and I made sure that all 12 mortars thoroughly raked the area several times.

Finally, I suspended the mortar fire, and our regiment and the 7th Marines went down in there, and I was glad to hear that resistance was not too heavy. The word later came down that the Jap 32nd Army was starting to retreat southward down the reverse ridges, and they had left a residual force to hold us up until the main body could get away safely.

We advanced up the northern side, cutting across the Army units (which I heard later really pissed them off), and finally took Shuri Castle.

Lt. Col. Ross, our battalion commander, even though snipers took a few shots at him, ran our flag up at the castle.[36] Which might have been a neat and daring thing to do, but it was also dumb, because the castle was on high ground that could be seen for miles around. Every damn Jap field piece that had the range opened up on our flag. It stayed up, but the area sure as hell took a pounding. We later found out that some smartass captain had first put up a Confederate flag.[37]

The next day, just after we had secured Shuri Castle, we were relieved. We moved back to rest and reorganize, and ended up back on top of Wana Ridge, where the Japs had fought us so hard. We set camp on the crest of the ridge, and I was just amazed at what I saw. The ground was

------

36 That morning, the division commander, General del Valle, had sent a G-2 (Intelligence) team from G-2 forward carrying the divisional colors (which the division had flown on Cape Gloucester and Peleliu) with orders to raise them on Shuri Castle.

37 An interesting story. Actually, the Confederate flag was raised on the 30th by members of "Rebel" A Company, 5th Marines. It had belonged to their company commander, Capt. Julius Dusenbury, a native of Clausen SC. He had carried the flag in his helmet. In heavy combat the day before though, he had been shot by a Japanese sniper and crippled. Not having anything else to raise, his men had raised his flag, partly in his honor, and partly to show that the castle had been taken. The commanding officer of the 1st Marine Division though, Maj. General Pedro del Valle, protested to his superior, Tenth Army General Buckner (whose father had been a famous Civil War general). Buckner told him with a smile, "How can I be sore at him? [Dusenbury]? My father fought under that flag." The flag stayed up for a couple hours, and amused by the whole thing, Buckner finally ordered it down, replacing it with the American flag in a formal ceremony on May 31st by Lt. Col. Richard Ross himself. Dusenbury, even though he was not present when his Dixie flag went up, was slated to be court-martialed over the offense. However, General Buckner himself intervened, and the charge was finally reduced to a reprimand. The Confederate flag was later given to Buckner as a souvenir, even though he would only have it for a short while before his death on June 18th. Dusenbury, who probably would have received the Medal of Honor for his actions were it not for this issue, was instead awarded the Navy Cross. He later went on to serve in the South Carolina state legislature and died in 1976.

all torn up, and there were craters everywhere. The whole area looked terrible, like some sort of weird moonscape.

I set my pack and gear down on that ridge and stood up to take a stretch. So far, so good, I thought as I gazed at what looked like a battle scene from one of those old World War I movies. A minute or so later, I went back to my pack and—son of a bitch—one of the guys had stolen my .45 right out from under me.

We rested on that ridge, and I sacked out for ten days. Then we went out looking for stray Japs. They mostly hid out either in caves, bunkers that they had built, or more than anything, in the hundreds of tombs all over the island. Most of them were either empty or had dead bodies. It didn't make any difference to us, though. We were told to assume that there were Japs in them, and to either check them out thoroughly, or else to either blow them up or seal them up. Since we knew that checking them out was most dangerous of the three choices, we opted for the last two. And in the end, it was easiest to just throw a couple grenades or some C4 into each entrance and take it out that way. We had learned from experience that as routine as this process seemed to get, that we should always be on our toes and expect the unexpected.

A few days after we had started patrolling, our unit came upon yet another one of these tombs. We checked out the front and a couple times called out to those inside to come out. When there was no response, we were told to set it off. So one Marine crept up to the entrance and listened. He motioned to us that he heard faint voices inside, so he pulled the pin on a grenade and threw it in. Unfortunately for him though, what he did not know was that there was a sizable ammo cache inside, and when the grenade blew up, all the ammo went up with it in a terrific set of explosions that shook the ground and took out the whole area.

When the debris stopped coming down and the smoke started to clear, we found nothing left of the tomb, and neither the Japs inside, nor the Marine who had tossed the grenade. What was left of him was a chunk of wood from the stock of his rifle sticking out of the dirt. That was it. He was gone.

June 1945

In the first two days of June, with the Shuri Castle area now ours, the 5th Marines continued attacking the retreating Japs. Our regiment stayed in the area to secure it, take out straggling enemy soldiers, remove the wounded, and bury our dead. During this time, replacements were brought in and given hasty training in weapons handling and in patrolling.

On June 5th, as part of a plan to keep constant pressure on the hard-pressed Japanese, 3rd Battalion, 1st Marines moved south, and after a day of sharp encounters, took the town of Iwa. They would pursue the Japanese for the next five days.

On June 4th, as we moved south in the rain, we received a nice surprise from, of all people, the Army. The guys in the 96th Infantry decided to share some of their rations with us. Which for us was a good thing, because we had almost nothing to eat at that point.

One thing about Marines: we had been taught to make do and, whenever necessary, to be innovative, whether it seemed possible or not. That, of course, went for drinking as well. Conditions being what they frequently were, alcohol would have for others been considered out of the question. However, we were Marines. We were taught to adapt. We usually did. On Pavuvu, Col. Puller had allowed us from time to time a ration of two beers. He sometimes withheld the rations until we had accumulated enough to have a few, and thus get a decent "buzz." Certainly no hard liquor, though. But now, on Okinawa, we had no alcoholic opportunities whatsoever, and we had been here for almost four months.

So, a couple of us came up with a classic solution: we built us a mobile still.

Many of us had the expertise. I had seen my old man run several in my youth. An amateur bootlegger, he would procure whiskey from questionable sources and hide it in a barrel buried in the ground, with a special lid over it. His main effort though was his own stuff. For years, my old man ran his own still, right up to the day he died. When I was a kid, the still was right in our house. I remember we would buy 30 or 40 pounds of lump brown sugar that came in burlap bags. He would then make a grain mash that he would cook before adding the heated sugar. Then came the distillation process. I clearly remember how the condensed clear liquid would slowly drip out the end of that lone spiral copper tube and into a bottle. I imagine the stuff was good enough to drink. He and his buddies sure as hell never had a problem swigging it down.

Usually he would get tipped off when a raid was coming (Dad was hooked up to a couple local judges), and so we would have time to scatter and hide the evidence, including the still components. Although I do remember one time, when my dad was not home, Alex and I got the word that the cops were coming. So we quickly took the still apart and waded out into the swamps to bury the equipment. Unfortunately, we got stuck on the bogs and the equipment got lost, sinking into the murky unknown. After it was safe, we went back and tried to find it, but we never could. When the old man found out, he liked to have killed us.

One time my dad actually did get caught with a still and was hauled off to the hoosegow. I was five or six years old at the time, and Mom took me and Alex down to get him out. Sure enough, the old man was in jail, locked in a fenced cage. After that, he made sure we were all on our toes for the law.

Now here on Okinawa, creating hooch was something I knew about. As did several others, and so we pooled our knowledge and resources. Howard Quarty and Fred O. Miller scrounged around wherever we went and soon found the parts to build the damn thing. They had found a copper pot and some copper tubing and had fashioned the whole thing together. Now all we needed was some ingredients to make the jungle juice. If we could steal a bottle of medicinal alcohol from the medics, we were nearly there.

Often though, we had to use other types of ingredients. Cans of fruit in their own juice worked, mixed with sugar and water. Other ingredients could include potato peels, coconut juice, raisins, and, in a pinch, very limited amounts of certain types of aftershave (I had learned from my incident on Pavuvu). We would thoroughly smash the entire concoction together, strain it through a T-shirt, and then Miller would cook the whole thing. Funny, but you would get these pieces of fruit in the mixture, even after you strained it clear like water out of the faucet. Then you heated sugar into it and it would color the whole thing up brown.

At that point, we were ready to distill. Up through the top of the pot the vapor would go, then spiral through the tubing and condense, and finally drip out the end into whatever bottles or canteens we could scrounge. Usually it cooled into a clear fluid. And there ya go. White lightning, Marine style. Man oh man, I can tell you that despite the sometimes really outlandish flavor, it sure took the edge off the evening. And it was sometimes even worth getting the heaves from a bad batch, or waking up the next morning with your head splitting in two.

Luckily for us, the officers were understanding and tolerant, for which of course, they sometimes were allowed to indulge as well. And whenever they got a whiskey ration, they would sometimes reciprocate. In that regard, we really appreciated Haggerty. He always shared his ration with us since he did not drink, bless him.

And the beauty of the whole thing was that whenever we moved out, the guys would pack the stuff all up, and the still went with us. I have to say, I would usually chuckle when I saw Miller walk by with that damn copper tube sticking out of his pack.

Like the other campaigns, food began to be an issue for us soon after we had engaged the enemy at the beginning of May. When we did have supplies, it was powdered crap all the time. Powdered eggs, milk, coffee, potatoes—just about all the food was powder. After all, it was easier to ship. Years later, I was asked if I ever got tired of eating spam. Hell, no. We very rarely got any. That for us was a delicacy. I was told that a good deal of it had been shipped over to us, but somehow, it all got siphoned off by others units before it came to us Marines on the front. The last really good meal I had eaten was steak and eggs that the Navy had given us the night before we went ashore.

So chow was getting to be a bit of a challenge. Rations were of course the normal staple for us, and once in a great while, we would get some hot meals—well, warm at least. But so much of the time, we were on our own and had to improvise.

When we had finally wrapped things up on Cape Gloucester in 1944 and a galley had at long last been set up, we were fed salmon patties for two meals every friggin' day, lunch and dinner, for two solid months. Salmon patties and more salmon patties, until they started coming out of our ears. I got so sick of eating it meal after meal. To this day, I cannot eat a salmon patty.

When reorganizing on Pavuvu, right before we were loaded up for Peleliu in September 1944, a refrigerator ship had come to the island. In it were tons of frozen liver. So we now were served liver every day Just like with the salmon patties, for two straight weeks before the operation. I got so damn sick of liver, but we were told to eat it, because it produces this chemical called fibrinogen, which supposedly is a blood coagulant. We were told that when we fought on those horribly hot beaches, if we were to get wounded, that fibrinogen would help keep us from bleeding to death. I supposed that it probably helped some, although it sure as hell did not do a damn thing for all the guys that got their heads blown off.

Now here on Okinawa, we found ourselves going days without regular rations. Since there were some animals on the island, we caught them whenever we could. Hogs, sometimes cattle, sheep, wild boar. Some were not fit to eat, because they were diseased or had bugs in them, like blow flies. Those we could though, we put to good use. We would slaughter them, then field dress them, cut them up, cook them, and then eat what we could stand. Any vegetables that we found, like yams, got sliced up and went into the pot as well. Other than that, warm meals were few and far between.

The K-rations kept us going, but were usually never delivered. We could pick some up whenever we went back to battalion headquarters for more ammo. So after loading down with shells and magazines and grenades and clips, you often did not have enough strength to carry very many K-rations, or not much room in your pockets, especially when you consider that we would have to share with the other guys when we got back. Sometimes, we were given chocolate bars. That, though, was rare.

Coffee was an absolute requirement for us, and we had some whenever we could. Bags of ground coffee were usually available. The problem was a fire to heat the water, especially when it was pouring rain all the damn time. So, being Marines, we came up with some novel solutions. We learned quickly that plastic C4 explosive was easy to mold, and generally safe to handle. More importantly though, when lit, C4 made a fierce burn that was pretty much impervious to rain. It came in these bars that were transported in canvas pouches. The bars were malleable, and so you could easily open a bar up and then could pull off whatever amount you needed. Lighting the C4 sometimes made for a challenge in the rain, but we used the negative paper range fuses off the 81mm and 60mm mortar shells.[38] They were somewhat difficult to keep dry, and it was hard to keep them from deteriorating, because they were made of thin paper and fell apart easily. Still, they lit up readily. Once the C4 was lit, it burned like hell, even in the pouring rain, and it stayed lit too until all the material was consumed. It was nice to be able to light one or two pieces and then heat our canteen cups over them.

To help with the cooking whenever we had the occasion, I now carried a little 8-ounce C-ration can that I kept lard in. Every time we cooked an animal, I would collect as much of its grease as I could. Usually, I would try to keep the can at least half full. In the evening, I would heat it up and we would take some huge island sweet potatoes, about the size of your head, and cut them up then slice them down into thin slices. We would then drop the slices into the hot grease, cook them, let them drain and *voila!* Sweet potato chips.

One or two of us also carried around a gallon can with a wire strap for cooking. We would fill it a third or half way with water and take any type of food "donations" and throw it all in for some eight to ten of us. We would cook it into whatever sort of stew we could, divide

---

38 Technically they were termed "propellant increments," and examples include Type M1, M2, M43, or M47. Each mortar shell had four to six of these thin square sheets of powder, located between the rear fins. Ignited along with the propellant charge, they were removable. The more that were removed, the less the total firing charge, and thus the less the distance the shell traveled (thus allowing the shell's range to be varied).

it up, and eat. That big old Texan Clarence Keele was our butcher (he had actually been one before the war), so he would cut up and prepare whatever meat we could kill. Howard Quarty was our cook.

I remember one night after a hard day of fighting, we were deciding what we wanted to do for chow. We hadn't received any K-rations, but we had a little meat and some vegetables between us. So should we pool our food and make our stew tonight, or wait until tomorrow morning and have a hearty breakfast?

I thought about it. I was pretty hungry. "Let's eat it tonight. Hell, we may get killed tonight. At least we'll have a full belly."

The guys were hungry too, so they agreed. We pooled all our perishable food and Howard made us this really savory stew over a low fire, and we all had a good meal. Next morning though, we had nothing left to eat, and naturally I caught hell for that. Figures.

So again I told those guys, "Well damn it, how the hell did you even know that you'd *be* alive this morning?"

They grumbled some after that, but that was the end of it.

Part of the time, we ended up surviving on the sugarcane that grew in the fields. We would hack the cane down and then cut the sticks up into one-foot lengths that we would stuff into our packs and pockets. Then, as we went along, if we wanted to, we would sometimes take one out of our pocket and chew on it. The sugar in the cane dissolved in our mouths, and the sweet taste helped.

Entertainment brews were scarce. Still, sometimes Providence had a way of helping us out. Like others in the unit, I had come to take a shine to our battalion doctor, Lt. Christopherson, and I would see him once in a while as we took wounded back to the aid station. Even though he was an officer, over time we had become friends. Now the doc had access occasionally to gallons of 190-proof alcohol. It was supposed to be for medicinal purposes, but sometimes he would give us some to brew up some brandy, for the guys recovering. We would occasionally give them shots of that homemade brandy made from this alcohol. So one time, after bringing back a few wounded guys, I talked Doc into giving me some. I said, "Hey doc, you know, we don't have any more brandy, and the guys are getting shot up pretty bad."

He thought about it, looked at my smiling face, and agreed. He then gave me a gallon. A whole friggin' gallon! It came in a shiny, plain silver, rectangular can. There was no sticker on it, no label of any kind. White lightning, U.S. Government brand.

I took it back and thought about what had happened. I decided to keep it all for myself. What the hell, they had plenty of alcohol at the medic tents. So even though I felt bad about it, I knew that I was going to keep the gallon myself. In the end, I fixed up and drank that entire can.

I still laugh today when I think about it. I would make up a one-quart batch at a time, stirring up a mixture of half alcohol and half Kool-Aid. I'd then carry this homemade elixir in two pint canteens that of course really should have held water. I do admit, I am ashamed of having kept the gallon and having done that. But at that time, any silly notions that I had carried about life were long gone, and mentally, I was in a bad place. I had lost so many friends, including Henry, and I had become isolated socially, doing everything very seriously. I felt that I had learned a lot about life, and so much of it was cold and impersonal. Funny, I hadn't yet even turned 23, but I sure felt a hell of a lot older than my years.

We continued attacking the Japs. On June 10th, with the Army on our left, 3rd Battalion advanced after I had coordinated an effective mortar attack on the Jap positions.

One night in mid-June, about a week before the fighting stopped on the island, I had a real scare put to me. Our battalion had set up our routine defensive line for the night. Not being around any other units, we just set up a big circular perimeter and made camp. We sort of circled the wagons so to speak—only we didn't have any wagons. After we had set up our perimeter, we dug in, prepared ourselves for the evening and then had chow.

Afterwards, a few of us settled in for some quiet sipping. The watch was set, our fields of fire were set, the trip wires were set, and we were set, ready for any kind of trouble.

It was really dark when my watch ended, and I went back to my foxhole to get some shuteye. Howard Quarty had the watch now. Yeah, he was drunk by now from the jungle juice he had belted down, but he was still alert.

Suddenly, a trip wire was pulled and its flare went off into the night. Howard turned his rifle in that direction and opened up, shooting into the dark. When he had emptied his clip, Lt. Haggerty, who had clearly heard the shots and knew who was firing, crept over to Howard's foxhole, saw his condition, and growled, "Quarty, there better be a gawddamn body out there when morning comes." He had a thing against anyone shooting out there just for the hell of it.

Luckily, there were no more incidents that night, and next morning we checked to see what if anything was out beyond the perimeter where Howard had fired. Sure enough, there was a body out there. But it wasn't a Jap. The warning wire had instead been tripped by a cow, and it lay out there, shot to hell and back. So naturally we cut it up and ate it. Quarty of course, got razzed for turning back a cow attack.

The next day, we continued north, and by sunset, we ended up closer to our original landing beaches. Even though we were not on the line now, we still had to maintain a constant alert, because there were so many Jap stragglers still around. So as usual, we had to set up our defenses at night.

Inside of our perimeter was this big cave. It was too big to blow up with the few explosives we had, so we just thoroughly checked out the entrance and then kept an eye on it, because we suspected that there were still Japs in it. We didn't find any though. Good thing.

That night, I stood my watch, doing my share of night duty standing guard. Along with the Thompson, I carried a shotgun that I had found—well, actually I had found it laying in the dirt in this hut. It was a civilian model, and someone on the island had used it at one time. It was a beautiful Model 97 Winchester.[39] It had a military bayonet lug and not the regular short barrel, but the long 28-inch barrel, with a perforated jacket over it to keep you from burning your hands after

---

39 Model 1897 Winchester pump-action 12-gauge shotgun. The trench model was quite popular with the Marines because of its close-action firepower. It was used effectively on Guadalcanal to repel Japanese banzai-style attacks.

you've fired eight or nine rounds. The magazine could hold six rounds, with another one in the chamber. It was a great piece to find, and the extra firepower it would give me in the jungle was considerable. It was though, in bad condition, having been in the dirt for some time. Still, I didn't care. I knew that it was quite a find, and I would make good use of it. After all, I was good with weapons.

The shotgun had built up some rust and crud on it, so I went to work. In my spare time, I tore it apart and carefully began to clean it up. I built a small fire and heated up in my helmet some oil that I had found. I then soaked the parts that I had cleaned in the oil for a couple hours. I then patiently cleaned each piece up again, and slowly I reassembled the shotgun. Then I went down to Division's ordnance and was able to get two boxes of big brass casing shells (not the paper or plastic ones), each one containing nine .32 cal. pellets. I was able to find some linseed oil, and I rubbed it on the stock like there was no tomorrow.

After I had cleaned it up, I immediately took it out and went pheasant hunting. I saw some, but I couldn't get any. So in the end, I started using it whenever I had nighttime sentry duty. It was a great weapon for jungle fighting so it was popular with the guys. Naturally, they all wanted to use it at night, and I was okay with that, so I let them all borrow it.

Tonight, when I was relieved, I turned over the Winchester to my relief and walked away from the line. Now it was my turn to nap, and I was tired. I walked over to a foxhole that I had found about ten yards in from the perimeter. Tired, I took off my gear. I laid my pack and my cartridge belt down in the shallow foxhole. I took my Thompson and laid it down on my pack, then turned to go take a piss. There was a steep bank nearby, with an elevated path around it. I walked over to it in the dark and stopped right next to the bank about 15 feet away, with the path up round my head. I leaned against the cliff, unzipped, and got ready to do my thing.

I didn't know it, but two of those Jap bastards were just coming out of that damn cave and were trying to leave the area. I don't think though, that they realized they were completely encircled by our battalion and so were trapped. I froze as I heard these muffled voices getting nearer and recognized they were Japs because I could hear them whispering to each other in their gibberish. What was worse, I realized that they were coming from the wrong direction, from the *inside* of our perimeter. I hunkered down and stayed quiet.

As I scrunched next to that cliff, frozen in place with my fly open, these two Japs began quietly to sneak round that path right beside me. They slowly tiptoed right next to where my head was at. They were so close that I swear I could have reached out and grabbed one of their ankles. I knew that they needed to be killed, but I was too damn far away from my Thompson to try for it. Now these Japs when they tried to infiltrate at night always carried grenades, or those bayonets attached to those long sticks, like the ones that we had seen on Peleliu. I hadn't seen any sticks as these two crept by (of course, with my face buried in the dirt along the cliff, I wasn't looking) so I figured that they must each be carrying a couple grenades. Therefore I didn't ask them for the password, because I was unarmed. I mean, the only thing I had in my right hand was definitely *not* my rifle. If I were to call out to them in the darkness, they'd throw their grenades down at me. So I crouched down and huddled up against the bank and kept quiet, listening for a click. That was the key, you know. If you heard that click, you knew that they had armed the grenade and were getting ready to throw it.[40]

These two Japs slowly crept by me, once in a while whispering in that damn drivel of theirs. I knew that there was a Marine guard about twenty yards away with a BAR, so I listened in the dark as they approached him. I waited to hear him ask for the password. But there was no sound. Nothing. I did not move.

All of a sudden, I faintly heard them whispering again as they seemed to be coming closer. They had apparently changed their minds. They

---

40 The fuse that the Japanese Type 97 or Type 99 grenade commonly used was in the 1½-inch-long cylindrical head at the top. It had a safety pin similar to an American grenade that when pulled would arm the weapon. The firing pin was set off by striking the head against a hard object like a rock or, more commonly, the enemy's helmet. They then immediately would throw the grenade. Japanese grenades were often unreliable, and in any event, were not as powerful as their American counterparts. The act of striking the head of course would make a loud clicking sound, which the Marines learned to key off.

had either seen our sentry or had just decided to turn back. Either way, they were coming round towards me, and damned if they didn't come again along that lousy path, right by me for the second time.

I clenched my teeth and just sat there in the dark, waiting, freaking out. Hell, I might have even pissed myself for all I knew. They slowly passed and I figured sooner or later they would come up on another guard. Sure enough, after a bit I heard somebody say something out loud. It was the other guard, no doubt asking them to give the password.

As soon as I heard his voice, I heard these two clicks, followed by two loud booms as the Jap grenades went off. At the same time, a BAR opened up, and I heard the rounds from his automatic weapon flying right over me and slamming into the dirt above and around me. Our guys rushed to the spot and found that the guard had been wounded by the grenade explosions, but he had survived. He did kill the two Japs though. I checked their bodies out. They had a couple more grenades with them. I had been right. If I had challenged them, I would have had them thrown at me. And I would not have been able to defend myself.

I shook my head. It was the only night on Okinawa that I did not have my Thompson in my hand or on my chest as I slept, and I almost got killed taking a leak.

Another night, it had been relatively quiet, when we got word passed down that some Japs were coming out of this cave and headed our way. We were supposed to look out for them, and when they came up to our position, we were going to let them have it. No shooting though, because we did not want to give our position away. So there we were crouched in the dark, waiting, waiting …

Suddenly, we heard one of them quietly crawling towards us. Clarence Keele, the big Texan, was nearest. He whispered, "Jesus Christ, here comes one of them."

Clarence drew back with his spade and was getting ready to let the guy have it. After a moment, he whispered, "Damn. I don't know how hard I'm going to have to hit that sonuvabitch so I can kill him."

Clarence stood there, his shovel gripped tight, waiting, and he was just about to let fly when the shadow crawling down there said something to him in English. It was one of our guys!

338 • 22 ON PELELIU

The last battle

The ground forces commander in the Okinawa campaign was 59-year-old Lt. General Simon Bolivar Buckner, Jr., commanding the Tenth Army. The general, who was the son of famous Confederate general Simon Bolivar Buckner, Sr., was unfortunately killed in the early afternoon of June 18th while inspecting advancing units at an 8th Marines frontline observation post at Hill 52. His open presence (especially the three stars on his jeep in plain sight) soon began drawing enemy artillery fire, and even when a nearby Marine post radioed that they could clearly see the general's jeep, the only thing he did was to exchange his 3-star helmet with an unmarked one.

A short time later, at 1315 hours, a salvo of five enemy 150mm artillery shells began to detonate nearby, and one of them hit an outcropping near the general. No one else was hurt, but the explosion from the shell hitting the coral slammed a few lethal fragments into the general's chest. He was taken to an aid station where he died on the table some ten minutes later. General Buckner became the highest-ranking U.S. officer to be killed by enemy fire during World War II.[41] Succeeding him in command was none other than Marine General Roy Geiger, George Peto's III Amphibious Corps commander. General Geiger immediately took command of the Tenth Army.

As it started to get dark on Tuesday, June 19th, we set up our positions on a hill. We were getting ready to attack a Jap ridge that was perpendicular to and adjacent to this mountain. The ridge was honeycombed with Jap bunkers, and we were going to hit them tomorrow. So we were setting up our positions as evening fell, when we saw a bunch of guys come down into this valley below us. From where we could see, they looked like were just milling around in the open and not seeming to be doing anything in particular, except maybe setting up camp. Evidently, they planned on staying down there for the whole night. We watched them for a while, trying to figure out who the hell they were and what

---

41 Three other senior officers of that rank were killed during the war. Two died in plane crashes (Lt. General Frank Andrews and Lt. General Millard Harmon), and the third (Lt. General Leslie McNair) was killed in a friendly fire bombardment near St. Lô.

they were up to. They certainly were not going about it very efficiently, and were taking their time.

Staring down below, Lt. Haggerty watched them for a while longer and finally he grumbled, "What the hell's that bunch of guys doing down there?" He looked over at me, but I just shrugged. I had no idea who they were.

He looked back down at them and shaking his head, he griped, "They're just farting around." After a couple more moments, he added, "They're gonna draw fire on us if they don't get their asses down."

We watched them some more, setting up for the night as it got darker.

Finally Haggerty muttered something under his breath and said, "I'm gonna find out what the hell those idiots are doing down there. They're gonna bring in fire on all of us."

He started down the hill to chew those guys out, and we watched him as he made his way down to the group and started talking to them. After a couple minutes, he began climbing back up the slope, and the guys down there went back to setting up camp.

Haggerty came up and, surprisingly, he had a kind of hang-dog look on his face. He looked at me and, pointing down the hill, he said in what could only be an embarrassed tone, "That's the corps commander."

"Huh?" was all I could say.

"That's General Geiger. He came up to check out the front area."

Major General Roy S. Geiger, commander of the III Amphibious Corps and currently commander of the entire Tenth Army was down there. Haggerty pointed him out to us. So much for bawling those guys out.

And that was the only time I ever saw our corps commander.

What turned out to be our last battle was the next morning, June 21st. It took place at the base of a big mountain. In front of and perpendicular to it was this long set of high ridges running south for about a quarter mile. At the end of it was a circle of firing pits dug into the ridge, all of which were connected by a mass of underground caves.

That morning, I hopped into a hole that was to the right of the ridge. I was facing the ridge on my left, about a hundred yards from it, and

I had a perfect view of the area. I never used binoculars. To me they were a burden to carry, and anyway, I never needed them. I had got rid of them long time ago. The same thing with the gas mask.

We knew that there was a mess of Japs in that ridge, and it was a tough position. We had made attacks on both sides to get into position for an assault. So now we concentrated our attention on that ridge before us. As mentioned it was on a large hill behind which was the base of this mountain. The Japs were going to defend the ridge, and we knew that it was peppered with all sorts of underground tunnels. Luckily for us though, there was only one escape hole: a square four-by-four-foot tunnel near the front of the ridge. There were four exit ladders, one on each of the sides. We figured that the Japs would defend the ridge until they were overrun. Then they would scurry out of the hole, run back to the base of the next ridge behind them, scamper up the ladders there, and take up new underground positions on that ridge to defend this new line. We had been through this ritual several times before, and we had lost a lot of Marines taking one position after another.

Well, not this time. I was going to put a stop to that. I was now going to zero in on the ridge, and if they tried to escape to defend the next higher one, I would be set. Granted, mortars are not exactly tack drivers.[42] But you only had to get close. If your 81mm shell struck within 25 yards of a designated target, that was considered a hit. It was not an accurate weapon, but it was damned effective. As usual, I was going to use 8-lb. 81mm HE anti-personnel PD shells.[43] They went off as soon as they hit the ground, and were so effective against open targets.

Unfortunately, we were suffering another shortage of mortar shells. Our 81mm shells were rationed, and a couple times we had sent Ernie Huxel on a midnight raid down to the beach areas to "commandeer" some shells—some of them destined for army units—from under the noses of the stingy beachmasters. Now though, our supply was

---

42 "Tack driver" is a term that refers to an extremely accurate firearm, usually a well-sighted rifle for hunting or a sniper.

43 Point detonating (on impact). Other shells available to this weapon were the 15 lb. delayed fuse M56 HE shell for buried positions, and the 11 lb. M57 WP round.

somewhat low, so I was only going to use one mortar. I chose the No. 2 gun because it had the best crew. Bill Mikel was the gun captain,[44] with Tom Avants the team's gunner, Matthew Frenchie as his assistant, and Americus Dirado, John Pollock, and Bob Dreckman as loaders. In my eyes, this gun crew was the best, the most consistently accurate of the four in the platoon.

Using Mikel's mortar, I started to zero in on the enemy ridge. We fired several smoke rounds, laying the bursts 50 feet apart. I locked my coordinates into the area. There was not much wind, so I had no trouble setting up for the upcoming fire missions. As I marked my map, Lt. Haggerty came over. I gave the order to fire one last smoke round onto a corner of the ridge ahead.

The lieutenant (I never called him "Red") saw where the round landed, looked at me, surprised, and said, "What the hell did you do that for?"

Since the round had landed exactly where I had expected it to, I knew that I had the area zeroed in tight, but the Japs would not realize it. I was ready now. Haggerty though, obviously thought I was not.

"No, that ain't right. You're way the hell off."

"No," I said. "That's at the base of that little ridge."

I told him that I had put the round there on the side of the ridge on purpose, and that I could put the next one on the other side of the ridge.

He just laughed at me and put his head down.

So I decided to give him demonstration. I had seen this pagoda-like shed with a short chimney about twenty yards to the left of the base of the enemy ridge. It was the only structure around. I asked Haggerty, "Hey, you wanna see me drop one down the chimney of that little building there?"

"Where?"

I told him that it was just to the left of the base of the ridge. He raised his binoculars, looked around, and spotted it.

"You're gonna hit that?" he asked, not convinced.

Confident (and perhaps just a little too cocky), I said, "Yup."

---

44 Mikel had returned to duty on May 12th.

He snickered. I looked back at him and said, "Watch." I knew I would probably not hit it square on top; hell, we're talking about mortar fire. But I knew that the shell would land very close.

I gave Mikel the coordinates with one small correction and ordered them to fire a heavy 15-lb. delayed-fuse round. We heard the shell coming in and sure enough, a few seconds later, it hit that pagoda dead center, and the building totally went up in smoke. Right on target! Granted, it was a one-in-a-hundred shot, a really lucky hit. Well, maybe it was only partly luck, because by then I was pretty good at my job. Still, I had to admit to myself that even I was surprised that the shell had hit so accurately. Haggerty looked at the smoke, then at me, shook his head, laughed, and walked off.

Early that afternoon, one of our rifle companies attacked the ridge, running up the valley next to it. I waited, giving the Japs time to go up their ladders and come out. I guess that there was a chance that with the island almost ours, they just might have thought about giving up, but I knew better. They weren't going to surrender. The little bastards had never done that before in all the months we had been fighting them, so I sure as hell didn't expect them to do that now. No, they were most likely just going to fall back to the next defensive bunker complex. So I was prepared to let them have it.

Sure enough, a while after the riflemen began moving in, the Japs started coming up the ladders. They began crawling up out of that hole four at time, and started running down the ridge. They were obviously falling back.

When I saw the first couple make it out and start to scurry back along the open ridge towards the bigger hill behind them, I was ready. Using my field phone, I confirmed the updated coordinates to Mikel and then told him, "Fire five rounds for effect."

Again, the No. 2 team was good; we had worked well together many times in what was now our fourth campaign together. So they performed like a well-oiled machine, and the fifth shell was already in the air before the first even hit. The 8-lb. anti-personnel rounds landed accurately and went off as soon as they hit the ground, one right after the other. Their effect was deadly, and the running Jap bastards were devastated.

A couple minutes later, another batch of them started to come up the ladders, and again, I gave the adjusted coordinates and ordered five more rounds. Once more, the mortar shells came *whooshing* in one after another in rapid succession, and to add to the party, as the rounds started to go off, I picked up my M1 Garand[45] and began to take shots at the running figures. I knew that I was too far away to get a good shot—hell, with an M1, over 100 yards is out of accurate range—but I didn't give a damn. This was personal for me.

I could tell that these Japs were not well trained, and I'm sure they were scared as hell, so taking them out was relatively easy. To be honest, I couldn't tell if some of them were dropping because of my rifle shots, or because of the shell bursts, but I didn't give a crap. They were going down, and that was the important thing.

More Japs came up, and I sent more rounds in. Then more, and the deadly pattern continued. Somewhere in the middle of our attack, Lt. Haggerty joined me, and stood watching it all. Then, with his binoculars, he spotted a native making his way towards the Jap ridge, carrying a sturdy metal pole across his shoulders. Hanging from each end was a net of some sort filled with boxes and other stuff.

Haggerty eyed him closely as he moved towards the ridge. I finally saw him shake his head and mumble, "Son of a BITCH!"

"What?" I asked him.

"That guy … that's about his eighth trip. He's hauling supplies or ammo for those Japs in the bunkers."

I looked out and could barely see the guy moving forward. It seemed obvious that he was not happy doing what he was doing. Clearly he was not hauling stuff of his own free will. The Japs must have pressed him into service.

Out of the clear blue, Haggerty said, "Shoot the sonuvabitch."

I had been firing my M1 over at the Japs on the left side of the ridge, so I dropped to a prone position, wheeled around to the right, and started to sight in on the distant figure. I noted that he was not running, but he was sure quick-stepping as fast as he could with that big heavy

---

45 George had replaced the carbine that he had carried at Wana Draw.

load. It didn't occur to me to ask why he was carrying supplies to the Japs if they were abandoning the ridge position. He was about 200 yards away, and I knew at that range, with him moving, it would be a hard shot to make. So I adjusted my sight and then carefully aimed my rifle at the guy. I squeezed off a round and saw a puff of dust just in front of him. Okay, I thought, I'm a little low.

I adjusted my aim a little higher and took another shot. This time, I saw a dust spurt go up just beyond him. Okay, I knew that I had the right elevation. Now I just had to get my windage right. I closed one eye, took aim, and shot again.

Another miss. Damn!

I gritted my teeth, aimed, and fired again. Another damn puff of dust—another miss. I slowly emptied all eight shots at that native. But before I could load another clip into the rifle, he made it to the brush line. I had missed him completely.

It turned out, that was his last trip. We never saw him come out again.

For quite a while, the Japs kept coming out of that tunnel regularly, about every two to three minutes. Early on, I began to try to time the shells to go off at the most opportune moment. Sometimes I did, catching them right out in the open, and the shell bursts would tear into them. Sometimes, I didn't quite. But none of them were making it back.

I continued the firing missions, sometimes giving corrected coordinates, with range and azimuth details. I continued using the HE shells.

When it finally got to where very few of the Japs were coming out of the hole, using my directions and coordinates, the mortar crews proceeded to lay a fire pattern going down the ridge.

Eventually, our riflemen, who had been advancing under cover of our fire, began moving up the ridge. I phoned in to the No. 2 gun the order for all crews to cease fire, but to remain on standby.

At that time, I had absolutely no idea that three-star Lt. General Geiger himself, along with several other of his senior officers, had decided to watch the 3rd Battalion's attack. He had been observing everything on a cliff located behind my position, looking down on that Jap hill in front of us. He had stood up there during the whole attack, and so he had

IN REPLYING
REFER TO No.

UNITED STATES MARINE CORPS
HEADQUARTERS,
FLEET MARINE FORCE, PACIFIC,
c/o FLEET POST OFFICE, SAN FRANCISCO

The Commanding General, Fleet Marine Force, Pacific,
takes pleasure in COMMENDING

SERGEANT GEORGE PETO,
UNITED STATES MARINE CORPS

for service as set forth in the following

CITATION

"For meritorious and efficient performance of duty while
serving as an observer of the 81mm mortar platoon of a Marine infantry
battalion during operations against the enemy on CAPE GLOUCESTER,
NEW BRITAIN, PELELIU, PALAU ISLANDS, and OKINAWA SHIMA,
RYUKYU ISLANDS, from 26 December, 1943, to 2 September, 1945.
Through all these campaigns, Sergeant PETO, though subjected many
times to intense enemy artillery and mortar fire, performed his duties in an
excellent manner, directing fire missions which were highly instrumental
to the successes of his battalion. His alertness and courage in combat were
outstanding and were in keeping with the highest traditions of the United
States Naval Service."

ROY S. GEIGER
Lieutenant General,
U. S. Marine Corps.

Commendation Ribbon Authorized

George Peto's commendation from General Geiger for his direction of the mortars on Okinawa, June 21, 1945. (Author's collection)

seen all of my mortar salvos landing on those Japs. You know, it isn't every day that your own personal actions get directly observed by your corps commander (especially in the Marine Corps), and evidently our barrage really impressed him. After I had stood down the mortars (I was told later), he had turned to one of his officers and said, "I want to see the officer responsible for these fire missions. I swear, I have *never* seen mortar fire like that in my thirty years in the Corps."

So his officers radioed inquiries and found out, and soon Lt. Haggerty, who had gone back to battalion headquarters, was ordered to report to them. He was taken up the mountain and brought up before the general. He came to attention with the usual "Reporting as ordered, sir," and stood there. Geiger congratulated him on the mortar salvos, repeating what he had said earlier.

To his credit, my buddy Haggerty was totally honest about it. A gentleman, he told the general, "Sir, I don't want the credit. My sergeant did that. You should give him the credit."

The general said, "Well, by damn, I sure will."

And damned if he didn't do just that. Six months later, after I had returned home to the States, I received a letter stating that I had received the Marine Corps Commendation Medal with Combat V (Valor) for my excellent fire direction. The accompanying certificate was signed by General Geiger himself. And since at that time he had taken over command of all the ground forces on Okinawa because General Bucker had been killed in action, technically I received the commendation from not only the commanding officer of the III Marine Amphibious Corps, but also the commander of the Tenth Army itself. For months after the war, my brother-in-law absolutely refused to believe that I received that high a commendation from an Army commander. It took a while to explain it to him …

Promotion as the fighting stops

After the Marine attack of June 21st, the battle of Okinawa essentially came to an end. Organized fighting on the island ceased. Although there were scores of Japanese still hiding in caves, holes, and hillside bunkers, enemy resistance had finally been broken for good.

The island was by now a shambles, with nearly all of the buildings destroyed, along with many historical artifacts and tombs. On the other hand, with Okinawa now secure, the Americans could take advantage of its fine airfield network, developing it to mount a massive strategic bombing campaign on the Japanese Home Islands. Okinawa would also provide an excellent staging area for the seemingly inevitable massive invasion of the mainland.

The morning of June 22nd, the Japanese 32nd Army commander defending the island, Gen. Mitsuru Ushijima, refused an official American plea to surrender. In accordance with Japanese tradition, he conceded loss of Okinawa to the Japanese high command and, along with his chief of staff, Lt. Gen. Isamu Cho, committed suicide by the ritual hara-kiri.

A few hours later at 1000 hours, an official American flag-raising ceremony occurred at the Tenth Army headquarters to officially proclaim that the island of Okinawa had been taken. The temporary army commander, Marine Corps General Roy Geiger, presided over the event.

With Geiger's new command came a promotion to lieutenant- general, giving him his third star. Still, it was a well-known rumor that the Army did not like him, and they certainly resented having a Marine command their operation. Thus, controversial four-star Army General Joe Stillwell (who had originally been slated to eventually take over from General Buckner) was hastily summoned to take command. He arrived in Okinawa on the morning of June 23rd and assumed command of the entire island on the next day.

General Geiger would become the only Marine Corps general in U.S. military history to ever command an entire army in a war.

The 8th Marines feinted and then moved towards our area, now detached to our First Marine Division. As far as I was concerned, we could let them come in and finish the job once and for all.

We finally pulled out of the line on the 22nd and spent the day moving north toward the rear area. That evening, we established our perimeter and set up for night. There were still Japs all over, so we set up a tight defensive circle. Each unit set up trip wires about 50 yards out and around our position and connected them to flares. Anything tripping the wire would set off a flare, and we would have something to shoot at. So now we were ready. I had the duty as evening fell. I stood an uneventful watch with my shotgun, then turned in for the night.

The next day, I was called aside by our new company commander, Lt. Koehler.[46] He told me that I had become eligible for promotion to sergeant, effective back on May 10th. He said, "George, you're the oldest in time here, and you're the best guy in the company, and so you're the most deserving for a promotion."

I didn't say a thing, as he went on. "Here's the story. Now, I've got three rank promotions for the company that I can give out. Two of them are to corporal, which you already are, and one of them to sergeant.

---

46 Charles J. Koehler, of Clifton Park NY. He died at the age of 84 from Alzheimer complications.

And I can also give out one medal." He did not say what the medal was. "So, you can either have a promotion or a medal."

I thought about it. It was unfair to make me decide. I was in no position to do that. Still, getting promoted to sergeant had been a major objective for me in my effort to reform as a good Marine, especially since I had already taken on the duties of one. So without even asking what the medal was for, I said, "Okay, you just keep your medal, and I'll take the sergeant's rank."

"Okay, but remember, then you can't have both. You can't have the medal. If you take the rank, you can't have the medal."

I thought about it more, and said again, "Well, I still want to take the rank." My reasoning was that since I was not sure at this point if I wanted to stay in the Marine Corps or not, the rank would be the much better choice. Besides, I might get awarded a medal later.

The corporal promotions ended up going to Pleasant V. Jones, gun captain on the No. 1 Mortar, and to my buddy Ernie Huxel, the gun captain on the No. 3 Mortar. I found out years later from Bob Johnson that the medal had been offered to Lt. Haggerty, but he wouldn't take it.

I was proud of myself. I had come out of the brig and had made sergeant in just 18 months, something not easy to do in the Corps. Of course, I could have made that rank a lot sooner if I had taken life more seriously before combat. But I considered that water under the bridge, and anyway, thinking about it, I did not regret a damn thing I'd done.

The next day, all the major fighting had stopped, and the island was declared secure. Relieved by the 8th Marines, our unit continued moving to the rear to set up camp. That evening, after walking for quite a while, we stopped to take a five-minute break. Everyone, about fifty of us, sat down to relax.

Near me was a group of three guys sitting next to the ditch beside the road. Two of them were our officers, one of them a company officer. The other was the new guy, our replacement platoon leader, 1st Lt. Curtis Beall. This guy Beall was an unusual fellow for a Marine, because he was quite the gentleman. Born and raised in Dublin, Georgia, he went to the University of Georgia.[47] He joined the Marines in September 1942, but was allowed to continue college until he was called up. He sometimes told us this story of when he was cheerleading, how Georgia beat UCLA in the Rose Bowl on January 2, 1943. All I could think of was: big deal. In July 1943 though, with only a couple more courses to go before he graduated, he was ordered to active duty, and because he was so far along in college, he became eligible to go to OCS at Duke University. There he got a commission as a 2nd looey in 1944, before shipping out to the Pacific.[48]

Sitting now with Beall and the other officer was this enlisted kid, around 18. He was a new guy. Okinawa was probably his first campaign.

Unknown to all of us, right next to these three in some thick brush next to the ditch were three Japs hiding. One of the Japs had a pistol in his hand, as the three of them crouched there silently, no doubt waiting for our unit to move on, and really hoping that they would not get spotted.

Unfortunately for them, that did not happen. After a couple minutes of sitting next to this ditch with the two officers, the kid happened to look down into the partly covered ditch and spotted the Jap with the pistol. The kid's eyes got wide and his mouth dropped as he saw the gun pointed at him, but before he could say anything, the Jap pulled the trigger and shot him in the head, killing him.

When we heard the shot, all hell broke loose. The other two Japs threw a couple grenades as guys jumped up and began taking off, trying to either find cover, or get the hell out of there, all of them trying to figure out what the hell was going on.

I had been sitting nearby at the time, checking my Thompson when I heard the pistol go off. I stood up and as grenades exploded, I ran over

---

47 Curtis had gone for a year to the Middle Georgia College with a basketball scholarship. He had then transferred to the University of Georgia, but was not eligible to continue playing basketball. So he instead ended up a male cheerleader.

48 George left out the part where after two semesters at Duke University, Beall was transferred to Parris Island for three months' basic training, and then another three at Camp Lejeune, before boarding the liner-converted-troop-transport for Saipan, and eventually, Okinawa.

to the kid. I looked round and saw the three Japs running away through a field. They took off over a rise and sliding down the slope, headed for a tomb in the gully below. I followed them and when they slipped down into the tomb, I crawled round the other side. My Thompson was loaded with that beautiful 50-round drum, so I just opened up on them. I strafed that whole inside, laying out an effective crisscross pattern. Then I fired a few up-and-down patterns. I finally stopped shooting with just a few rounds left, and walked into the tomb. Sure enough, all three of them were dead.

I came out, looked round, and cursed. Not one sonuvabitch had come down to help me, or had even come over to try. Ungrateful bastards.

Afterward though, one of the officers, the new guy, Lt. Beall (who I found out was only four days younger than me) came over to me walking back from the tomb. "Did you get them?" he asked.

I glared at him, "Sure as hell did," I grumbled.

He gave me a real serious look and took my hand to shake it. "If it hadn't been for you, I'd be dead. You saved my life," he added quietly.

Island victory

The nearly three-month, savagely fought battle for Okinawa was the last major campaign of World War II, and when it was over, more casualties had been accumulated on both sides than in any Pacific battle of the war. As usual, the statistics over the years have varied with each source, but it is generally acknowledged that over 77,000 Japanese and yet another 40,000 Okinawan draftees who had been pressed into service were killed, executed, or committed suicide. Another 20,000 islanders were lost as well. Only about 10,000 of the enemy were captured.

The losses to the Allies were staggering as well. The Americans had over 80,000 confirmed casualties. This included 20,190 dead, 12,500 of which were killed in action. Some 3,000 of the KIA, or over 25 percent, were Marines. There were another 500 missing, presumed dead. Additionally, of the 60,000 casualties who survived, over 25,000 would later diagnosed with psychiatric problems directly attributed to the battle.

Another famous casualty of the operation, besides General Buckner, was famed war correspondent Ernie Pyle. On the tiny island of Ie Shima, just off the northwestern tip of Okinawa, Pyle was ashore with the 305th Regiment of the Army's 77th Infantry Division. His jeep was heading towards the regiment's command post on the morning of April 18th with the regimental commander, Lt. Col. Joseph B. Coolidge. Suddenly, the jeep was fired upon by a Japanese machine gun located on a ridge overlooking the road. They immediately took cover in a nearby ditch on the other side of the road. The firing stopped, and after a half minute or so, Pyle and the regiment's commanding officer both cautiously raised their heads to see if the coast was clear to get back into the jeep. The machine gun opened up again. Coolidge immediately dived down to safety, but Pyle was struck by a bullet in the left temple just below his helmet. He was killed instantly. For a few hours his body lay alongside the road, until a combat photographer managed to pull it into the ditch. News of his death went round the world, and people everywhere, from heads of state to senior generals to buck privates, mourned his passing.

The Army buried him alongside other GIs there on the island.

We heard that Ernie Pyle had been killed. I remember meeting him several times, especially when he once spent a week with our 1st Battalion. Often I would see him in our chow line and get to talk to him. And he loved to hang out with us peons. I was surprised to find that although he was now famous, he was a little guy, about my size, skinny as hell, and looked old. And he seemed sad a lot. As serious as we were under fire though, we would laugh and joke after combat to relieve our stress. He usually did not smile, but he sure enjoyed being with us. Later on, he wrote a bunch about his time with us.

I heard later that he had been killed on some island, and I wondered about that. He really had enjoyed being with us Marines. Oh, he said he liked the Army, but the Marines he would say with a grin, were hell on wheels. I think that being with us might have instilled in him some charisma and macho B.S. I hope that didn't make him get careless.

Looking back, for me it was just as well that the fighting ended when it did in June. I think that a couple more weeks of heavy combat might very well have done me in. I had been on the island now for 82 days, 52 of which were intense combat. We had been sniped at on and off for the first month, and that was not too bad. But on May 1st, when we relieved the 106th Infantry Regiment, we had started to take more casualties. And then on steadily.

Men of George's mortar platoon, taken on Okinawa after the island had been secured on June 22nd. Bottom center: Lt. James "Red" Haggerty, mortar platoon commander; Second row l-r: Robert R. ("Railroad") Johnson, Ass't Communications Section Leader; George Peto (Code Name "Xray"), Forward Observer; Fred O. Miller, wireman; and Howard Quarty, ammo carrier. Third row: Ernie Huxel, Gunner, No. 3 Mortar, and John Skoglie, Ass't Gunner, No. 2 Mortar. Top row: Harry Owens, Gunner, No. 4 Mortar. (Author's Collection)

Since then, we had mostly been in combat non-stop, sometimes for a couple weeks at a stretch, sometimes less, and it was having an effect. With all the action I had seen and all the friends I had lost, my combat efficiency had gone down, even though, strangely, I was now so much better at my job. But more and more I was detaching myself from the other guys. I found myself becoming more isolated, and I usually avoided people. Being a forward observer made that possible, because nine times out of ten, I found myself alone, scouting the area ahead for Jap positions that I could call a mission onto. Lt. Haggerty would come up with me once in a while, but usually he was off somewhere else. Besides, no one else wanted to go with me, especially since both Rucker and McGuire had gotten killed. My radio operator, Bob Sprangle, had often been with me for the first half of the campaign. No matter where I went, he eventually showed up. Then one day in mid-May, he just disappeared, and I never saw him again.

As the miserable days went by, the pressure of being in combat again, only now for longer periods, was really starting to get to me. I mean, on Peleliu, it had been one huge intensive bang for us over a week or so and then it was over. Everyone was either exhausted, wounded, or dead.

Okinawa was a very long, drawn-out campaign, made up of dozens of three- or four-day actions that were stretched out over a much longer period. In between them, you had more time to think about stuff—to worry about what could happen to you. Another point that drove this home was that unlike before, or probably much more developed than before, I had a much closer relationship with the guys getting killed or wounded. I knew them so much better, their habits, what made them laugh, their families back home. We had shared some good times together in Samoa, in Melbourne. And we had been through so much more together. We had deepened our relationships, and so their dying or getting blown apart became a much more personal loss. Hell, sometimes you spotted a familiar face getting carried off to the rear with painful wounds, and you never saw them again. You only could wonder if they died or survived.

What was worse maybe was the fact that we were getting replacements almost as fast as we were losing men. And many of the replacements that we tried to train on the job, so to speak, were getting knocked off. I found that I was getting to the point where I didn't want to get to know anybody, because there was a good chance that they might be dead in a couple days' time.

On June 23, 1945, the Tenth Army began a systematic, comprehensive operation to mop up the southern part of the island and ferret out any last-ditch elements of what once had been the Japanese 32nd Army. Two days later, units of the First Marine Division began a similar sweep to the north, to remove enemy holdouts—one way or another. Specific instructions were handed down on the procedures to be used to do this. Additionally, units were to begin to police areas in an effort to make the island safe.

By Saturday, June 23rd, we had settled into our new camp and started to recuperate from the action. I mostly just ate and slept. On Sunday morning, Lt. Haggerty asked me what I was going to do today. I told him I was just resting.

He looked round, then back at me and said, "Look, I know we're recovering from combat, but we can't have these guys just sitting around. We gotta keep them busy." He suggested we do some training or something.

So for the next two days, a few of us gave classes to the new guys. I myself gave a few classes on disassembling the .45 and first aid. Just something to keep their minds occupied while keeping the brass happy. I found it hard to believe though, that I was teaching first aid now that the fighting had stopped.

On Wednesday the 27th, Haggerty gave me permission to go on a 24-hour liberty. Big deal, it wasn't like I could leave the island or anything. Still, I took my souvenir saber and captured Jap .25 cal rifle and hitched a ride up to the docks to trade with some squids. I went aboard a couple of the ships and talked to some sailors. One thing about the Navy: they always ate good. So I had a great lunch with them, and while I did, a number of them came over to where I was sitting and started making me offers on my stuff. We did some horse trading, and I ended up getting two fifths of good whiskey.

We shot the breeze some more, and I then left the ship. I walked away from the docks and started back south towards my unit with my two bottles and a belly full of great chow. I had gone two or three blocks up a dirt road when I saw some tents over on the right. It was some sort of Army administrative unit. One of the tent flaps was tied up, probably for air circulation, and as I got closer, I saw something at the bottom of the tent that absolutely made my eyes bug out.

A pair of gams. And I mean, a really *nice* set of gams.

I was stunned. I had not seen a woman since we had left Melbourne. That was—wow—almost two years ago. And the last American gal I had seen was over three years ago. But now I was looking at what seemed to be a very nice pair of female legs. The shooting had just ended. But from what I saw, that *had* to be an American woman, for crissakes.

Curious, I walked over to the tent. Sure as hell, there was an attractive Army WAC sitting in a chair across from some sort of technical sergeant. She was wearing a field jacket, a nice skirt, and those Army high heels.

I stared at her. I knew that with my Thompson over my shoulder, scraggly, dirty, and my worn uniform and all, I must have looked like a ragged scarecrow to the two of them, but I didn't care. Holy crap, a woman!

I smiled, introduced myself, and offered them a drink of whiskey. Hell, I hadn't opened the bottle yet, but I would have gladly given both bottles to this gal just for the chance to talk to her for a while.

The tech sergeant was naturally pretty leery of me and declined. Still, he wasn't rude. Maybe the Thompson might have had something to do with that. The WAC though, smiled at me and was very nice. She kept typing and working there at her desk.

I sat down, poured me a drink. I began talking to her, about anything, just enjoying being with her. I ended up spending the whole afternoon there, drinking. The WAC after a while relented and had a couple drinks too, and finally the tech sergeant had one too. Me though, I went full bore for several hours.

By sunset, they started shutting down for the night. It was getting dark anyway, so I was ready to go back to my unit. I gave them what very little was left of the whiskey and said a fond goodbye. I left there drunk as a skunk and somehow got up onto the main road. I think they called it Highway 1. They had recently widened it with bulldozers to about three times its original width for the extra traffic, and had pushed the extra dirt high up along each side of the road. I had to take a leak pretty badly, so I climbed up and over the left side embankment to do my thing.

I staggered down the other side, took a long piss, climbed back over that embankment, and back onto the road. I started back to my unit, but somehow, I must have gotten confused (in my condition, it was no wonder). I began heading north instead of south. I managed to bum a ride on an army supply truck. I jumped in and laid my head back. The driver was a nice guy, and soon I was asleep in the cab. All the while, I was unaware we were going in the wrong direction—north, past Kadena, and on towards the big Yontan airfield.

Finally, as we neared the airfield the driver turned, shook me awake, and asked, "Hey, where you plan to get off?"

Groggy, all I could say was, "Uh ..."

"Where'd you say you were going?"

I told him.

He thought about it a moment and said, "Aw hell, you're going the wrong way." He looked out the window and realized that it was getting dark. "Well, it's dark now. You don't wanna be out there walking around by yourself. There are Jap stragglers everywhere."

He thought about it and added, "Look, come on back with me, and you can spend the night on one of the guys' cots that's out making a run. And get yerself some breakfast, and then you can go back."

That sounded good to me. I agreed that it was not safe for me to try to go the other way and try to make it back. So I did what he suggested and slept the night off in his tent. The next morning I had a good meal and then hitchhiked south all the way back to my unit. Man, was I hung over. After all, the biggest part of two fifths of whiskey had gone into me.

I got back to the unit and was sitting at my tent shelter on a hill, my head splitting, feeling sorry for myself. Lt. Haggerty came walking up, saw me, and with a trace of a smile, said, "So, you're back, eh?"

I just looked up at him.

"Well, it looks like you did it now," he said. "The damn war hasn't been over for two days, and you're AWOL again." He paused and said, "Yer gonna have to dig a six by six for this."[49]

Figures.

I looked at him, feeling miserable, and said, "Well, do whatever you got do, and then leave me the hell alone, cuz I got a helluva headache."

He smiled. "Well, hell," he said. "Forget about it. I guess yer entitled to it."

I thanked him and really meant it.

He then said, "I just come up to say goodbye." He smiled again. "I'm shipping back home," he said simply.

---

49 A typical type of non-judicial punishment, whereby the individual has to dig a hole that is six feet long by six feet deep, a laborsome task. After the hole was inspected, the individual would have to then fill it in again. This task was then sometimes repeated.

Wow. The good lieutenant had his ticket back to the States. I had been in his platoon since Melbourne in July of 1943, and now he was leaving. I stood up and we shook hands in silence.

We said goodbye. He looked at me, and the last thing he said to me was, "Don't take any wooden nickels."

He turned and walked away. My hungover mind was in a whirl as I sat down again. After two long years of working together, fighting together, laughing at each other, sending mortar shells over to the enemy together, we were splitting up. I found out later that I was the only enlisted man in the platoon that he had bothered to say goodbye to. Years later, Lt. Beall at one of the reunions told me, "You know, he really had a healthy respect for you." He had actually seen potential in me and had given me a chance back when I had been such a screw-up. Now the lieutenant was gone.

I would never see Lieutenant James J. Haggerty ever again.

The hamlet

The mop-up operations in late June and July were often just as dangerous as the battle phase had been, because many enemy soldiers were ready to conduct a last-ditch defense of their positions. Outside shouts from American units to surrender were often ignored. Unfortunately, caught between the two sides were the civilians of Okinawa.

Although Okinawa and the other Ryukyu Islands had been annexed by the Japanese Empire in 1879, the islanders had always been looked down upon by the Japanese as foreigners and an inferior people, and were treated as such. After the war had begun, the Japanese government had made great efforts to force the "coarse" Okinawans to abandon their language, culture, and society to be assimilated into those of Japan. They were pressed to adopt Japanese customs and beliefs, which the easygoing yet proud Okinawans resented a great deal.

As the war went on and the Americans began to close in on the Home Islands, the Japanese Army conscripted Okinawan men into military service (where they were usually discriminated against), and all Okinawans into wartime production or into civilian militias. At every turn, the Okinawans were exploited and mistreated, and towards the end of the campaign, ruthlessly sacrificed. Refugee women and children were held hostage, or forced at gunpoint to fight alongside the Japanese, including defending miserable caves. Many were forced out of shelters and caves so that Japanese soldiers could use them for protection. Moving around at night was just as dangerous as during the day, because Marines often mistook them for Japanese soldiers. Worse, some Japanese would don kimonos over their uniforms to try and infiltrate American lines.

Civilians were prohibited from surrendering, and were given hand grenades and orders to instead kill themselves and their families. They were told repeatedly that death was more honorable than a shameful surrender. The Japanese also did their best to convince the Okinawans that the invading Americans were ruthless, bloodthirsty savages, and so an honorable suicide would be less painful for wives and children than to suffer unspeakable torture by the enemy. That was one reason in the last few days that so many island women jumped off cliffs instead of capitulating to the Americans. Many surviving civilians later confirmed to their captors that they never responded to calls for surrender because of what they had been told would happen to them if they came out of their hiding places.

We moved north again and finally approached the landing beaches. We set up and made camp. The more we searched for enemy strays, the more we interacted with civilians, and we saw how terrified they were of us. They figured that we were three times worse than the Japs.

For instance, one morning, I took a patrol out to search this nearby hamlet for Jap holdouts. The minute the people saw our patrol coming, they did something that surprised the hell out of us. Those outside dropped what they were doing and rushed out to meet us, accompanied by others who ran out of their huts. They all quickly lined up in formation on the road through the hamlet, unbuttoned their clothes, and dropped them to the ground. There they stood, about thirty or forty villagers, all at rigid attention, like this weird civilian platoon, as if for some sort of an inspection, and every one of them was totally buck naked. Old men (the young males were probably dead or missing), women, boys and girls, all of them standing there in one line without a damn thing on, and every one of them with a nervous or scared look on their face.

I stood there surprised. Evidently, this is what the Japs had required of them whenever they entered a village. Maybe it was as an act of forced humiliation, or maybe it was just to show that the villagers were not armed or carrying explosives. More likely though, they expected us to do terrible things. We knew that they had been mistreated by the Jap soldiers, who in turn had pounded into their heads the nightmare stories that Americans were marauding beasts.

I noticed out of the corner of my eye some sort of movement between two of the huts. I motioned to a couple of my guys to come with me, and told the others to keep the civilians there until I got back. Moving cautiously with our weapons ready round the corner of the nearer hut, we saw the back of this girl crouched between the two buildings. About 18, she was as pretty as I had ever laid eyes on, about medium height, and with a great build, I mean, like a brick outhouse. With her back to us, she appeared to be burning some garbage over a fire in some sort of wire basket.

She must have heard our steps, because she turned round and saw us. Her hands flew up and her eyes got as big as saucers and impulsively she cried out, "Uhhh!"

She slumped back against a hut with a look in her eyes that seemed to say, oh well, I'm gonna die. Then she got a determined look on her face,

George with two Okinawan children. Taken some time in late July. (Author's collection).

gathered her composure and stood up. Looking at me, she unzipped her garment. She wriggled out of it and stood there at attention, naked, silent. Now none of us had seen any kind of a gal in nearly two years, so all we could do was just stare.

I looked into her eyes. She seemed to be resigned to her fate. Obviously, she was waiting for whatever hell these devil Americans were going to do to her.

I just shook my head because I felt so sorry for her, standing there in that humiliating way, scared out of her wits.

I motioned to her dress on the ground and told her, "Put that back on," although I knew she didn't understand English, and I sure as hell did not know Japanese. So in sign language, I again pointed to her garment and motioned her to get dressed.

Keeping a wary eye on me, she bent down and put the gown back on. As she did, I tried to communicate with her that we were okay, making sure that I did not make any sudden scary moves. I tried to let her know and that we were not going to hurt her. Then I motioned for her to go back with the rest of them and let them know that we meant them no harm. She slowly walked back with them and spoke to them, although she still seemed wary. I had no idea what she said to them.

Later, after weeks of meeting many civilians, I realized how terrible the images of Americans had been. They must have been told that it would be better to die in some kind of suicidal rush at us with a grenade, rather be captured, because if they were ever taken alive, we Americans would torture them and then execute them. While that of course was never true, I could see how a bunch of ragged dirtball killers like us might intimidate them, and we tried our best to be friendly to them. At least, my men did.

July 1945

By the end of June, reports indicated that most of the Japanese stragglers had surrendered or been killed. Those still holed up in caves and bunkers refusing to surrender were slowly and methodically eliminated. The caves openings were either sealed with explosives, burying those alive inside, or the interiors burned out with flamethrowers and napalm. Other small groups were found hiding in tall sugarcane fields, or lying low in rice paddies.

There were a number of firefights as enemy soldiers desperately fought until the bitter end. Some small groups tried to infiltrate American lines, and when discovered, died attacking their foe. On July 2nd, although the patrols would continue, mop-up operations of all organized enemy resistance were declared successful. Since the official end of organized resistance on the 22nd, about 9,000 more Japanese had been killed and nearly 3,000 taken prisoner. These sweeps in turn had cost the soldiers and Marines some 800 casualties, most of which occurred in the earlier operations.

With the fighting over, I started recovering from some from my dark moods. I began to do some night exploring, just to see what I could find. Although the island was secure, I always took someone with me. Usually John Skoglie.

One night we went down to this small town north of the Yontan airfield. Even though the area was not yet officially declared secure, we went to see if we could hook up with a couple native women. Although it was dark, we noticed people moving around between the huts. Whenever we approached someone, at first they did not know who we were, but seeing my Thompson and realizing that we were Americans, they would get scared as hell and *zhoom!* They'd take off in terror.

Unsuccessful in our attempts, we walked into this long thatched hut. From the lamps, we saw a long, low table with over forty guys at it, sitting cross-legged on the floor. They seemed to be having some sort of meeting, but for some reason, the spot at one end with a small chair was vacant.

Skoglie and I looked at each other and, feeling daring, I told him, "The hell with it. I'm gonna sit at the head of that table."

He looked at me and shook his head.

I walked over to the empty spot and sat down there on the floor. I put the Thompson across my lap and sat there. I looked at the guy to my left and grinned. He grinned back. Skoglie, armed with just a .45 pistol, with a wall to his back, stood behind me as if he was my bodyguard, silent, unsmiling. I felt safer. Several people at the table were drinking tea, and to my surprise, a native came over and served me a cup.

I was a little leery of drinking it, but I did take a few sips as these two rows of guys sat there, watching me. Surprisingly, the tea was warm and good.

John and I stayed there for about fifteen minutes while them locals continued with their meeting. Finally, my tea finished, I stood up and nodding solemnly to them, we left. We figured that we'd better get the hell out of there before they had second thoughts, so we took off. I guess they were afraid we'd kill them if they were impolite. That's probably the only thing that saved our ass.

The Japs were not too aggressive after June 22nd, but there were a hell of a lot of stragglers and holdouts all over the island. So it was still not safe to go anywhere by yourself.

Having been promoted to sergeant and one of the older survivors, I now had some authority, as well as respect in the battalion. One of my main duties now was to help organize search parties to look for stragglers, because they were all over the damn place. Every other day, I took out patrols of 15 to 20 men (you needed enough men to be able to get yourself out of any serious situation), and we perfected the art of ferrying the bastards out. Our techniques were also based on what we had learned on Peleliu, as well as Okinawa. In doing so, we also got to mingle a lot with the Okinawans. With the fighting all but over, they were grateful to us for having rid the island of the Japanese. We learned a lot about what they had suffered.

Whenever we could, we tried to avoid hitting civilians, or at least to move them out of the danger area. Especially me, because I knew that these poor people had not asked to be caught up in this hell, and I had always had a soft spot for the helpless, and I sure as hell did not like to see any of them get hurt.

I remember one time in the middle of the fighting, we accidently hit this teenage Okinawan gal. She had been caught in a crossfire, and one of our riflemen shot her up. I helped carry her back out of the combat area. Poor kid, she was in a bad way. Our corpsmen did what they could, including a couple shots of morphine for her pain. They had to leave her though, to go tend our own wounded, so a couple of us took turns watching over her that night, trying to save her, to soothe her and help her with the pain. But she died the next morning.

Once in a while, we would encounter a straggler in the oddest sort of way. I remember once, our patrol had stopped to take a break. We were next to this field that the engineers had plowed up to make a garden or something like that. The soil had been banked into some type of jagged ridge. There were four or five of us sitting next to this ridge eating snacks, my Thompson leaning against a bank. All of a sudden, this Jap about fifty yards away tossed his rifle over the top of it and then rolled over it. He came to his feet, grabbed his weapon, and just stood there, looking down at us. We were in shock for a couple moments, our mouths half open with chewed food, before we could react. We dropped our rations and went for our weapons. As I grabbed my Thompson, the sonuvabitch, quick as a flash, rolled back over the top of that ridge and disappeared. We ran up the embankment, but by the time we got to the top, he was long gone.

Another time, I was going up a small rise. Skoglie was with me. Suddenly I came face to face with a Jap standing there in front of me, just twenty yards away. He looked at me and immediately took off. When I started over the top, he disappeared, going down some hole like a groundhog. I never did find him.

Often, we would see a little opening in the ground or in the side of hill, and as we crept up on it, we would listen and might hear faint voices inside. I mean, they were living in there, and usually had no idea we were right outside. We would position ourselves round the hole, and when we were ready, we would call them out, telling them to surrender. We used phrases that were given to us, like "*Kosahn!*" which means "Surrender," or "*Tay-oh AH geh-roh!*" (Hands up").[50]

If they shot at us, we'd fire back and get close enough to lob some grenades in. Then we would seal the hole with C4, keeping an eye out, of course, for some back exit. If they came out with their hands up, we would frisk them and then march their butts back to camp. If they did not come out and just stayed in there, we would warn them again. If they still did not come out, then, per our orders, we would either seal the opening or else blow those up inside with a couple hand grenades.

I always hated to do that, because I knew in some of those caves were Okinawan civilians, either too scared to come out, or held prisoner in

---

50 Other phrases that were given to the Marines to use were "*Boo-kee OH steh-roh*" ("Drop your weapons"), "*Deh-the KOH-ee*" ("Come out"), "*Dah-mah REH*" ("Shut up") and "*Koh-roh sah-NAH ee-yoh*" ("We will not murder you").

there by Jap soldiers. But we had our orders, and I always looked back on sealing the caves with a good deal of regret.[51]

Little by little, the Japs began to get the idea that the war was over, and a few of them actually surrendered. Many of them though held out, and once in a while, we would come across a lair or cave that they were holed up in. One way or another, we resolved the issue.

The grave

On the 4th of July, the First Marine Division Cemetery on Okinawa was dedicated. Located near the Machinato airfield, the simple memorial park had been created by using a large bulldozer to dig a long ditch. The bodies of the dead Marines, enshrouded in canvas body bags, were then one by one carried into the ditch by stretcher and deposited there next to each other in an evenly spaced, certain specific order. The bodies were then covered over by a detail of men shoveling thick slabs of dirt over them. The bulldozer then dug a second long row next to the first, and the process was repeated. The list carrying the order of the names of the fallen was then used to create simple white crosses that were erected for each fallen Marine.

One day, Capt. Bennett, the guy who had been relieved on May 13th for not wanting to take L Company and attack Hill 55, came into our area. He was being court-martialed for the incident, and was looking for witnesses to back up his story. Some of the guys talked to him. Haggerty was gone though, along with a number of other officers. It was officers that Bennett really wanted to bear witness on his behalf, since we enlisted pukes were not considered reliable testimonies. Oh well …

When we were not on patrol, we were busy doing other labor. Most of the time it consisted of either training or going on working parties. Now that I had been promoted, I was a squad leader, and so organizing

---

51 It was a sad episode in the Battle for Okinawa that both during and after the battle, Americans were instructed to kill unidentified occupants of caves and bunkers who chose not to surrender. This unfortunately included many Okinawan civilians of all ages who were either too terrified to come out and surrender to what they had been told was a savage enemy, or were forced at gunpoint to stay in the caves with the Japanese soldiers.

and overseeing these work details was up to me. That did not sit too well with me, because most of these guys that I had to supervise and put on these jobs were seasoned combat veterans like me, some of them noncoms with two or three campaigns under their belts. Still, orders were orders.

Now although commanding a small group was not new for me, I had never done it as a sergeant. Several of the guys were not happy taking orders from their new squad leader, and some just flat out did not want to work, especially now that the fighting was over. There was this one guy in particular in our battery who really resisted going out on details. A solid-looking guy with a sour disposition, he always seemed to be scowling. He kept to himself and liked to drink, sleep late, and generally avoid work. He had a few of the guys spooked, too.

One evening early on, we were given a work assignment to start the next morning. After chow that night, I told my squad that we were going on an extended detail tomorrow, and that all of us would be on it. One noncom pointed to that loner snoozing in his rack, and asked if that included him. I told them damn right. All of us.

A couple of them shook their heads and told me to just leave him be. "Why?" I asked them.

One of the guys said he thought that he was nuts.

"What?" I said. "Hell, we're all a little fruity over here." But I hit the rack that night wondering if this guy would give me any problems the next day. I decided I would get the problem resolved and make damn sure this fellow came with us.

Sure enough, the next morning after chow, all the other guys were up and getting ready to start, but this fellow was still in his bunk. This was going to be a tough work detail, a nasty one, and we were going to need him. Besides and I wasn't about to give this joker any slack.

When I started over to get him, one of the fellows grabbed my arm. "Hey," he said, "don't bother that guy."

"Why not?"

Another guy made a couple circles with his finger next to his head and said, "That guy's a little wacky over there. If you wake him up this morning, he's apt to go nuts and shoot you. Hell, you don't know what he's gonna do."

We'll see, I said to myself. I had no time for any kind of crap like that, and so I just said, "Is that right?"

Clenching my teeth, I walked into his tent, determined to straighten this guy out right quick, and looked down at him. He might have been sleeping, but I figured that there was a good chance he'd heard us and was just lying there, faking it. I thought, the sonuvabitch. He isn't sleeping. He's just trying to play games with me.

So I walked up to his cot and set my leg right up against the rack's frame, so that if he raised up, he would not be able to go anywhere. He would just bump into me. I reached down, grabbed him by his lapels, and growled, "Get up. You're going on a working party with me."

His eyes popped open and he looked up at me. He could see I was ready for anything he had to give me. He scowled and stayed silent as he got up and got ready.

We carried out our two-day working party, and sure enough, he did his part, although he sure as hell was not happy about it. Actually, none of us were. They worked the crap out of us, especially him. I realized that he was not a rough guy. He had just been running his bluff for a while. Everybody had just stayed away from him because they thought he was off his rocker and capable of anything. There were a couple of guys like that who had tried that in different units. You know, making you think that they were nutty or something, and if you woke them up out of a dead sleep, they'd come up shooting or something. This guy turned out to be just a deadbeat who had something going for him. He was just another phony. But he never gave me any trouble after that. He had seen the light. I mean, I'd made a Christian out of him.

July went by slowly. We rested and recuperated for part of that month. Even though we had initially been assigned to this antiaircraft battery, as we packed up the equipment and sent it off, we had more time for other things. When it rained, I'd give classes on disassembling weapons. And every week or so, I would read sections of the Rocks and Shoals.[52]

---

52 Marine nickname for the *Uniform Code of Military Justice* (UCMJ).

We continued our patrols looking to pick up or get rid of Jap stragglers. They hid in these holes, tunnels, or caves, and they sure as hell knew we were looking for them.

Around mid-August, rumors began again. Some said the division was shipping out for China. Others said we were getting ready to go home, or Australia again. No one really knew anything, but since it seemed likely that we would be moving out soon, Bob Johnson and I decided that it was time to visit the First Marine Division cemetery. We were joined by a friend of Bob's, who brought with him a camera.

Emotionally charged, we started out. I was wearing a clean blouse that I had liberated from the rear of an Army hospital. Walking round there one day, I found these mounds of clothes. They had been taken off various guys who had been admitted to the hospital, most of them obviously wounded. Naturally, a lot of the trousers and shirts had bullet holes and blood on them. A few of them though did not, and I picked out a really nice blouse to wear to Rucker's grave. The shirt's previous owner had been a sergeant, an E-5, and when I started to put it on, a couple of G.I.s saw me.

"Hey," one of them warned, "you'd better not get caught wearing that shirt."

"Why not?" I asked.

"Because it's got sergeant stripes on it, moron!" You're just a corporal." The Army guys of course did not know that I had been promoted.

"It'll be okay," I said. And anyway, I didn't have given a damn. I was too worked up about going to seeing Rucker again.

The three of us walked over to the cemetery. I stopped just inside the entrance and shook my head as I saw all those crosses. Each one of those represented a guy that I had gone into combat with. I'd known quite a few of them.

We slowly walked around and found PFC Jim McGuire's grave. Jim had been Rucker's assistant FO, and had been killed at the ammo dump explosion on May 11th, eight days after Rucker. Bob and I crouched, and his buddy took a picture of us next to his cross.

We began walking again, and I was apprehensive. Then I froze. There it was. We had finally found Henry Rucker's grave—Number 259.

George at the grave of his friend, Henry Rucker, at the Okinawa cemetery. (Author's collection)

I stood there, mute, staring at his cross, and as I did, I realized that I would never return to this place again, because I was never going to come back to this damn island. So this would be my last goodbye to my good friend—the Hard Luck Kid.

I knelt down and looked intensely at the small wooden cross. I got all sentimental as the memories flowed. Henry and I had done so much together. Tears in my eyes, I stood up and gazed around. From where I was standing, I could see the road that went south toward Naha, and off in the distance the area where Henry had been killed. I turned round and looked back at his cross.

Bob's friend suggested we take a photo. Gathering myself emotionally, I squatted down behind Henry's cross and let him take the picture. Then I stood up and we walked away. I didn't look back.

Later, as we headed back to our unit, I wondered again why I had been spared, while so many like Henry had died. I would wonder that for the rest of my life. And even now I still get choked up.

September 1945

As July turned into August, the First Marine Division continued patrols to take out the Japanese stragglers. Rumors circulated that the division was going to move out. The question was where. One rumor was that they were going to be shipped home. Another was back to Pavuvu for rest and relaxation. Australia was another.

Division morale understandably took a hit when official word came down that they were to remain on Okinawa for the time being to get ready for the final assault on Japan. Along with the rest of the III Amphibious Corps, the division had actually started training when it was announced the second week in August that Japan had surrendered and that the war was officially over.

Then a couple weeks later came another disappointment. They were told that they were not going home or to some exotic port, but rather were going to be shipped to northern China as an occupational force, and to oversee the surrender of Japanese forces up there. Also going would be the Sixth Marine Division and the 1st Marine Air Wing.

On September 8, 1945, the III Amphibious Corps was given official orders to embark for China as part of the Hopeh Occupation Force. Senior Marine officers were to fly out immediately to coordinate the move. Additionally, the Third Marine Division on Guam and the Fourth Marine Division on Maui were designated as reserves for the operation. The First Marine Division received its embarkation orders to be gone by September 30th. With its headquarters to be located in Tientsin, they would remain there for at least two years before elements began going home, and even then, the process would take many months.

By September, the Okinawa operation was over and our division had orders to head for China. Me though, I had seen four campaigns, and even though the last big operation, the invasion of Japan, had been canceled with the war's end, there were still Jap holdouts in China and other places. Anyway, just like the guys who had fought at Guadalcanal, those of us in the division that had served longest were getting to go home. So while my division had been packing for mainland China, I had gone through enough combat to qualify for rotation back to the States. Yeah, my time was almost up, thank God.

There was a snag though. While I did not have enough time left to go to China with the rest of the division, I was not so short that I could be allowed to return to the States yet. I was told that I either had to ship over and extend for two more years with the division, or stay on Okinawa until my enlistment was up. As far as I was concerned, there was nothing to think about. I basically said the hell with the government. I had been on only one leave in four years, and that had only been for eight days. No, I had had all the living as a U.S. Marine that I would ever want. So when the division embarked on ships and left Okinawa, I stayed behind.

On September 15th, as the division started moving out to China, to work off the rest of my time in the service, I was transferred to a coastal defense unit: the 16th AA Battalion. I was assigned to a 90mm antiaircraft battery of four guns.[53] The unit had been disbanded a month ago, and those who had manned the battery were gone, either off to China or else shipped back home.

Along with other Marines, I was assigned to that unit to help take apart the guns for shipment off the island. As a newly promoted sergeant, the command put me in charge of a squad to dismantle the sites. My new squad was made up of a couple corporals and the rest sergeants like me. Although I had just been promoted, because of my seniority in service, I was put in charge. Overseeing the work squad was a bit tricky, because there were some salty guys in it. I mean, all of these guys had been overseas for a couple of years like me, and most of them were slated to rotate back to the states.

Our squad was indoctrinated on how the 90mm gun worked. The 90mm was our answer to those infamous German 88s. The gun itself

---

53 Before the war, a Marine antiaircraft battalion, designated a "defense battalion," included an antiaircraft unit that consisted of three or four batteries of 3-inch AAA guns, a group of eight .50 cal. heavy machine gun units, and a group of eight .30 cal. machine gun units. After 1943, the 3-inch guns were replaced by 90mm (about 3½-inch) guns, the .50 cal. machine guns by 40mm AA guns, and the .30 cal. machine guns by 20mm AA guns.

was fairly good size, about 16 feet tall. The barrel itself weight over a ton, and each round weighed about 23 lb. The gun only fired a single round at a time (unlike those pom-pom guns). Still, each gun crew could fire up to 20 rounds per minute.

For a few days, I was taught a great deal about that antiaircraft weapon, including how to fire one, and I actually got to shoot off a few rounds. I learned that the 90mm fired a relatively new type of shell, with something called a proximity fuse, which I'm sure was expensive as hell. We then began to dismantle the guns themselves, package them, and prepare them for shipment elsewhere. A good deal of the ammo though, was not to be taken off the island. So it either had to be ditched or dumped somewhere. This included dozens of cases of those new right-off-the-assembly-line proximity fuses that had recently been developed. Each fuse screwed in to the top of a 90mm antiaircraft shell. The fuses, I was told, were new technology. They were designed to explode the warhead if it came within 50 yards of an enemy aircraft. Worth thousands of dollars, we now we had to get rid of them, mostly to keep them out of the hands of civilians and the military of other countries. What a damn waste.

Still, we had our orders. So while the division left the island and sailed off to China, day after day, we loaded these crates of ammo, including those proximity fuses, into a Duck. Then we would get its crew to sail us out three miles into the bay, where we would start dumping the crates into the ocean. Then we went back to taking the emplacements apart.

Louise and the lucky Lavaca

On Thursday, October 4th, a typhoon named "Louise" by the Navy Weather Central was detected developing in the Caroline Islands. The Navy tracked it as it headed northwest, the storm predicted to pass a good 150 miles west of Okinawa. Four days later though, as it entered the East China Sea, it caught the Americans off guard by unpredictably veering to the right. It started to move north, up towards Okinawa. The next day, as it continued to increase in strength, it began to slow down, and the typhoon hit the island with full fury. By 1000 hours, the winds had already risen to over 40 mph, and four hours later, they were whipping across the island at a staggering 92 mph, creating waves over

30 feet high. Visibility was near zero, and ships and small craft were battered like toys, especially those caught in narrow waters.

At 1600 hours, the typhoon reached its peak as it traveled over the island at 15 knots. Sustained winds of 115 mph, with gusts up to 140 mph continued without a break for another few hours as the storm continued northward. Ships in the area desperately struggled to stay afloat, but periodic shifts in the wind direction made things worse as the vessels bobbed about in the water in the near darkness, many dragging their anchors as they drifted. Erratic zigs and zags created havoc with both ships that had functional engines struggling to navigate and those that had lost power and were wildly drifting. These unpredictable gyrations caused terrible collisions and near-misses as vessels suddenly loomed out of the darkness headed for each other and smashed into one another, either directly or with glancing blows. Dozens of vessels were driven ashore and beached, many by now reduced to mangled piles of junk. Others began sinking and had to be abandoned, as their crews desperately tried to swim ashore and spend the night in fields or shivering in trenches.

On the island, horizontal rain and fierce howling winds blew away food and medical supplies, and other provisions were ravaged as pallets and cases were torn apart. Brutal, blasting gusts tore into Quonset huts and buildings, and anything not firmly secured down went sailing away into the night. The winds finally began to die down around 2030 hours, but it was not until 1000 the next day that the winds would die down to 40 mph.

At the beginning of the second week of October, we were told a storm was about to hit the island, and we had instructions to firmly tie everything down. We did, but that didn't prepare us for what was about to hit. That Tuesday, the wind really began to pick up and the rain got heavy. Most of our tents were sitting on wooden platforms, and the tents were secured to them. Most of the smaller ones were tied to the platform, with a sturdy six-inch-round center pole bolted into it. The platform in turn was anchored securely to the ground.

The five or six of us in our tent were kind of lucky. First of all, we were glad we even had a tent. The unit had just been issued these tents, and this was the first we had. In addition, our tent was in a sort of corner, with a five-foot mound of earth behind us to partially shield us from the wind. The tent across from us though, was in an open field and exposed to the elements.

The storm started on a Tuesday morning, coming in from the south, and it kept getting stronger as the day went on. Around 4 p.m., the downpour began to get a lot worse. I was peeking out through the flap, seeing all kinds of small stuff flying around. I turned to the guys in with me and said, "Hey fellas, this wind is really getting bad."

Suddenly, we heard a few *whaps* come from outside. A couple of us lifted the flap to see what was going on. I saw the tent across from us getting pulled up as guys started running out of it. The tent rose up a couple feet off the ground and started sailing off across that field.

I looked at the guys inside and said, "The other tent's gone."

As the hours went on, the storm just got worse. To keep from getting blown away like the other guys, we started to take shifts holding on to the center pole. It took two of us to hold it down securely, so in teams of two, we took turns standing at the pole, holding it down. None of us got any sleep. We just rested up until it was our turn to hold that center pole again. The tempest went on like that clear through the night, and we spent the whole night holding onto that pole. Outside, we sometimes heard stuff go tumbling by, so we stayed where we were. None of us really could get any sort of rest, and it became one really long stormy night.

Early the next morning before dawn—not that we would have been able to see a sun or anything—we saw that our tent was starting to rip at the top. With all of us up, we struggled to catch each ripped streamer of cloth to pull it down and hold it. More and more of the tent started to rip and the center ring began to come down as we held on, huddled down around the pole.

The storm had been raging for over 14 hours now, and it was only when morning came did the wind started to decrease in intensity. By then, the tent was almost down over us as we sat on the ground, holding on to as much of it as we could.

I finally got up with a couple other guys and we looked out of what was left of our tent. It was still really windy, and we could not see anyone around or moving about. We ducked our heads back under the canvas.

One of us finally said, "Well, it'd be nice to have some coffee."

The mess tent was down the road from us, so we started talking about who was going to go and get some coffee and maybe something to munch on.

Suddenly, this ten-foot-long 2x12-inch plank came sailing in and banged into the side of the tent, smacking into us below. We sat in shocked silence as the board rolled over the top of the tent and then sailed away to heaven knows where.

Finally, one of us said, "Ah the *hell* with the coffee." We had lost our appetite too. And that's how we stayed until around noon. It finally quieted down enough so that we could get out and look around. Holy crap, what a mess. Most of the tents were down or just gone, and there was stuff lying all over the place. There were a lot of boats sitting out of the water. The Army Air Corps had a solid metal 30-foot flagpole that was bent 90 degrees over, about a third of the way up.

When Typhoon Louise was finally over, a dozen U.S. Navy ships and craft had been lost, including two destroyers. Another 200 vessels were grounded (half of which were amphibious ships and craft), and another three dozen had been heavily damaged. The island was half flooded, with mud and salt-water swamps everywhere. Some five dozen aircraft had been destroyed or heavily damaged. About 80 percent of the housing and billeting structures were knocked down, and dozens of tents and Quonset huts were moved hundreds of feet from where they had been set up.

Casualties from the storm included 36 dead, 100 wounded, and 47 missing. Those that survived, after occasionally dodging flying timbers, beams, and crates, ended up either in trenches, in ditches, or, in an ironic twist, huddled in what turned out to be the safest spots on the island: the very caves and bunkers that the enemy had occupied.

Because I had been on Okinawa over 30 days after the end of hostilities, I was awarded another ribbon for being a part of the occupational forces. Big deal. Finally, near the middle of October, word came down: we were to pack our gear, because a ship was coming to pick us up and take us back home.

Home!

It sure as hell was way past time for me. I had left the states some two and a half years ago, and had hit the beach here on D+1, Monday, April 2, 1945. Finally, over six months later, at long last I would be leaving that crappy miserable island.

About 600 of us Marines, mostly sergeants and corporals, boarded the USS *Lavaca*[54] on the 15th, and the next day, we sailed away from the island of Okinawa. I had mixed emotions as I stared at the receding image. I had spent 188 days on that hellhole, and over two months of it had been nothing but intense combat in which I had lost many good buddies. Looking back on that time, there seemed to have been very few moments, either day or night, that we were not getting attacked, shelled, shot at, or bombed. As forward observer for the heavy mortars, I had ended up at one time or another being a part of all three of 3rd Battalions rifle companies: Item, King, and Love.[55] And each of them had at one time or another been decimated.

Now as we headed out to sea, I looked back at that wretched, atrocious, stinking island. I knew I would never see it again.

We sailed across the Pacific towards California, towards home. Naturally, because we were anxious to get back, after being a day at sea, one of the ship's main boilers broke down. This knocked our speed down to 10 knots, so we would not get back to the States until the beginning of November.

Chugging along at a slow speed, the time seemed to crawl. The food for us enlisted was bad, and the cramped living quarters were terrible;

---

54 USS *Lavaca* (PA-180) was an attack transport of the Haskell class, named after Lavaca County, Texas. Commissioned on December 17, 1944, she could make 17 knots with her one propeller. She carried a crew of 690 and could carry 1,550 men, along with two dozen landing craft. She was armed with a 5-inch/38 cal. gun, a quad 40mm mount, two twin 40mm AA mounts, and ten .50 cal machine guns. She was placed in mothballs in October 1958, and scrapped in November 1992.

55 U.S. World War II phonetic identifiers differ from today's NATO identifiers. Leaning to the superstitious, Marine regiments never had a Company J (as in "J" for "Jinx"), just like tall buildings did not have a 13th floor.

as bad as I had ever seen aboard any ship. We sarcastically began calling her "Ole Lucky Lavaca," with no speck of affection. Still, the swabbies treated us okay, and we talked about getting back to the States.

Besides us Marines, the ship carried a number of civilians coming from the Far East, including several women. Some were Oriental, some looked like they were Russian gals. Many were beautiful ladies. Well, to us love-starved Marines, they looked beautiful. But the captain[56] wanted us to have a minimal "disturbing" impact on them, so we Marines had to stow our gear in the lower decks, and whenever we were allowed on deck, we had strict instructions to limit ourselves to the fantail. To enforce this, guards were posted between the civilians and us, and there were ropes across the forward areas.

This of course did not sit well with us. I mean, for crissakes, we had been overseas for over two years and some of us had five campaigns to our credit. And these were the first non-native women that we had seen since Melbourne two years ago (okay, except for that WAC I had seen four months ago). So this was no way to treat Uncle Sam's finest. We spent a good deal of time on the fantail, looking at them damn flying fish or whales, but trying to get a couple glimpses of the ladies on the upper decks.

The captain though, must have had it in for us Marines, because he did not give us any consideration. In fact one day, incredibly, word came down that he wanted us to do some close order drill. We did not know if it was just to keep us busy, to show off for the civilians around, or just to piss us off even more. We figured the third choice, and we really began to boil. I mean, no matter how damn rough and raggedy we may have looked to him, most of us were NCOs, seasoned Marines from the finest divisions in the Corps, veterans of several campaigns. So to us, that boot camp crap was for the birds. To make matters worse, there was not a single Marine officer on board to stick up for us. We were at the mercy of this dumbass navy reservist. We grumbled how it was too bad that we had all turned in our weapons on Okinawa and had left them all behind. We were unarmed.

---

56 Captain Walter S. Gabel, USNR, commanded the *Lavaca* from December 1944 to April 1946.

Fed up, our senior gunny went up to the bridge to see the captain and talk to him. From what we heard later, he basically told the skipper that weapons or not, he was about to have a real mutiny on his hands from men who had done plenty of hand-to-hand combat. The gunny told him, "Captain, with all due respect sir, these guys are all combat veterans. Sir, they're not going to put up with anything like that after what they've been through."

Evidently, the captain saw the logic in that, so he backed off. It was just as well. We didn't need any more of his bullshit, captain or not. We did though, have to do menial crap like swabbing the deck.

Finally, on November 4th, we sighted land, and everyone got excited and began to cheer. We were laughing like schoolboys and singing "Bless 'em All"[57] as we steamed under the Golden Gate Bridge, and approached the piers of San Francisco. As we came in, we saw and heard a band playing patriotic music on a yacht that we passed.

We grinned at each other as the *Lavaca* approached the dock. We all thought we were for once going to be treated like the heroes we were. Every one of us 600 grunts was eager as hell to get ashore and see the glamour of this wonderful city. I mean, we were finally back in the States!

Well, not quite.

The ship docked, lines were tied off, and that beautiful gangplank was lowered and secured. Instructions were that the civilians were to be allowed to leave first. Okay, we went along with that. As the last of them were departing though, a detachment of Marines from shore marched up to the ship. As they took positions next to it and on both sides of the gangway, I got suspicious. They sure as hell didn't look like any damn honor guard to me.

Then the bad news came. It was announced that no Marine under any circumstance whatsoever was to leave the ship, and we were actually barred from going near the gangplank. The posted stateside Marine

---

57 A popular British song sung in World War II. George could only remember the chorus and the first verse: "There is a troopship just leaving Bombay, bound for a distant shore; heavily laden with the time expired men, bound for the land they adore."

guards on the dock emphasized that. We knew that our navy captain hated us, and in response to his restriction, he probably now would have had that mutiny on his hands that he had nearly triggered a couple weeks before. Luckily for him we Marines were considered part of his crew and therefore under his direct command. So we stayed restricted to the ship. We could go back into the hold below and be miserable down there. Or, just like on the trip home, the best we could do was to stay on deck on that damned fantail. That was it. Nowhere else on the ship. Just stand there and fantasize about what it was like ashore. I mean, *man!* San Francisco! I thought back to when I had been there as a teenager. About the hot gals. And the booze ...

I sighed. It wasn't fair.

As night fell, some cargo was offloaded, and a few officers, and some more civilian passengers left. Those stateside Marines on the dock remained on guard, standing with their M1s. And while we Marines onboard could clearly see the bright lights of the city, we remained penned up on that damn transport.[58] Again, it sure was a helluva good thing that we were not armed. If we had been ... Damn!

Fortunately for all, we only sat in harbor for just a short time. Several hours later, we made preparations for getting underway. Finally, we weighed anchor, left San Francisco Bay, and turned southward. The ship's broken boiler had not been repaired in harbor; there had been no time. So we kept limping along down the Californian coast. We were at sea for four more days, pent up on that transport, grumbling, stewing, wondering where the hell we were going. Who knew? Mexico?

---

58 In the captain's defense, he was a naval reservist, and this was his first sea command. These 1st Marines he was bringing home were a rough, intimidating lot, and they had just endured a prolonged, intense combat campaign. According to a radioman stationed aboard the *Lavaca* at the time, K. F. Desha, the captain sometimes gave his crew instructions to avoid going on deck at night, and the Marines were to be fed well and allowed to sleep just about wherever they wanted. Desha described it that these Marines had "been in hand-to-hand contact with Japs ... I mean, they were wild looking, oh man! They'd walk around rattling their pockets sometimes where they had killed Japs, taken the butt of their gun and busted their mouths—they were dead, you know—and taken out the gold from their teeth."

Maybe they were taking us to some remote island to get indoctrination courses on how to re-enter society or something. I remember that Mrs. Roosevelt had made that comment once in Melbourne. There were rumors ...

At long last, on November 8th, we turned and steamed towards the land. As we approached, we got the word: it was San Diego. But there were no cheers now, no celebrations on deck, no laughter. We just wanted off that gawddamned ship.

We pulled into San Diego Harbor and tied up to the docks. The gangplank went down again, and this time, the Navy finally, reluctantly, turned us war veterans loose. We gratefully walked down the gangplank carrying our seabags. Our ordeal on that damned "Lucky Lavaca" was finally over, and once again, we were standing on American soil. Home at last.

Of my friends in the platoon that had made it through Okinawa alive, most had shipped off to China with the rest of the division. I was alone again. Still, I was back in the States, and I was ready to hit the bright lights of San Diego, although I would be doing it by myself. As I stood there, with bunches of Marine veterans around me, none of whom I knew, I thought about the buddies I had served with that had died on Peleliu and Okinawa. I felt isolated.

Suddenly, in that swarm of Marines on that dock, I heard behind me my name being yelled: "PETO! PETO!"

I looked back at the crowd of green, and way off in the distance, I saw a familiar face. It was John Skoglie, smiling and waving at me. Grinning, I waved back and struggled my way over through the crowd to meet him. He had already been transferred to another unit, but I didn't give a crap. I was happy to see his ugly mug. We stowed our gear and laughing, we took off for a well-deserved and long-overdue liberty. We went out to a bar, and had a few drinks. We picked up two nurses, and spent the night with them.

The next day, I returned to my unit. They put us in Camp Pendleton, and there I saw my first lady marines. We called them "banders." They were rough-looking, too. All I could think of was, what the hell were they turning these gals into? It left a bad taste in my mouth.

Although we were on the base, we were allowed to go on liberty, and I spent some two weeks there in San Diego, reintroducing myself to life again, before we all left for home. With the war over, and me back in the U.S., we were all going to be processed out. Around November 22nd, I was shipped back to Great Lakes Naval Station, on the north side of Chicago. Finally, almost like a dream, I was processed out, and on November 25, 1945, I was honorably discharged from the United States Marine Corps.

After I signed the papers, some officer asked me to read the discharge agreement, then shook my hand, and said, "Yeah you're alive. You're in pretty good shape."

All I could say was, "Thanks."

Still shaking my hand, he said, "You've always got a home in the Marine Corp if you want to come back."

And that was it. I was out. I had served a total of four years, three months, and 20 days on active duty, most of World War II, and all through America's participation. I had been through some staggering ordeals of war, often in really hot climates. I had seen things no human should ever see and run such a gamut of terrible sounds, smells, shocks and pain that few individuals had been through. And somehow, I had survived, and incredibly, without any wounds. The closest I had ever come was when that mortar shell had glanced off my back on Okinawa.

After I was given a boatload of decorations, my records were closed. I received the Navy Marine Corps Commendation Medal with Combat V, the Combat Action Ribbon, the Navy Presidential Unit Citation with two bronze stars, a Good Conduct Medal, the American Defense Service Medal, the American Campaign Medal, the Asiatic Pacific Medal with four bronze stars (one for each campaign), the World War II Victory Medal, the Navy Occupation Medal, and (unofficially) the Solomon Islands Medal.

CHAPTER 8

After the War

My first act as a civilian was to proceed to the nearest bar in down-town Chicago, which happened to be the Hotel Sherman. I was still in uniform, although I did not wear any medals or ribbons, just my First Marine Division shoulder patch, my ruptured duck,[1] and what I hoped was a sweet smile.

It worked, and I later thanked each of those two ladies that I met during those first couple weeks. They gave me their special, effective treatment for my own minor version of PTSD. The first gal was built real

---

1   The pejorative term refers to the Honorable Service Lapel Button awarded to U.S. veterans who had served in World War II and subsequently were honorably discharged. Issued from September of 1939 to December of 1946, it was a gilded brass (or plastic, when there were brass shortages) ring through which an eagle was getting ready to take flight. The pin was an official indicator to honor the veteran and to prove that he was not a deserter or AWOL. Since Federal law prohibited discharged veterans from wearing their uniforms, this pin allowed one to identify veterans separated from active duty. As such, the official pin commonly served to identify honorably discharged veterans to railroad and bus companies, because most of them honored such veterans by giving them either free or reduced cost transportation. While the term "ruptured duck" was enthusiastically taken up by the veterans by its very nature, its source is somewhat hazy. One version has it that during the war, the manufacturing plant that made the pins stamped it on the boxes they were shipped in, so that any enemy agents in the area would not know what was in them. Another is that because, as many remarked with a laugh, the term was accurately descriptive of the image, as the bird's head is turned to the right during a hernia exam when the patient is told to "cough." Naturally, the term was a huge hit with the sardonic veterans and immediately adopted.

nice, but not too bright; what we would call today no rocket scientist. So what? I was not particular at the time. Actually, I never was. This nice lady turned out to be a memorable one-night stand.

The second gal I hooked up with the next day turned out to be some bandleader's wife, and like it happens so frequently, he was on the road and this pretty lady, neglected even when he was around, was now alone and depressed. We were immediately attracted to each other, her because she was just lonely, me because—well, because I was me.

We spent our initial night together in an apartment I was able to get for a short time, and I must say, those first couple nights, she really put her heart into making me well and we gently made love. At one point, she teased me by saying, "You know, sometimes I like my sex a little rough." I thought she was serious, so I tried to accommodate her, although I must admit, most of the time I was embarrassed because I had never done anything like that, and I was not used to it. Of course, nothing really kinky happened, and we both ended up laughing about it. I really liked her, and she in turn was so happy to be with me, that she happily paid for my room for some five days. Hell, she easily could afford it, and I didn't argue.

That week with those two "nursing ladies" for the most part washed away most of those bad memories that had been swimming around in my head. I still might have an occasional nightmare of being in combat. But each of the two ladies did a lot to bring my humor back, and to put a big old smile back on my face.

When that week was over though, I had spent all my mustering-out money. I was hung over and now I was also broke. Still, mentally, I was in a much better place than I had been. So I hitchhiked back home to Akron. It was 2 o'clock in the morning when I walked up my street to our house. Tired, I went up the steps and knocked. Finally, my mother came to the door and gave a big *whoop*. She then hollered for Liz to come down and see who was back. We then sat down on the steps and began talking.

For several years after returning home, I would continue to have occasional nightmares. While they mostly varied in specific details, there were common themes in them. In the dream, I would find myself being chased by one or two Japs. They would have these caricature features, with big glasses, buck teeth, and big maniacal grins as they chased me. I would usually have some sort of weapon with me, but something would always be wrong with it. Either it would have no ammo, be jammed, or missing a piece. Anyway, I wouldn't be able to use it and would have to run. One of my biggest fears when I had been in combat was that I would run out of ammo. That was why I always carried around an extra weapon. Now, in my dreams, carrying a useless weapon, I would be reduced to running in fear. I would usually wake up scared, sweating, and totally exhausted.

Still I resolved that I was not going to let the nightmares get to me, and I was not going to get to the point where they really bothered me. I did not want to get reduced into a state of constant terror of sleeping. After about five years, the nightmares ceased, and for decades, the war became a foggy, distant memory.

After Melbourne, I had tried to toe the line and stay out of trouble—well, okay, except for that one time on Okinawa at the end of June. Still, I think that I had turned out to be a fine NCO, and if it had been a longer war, I probably would have ended up being an officer. After all, I had acted like one on Okinawa. I had ended up second in command of L Company. I had no intentions though, of staying in the Marine Corps. I knew that I would always be a Marine, but regarding the travel and adventure that I had signed up for back in August of 1941, well, I had damn sure gotten my belly full of it. And I knew if I reenlisted, I would not stay at just one duty station. I would be moving around a lot, with not much of a life.

The hell with that. I was now out of the service.

I had just returned home when I got a surprise. My old girlfriend Phyllis and her mother came over to see me. With Phyllis sheepishly sitting next to her, her mom broke the news that Phyllis was three months pregnant. I think that they were nervous about how I would react. I took it in stride, though. Actually, the truth was that I still was not ready to settle down, and so her getting pregnant was an easy out for me.

For a short time, I lived there with Mom in the house that Alex and I had bought during the war and were making joint payments on. Also living there were my sister Liz, her new husband, and our kid brother, Steve. I found out that Alex had left Chicago and moved to Florida.

My sister Liz filled me in on her new marriage. During the war, she had married a 27-year-old Jewish fellow named Samuel E. Rosker. Pop hated the guy and refused to ever talk to him. Sam had joined the National Guard in 1937, and had become an officer. After he married Liz, he was shipped off overseas and served somewhere in France, doing something in the rear with supply. Now he was a captain, stationed in New Orleans. He had served in France, but had not seen any action. On the contrary, he was stationed in Paris after the city was taken, and because he was a supply guy, he never had to be in combat. His two brothers-in-law though, as Marines, had seen all kinds of combat and had earned medals for valor, and I was told that this was driving him crazy. I laughed when I heard that.

Around this time, Waddy returned home too and came over to see me. Naturally, we wanted to trade stories, celebrate the end of the war and being alive, and the good fortune to be able to get together again. We had to get stamps to purchase whiskey because it was still being rationed.[2] We pooled our ration stamps and found that we had enough to get us each a fifth of cheap PM.[3]

---

2   Rationing in the U.S. during the war encompassed a wide variety of critical products such as rubber, nylon, silk, sugar, shoes, coffee, tobacco, fuel, and a host of other conveniences as well. This included such things as new cars, zippers, bicycles, vacuum cleaners, stoves, phonograph records, and typewriters. Whiskey distilleries were put into the rationing program as well, because critical components such as sugar and grain became valuable commodities. All distilleries were modified to mostly produce industrial alcohol. This was a vital component in the production of such wartime products as torpedo fuel, smokeless powder, bomb components, fuel additives, life vests, and gas masks. Whiskey chemists were channeled into working on yeast-similar drugs, such as penicillin. Fortunately for the alcoholics, the President's "Good Neighbor Policy" with Latin America made some spirits like tequila, rum and vodka readily available. It did though by necessity, require a change in one's drinking preferences.

3   "Pleasant Moments." A low-end National Distillers blend that came in different sizes and was comprised of anywhere from 49% to 71% distilled grain spirits, and the rest straight whiskey.

We went to my house and sat in the kitchen. We had a great time shooting the bull as we drank our fifths, with Mom *tsk-tsking* us once in a while. When our whiskey was gone (the bottles were only pints), we decided to go into town, despite Mom's protests. We started out, planning to go all over the neighborhood: Kenmore, Portage Lakes …

We walked four or five blocks east and ended up at a Portage Lakes nightclub. We got into a scuffle somewhere for badmouthing someone. Both of us drunk, we came across a car parked off Kenmore Boulevard. Surprisingly, the key was in the ignition and it was running. Waddy looked at me and smiled. "Let's go for a ride," he said.

He jumped in behind the wheel, and I climbed into the passenger seat. He put the engine in gear and roared off. Now you have to understand that Waddy was a wild enough driver when sober, so you can imagine how terrible his driving was now that he was smashed. To me, it was borderline suicidal.

"He's gonna wreck us," I thought to myself (as best as I could, given my condition). Another screech of tires as he merrily took a curve, and I thought, "Wreck us, hell! The sonuvabitch is going to kill us!" I offered to drive instead, but he just laughed and shook his head. Obviously, Waddy was having a ball.

Finally, when he was looking out to his left at the night scenery, I discreetly reached over and turned off the ignition key. We slowly coasted to a stop in the middle of the road as we looked around to see where we were. I somehow realized that in his crazy driving, Waddy had sideswiped another car.

As we sat there, we heard sirens away off in the distance. We tried to start the car again, but it stalled and wouldn't start. So we got out, recognized that our "borrowed" car was still sitting in the middle of the road next to a bridge, and realized that we had to get the hell out of there. Not, of course, before we staggered into a nearby bar and had a drink first. We were really plastered. Three guys followed us into the bar and sat down, watching us. We didn't know it, but they had been in the car that we had sideswiped down the road. They just sat there, staring at us.

We finished our drinks and walked back out to the car. We stumbled to the front of it and popped the hood. While we were looking at the engine, the three guys came up to us. They seemed calm as they talked to us. Suddenly, one of them busted a beer bottle over my head and they started to jump us. Despite the glass breaking on my noggin, I didn't go down. This made them hesitate, probably wondering if attacking us was the right move, and they stood off for a few moments. There were three of them versus us two, but what the hell, we were Marines. Still, we were drunk and caught off guard, so we backed off. After all, there was still the highway.

I shook off the blow and tried to think. I knew that we were fighters, but we were outmatched. The cops were coming and we had stolen a car while drunk. And we were clearly in no condition to take on these three bastards. So I decided to make a strategic maneuver. "Let's get the hell out of here. Jump over the rail."

We ran over to the highway railing and bolted over it, tumbling down the embankment. Luck though, was against us. This was not some gentle, five-foot grassy slope, like our booze-addled brains had just assumed. It was instead a ten-foot steep drop with bunches of rocks and stones, and I swear, we must have hit every other one going down the slope.

We got up, woozy, shook ourselves off, and took off down the creek. Discretion, we clearly felt, was in this instance definitely the better part valor, and when we had to, we were masters at eluding folks. So after a while running down the creek, we fled into the woods. Once in the trees, we were safe.

For a while I drove a truck delivering beer. I never told friends or family about my wartime experiences and what I had gone through, but once in a while, when I'd be over at Waddy's house, his mom would catch me staring off at the wall. She'd smile, and say something nice, like, "Oh, you just grab yer fishing pole. Go down to the canal and go fishing, and you'll get back to normal."

I'd look at her and smile, but I would be wondering what the hell she talking about. I mean, I felt okay. After all, the war was over with. Still, for the next forty years, I would never reminisce. Except of course, with my buddies at the reunions. But even then we kept it light. Other than that, there was no one around us to talk to about it. I did though,

George, Sam, and Alex, taken in late 1945 in Akron. (Author's collection)

think about those years once in a while. Sometimes, I would get a little peeved at historical accounts. It seemed like only sob stories were getting written up. The regular guys, we got nothing, even though that was for most of us the way we wanted it. Just leave us the hell alone. Some guys used the public thing as a crutch so they tried making something about it. Me, I was okay, and did not want anyone thinking I was messed up or anything.

Job wise, I found that being a war veteran did not necessarily open any doors for you, especially now that the war was over. There were so many veterans now back as civilians. Before I had joined the Marines, my job experience had mostly been in soil conservation. That had provided me a good education on life, but just like veteran status, it did not automatically open any doors for you, and you could not use it to further a career.

When I first got home, I probably had four or five jobs in just a couple months, because none interested me. I didn't know what I wanted to do for the rest of my life. A stubborn fellow to begin with, I guess that I still had a problem with authority. After taking orders—and some of them were really stupid—in combat for 32 months, I found it difficult letting anybody tell me what to do.

Now my brother-in-law Sam Rosker had a 1941 Plymouth that he had left with mom. It was in reasonable condition, and in late December of 1945, he wrote to us, asking if I would drive it down to him in New Orleans. We negotiated "expenses," and I finally agreed to do it.

I left Akron on a freezing morning at the end of January and headed south down U.S. Route 21, through Marietta, and into West Virginia, then turned and headed southwest down some older roads; remember there were no freeways in those days. Unfortunately, the Plymouth's defroster did not work, so between that and the cold, the windshield kept fogging up from my breathing. I had to drive slow, because I was having trouble seeing the highway. Once in a while, I had to stop and wipe a hole on the inside of the windshield with a cloth to clear the condensation so that I could see. Naturally this got worse as night came on, but since there was little or no traffic around, I managed to keep going. So there I was, driving down a dark road, now somewhere in Tennessee, wiping the windshield, driving and then wiping again.

Finally, cold and miserable, I saw a light up ahead. I pulled over to what looked like a little restaurant, and I went inside to warm up. Shivering, I ignored the couple of people in there, walked over to the counter and sat down. I ordered a cup of hot coffee.

The attendant stood there and looked at me. After a moment, he said, "You ... you don't want any coffee. You don't wanna drink in here, do ya?"

I looked up at this fellow and thought, "What the hell's the matter with this guy? Is he crazy?" So I said, "Yeah, I wanna cup of coffee."

He looked at me, paused, and said, "Ah, I ... I don't think you better have one in here."

I stared at him and then slowly looked around the room. It suddenly hit me. Everyone in there was black, the guy that was waiting on me, the folks at the tables ... I was in the South now. If word got out that this guy had served me and was now serving white guys in here, he would really catch hell.

I looked back at him, having realized what was going on, and said quietly, "Well, I'll be damned." I got up and packed my crap. I thanked him for making me aware of my mistake—he was real nice about it—and I left.

As I started driving on, I thought about what had happened. I sure as hell wasn't tuned into that damn racial crap. I had not been around many black folks in my life, so I hadn't been exposed to that way of thinking. Even when I was hitchhiking through the South in 1941, I hadn't seen much of it. Oh, I knew the South was segregated, but that was about as far as my thinking had ever gone. I remember that there had been one or two Negroes in our high school, and it was almost a novelty when you saw one in Akron, let alone our school. But so what?

I shook my head and continued on in the cold, as night turned into dawn. I only stopped for gas and to check the car fluids. Luckily, the weather warmed up, so I didn't have to wipe the windshield anymore. I kept going and finally made it to New Orleans and met my brother-in-law. He greeted me and escorted me into the army base there.[4] I stayed there for a couple days in one of the empty cots, visiting with Sam and Liz.

It was still winter, and for weeks now, I had realized that I was not yet used to Ohio winters again. Between the snow and the ice and the cold, my body, accustomed to tropical weather, had not yet acclimated again. So I figured I stay down South where it was warm for a while. Before the war, seeing those chain gangs and hearing those stories, I had just wanted to get the hell out of there. Now though, having gone through all that hell in the Pacific, I really did not give a damn about the conditions and went through the South without a fear.

Since Alex had since moved south from Chicago to Miami, I decided to go see him. I guess that I loved to travel and was still looking for adventure. I had grown up with a roadmap in my hip pocket, and it

---

4   The Jackson Barracks Army base. It was later turned over to the Louisiana National
    Guard.

was still there. So after a few days visiting with Sam and Liz, I took what clothes I had brought, and left them to go see Alex. I hitchhiked my way eastward from New Orleans to Miami and found my brother working there. He had landed a job singing in some theater bar, and working with him was this new comedian, a guy named Jan Murray.[5] I stayed with Alex for two weeks or so before hitchhiking back to Akron and doing more odd jobs.

Around this time, I stopped drinking. I mean, I just stopped, cold turkey. Looking back on it, this seems a strange thing to me now. From when I was 15 years old until I was 24, I would drink—well, shall we say, rather liberally. Then one day, I abruptly decided that it was over. I totally quit drinking. A large part of the reason was the fact that I woke up one morning with a terrible hangover. Then, through the cobwebs of my memory, I realized I had spent all night with this really pretty girl, and I could not remember if we had actually messed around or not. That was it, I said to myself firmly. No more alcohol. And I haven't had a drink ever since.

I guess that in many ways, 1946 was a momentous year for me. For one thing, I was still adjusting to civilian life, and trying to forge some sort of future. I moved south from Akron Ohio to Columbus in September to go to school. I had decided that I wanted to get some more education, so I enrolled at The Ohio State University in September of 1946 to take some business courses. Then something happened in my social life, something that was to take me down a whole new path.

Being a veteran, I had begun making visits to the VA for various medical issues that came up. Near the end of November, I went there to have some work done on my teeth.

During my visits, I became acquainted a sweet lady working as a stenographer and a secretary. Her name was Juanita Shilling. She was two years older than me. We struck up a conversation and I came away

---

5   Jan Murray, 24 years old at the time, began as a standup comic before he moved up to star in various early television shows. He later became a game show host for such programs as *Dollar a Second* and one that he created called *Treasure Hunt*. He also starred in a number of TV dramas and movies. He died in 2006 at the age of 89.

liking her. After that, every time I went to the VA, I would chat with her. One day she mentioned that she played on a bowling team with several of her friends there at work. She asked me if I bowled. I was not into that sort of sport, but I faked it and told her that I guess I did sometimes. She then asked me if I would want to go bowling with her and her team some night.

I shrugged and said, "Sure, why not?"

So she gave me the specifics, and that night, I went bowling with her. I suppose that I did all right for an amateur, because the next thing that I knew, I was on their team. That night, we crossed the street from the Olympic Bowling Alley and went into this bar. We sat down, had a couple drinks, and listened to this gal singing at the piano.

We started dating, and that became a regular haunt for us. I continued going to Ohio State, as well as working two jobs. I dated Juanita for about a year and a half, and the more we went out, the more we talked about our future. Finally we talked about getting married. Well, technically, she proposed to me, but what the hell—we weren't kids by then. Anyway, I told her it was something I had to think about. I mean, it was a big step for me.

That night, I mulled it over. Crap, something inside of me said that I didn't want to get married. But then I reconsidered. I was 25 years old and not getting any younger, and I wasn't going anywhere in life. So I finally agreed, and we got married on June 27, 1948 in the town she grew up in, Ada, Ohio. We were married in this big church across the street from Ohio Northern University. Over the years, Juanita and I would have two children: Nancy, born two days after Christmas 1950, and George Lee, born some ten years later on February 16, 1961.

A little after we got married, I quit going to Ohio State and took a job in the evenings selling vacuum cleaners and then a third job at Ranco Controls.[6] I kept selling vacuum cleaners in the evenings as backup, because Ranco had a bad reputation for laying people off. And that's how it went for the next five years. In the spring of 1952, I finally got fed up with all three jobs. The sweepers were not bringing me in any

---

6   Ranco moved to Plain City, Ohio in April 1980.

decent money to speak of, and Ranco was jerking me around. I was going crazy. I was in Production in that plant over on Russell Street, weighing screws that came off its production line.

We had often been told that we should try to become salaried employees, because no one on salary got laid off. So, one day, disillusioned with my job and again being told I might get laid off, I got sick and tired of the whole lousy thing. Mad, I decided to take a gamble and complain. I went over to my superintendent's office. I walked in and he asked me what the trouble was. I started in.

"You know, no disrespect or anything, but I'm sick of this gawddamn job. I've got a little education and I think that I can do better."

"Yeah?" he said, looking at me.

"Yeah. I've been working here for about four years. You could teach a monkey to do what the hell I'm doing. It's just setting there doing the same damn thing over and over. So I'd like to be a machinist."

He expressed doubt as to whether I could do that.

Looking him straight in the eye, I told him, "Well, if I gotta keep doing what I've been doing, you pretty much got my two weeks' notice."

So he made some calls, and by damn, he somehow made it happen. I was happy and thanked him. As luck would have it though, two weeks later, I still got laid off, the first salaried employee in that plant that did. Just my luck …

So that June, with me laid off, Juanita and I took a daring risk. We pooled all our savings together and invested in a small convenience store. It was in the Short North, on North High Street. We called it "The Loop Carryout." I would run it, and Juanita would be our bookkeeper.

I was taking a risk owning a store, but at least I could be my own boss and no longer have to take crap from some self-inflated jerk full of himself. Still, The Loop Carryout was sure as hell not anything fancy. When we first opened, all we sold was beer and wine. Our suppliers included five wine companies and eight or nine beer distributors that delivered to the store. Soon after we expanded to include pop, candy, some canned food, cigarettes, cigars, paperbacks, some magazines, and some convenience items. I later included some liquor, but only that watered-down stuff that you find in big grocery stores and tastes like crap; nothing over 40 proof.

I also sometimes sold firearms out of the store, but mostly using catalogs and brochures: special orders. I did have a small inventory of pistols, shotguns, and rifles, but I sure as hell never had any in the store—well, except of course, the one I carried on me. It was a 1911 model .45 cal. semi-automatic. I had purchased it through the NRA from the Redfield arsenal for just $14 (I still have it, in fact). But that was the only gun I carried in the store. And it was always loaded—cocked and locked.

Perhaps inevitably, I sometimes got into trouble. I soon learned that the liquor agents were a nasty group of guys, and many of them were shakedown artists in one way or another. Today these dirty bastards would get exposed quickly, but not so back them. Most of them it seemed were rejects from various police departments, or were cop wannabes.

One day an agent from the ATF Bureau[7] name Pugh came into the store, showed me his badge, and said, "Let me see your inventory."

I told him that I couldn't do that because. I kept my inventory at home.

His look was one of skepticism.

I smiled and added, "I think you can see why." Hell, if I kept firearms in the store, especially in this part of town, I'd be getting broken into a lot.

"Oh," he said sternly, "you can't keep them there. You gotta keep them here."

I gave him a puzzled look and said, "Uh, no, I don't."

At least he was not bellowing at me. "Yes you do," he insisted.

I had already checked on this long before, so I stared back at him, nodded, and said, "I'm pretty sure you're wrong."

Well, we talked some more, but he kept telling me that I would have to store the guns in the store.

Amazingly, a couple days later, he came back and apologized to me. "By God, you know, you were right. You can keep them in your home."

---

7   Alcohol, Tobacco and Firearms.

I was shocked. I think that was the first time that anyone in civil government was actually decent enough to do that. I had concluded a while back that most of those officials were dirtbags. I thanked him and again pointed out that he could see why I did that, and he agreed with me. All in all, a nice guy. Unusual, for a liquor agent.

In 1969, I had a squabble with the State of Ohio. These three state liquor-control agents that liked to frequent my convenience store in Columbus, Ohio had a real beef with me and were always trying to pin something on me. They often came into the store and inspected it, looking for signs of illegal alcohol, gambling, or anything else that they could find.

Finally one day, frustrated at all their unsuccessful attempts, they accused me of selling pornographic material. They charged me on the spot, immediately revoked my liquor license, and confiscated all my magazines. As it turned out (unknown to me), some of the magazines actually did have some "inappropriate photography." Naturally, I tried to tell them that I didn't know about it, but that did not matter to the State of Ohio, and I was charged and fined.

Angered over the injustice, I appealed the verdict. My defense centered around two points. First, the liquor-control agents actually had no jurisdiction over anything in the magazines I was selling. Second, I had not been aware that there was pornographic material in any of my stock, and even if I thought there might have been something there that could have fallen into that category, that I was no authority on what was legally obscene and what was not. Nor were they. When I won the case, the state appealed. The Ohio Supreme Court in the end decided that they would not take my case, so the state stubbornly appealed the case to the U.S. Supreme Court. Surprisingly, they actually did agree to take it, and after more years of litigation, I successfully had the charge appealed in 1979.[8] My liquor license and the stuff that had been confiscated was

---

8   Cook, Donald vs. Peto, Jr., George, U.S. Supreme Court Ohio Southern District Court, Case No. Civ. No. 70-57, docket://gov.uscourts.ohsd.Civ. No. 70-5; 409 U.S. 1071 / 93 S.Ct. 675 / 34 L.Ed.2d 659 / 5-19-1972. The court ruled against the agents (under Donald Cook, Director of the State's Department of Liquor Control at the time), and the department's declared claim to have the authority to

returned, and my article was in several newspapers. But it had been a ten-year fight that had cost me a good $20,000.

Alex had been wounded at Guadalcanal in the summer of 1942 under the command of Lt. Col. Herman Hannekin, an old-timer.[9] According to Alex, during a firefight with the Japs, his unit was forced to fall back. As they did, Alex was shot in the knee and left behind, sitting there in pain, stranded, alone, and barely able to move. Things got even worse when a mortar barrage began.[10] A nearby shellburst flung a few pieces of shrapnel into his ribs and started more bleeding. Somehow though, by some miracle, he managed to control the bleeding, dodge enemy patrols, and survive through the night. The next day, his unit went looking for him and found him. They immediately sent him to the rear for treatment. Alex was soon evacuated off the island on the USS *Solace*[11]

---

regulate the Loop Carry Out's magazine material was wrong. The court stated that the state's liquor control agency had no authority to control the material in the magazines George sold, and to do so was to the court a threat to free speech, stating that the "seizure of material was based solely on the personal predilections of the liquor control agents."

9   Lt. Col. Lewis Puller at the time commanded the regiment's 1st Battalion.

10   Alex Peto never found out if the mortar barrage that came in was from the Japanese or friendly fire from the Marines to slow down the enemy advance.

11   The USS *Solace* (AH-5) was a famous ship that saw a good deal of action in the Pacific. Commissioned as the passenger liner the SS *Iroquois* in 1927, she was purchased by the U.S. Navy in 1940 and renamed the USS *Solace* on July 22nd. Refitted as a hospital ship, she was commissioned on August 7, 1941 (just two days after Alex and George were sworn into the Marine Corps). With a crew of 470, she could make up to 18 knots and could accommodate 425 patients. On the morning of 7 December 1941 when the Japanese attack began, the *Solace* happened to be at Pearl Harbor, moored northeast of Ford Island and about 125 yards north of the USS *Arizona*. It was a visiting Army doctor aboard her, Dr. Eric Hakenson, who went topside and shot the famous 8mm film footage of the *Arizona* blowing up. The *Solace* immediately went into action and lowered her two motor launches with medics and aides to evacuate wounded off the stricken ships. Risking their lives under attack, they rescued struggling and wounded men covered with oil, taking many off the *Arizona* and pulling others out of the burning water. They took them to their ship, where a makeshift emergency room was hurriedly put together. The boats went out and returned again and again, rescuing hundreds from the water

and sent to New Zealand, where he spent nine months recovering. While recuperating, he was transferred to the Brooklyn Navy Yard. As a wounded hero, he went on a couple bond tours, and a prominent article was written up about him in the *Akron Beacon Journal*. When the reporter asked Alex what he wanted to do now, he supposedly replied, "I want to go back there and kill some more Japs."

After the war, when I ribbed him about that, he looked at me sheepishly and said, "Hell, I never said that! That damn reporter added that."

Alex was processed out in 1943 and after the war, he moved to Miami to get into entertainment. He landed that job as a singer in a Miami nightclub, working with comedian Jan Murray. When he was offered a screen test in Hollywood, he jumped at the chance. Over several years, he did a number of commercials out there for different products, such as cologne. As many starting out there did, he decided that Alex Peto was not snazzy enough a name and did not have enough pizzazz. So he changed it to Alexander Darson. Now sporting this thin moustache, he had a sort of Errol Flynn look about him, so he had a few opportunities to make it to the silver screen. He also did a number of films working as a stunt man, and once in a while, a few voiceovers and commercials. When Walt Disney's "Zorro" series began in 1957, Alex was lucky enough to get hired as a backstage assistant fencer who helped many of the characters learn how to fence. Alex's name though, never appeared in the credits.[12] He later married and raised two boys and eventually retired after a half century of being in television and film.

My younger brother Steve did not serve in the war, because he was diagnosed as having a bad kidney. He had always been a sickly kid, and his health remained an issue the rest of his life. Still, he tried to make

---

and from the burning hulks in Battleship Row. The *Solace* served throughout the entire war, sailed some 170,000 nautical miles, treated over 25,000 service members, and evacuated thousands of wounded men, ultimately shuttling many back to the United States. She earned seven battle stars and was finally decommissioned in February 1946 at Norfolk, Virginia. In August 1947, she was sold to a Turkish ship company, refitted once again as a passenger liner, and renamed the SS *Ankara*. This historic vessel was finally scrapped in Turkey in 1981.

12 Head trainer Fred Cravens received credit for Guy Williams's fencing lessons and choreographing those scenes.

the best of things. A natural pilot, he became a pilot instructor at the nearby Barberton Airport. In his condition, he probably never should have been given a pilot's license, but his flying skills were well qualified. Somehow, he got a doctor friend to sign the physical part to his pilot's license application.

Not just a flyer, he also became experienced at working on aircraft as well. In November of 1945, just as I was coming home from the war, Steve was lucky enough to land a job working for an aviator named Cook Cleland, who had been a decorated navy pilot during the war.[13] Cook's company owned these four Corsair ex-fighters in this huge

---

13 Cleland received his wings just before Pearl Harbor. During the war, he flew an SBD dive bomber off the USS *Wasp* (CV-7) in the Guadalcanal campaign. On September 15, 1942, flying ASW cover for the carrier, he spotted a submarine periscope. Flying down, they marked the spot with a smoke flare, but could not notify the carrier because his radio was out. Cook (nicknamed "Cookie") landed on *Wasp* as it started turning into the wind at 1445 hours to launch an air raid, when that Japanese submarine IJN *I-19,* having maneuvered close in, fired a full spread of six torpedoes as Cleland was just walking away from his aircraft. The first passed in front of *Wasp* and hit the destroyer *O'Brien*. The next three torpedoes though, struck the carrier's port side, and the sixth finally hit the USS *North Carolina* some seven minutes later. Cook, injured by an explosion, managed to make it back to the stern, and along with the task group commander (Rear Admiral Leigh Noyes, Commander Task Group 61.1) jumped into the water. He floated for four hours in his life preserver, while destroyers depth-charged the area, trying to get the sub that had fatally crippled the carrier. It was a painful experience for the men, because every time a depth charge exploded the shock wave would slam against their bodies. Cook later claimed that each time there was an explosion, the concussive shock would force water up his butt. So he had to actually put his finger in his rectum to prevent that. He wryly added, "I guess this is where you would say, 'Desperate times calls for desperate measures.'" The *Wasp* finally went down at 2100 hours that evening. The next year, on the second USS *Lexington* (CV-16), Cleland distinguished himself by becoming an ace, with five enemy aircraft to his credit, an extraordinary accomplishment for any pilot who flew any aircraft that was not a fighter. He was later awarded the Navy Cross for having crippled the Japanese aircraft carrier *Junyō* in the Battle of the Philippine Sea in June, 1943. Near the end of the war, the Navy made him a test pilot for various captured enemy aircraft to assess their capabilities. Cook went back to flying a Corsair when the Korean War broke out, and, in 1951, he was shot down and later rescued at sea. He died on June 13, 2007.

hangar located along Route 224, southeast of Akron. Designed to be the single biggest one-room hangar in the world, it had been designed to build dirigibles and later on, blimps. Because this damn thing was so huge, small clouds actually sometimes formed inside of it, and once in a while, they actually created some light drizzle.[14]

Since Steve did not have his own car, I usually drove him to work, and he took great pleasure in showing me around and getting me in with his co-workers there. Eventually, the work that they did on those Corsairs paid off. Cook Cleland came in sixth in the R Division in 1946 with the Corsair FG-1D, and won first place in 1947 and again in 1949 with the F2G Corsair.[15]

Steve moved to California in 1950 to live with Alex, and for a while, they shared an apartment. He pursued his career in flying instruction, teaching Roy Rogers how to fly, and eventually in charge of Veronica Lake's aircraft.

In early March 1953, Alex got a phone call from mom, telling him that Steve was really ill and needed us. Alex at that time had a short-time job in New York City, selling coin-operated oxygen machines. When he got mom's call, he called me immediately and told me he was going to come get me, so that we could drive out to California together. Although I had only had my convenience store for nine months, I agreed to go, and he ended the phone conversation with a simple, "I'll pick you up in the morning."

Alex drove all night to Ohio, and the next morning, we left. We drove straight through, only stopping for gas and some coffee. Unfortunately,

---

14 The Goodyear Airdock, built in 1929. Sudden changes in the temperature could cause condensation inside, resulting in a type of fine mist rain.

15 With the war over, the Cleveland Air Foundation was created to reestablish air racing. Taking advantage of advanced military technology, and a surplus of aircraft, the military services took a keen interest in these races. Cleland bought four new Corsairs, promising to soup them up and fly them to give the Army P-51s that were being entered some competition. These Corsairs were not built by Vought (F4Us). Because of war production demands, Corsairs were also built by the nearby Akron-based Goodyear. Cleland bought four, each for about $1,400, although each one had cost the government today's equivalent of a million dollars.

we were delayed in Texas by a sandstorm that was so fierce, it sandblasted a good part of the paint off Alex's car, and pitted the windshield.

When we finally arrived, we were told that Steve's prognosis was not good. He had contracted a serious case of uremic poisoning.[16] He was still alive, but the doctors told us he was going fast. There was not much that could be done, especially since there were no kidney transplants back then, even though Alex and I each volunteered to donate one of ours. We sat with Steve for a while, but Alex absolutely hated hospitals and finally just had to leave. I remained with Steve though, and his girlfriend. We stayed with my little brother for four long days, never leaving the hospital. We ate at the cafeteria and slept on chairs or sofas. Mom and Alex visited occasionally. Steve's condition continued to worsen, and occasionally the poor guy became delirious. I sometimes held his fevered hand, and once in a while, I'd put ice on his lips to cool him down. At times, he thought that his bed was an airplane, and that we were flying it high over the country. To make him more comfortable, I every now and then would raise or lower the front of his bed end by cranking on a wheel at the side, and he would sometimes blurt out, "Crank that wheel!" Those were his flying instructions to me.

Discouraged to see that he was not getting any better, I finally went to talk to his doctor. "Do something, fer crissakes," I said.

The doctor looked at me sadly, shrugged, and said, "Nothing much else that we can do."

Frustrated, I grumbled, "Well, he's not getting better. Try something. Anything."

My insisting finally got them off the fence. As a last-ditch attempt, the medical staff decided to give Steve a whole blood transfusion. He had been a likable patient, and I could tell that the nurses liked him and felt sorry for him. In fact, as they readied him for the procedure, one of them actually looked away and started crying. On March 25, 1953, Steve died at the age of 26. He slipped away as I sat next to him, holding his

---

16 A condition where high levels of uric acid contaminate the bloodstream. Symptoms include weakness, fatigue, nausea, shakes, deliria, and high levels of acid. Severe conditions can cause renal failure, coma, and death.

hand. I would do the same thing with my wife Juanita when she would pass away almost exactly sixty years later.

At Steve's funeral, his pilot friends flew their aircraft over the service, performing the missing-man formation. He was buried in a cemetery near the National Guard Armory in Burbank, California.

In 2004, at age 84, Alex became ill. When I talked to his doctor by phone in Columbus, the physician did not pull any punches. He told me that Alex was so full of cholesterol that there was not much they could do for him. I knew that there was nothing that he could do, so I decided not to go out for the end. Alex died on September 5, 2004 in Tehacapi, California.[17] He had wanted to be cremated and his ashes spread into the Pacific Ocean, but his son thought it would be more appropriate if his ashes were dispersed on a military base. So Gregory took his father's urn and traveled south to the Marine base of Camp Pendleton. He drove up the back road behind the base, and had Alex's ashes scattered along the road.

Because my brother-in-law Sam was in the Army and then later the National Guard, he traveled quite a bit. When the Korean War broke out, I went to visit them and found out that Sam had gone back into the Army and was on his way overseas. Liz confessed to me that since the end of World War II, he had been considerably bothered by the fact that both Alex and I had seen heavy combat in the war, while he had not. It really ate at him to the point where, not to be outdone by his brothers-in-law (and maybe to look more like a patriot to his wife, although he never admitted that), he had signed up again and had volunteered to serve over in Korea.

He got his wish, and went over as an artillery observer, not too different from what I had done with the mortars (I guess it ran in the family). He stayed over there until the conflict ended in 1953. Elizabeth and Sam eventually moved to Burbank, California and had a boy and a girl. My sister passed away on March 6, 2004 at the age of 87, even

---

17 106 miles north of Los Angeles.

though she had been a chain smoker in her later years. Sam died on March 1, 2010 at the age of 93.

My father had been a wild man all his life, with a good many of his crazy quirks. On top of that, he was an alcoholic, and the combination finally ended up to be more than my mother could bear, despite the fact that she loved him. Finally, in 1943, she had enough and left him. Mother moved out to California, and Pop stayed in Akron, where Alex and I eventually bought a 12-acre farm for him just south of Barberton. He built a small house on it, where he lived alone. Even though he still drank a lot, he mellowed some later on, and with my combat experiences, he developed a new respect for me, and so despite the fact that he was still a drunk, we managed to have a working relationship.

After the war, Pop sold firewood. Sometimes, we would start in the morning and cut wood all day. We had plenty of trees on those 12 acres, and we made sure that we planted trees to replace the ones that we cut down. In the end, we ended up with more than we had sold. One of our special products was wild cherry wood, which we kept and sold two cords at a good price for one special customer.

Later on, Pop developed serious problems with his stomach and digestive system and had to have an operation. Recovering, he struggled to continue on his own. I occasionally helped him at the house and often paid his hospital bills, since I could afford to. Mother had regrets that she could not come back to Ohio to help him.

Again, Fate took a hand. She somehow landed a ticket to see a TV game show back then called "Queen for a Day." The show's premise was simple: several female contestants for a number of prizes would be introduced and questioned about their lives, and what she needed most in her life, usually something medical or financial. Then at the end the audience voted by means of an applause meter. The winner would be crowned and given roses like a queen, and her need would be taken care of. She would also get a lot of extra prizes.

So Mom went as part of the audience, and on one show, she was lucky enough to be selected as a contestant. She gave her spiel about her simple life, and at the end, when they asked her what she would like most in the world, she stated simply that she be able to afford to go back to Ohio and take care of her ex-husband until he recuperated. Incredibly, Mom won, and the program granted her request. They agreed to pay for a round-trip ticket to Ohio and back. Sure enough, she returned to Akron and took care of Pop until he recovered. Then she went back to California.

Dad lived for years on my farm. In 1981, his health started going downhill. Four years later, on Saturday, April 6, 1985, he called me up at 11 p.m. "George, come on up. I want to talk to you."

I was tired though. I had worked at the convenience store for eleven hours that day, and I did not feel like taking a trip up to Barberton. So I told him, "Pop, how about I just see you in morning."

He paused and said quietly, "I won't be here." I realized at once that he knew he was dying.

I told Juanita, made me a thermos of coffee, and left. I drove up to Barberton, worn-out, my mind wondering all kinds of things. I got up to the farm at a little after 1 a.m. I went inside and confirmed my suspicions. I told him that he should go to the hospital. No, stubborn bastard that he was, he didn't want to. But he did want me to hang up a clean shirt for him, so that if he had to make a trip to the hospital in the morning, "I'll be ready."

I looked at him and said, "Hell pop, let's go now."

"No, if I do, they'll keep me. Let's just stay here for now."

Not wanting to start an argument, I gave in and said, "Okay." I thought about it, and added, "Let me know if you change your mind."

A while later, exhausted from not getting to sleep, the drive up, and the stress over his condition became too much. I yawned, stood up, and told him, "Pop, I'm tired. I'm gonna lay down on the davenport for a while."

He looked at me and nodded. I went over to the sofa, collapsed, and quickly fell asleep. I remember that, a couple hours or so later, half awake, I felt him brush by me as he walked by, headed for the bedroom. A while later, I woke and heard him quietly moaning in the bedroom. I listened for a bit and then fell asleep again.

I finally woke at 8 a.m. It was Sunday, the 7th. My bladder was full from all that coffee, and I had to go real bad. The bathroom was down the hall and to the right. I paused at dad's bedroom and listened. I didn't hear him breathing or anything. I thought, uh oh, that ain't good.

I walked around the corner and saw Pop there in the bathroom, sitting on the toilet, leaning against the wall with his eyes closed. I could tell that he had died. I stood there, looking at him. Despite finding Dad like that, I could not wait. I quickly went outside, took two steps, and relieved myself. I finished, went back inside, my mind numb, and sat down. I tried to think, but my mind drew a blank. So I got up, made myself a cup coffee, sat down again, and wondered what the hell I was going to do now.

I decided to call his second ex-wife. Then I changed my mind and decided to call her daughter, Ruby Bedita. She and her husband John lived over the hill about a half mile. Luckily, Ruby was home. I told her that Pop had passed away in the night, and after being shocked for a few moments, she told me that she and John would take care of everything. And they did. The funeral parlor, the showing, all of it.

After the funeral, as the hearse pulled away with Pop, I stood outside with Ruby's husband, John. The sky had suddenly gotten dark, and it began to snow. It really came down, a heavy, wet snow, with the damn biggest thick snowflakes I had ever seen.

We both stared out into the dark sky without saying a word. John finally looked over at me, took a deep breath, and said quietly, "Well … the old man's raising hell now somewhere."

I watched the snow coming down and nodded. Pop had been a wild, crazy, mean drunk—quite an instigator.

Mom died 17 months later in Burbank California in September 1986 at 90. We had been told her health was failing, so Juanita and I decided to go see her one last time. Unfortunately, Mom passed away while we were in New Mexico, and we did not get to California until the next day.

Five years after World War II ended, I had another close call with the Marines. I had toyed with the idea of joining the Marine Corps Reserve.

I had talked to a recruiter about it, and he told me that if I did reaffiliate, I could get my old rank of sergeant back. It would not only bring in a couple extra bucks every month, but as a World War II veteran, I would have something to do one weekend a month, with a prestigious reputation in whatever unit I went into. My buddy Alvin Ott had been in the Navy during the war, and he had decided to go back into the Naval Reserve.

We talked a couple times about reaffiliating, and finally we agreed towards the end of June that we would go downtown together and join up again. There was a small Marine Corps company barracks located on the Scioto River in the southwest part of Columbus. I had already been down there once to fill out some preliminary forms. So we decided we would go down, and I would sign my final papers to reenlist. Then we would go over to the naval reserve center, and Alvin would sign his papers.

As it turned out though, something came up that Alvin had to do that Saturday, so he suggested that we wait until Monday, the 26th. I was in no hurry, so I agreed.

But on Sunday, June 25, 1950, the North Koreans invaded South Korea, and the balloon went up over there. The U.S. started to actively support the South Koreans. Things looked like they were escalating quickly. I figured that the U.S. would put a huge effort into this, and thought about going to war again. I definitely did not want to do that. I had been married a year and a half, and I had just planned on joining the reserve for something to do.

It was one of the best and luckiest decisions I ever made in my life. Had Alvin and I joined that Saturday or a week before, I most likely would have been shipped over there to fight again with the First Marine Division. Training onboard ship was their boot camp. The only plus to that would have been that I would have been serving under Chesty Puller again. In hindsight though, balanced against that would have been the misery of the Pusan perimeter, the Inchon landing, that miserable freezing Chosin Reservoir, a thousand screaming Orientals coming at me again. On top of that, my reoccurring nightmares from World War II had finally gone. I did not need new ones. No thanks.

So once again, I was lucky. I had been saved by the bell. Even so, I still explored some possibilities. I later went down to the recruiting station at King and North High Street. They told me if I pressed the issue, I could probably get back into the Corps. But as it was, my record was too "overloaded" as they put it, with my time from World War II. That was good enough for me. If I went in, I would have something to prove. I would have had to stick my neck out to show them what the Old Breed was like. I probably would have been killed.

No, no more war for me. I had seen enough.

CHAPTER 9

Old Friends

A couple decades later, after having retired from the convenience store, I started trying to find out what had happened to my war buddies. Some I knew where they were, but many I did not.

Melvin "Waddy" Getz served in Panama during the war and never saw any action. He got married to Betty on July 24, 1950 and had three daughters: Margie, Jeanette, and Laura. Waddy's brother **Danny**, served with Merrill's Marauders in the CBI[1] and was later sent back to the United States, diagnosed with battle fatigue—PTSD. He finally recovered enough to work in a factory for a few years. He later bought a 250-acre backwoods ranch north of Cambridge, near Londonderry. Waddy's younger brother **Warren ("Boysee")** joined the Navy after the war began and got married. Some 50 years after that, Boysee and his wife decided to renew their vows at Lake Ann. Waddy came to the ceremony. It was an unusually hot day, and near the lake, the two brothers sat down on a wall to rest. They were talking as Boysee, uncomfortably hot, collapsed to the ground from a heart attack and died right there. Waddy passed away on Monday, January 26, 2009 in Cambridge.

---

1   China–Burma–India. This was a term used during the war to differentiate actions, supply points, and individuals serving from those in the Pacific Theater, even though it was technically never classified as a "theater" in an organizational sense. It encompassed China and Southeast Asia. The most famous units to serve there were the prewar Flying Tigers, Merrill's Marauders, and Army Air Corps units flying the "Hump" over Burma. After Okinawa, the 1st Marine Division was sent there.

Jefferson Davis ("Jeff") Watson, Jr., who I had gone on several liberties with in Davisville, Rhode Island, had joined the Marine Raiders, as a part of C Company, 4th Raider Battalion.[2] He was killed in action on July 20, 1943 during the battle at Bairoko in New Georgia. His body was never recovered. He does not have a grave there on the island, but he does have a vase (but no actual body) within a mausoleum in Manila's big national cemetery.

After he had been shot up on Peleliu and evacuated, I never saw my buddy **Jim Olivera** again. Last I heard, he was living in Fall River, Massachusetts.

After Parris Island, I never bumped into **John Siler** again, the guy we had coerced into joining with up back in August 1941. I did find out that he had landed on Iwo Jima.

I never met **Richard Tomkins** again either, the guy who had introduced me to Phyllis Carpenter in the fall of 1939. All I ever heard of him was that he had been shot up in the Gilberts.

Bob Johnson, who had been one of our platoon's communicators, after the war went back to Godfrey, Illinois[3] and became a barge inspector. He came to visit me a couple times just after I returned, and we had some real good "liberties" in Akron. I saw him occasionally after that whenever I traveled west. On my way to California, I would stop and visit him in Godfrey.

Carl Jenkins went back to Cleveland. I, years later, went to his wedding.

One of our corpsman, **Al (Alfonso) Romero**, became a prominent federal judge in San José California. He lives with his wife Lucy in Aptos, just east of Santa Cruz.

Joe Rzasa survived the war and eventually moved from Massachusetts, New Hampshire to Laconia, Florida, and became a machinist. He was married for some 60 years to Alice before he died on October 22, 2005.

I never did see **Lt. James Haggerty** again after he left me on Okinawa at the end of June. A few decades after the war, I met **W. A. Young**, the officer who had fired the rockets on that LCI at Peleliu. As a lieutenant,

---

2   Originally 1st Raider Battalion, and later designated 4th Battalion, 1st Marines.
3   Across the Mississippi River and just north of St. Louis.

he had come into our mortar platoon for a week or so on Okinawa. When he was with I Company, he had been shot in the back. We assumed it had been by the Japs, although he had been a caustic sort of fellow, kind of nasty to everybody, so who knows? Anyway, I met him many years later, and he claimed that he had run into Haggerty in New York right after the end of the war, somewhere around the end of August. That was the only instance that I heard of anyone ever being in contact with the lieutenant. Many years later, Bill Mikel told me that Haggerty had passed away not long after he had returned to the States. According to Bill, he had gone into hospital for a minor operation and he had died. Apparently, so had **Lt. Joe Murphy**. I never found out anything else about him.

Clarence G. Keele, one of our platoon's ammo carriers, after the war moved to Detroit and went into law enforcement, like his father, who was a sheriff in Texas. Clarence himself later became a Texas highway patrolman, and eventually landed a policing job with General Motors. He made a career with GM, and years later, became the head of their Investigative Division. I remember that big Texan S.O.B. with these huge hands. He was a quiet guy, not very chummy with many, but he and I always did get along, and he always defended me. When he died in 2007 in Grosse Point, Michigan, a lot of GM big shots attended his funeral. They presented his casket with a Marine Corps white barracks cap, and, strange as it seems, that was the first time anyone was aware of his service in the Marines.

Bob Sprangle, who had been my calm phone man on Okinawa and had followed me along the line, survived the war and went back to his wife and kids in Toledo. In 1947, I found out that he was running a grocery store that he had inherited from his father. I once went up to visit him, and we had a nice couple of days. A little after that, he died.

Albert J. ("Al") Cook, who had been in charge of the platoon's communications, ended up in I Company. He survived the war, went back home to Erie, Pennsylvania, married a great gal named Mary Ann, and became a banker. I saw him occasionally when we went hunting together out of his cabin, and also when he attended a number of our reunions. He wrote a short autobiography in 2009, and died five years later.

Albert William ("Bill") Mikel, the mortar gunner who had joined us just before Peleliu, lived to be old like me. Like a number of survivors after the war, Bill wrote a few articles about our experiences on Peleliu. Before he went off to war, he had already acquired a wife and kids, and so he wrote home almost every day, and in doing so, had kept a secret diary. Now Bill had a good eye for detail and an accurate memory, so he used his notes and memory to write a few stories of our encounters. One was about Lt. Haggerty on Peleliu in *The Old Breed* July 2015 issue, entitled, "A Salute to Lt. Haggerty."

Norman L. Leishman, the No. 4 mortar assistant, returned home to Santa Monica, California. His family had considerable influence in the area. His father, Lathrop Leishman, was a VIP with the Rose Bowl in Pasadena.[4] His father brought Norman into the family construction business, where he pursued a successful career.

Russell Diefenbach, who had been the loader for the No. 3 mortar in our platoon on Peleliu, and later on Okinawa our No. 3 Gunner, survived wounds that he received in each campaign. In his later years, he wrote a self-published book on his wartime experiences, and stayed in his hometown of Aurora, Illinois.

Joe Miceli, who had been a key part of the platoon's communications team, returned to Cambridge Massachusetts and became a police officer for the City of Cambridge. For many years, Joe was a fervent part of our reunions. He passed away on March 19, 2016.

Joe LaCoy, K Company's 60mm mortar chief, survived the war and went back to Alabama. I get a Christmas card from him every year. I heard that a few years ago, the old buzzard skydived out of an airplane.

After Cape Gloucester, I never heard anything about those crazy **Woodring brothers** until after the war. I was working down at the Silver Dollar Bar at Broad and High Street in Columbus at the time, and I was on my way in to work. Starting to walk into revolving door of the Gray Drug Store on the corner, I saw what seemed like a familiar face

---

4   Norman's grandfather, William Leishman had overseen construction of the Rose Bowl Stadium in the early 1920s. The Tiffany-designed Leishman Trophy, which is given each year to the winning team at the Rose Bowl, is named after him.

coming out. Stunned, I realized it was one of the Woodring brothers. He recognized me, and after a couple hearty greetings, we talked briefly. He was the twin who had been hit by that tree branch that stormy night back at Cape Gloucester in December 1943. Today, he had come down from his home in Paulding, Ohio to go to the VA facility for a health problem—no doubt related to that injury from that tree limb. Me, I was so happy to see him, I tactfully decided not to bring up the five dollars that he (or his brother) still owed me. And funny, all these years, not only could I not tell them apart, but I could never remember their names.

Lt. Curtis Beall after the war for a few years was some sort of government agent. During the rest of his life, he owned a Christmas tree farm and for while he raised and sold catfish.[5] For years afterward though, whenever I had occasion to visit him, he would tell his family with pride that I was the guy that saved his life, and his son Al grew up with that. After Curtis died in 2013, Al again thanked me for saving his life.

Twenty-year-old **Raymond Gilder Kelley**, who had been on the No. 4 mortar crew, went back to his job with the railroad in Eldridge, Alabama. One day, working in the railroad yard, he was hit by a train. Even though it had been slow moving, it messed him up. R.G. was a quiet sort of fellow. He stood about six four although he was always hunched over. His wife's family had money, and they ended up owning the fire department and two old grocery stores.

I remember taking a camper down there around 1990 to visit him. His wife Helen was a schoolteacher, but worked part-time in the town post office in the summer. When she heard me telling someone my name, she came out right away.

---

5   After the war, Curtis Beall was sent to China, where he was wounded and received the Purple Heart in 1945. He returned home in 1946 and went back to the University of Georgia, where he finally graduated in 1947. He also went back to being a cheerleader, and at 24½, he ended up the oldest student ever to cheerlead there. For several years he worked as a government instructor on agriculture to veterans and later became president of Federal Land Bank, before going into business on his own. His firm, Beall's Christmas Trees, started in the late 1970s, once boasted over 48,000 Christmas trees. He also served for nearly three decades as the president of Dublin's Federal Land Bank Association. Beall died on January 10, 2013 from prostate cancer at the age of 90. He was buried in the Brewton Community Cemetery in Dublin, Georgia.

"Peto?" she exclaimed. "I know HIM!"

I grinned and said, "Well, I'm it."

A crowd gathered around us as she gave me these big hugs. She had heard so much about me that she thought she knew me. I guess she expected me to be 10 feet tall or something from Guilder's stories. Kelley died November 10, 1995 and was buried in the town's ten-acre cemetery that his family owned.

After **John Skoglie** and I did our wild stint in San Diego in November 1945, I never saw him again for some 60 years. In 2005, I drove out to Burbank, California to visit my mom and my sister. Afterwards, instead of heading home, I decided to try and find Skoglie. His father had been a northern California miner, which explained why John had been fascinated with mineral exploration and ores all his life. I knew that he had returned there, but where, I did not know.

I drove north up to the backwater areas of northern California where supposedly John lived. No one knew of him, and his name was not in any of the phonebooks. I finally ended up in this little town where Al Cook had found some report that a guy named John Skoglie had committed suicide. I hoped that it was not my friend, but I had to find out. I walked into the little police station and asked the lady at the desk if they had any information on a John D. Skoglie. She checked her records and confirmed that there was a report of a John Skoglie that had committed suicide. From what she told me though, this fellow was much younger and could possibly have been my buddy's son. She printed out a copy of that record for a buck and I thanked her. Using the information on the sheet, I made a few phone calls, but again, no luck. No one knew anything.

Depressed, I finally drove back to Ohio. But I was not going to give up. I made a couple more calls to some other names on the report. Finally, I struck oil. One lady told me that she knew John, and that he now lived in a small crossroads town called Imlay in Nevada.[6] She gave me his phone number, and I finally was able to get a hold of him.

6   Imlay is located along Interstate 80, about 15 miles south of the Thunder Mountain Indian Monument and some 130 miles northeast of Reno. It has a population of about 170. It was once a modest railroad town, now all but abandoned.

Excited, I told John that I would like to get Al Cook and drive out to see him soon. Skoglie loved the idea, so we started to make plans. We drove across the country, through Colorado, to Oregon, and picked up another one of our old platoon buddies, **Ernie Huxel**, who lived in "The Dalles."[7] Then we all left in Huxel's car headed south, to go down about 500 miles to Imlay, Nevada.

Ernie told us that he had gone into construction running a bulldozer. As he put it, "Hell, anyone can do that. But not many guys can maintain an even grade like I do."

Even though Ernie drove a slow dozer—or maybe because of that—one of his favorite hobbies became auto racing. He owned a couple cars that he had bought and souped up. So as you can imagine, he drove fast and perhaps to some people, somewhat recklessly.

Al Cook was one of those folks, now nervously sitting in the front on the passenger side. Now let me explain that Al was a strange sort of fellow. He had joined the Marines around the same time as I had, but he had been assigned to the First Marine Division in mid-1942, and as such, had been on Guadalcanal. On Peleliu, he had been the section leader of our mortar platoon's communications group, and like his comrades, after Peleliu, he had been rotated back to the States.

I think that was just as well. Albert was a good Marine, all right. But it seemed to me that he didn't have the temperament to be a gung ho combat soldier. Since he had been in charge of wires and field phones and such, his job had never been to mix it up with the Japs and kick ass. He had just been in charge of the linemen.

Another thing about Al I found downright spooky. He had a sort of tunnel vision.

He didn't use his peripheral vision very much, not like me. Al was the sort to always look forward. I remember one time on the way out to get Huxel when I was driving, I had spotted a deer off to the right, on his side. "Hey, did you see that deer?" I asked him.

---

7   The Dalles (pronounced "Dales") is a city in Oregon about 84 miles east of Portland, with a population of 13,600.

Without batting an eye, looking straight ahead, he had said, "No." He didn't even turn his head to talk to me, much less to view the scenery. It was peculiar as hell.

Huxel was in a carefree mood, and his driving showed it, and while comparatively tame, Al in the front passenger seat was getting nervous. Watching him sometimes shake his head, I imagined Al thinking, "Man, I survived all them damn Japs and now I'm going to get killed with this maniac driving." I don't know why, but that thought amused the hell out of me. At one point Al said, "Ernie, you're gonna get a cop on our tail." But Huxel just smiled and drove on as if he wanted to break some sort of speed record.

We got into Nevada. Every once in a while, Huxel would approach a curve that Al figured deserved a little more respect, and as Huxel veered the car around the curve, the tires growling over the road, Al would sometimes thump his left foot onto the car's floor in a vain attempt to find his own brake pedal. This went on for a number of curves.

Finally, Ernie screeched the car to a halt and turned to Cook. "Now look Al, I'm doing the damn driving, so let me do the damn braking."

I don't think I ever laughed so much in my life.

And that's how we continued on our way to Skoglie's, with Huxel racing along, and wide-eyed Al staring at the road ahead, sometimes gripping the door handle.

We drove through swamps, with thick groves of tules[8] round them. They looked like cattails, but round instead of flat. Huxel's little car had no air conditioning, so we were all sweating.

Finally Huxel growled, "It's hotter than hell. Roll all the windows down. I'm gonna air this damn thing out."

We rolled our windows down and he took off down the road like a bat out of hell. I thought old Al was going to have a heart attack right there, with Huxel driving like crazy to keep the dust from whipping into the car.

---

8 Tules (pronounced tOO-lees) are country plants that thrive in swamps and marsh areas on the West Coast. Western Indian tribes used to harvest them and fashion them by dyeing and weaving them into baskets, bowls, sleeping mats, and head coverings.

We reached John's ranch in Nevada and he came running out in his blue bib overalls. I could tell by the big grin on his face that he was happy to see us. He had always been a quiet sort of guy, but he had always been ready to go on an adventure with me. Now he beamed from ear to ear, ecstatic to see some old Marine buddies.

As we approached, John pointed to his chest and said proudly, "I was one of Peto's raiders," referring to the many night excursions we had taken in the Pacific islands. Yes, Skoglie too had always been an explorer. So many times we had gone off at night just to see what we could find, and what mischief we could get up to. It looked like he had continued to be the explorer, now out West. He sure as hell dressed the part. With his big overalls and this huge moustache and beard, he looked just like a gold miner. All he needed was a mule to drag along.

We talked a bit, and then he gave us a tour of his ranch. That evening, he had an indoor barbecue and cooked us these huge, juicy steaks. We stayed a couple of days at his ranch and had a great time before we started heading back in a heavy snowstorm. That was the last and only time I ever saw John Skoglie again. He died at the age of 83.[9]

There was one good friend that had served alongside my division in the war. A funny thing though, I did not actually meet him until fifty years later. His name was **Joe Dodge**, and he lived not far from me in Marysville, Ohio. Joe had fought with MAG-12[10] in the Pacific as a flamethrower operator, and he saw action on Cape Gloucester and later on Peleliu. It was there that he came down with an infection of some sort, and Joe spent the next six months after the campaign recuperating. When he was well enough, they sent him home to the States. It was there that he found out from his family doctor that he had contracted a case of acute jaundice.

I met Joe when I joined the Marine Corps League in the summer of 1995. Joe was two years younger than me. We hit it off right away. This guy really lived at the foot of the cross, so to speak, and I really liked him. After the war, Joe worked for 20 years at the Scott's Fertilizer

---

9   Cpl. John Donald Skoglie died on December 2, 2007, and was buried in the Northern Nevada Veterans Memorial Cemetery in Fernley, Nevada.

10 Marine Aircraft Group 12, created in March 1942 in San Diego.

plant, before he turned to farming. He and Karen bought this big farm right next to his aunt's farm, located just outside of New California, Ohio, which is about halfway between Dublin, Ohio and Marysville. There were plenty of woods, which I found out, were great for all sorts of hunting. So Joe and I would often go out for hours in their woods, hunting for all sorts of critters: deer, coyote, groundhog, squirrel and the like. My great hunting buddy Joe passed away in the fall of 2013.[11]

Every now and then, we living survivors of our mortar platoon would have reunions. There was quite a showing for the first one, with 41 people attending. Of course, that included all those guys that had served in the platoon at various times over five years, including some 30 replacements just before the division had shipped off to China in 1945. So some of these guys I did not even know. Like for instance, **Karl Tangeman**, who I found nice to talk to and had a good memory. For many years, he was the chaplain at our platoon's reunions. After the war he became a Baptist minister, so we figured he knew what he was doing in the prayer department. I had never had a chance to know him, because he was gone from the platoon before I was assigned to it.[12]

We also had our share of personality conflicts, a couple of which probably had their origins in the Pacific. A few of these guys had idiosyncrasies in their personalities, and so sometimes a couple of us would have to step in and play the diplomat. And as we got older, our strange behaviors intensified. **Howard Quarty**, for instance, had always had a bit of a mean streak in him, and it would come out whenever he drank. Joe Miceli had been a cop for 25 years, so we assigned him the job of watching Quarty whenever he got drunk.

---

11 Joe B. Dodge was born September 9, 1924, and died of cancer November 26, 2013 at the age of 89.

12 Karl Tangeman had been on one of the mortar teams, and had seen action with them on Guadalcanal. Wounded twice, he was evacuated to Brisbane, Australia. When it was discovered that Karl was only 15 years of age, he was immediately transferred out of the platoon and sent back home. As soon as he turned of age, he reenlisted in the Marines. He was though, never reassigned to the mortar platoon.

The Columbus Dispatch
SUNDAY
AUGUST 30, 2009
B

METRO&STATE

Veterans decide not to toast buddies alone

Instead of saving brandy for the last man, they all have a drink at their last reunion

By Dave Hendricks
THE COLUMBUS DISPATCH

The men who fought some of World War II's fiercest battles in the Pacific bought a bottle of brandy 20 years ago and made a pact: The last man alive would drink the bottle and toast his fallen comrades.

But yesterday, the unit's 11 surviving members decided they'd rather drink it together.

"Now we've gotten so old we're going to give it up," said Russell Diefenbach, 84, of Aurora, Ill., who paid $200 for the brandy in 1989. "That's about the best (as far as) I can tell you, being a martini drinker."

So hours after the group voted to stop holding reunions — acknowledging they've become too old to jet across the country each year — they cracked the bottle of Marquis de Caussade Armagnac.

"I'm going to be the last guy anyway and I don't want to drink it alone," joked George Peto, 86, of Columbus.

The men met in the 81mm Mortars, 3rd Battalion, 1st Marines. Together they wrested Okinawa, Peleliu and Guadalcanal from the Japanese.

Positioned behind the riflemen on the front lines, the mortar unit rained shells onto Japanese positions to clear the way for American offensives. At times, they were positioned just feet behind the front.

See VETERANS Page B2

KELLIE MANIER | DISPATCH

Members of the 81mm Mortar Unit of the 3rd Battalion, 1st Marines with the bottle of brandy that, originally, was being saved for the last man alive to drink in the group's honor

Last Man Reunion for George's Mortar Platoon, 3rd Battalion, 1st Marines. Columbus Dispatch (August 30, 2009).

In 1989, we had our first big reunion in Columbus, at the Harley Hotel on Route 161. In the next years, we had more in other big cities all over the country and each time we had a blast.

Over the years, we held our reunions in fancy cities all over the country—Las Vegas (that one was a blast), New Orleans, San Diego … These get-togethers were always fun, and I enjoyed spending time with these guys, fellows I once saw combat with. We never had what I would call a bad reunion. Of course, money was often a problem. It was sometimes difficult to get hotels to give us a price break on our stays, so that we could afford to go. Naturally, I did my best to put a guilt trip on the manager, and it usually worked, especially if he was a veteran.

In 1995, having had reunions all around the country we had one again at the Harley Hotel. **Russ Diefenbach**, now 70 (I was 73), our No. 3 gun loader, was there, he bought an expensive $250 bottle of cognac, something called Marquis de Caussade Armagnac.[13] We decided at that reunion that the last living survivor of the unit would drink that bottle for all of us—sort of like a tontine.[14] At the end of the reunion, Russ decided to turn the bottle over to me for safekeeping. I was its caretaker for 14 years. As the years kept rolling though, and we passed our sixth decade since the war had ended, and as more and more of us died,

---

13 It is considered by connoisseurs as one of the oldest, finest VSOP (very superior old pale) distilled brandies in the world. It is similar to cognac, averaging 84 proof. Once consumed for medicinal purposes (really), it is still produced in the Armagnac region of southwest France near the Pyrenees.

14 A tontine is a dedicatory custom in which survivors of a war unite together create a fund or, in this case, purchase a rare vintage bottle of wine or spirits, with the idea that the last living survivor drink it on behalf of his other departed comrades and to commemorate their memories in a toast. The idea perhaps came to Diefenbach after watching a similarly themed 1980 *M★A★S★H* episode entitled "Old Soldiers." In the TV show, the 4077th's commanding officer, Sherman Potter, is involved in such an experience on behalf of the old war buddies he served with in France in World War I. More likely though, the last-man bottle idea was borrowed from a similar arrangement for the 1st Marine Division Association. In 1946, the association was donated a bottle of rare 50-year-old Jph. Etournaud cognac (insured for $25,000), a gift from World War I Marine veteran Ralph McGill, editor of the *Atlanta Constitution*. Presumably, the bottle, last reported to be at the Marines Memorial Club in San Francisco, is still unopened.

I realized that we were getting close to the end, and to be honest, I did not want to be the last Marine that would be drinking to his buddies.

I finally decided that that was not going to happen. Those few of us that were left, about 15 guys, could have one last reunion and all share the bottle. I proposed that idea to them. I told them with a chuckle that I figured I would probably be the last guy anyway, and that I didn't want to drink that damn bottle all alone.

They mostly laughed at that, but they all agreed. On Saturday, August 29, 2009, 64 years after the war's end, we had one last get-together in Columbus. We met at that nice Hotel Hilton in the Easton Shopping Center. I drove over there wearing my bright red Marine Corps League jacket and my ribbons, of course. Finally, the time came, and we cracked open the brandy. Unfortunately, the flavor was disappointing. I guess you're not supposed to keep good brandy in the refrigerator, especially for some 14 years.

The guys stayed at the Hilton that night, and we had a few more "sessions" in a couple of the rooms. In the end though, I was sorry to see my buddies leave, because I figured it would be the last time that I would see most of them, well, alive. I was right. Two of them died right after that reunion: **Wilber Cox**, a replacement corpsman, and **Richard Radke** who had been one of our ammo carriers and later had retired as a lieutenant colonel in the Army. And since that time, another eight or nine have gone on.

Postscript

As I often discuss with school kids, no matter how much someone wonders about it, they never know how they will act in combat until they're actually in it. There is no test to tell who will perform and who won't. Some of the biggest, gung-ho guys turn out to not be worth a damn, while some sheepish, quiet, seemingly no-good fellow will come through with flying colors and end up a skilled combat veteran. There were a lot of guys in our battalion who would fight anyone at the drop of the hat, but were scared to death in combat. You just never knew beforehand.

I am still not quite sure why I survived the war. Maybe because I did everything right and did not expose myself needlessly. But a lot of us did that and still got killed. On the other hand, I saw so many guys get hit because they were doing something wrong at the time, occasionally on purpose. I mean, for crying out loud, when enemy shells are landing around you, the dumbest thing to do is to get up and start sprinting away from them. I know that these guys were running because they were scared. However, that's the last thing you should ever do. You stay down, protect yourself.

Some guys just freaked out and froze or locked up out in the open. I sympathized with them, I really did. On the other hand, they were just inviting what they were so afraid might happen to happen.

On the other side of the coin, other guys, like ostriches, would just dig their heads in the sand and pray that the shooting be over. You can pray all you want, but I had learned on Peleliu that the Lord won't most likely help you until you until you make the effort to help yourself.

I remembered back to one time in mid-May 1945 on Okinawa when we had been attacked. Towards the end of the action, I moved around our slope to get a better bead on a hidden Jap position, and as I did, I walked past one of our foxholes. I looked down and saw a figure crouched down in it, curled up in a fetal position, his rifle on the ground, a few feet away from his hole. He was hunkered over with his hands over his ears, and he was shaking with fright.

I paused above and snarled at him, "What the hell are you doing down there?"

He just lay there, trembling, obviously wanting the world to go away.

"Get up and shoot!" I yelled.

He still did not move.

"Cmon!" I said. "Christ, if I had been a Jap, you'd be dead right now."

He stayed where he was, scared shitless. I shook my head and moved on, muttering to myself. If he was not going to fight, he should at least tell the officers, so that they could put him in a rear job or something, and replace him. Otherwise, just lying there put both of us at risk of getting killed. It was not like I did not sympathize with the guy, because I really did. I understood fear. It was normal to be frightened on the line, but to be a good combat soldier, you had to recognize that fear and still function under those scary conditions. I'd rather have 10 riflemen who can shoot (groundhog hunters, as I called them), instead of 40 guys who don't know if they wanted to be there.

This guy was in my mind, depriving the unit out of his support, cheating other guys who might be killed if he did not doing their job. If he couldn't help us, he had no business being there for the guys who needed him. He was just a drag to the unit. Still, I did feel sorry for him, even as I was grumbling.[1]

I think in most ways, Peleliu was my worst combat operation of the war. It was just a slaughter ground, based on one set of screw-ups after another. I mean, from the Navy bigwigs on down to our own division

---

1 After the war, perhaps out of shame, he never attended any of the unit reunions.

commander. And we riflemen were the ones that suffered the worst. The 1st Marines at Peleliu went on record as the regiment that took the highest percentage of casualties ever in Marine Corps history. And of the three battalions, mine, the 3rd, had taken the worst of it. A lot of the Old Breed died those first few days.

I know that I was often scared to the point where I sometimes shivered with fright. Today though, having gone through all of that, I can say that I have had every damn experience that you can have. I remember when the *Pinkney* began sailing away from Peleliu, I swore that I would never to go back to that damn island of hell again.

Many times in the last few decades I have been asked why I never returned. I wouldn't go back, not even to pay homage to my buddies who had died there. I mean, what for? The reason for not going is in my mind, simple. In the years since, Peleliu has gone back to being a tropical island. And I hear it's real nice now, a type of tourist resort. That shoreline that we had been evacuated from in early October, Purple Beach, is a good example. It is now called "Honeymoon Beach."[2] You would probably see couples vacationing, walking along the sand holding hands, sitting under some umbrella sipping tropical rum drinks. There would be some native girls dancing in their *lavalava* skirts with pretty smiles, waving their arms to the music, gazing at you with dreamy eyes, with the gentle sea behind them.

Me, I figure that I would look right next to where the tourists were sitting and imagine seeing bodies lying in the sand, or rolling around in the surf. Tourists would hear soft Polynesian music; me, I'd hear mortar shells echoing in my head. The vacationers would see the beauty of a tropical island, and I would just see shattered mangroves, burnt amtracs, craters, and corpses—lifeless friends lying face down in the wet sand.

One time, a friend of mine sent me a small plastic tube with some sand inside that had come from Peleliu. I looked at the tube and almost pitched it. No, I guess I think differently on this than most veterans do ...

---

2   Peleliu, today known as the Palau state of Bliliou, remains a point of visitation for many Marines. Nearby Angaur Island is today the island state of Ngeaur.

I sometimes think back to that second morning when I was sitting in that crater, frightened, shells landing everywhere, and I had turned to God for help. When nothing visibly happened right away and I was still lying there, mortar rounds continuing to come down around me, I mentally gave up on Him and went on, hoping that I would not get blown to bits. Looking back on it now with hindsight, I guess He was riding shotgun with me all along, and I had just been too damned stupid to realize it. How else could I have gone through some 24 months of combat, seen so many of my comrades getting killed, and never even get a scratch?

On Okinawa, I went through a different type of hell. The fighting was not quite as vicious and deadly as it had been on Peleliu, and the enemy fire most of the time was not nearly as intense. On the other hand, Peleliu for us was only a couple of weeks long before we were relieved. Okinawa though had been almost seven months long, of which eight weeks had been in rigorous combat.

I can say one thing with pride. I never did anything in combat that I was ashamed of. I saw some brutal, savage stuff happen, most of it by the enemy, but some of it by us. I was never happy about it, but I never lost sleep over it. That is how real war is: vicious, no matter who you are.

The only regret that I have in that regard was not being there when my close buddy died on Okinawa. Henry Vastine Rucker. Yeah, I miss old Henry …

I was not any kind of a gunfighter, but I like to think that I was a thorough, cold-blooded killer when I had to be. I know that I was an efficient shooter. I don't know how many Japs I killed or had killed, but I know there were many. And I would kill them any way I could. I think that the instincts I picked up in my early life outdoors did a great deal to help me survive the island campaigns. And my Marine training helped even more.

Like one of my drill instructors at Parris Island once told me: "Ya gotta be like a cattail in a swamp and bend with the wind. And you gotta be able to creep like a baby and crawl like a snake."

On November 9, 2009, I was lucky enough to be inducted into the Ohio Veterans Hall of Fame. I was told that it was recognition for my service to the country and my contributions to fellow veterans. I was quite humbled by that.

In December 2015, I was given an honorary trip to the National World War II Museum in New Orleans. Along with a few dozen other veterans, we were honored as a part of the unveiling of its new Pacific Theater wing. I myself had my own kiosk there, featuring an audio recording of mine about Okinawa. I had several occasions to talk to co-founder Gary Sinise, and all us old veterans had a great time.

Perhaps just as satisfying to me was that fact that my son George Lee came down with me. Both of us are stubborn cusses, and we had from time to time had some head butting. We were not at odds in life, but over the years, we could have had a better relationship. This trip helped us a lot. And I think George Lee got a better idea of what I did. When we returned to Columbus, he told me that he was proud of me for what I did during the war. That went a long way with me. It meant a lot.

For almost 40 years, I rarely talked much about my experiences in World War II, except of course with my friends at our reunions. All that changed though, a half century after the war ended.

1995 was to be our mortar platoon's 50-year reunion. We decided to hold it where it the whole Marine experience began for us: Parris Island, South Carolina. We planned as a part of the reunion to attend a boot camp graduation, something none of us had been given when we had gone through. In those days before the war, when you finished boot, you were just given your orders and that was that. Now they have a whole day of ceremony and stuff for these guys.[3]

The training command was thrilled for us to want to come, and so we planned accordingly. We would have our actual reunion in nearby Savannah, and the base would make transportation arrangements to get us out there.

---

3   Today, the end of boot camp at Marine Corps Recruit Depot (MCRD) is indeed capped off at the end of the last week with a formal graduation ceremony. Thursday of that week is considered Family Day, and those graduating are granted on-base liberty to visit with friends and relatives who attend. Friday is Graduation Day. The day consists of a parade and formal ceremony on the parade field, with friends and family in attendance.

George Peto, along with about 40 other World War II veterans, is honored at the opening ceremony for the new Pacific wing of the National World War II Museum in New Orleans, December 11, 2015. Standing second to his left is Gary Sinise, who played Vietnam veteran "Lieutenant Dan" in the award-winning movie Forrest Gump. *Mr. Sinise is a major sponsor of the museum and founder of the Gary Sinise Foundation for Veterans. George's oral account of the Hill 55 attack on May 13, 1945 featured in the Okinawa section of the new wing. (Photo courtesy of George Peto Jr.)*

We all arrived separately, about 21 of us, and the first night of our reunion (as you can imagine) was a roaring success. The next day, the recruit training center sent a bus, and we traveled out to Parris Island. From the moment we arrived, we were given the red carpet treatment. As guests, several officers there gave us the rare opportunity to actually see some of the activities that the new recruits were going through. We saw some exercises in personal combat. Another interesting exercise was the hand grenade training. For safety (and probably because of liability), when they started throwing those grenades, we had to observe behind bulletproof glass, which we veterans found amusing, seeing how we had thrown hundreds of the damn things in the war. However, the grenades these kids threw were different than ours. These grenades were round, where our olive-green pineapples had been more oblong. And it surprised me how much louder these exploded than ours had. They made a horrendous noise, even though these suckers were much smaller than the ones we used.[4]

We watched the graduation and really enjoyed it. After the main ceremony ended, we were supposed to have our picture taken with the ranking officer present, the colonel of the graduating class. Somehow, the base commander, General Klimp,[5] got the word that there was a platoon of old World War II veterans there, and he decided he was going to have his picture taken with us as well.

A week or two after I got back home, I got a personal letter from the general. Since I was one of the organizers of our reunions, the letter had been sent to me. In it, General Klimp asked for our reunion organization to assist the Corps in spreading the word about how great the Marines were, and about my experiences in it. In essence, he wanted us to be a sort of recruiting tool, and to give the Marine Corps recruiters a hand as such. According to the general, the recruiters were having trouble filling their enlistment billets. I never did get around to writing back to the general, but I did think about what he had written, and I finally decided that the least I could do was tell folks about my experiences and to indirectly make a pitch for the Corps.

Having made the decision, I started to get involved. I put the word out to a couple schools that I would be willing to show up with some

---

4   George's unit used the famous 1½ lb. Mark 2 fragmentation grenade, affectionately nicknamed the "pineapple" because of the cast-iron-groove pattern's resemblance to the fruit. The recruits were probably using the Mark 67 grenade, which although some 12 ounces lighter, packs a more powerful explosive. Its shape is round and much shorter.

5   Lt. General Jack W. Klimp, now retired. He served as the Parris Island commander from June 1993 until July 1995.

Two items that George showed to school children as a guest speaker. At bottom the compass he carried in all four Pacific campaigns to calculate coordinates as a forward observer for 3rd Battalion's 81mm mortars. Above it is the small notebook that, located in his left front pocket, absorbed shrapnel from a mortar blast on Okinawa, May 11, 1945, saving his life. A couple pieces are still embedded in the notebook, although most have fallen out over the years from the notebook being handled. (Author's collection)

props and tell the kids of my exploits. What the hell, I liked to talk to people anyway, and I had no problems speaking to a group. I was surprised that a couple high schools responded to my invitation. So I started speaking at them on veteran holidays. I soon got my buddy Joe Dodge to start coming to these show-and-tells with me, and for about ten years, we were quite popular. We spoke at high schools, middle schools, veteran organizations like the VFW and the American Legion, the Wooster and Urbana Historical Societies, and even to some junior colleges. I have been doing these presentations ever since. I find it fun, and the kids are amazed at some of the stuff we did on those islands.

Besides the gratification that I get from these guest appearances (often with a free meal, even if it is only pizza), I occasionally see other benefits. Like for instance, just before Veterans Day in 2013, I went to Thomas Worthington High School, about three miles away from where I live in Columbus. Just before I was scheduled to speak, I met a Marine recruiter in his dress blues. He came up to me with a big grin, introduced himself, and shook my hand. We stood there and he started talking about the occasion, recruiting, and other stuff.

I finally smiled at him and asked, "Well, what's your story? How'd you get into the Marine Corps?"

He told me that he had joined the Corps because as a teenager, he had become captivated with the idea of becoming a Marine.

"Really," I said. "What got you fired up to be a Marine?"

He looked at me and cracked a big-assed grin. "From listening to you tell them sea stories."

I looked at him surprised. "Huh?"

He smiled again and spread his hands out as he looked around us. "I graduated from here," he said. "I listened to you, and you're the one that talked me into going."

I was stunned, and all I could say was "Wow." He had attended Thomas Worthington and had joined the Marines because of hearing the things that I had said. I had actually recruited what was now a recruiter. General Klimp would be proud. Maybe I was doing some good after all.

Over the decades, I have seen nearly all of my buddies—those that survived the war—pass away from one thing or another. I have attended so many of their funerals, and yet for some reason I still go on. I have been asked a number of times how I feel at one of these funerals, and to be honest, I feel kind of numb. I think to myself that it must have been his time to go, and I let it go at that. I was though, really messed up when I lost Juanita on March 9, 2013, at the age of 92. We had been happily married 65 years.

George with some of his artifacts, talking to students of Fairbanks Middle School on May 4, 2016, about his experiences in World War II. (Author's collection)

I continue to support local veteran groups. I'm a member of the VFW and the American Legion. But I try to attend every monthly meeting of my local detachment of the Marine Corps League.[6] I suppose that doing stuff for the Corps will always be in my blood. I may be retired, but what the hell. I'll always be a Marine.

Semper Fi.

---

6   Belleau Wood Detachment #508, Columbus, Ohio.

Epilogue

On Independence Day, 2016, with the first draft of his autobiography now complete, George Peto, driven by his daughter Nancy, went over to a Worthington home in the late afternoon to attend a picnic and then watch the evening fireworks. The home had a magnificent view of the display. It was owned by the principal of nearby Thomas Worthington High School, where George had spoken on several veteran occasions.

Now considered somewhat a local celebrity as a special World War II veteran, George was singled out and honored that evening. Two attending young ladies happened to be school alumni and recognized him from when he had spoken at the school over the years. Bubbling, the girls gushed over him and gave him several big hugs. Pleased and happy, George was his usual, talkative self. It turned out to be a very pleasant, satisfying evening.

Nancy drove him home. He was tired from the evening, but he was feeling normal. Knowing that he had another book interview session with co-author Pete Margaritis the next morning, he kissed his daughter goodnight and climbed the stairs to go to sleep, accompanied as usual by his ever-faithful companion, Trixie.

George Peto passed away in his bed that night at 12:51 a.m.

At his funeral service on Tuesday, July 12th, he was given full military honors by his Marine comrades. The next day, he was interred next to his wife Juanita in Hasson Cemetery, in Jenera, Ohio. George had left specific instructions that when Trixie, that vivacious little dog that

George Peto on his back porch with Trixie, 2015. (Author's collection)

he loved so much, passes as well, Nancy would have her cremated and buried next to George and his wife, with her image set on the gravestone between George's and Juanita's names.

> *When your time comes to die, be not like those*
> *whose hearts are filled with fear of death, so that when*
> *their time comes, they weep and pray for a little more time*
> *to live their lives over again in a different way.*
> *Sing your death song, and die like a hero going home.*
>
> Tecumseh

Sources

Main Resources

By far the main source of information for this book was George Peto himself, an extraordinary individual who, even at 93 years old, retained a remarkable, consistent memory for detail, including events that occurred over eight decades before. Most of his memoirs were obtained through a series of interviews with him in his home in Columbus, Ohio by Pete Margaritis between June 2015 and June 2016. A second good source of information was an audio set of two interviews taken of Mr. Peto on March 31, 2015, by Fairbanks Middle School teacher Claudia Bartow, also a veteran. Claudia's excellent, detailed interviews augmented to a considerable extent the information subsequently obtained by Mr. Margaritis.

In addition, Mr. Peto's sources include articles over the years that he has either written or contributed to. These include his "Combat Action Report" of November 1, 2014, "The Hard Luck Kid," "The Real Heroes," "The Long Voyage Home," and "The Battle for Peleliu" (August 25, 2011). Also helpful were a few sources in which his personal actions have been included, including several books listed below.

A few additional sources for Mr. Peto's unit detailed a good deal of information that was so valuable in filling in a few holes of Mr. Peto's accounts. One useful resource was Russell Diefenbach's privately published *Autobiography of a Common American*, R. E. Diefenbach, c.1997. This work, although at times (according to Mr. Peto) slightly more imaginative than accurate, provided a fairly good account of many of the day-to-day, intricate details of the 3rd Battalion's heavy mortar platoon.

George P. Hunt's *Coral Comes High*, Harper & Brothers, NY, NY, c.1946, gave excellent first-hand details of Company K (K/3/1) at Peleliu, to which George was briefly attached.

Curtis Beall's *Memoirs of a Marine Dawg: From Rose Bowl to Pacific Theater*, Indigo Custom Publishing LLC, Macon, GA, c.2006, provided additional accounts of the mortar platoon's combat experience on Okinawa.

Albert C Cook's *Between Shots—A Memoir: Experiences and Reflections, South Pacific, World War II*, Albert C. Cook Publishing, c.2009, provided a fair amount of additional information on George's mortar platoon starting from 1943.

Unless otherwise indicated, most of the informational footnotes came either from Mr. Peto or crosschecked open Internet sources such as Wikipedia.

Additional Sources

Albers, Col. Ron, USAF Ret., "FOCUS FEATURE: Sgt. George Peto, Jr., 3rd Battalion, 1st Marines, 1st Marine Division, Pacific Theatre, WWII," *From the Trenches: Official Newsletter of Motts Military Museum, Inc.*, Fall issue, 2012, Groveport, OH.

Alexander, Joseph H., Col., USMC, *Storm Landings: Epic Amphibious Battles in the Central Pacific*, Naval Institute Press, Annapolis, MD., c.1997. **(A)**

———————————————————, "What Was Nimitz Thinking?" Proceedings: U.S. Naval Institute, Vol. 124/11/1,149, November 1998. **(B)**

Appleman, Roy E., Burns, James M., Gugeler, Russell A, and Stevens, John, *Okinawa: The Last Battle, U.S. Army in World War II—The War in the Pacific*, Center of Military History, United States Army, Washington, D.C., c.2000.

Bevilacqua, Maj. Allan C., USMC (Ret), "Brothers in Arms," *Leatherneck* Magazine, April, 2007, Vol. LXXXX, No. 4.

Cameron, Craig, M, *American Samurai—Myth, Imagination, and the Conduct of Battle in the First Marine Division, 1941–1951*, Cambridge University Press, Cambridge, United Kingdom, c.1994.

Camp, Dick, *Last Man Standing: The 1st Marine Regiment on Peleliu*, Zenith Press Division of MBI Publishing, Minneapolis, MN, c.2008

Davis, Burke, *Marine! The Life of Chesty Puller*, Bantam Books, NY, NY, c.1962.

Deen Jr., Braswell D., *Trial by Combat*, CreateSpace Independent Publishing Platform, c.2011.

Fox, Fred K., "My Ten Foot Circle of Space," *The Transfer Case* Magazine (Lone Star Military Vehicle Preservation), Austin, TX, reprinted from *The Old Breed News*, August, 1997, Beaufort, SC, c.1996.

Frank, Benis M. and Shaw Jr., Henry I., *History of U. S. Marine Corps Operations in World War II. Vol. V. Victory & Occupation*, Historical Branch, G-3 Division Headquarters, U.S. Marine Corps, Washington, DC, c.1968.

Gailey, Harry A., *Peleliu 1944*, The Nautical & Aviation Publishing Company of America, Annapolis, MD., c.1983.

Garand, George W. and Strobridge, Truman R., *History of the U.S. Marine Corps Operations in World War II, Vol. IV: Western Pacific Operations*, Historical Division, Headquarters, U.S. Marine Corps, Washington, D.C., c.1971.

Gayle, Brig. Gen. Gordon D., USMC, *Bloody Beaches: The Marines at Peleliu*, Didactic Press, c.2015.

Haines, LCDR Joseph D., Medical Corps, USN, "Planting the Confederate Flag at Shuri Castle, Okinawa", *Confederate Digest*, January 4, 2012.

Hallas, James H., *The Devil's Anvil: The Assault on Peleliu*, Praeger Publishers, Westport, CT, c.1994.

Hoffman, Lt. Col. Jon T., USMCR, *Chesty: The Story of Lieutenant General Lewis B. Puller, USMC*, Random House, NY, NY, c.2001.

Hough, Maj. Frank O, USMC, *The Seizure of Peleliu* (also printed as *The Assault on Peleliu*), Historical Branch, G-3 Division, Headquarters, U.S. Marine Corps, c.1950.

Johnstone, Maj. John H., *USMC, A Brief History of The First Marines*, Historical Branch, G-3 Division Headquarters, U.S. Marine Corps, Washington, DC, c.1962.

Makos, Adam, *Voices of the Pacific: Untold Stories from the Marine Heroes of World War II*, The Berkeley Publishing Group, London, England, c.2013.

McEnery, Jim, and Sloan, Bill, *Hell in the Pacific: A Marine Rifleman's Journey from Guadalcanal to Peleliu*, Simon & Schuster, NY, NY, c.2012.

McMillan, George, *The Old Breed—A History of The First Marine Division In World War II*, Infantry Journal Press, Washington, DC, c.1949.

Mikel, Cpl. Albert William, "A Salute to Lt. Haggerty," *The Old Breed News*, Vol. LXIV, No. 3, July–August–September, 2015, Beaufort, SC, c.2015.

_____, "The Rest of the Story," c.2009.

Miller Jr., John, *United States Army in World War II: The War in the Pacific—CARTWHEEL: The Reduction of Rabaul*, Office of the Chief of Military History, Department of the Army, Washington, D.C., c.1959.

Miller, Thurman, *Earned in Blood: My Journey from Old-Breed Marine in the Most Dangerous Job in America*, St. Martin's Press, NY, NY, c.2013.

Moran, Jim, and Rottman, Gordon L., *Peleliu 1944: The Forgotten Corner of Hell*, Osprey Publishing, Oxford, England, c.2002.

Nalty, Bernard, *Cape Gloucester: The Green Inferno*, Marines in World War II Commemorative Series, United States Marine Corps Historical Center, Washington, DC, c.1994.

Nichols, Major Charles S. Jr., and Shaw, Henry I. Jr., *Okinawa: Victory in the Pacific*, Historical Branch, G-3 Division, Headquarters, U.S. Marine Corps, Washington, DC, c.1955.

North, Oliver L. and Musser, Joe, *War Stories II: Heroism in the Pacific*, Regnery Publishing, Inc., Washington, DC, c.2004.

Parks, Kevin, "Peto beats the odds again—as he's inducted into vets' Hall of Fame," *Northland News*, ThisWeek Community News, November 16, 2009, 2:24 p.m.

Potter, E.B., *Bull Halsey: A Biography*, U.S. Naval Institute Press, c.1985.

_____, *Nimitz*, U.S. Naval Institute Press, Annapolis, MD, c.1976.

Robinson, Claudia (compiler), *Heroes from the Heartland, Union County, Ohio*, Copy Source, Marysville, OH, c.2002.

Ross, Bill D., *Peleliu: Tragic Triumph*, Random House, c.1991.

Rottman, Gordon L., *Okinawa 1945: The Last Battle*, Osprey Publishing, Oxford, England, c.2002.

Shaw, Henry I Jr., *The United States Marines in North China, 1945–1949*, Historical Division, Headquarters, U.S. Marine Corps, Washington, DC, c.1960. (A)

Shaw Jr., Henry I. and Kane Major Douglas T., USMC, *History of the U.S. Marine Corps Operations in World War II, Vol. II: Isolation of Rabaul*, Historical Division, Headquarters, U.S. Marine Corps, Washington, D.C., c.1963. (B)

Shisler, Gail P., *For Country and Corps: The Life of General Oliver P. Smith*, U.S. Naval Institute Press, Annapolis, MD, c.2009.

Simonsen, Robert A., *Marines Dodging Death: Sixty-Two Accounts of Close Calls in World War II, Korea, Vietnam, Lebanon, Iraq and Afghanistan*, McFarland & Company, Inc, Jefferson, NC, c.2008.

Sledge, E.B., *With the Old Breed: At Peleliu and Okinawa*, Presidio Press Division of Random House, NY, NY, c.1981.

Sloan, Bill, *Brotherhood of Heroes: The Marines at Peleliu, 1944*, Simon & Schuster, NY, NY, c.2005. **(A)**

_____, *The Ultimate Battle: Okinawa 1945—The Last Epic Struggle of World War II*, Simon & Schuster, NY, NY, c.2007. **(B)**

Standring, William, "Everyone Knew Ernie," *Marine Corps League Magazine*, Vol. 51, No. 1, Spring, 1995, pp.28–32, Merrifield, VA.

Stockman, Capt. James R, USMC, *The First Marine Division On Okinawa: I April–30 June, 1945*, Historical Division, Headquarters, U.S. Marine Corps, Washington, DC, c.1946.

Yenne, Bill, *Tommy Gun: How General Thompson's Submachine Gun Wrote History*, St. Martin's Press, NY, NY, c.2009.

(No editor), *H-3-1: The Life and Times of H-3-1*, USMC, (private publishing), c.2000.

(No editor), Civilian Conservation Corps Camp of Vernal records, 1937–1939, http://archiveswest.orbiscascade.org/ark:/80444/xv81680